MODERN EDUCATION IN THE SMALL RURAL SCHOOL

THE MACMILLAN COMPANY
NEW YORK · BOSTON · CHICAGO · DALLAS
ATLANTA · SAN FRANCISCO

MACMILLAN AND CO., Limited
LONDON · BOMBAY · CALCUTTA · MADRAS
MELBOURNE

THE MACMILLAN COMPANY
OF CANADA, Limited
TORONTO

The original pattern of public education in America exists today in large numbers.

MODERN EDUCATION
IN THE
SMALL RURAL SCHOOL

BY

KATE V. WOFFORD

Director of Rural Education
State Teachers College at Buffalo, N. Y.

THE MACMILLAN COMPANY

New York

Published June, 1938

Sixth Printing March, 1945.

Printed in the United States of America

DEDICATION

*To my father and mother
who exemplified, in their day and generation, all that is
best in modern education*

THERE WAS A CHILD WENT FORTH

by *Walt Whitman*

"There was a child went forth every day,
And the first object he look'd upon, that object he became,
And that object became part of him for the day, or a certain part of
the day,
Or for many years, or stretching cycles of years.

"The early lilacs became part of this child,
And grass and white and red morning-glories, and white and red
clover, and the song of the phoebe-bird,
And the Third-month lambs, and the sow's pink-faint litter, and the
mare's foal, and the cow's calf,
And the noisy brood of the barn-yard, or by the mire of the pond-side,
And the fish suspending themselves so curiously below there, and
the beautiful curious liquid,
And the water-plants with their graceful flat heads, all became part
of him.

* * *

"The hurrying tumbling waves, quick-broken crests, slapping,
The strata of color'd clouds, the long bar of maroon-tint, away solitary
by itself, the spread of purity it lies motionless in,
The horizon's edge, the flying sea-crow, the fragrance of salt marsh
and shore mud,
These became part of that child who went forth every day, and who
now goes, and will always go forth every day."

PREFACE

PREFACE viii

THE small rural school is a persistent problem in the field of education. Originally the pattern of public education in America it has yielded slowly to reform. Reforms came to it first in a program of consolidation, an administrative device which developed large teaching units from small ones. Beginning slowly in the early years of the twentieth century the consolidation movement has gathered enough momentum to establish consolidated schools in every state in the union. In 1928 there were approximately 17,000 such schools scattered throughout the several states. As efficacious as this reform has proven to be, however, small schools exist in the present and in large numbers.

In 1934, according to the United States Office of Education, 13,024,021 children attended rural schools. Of this number 10,821,777 attended elementary rural schools and 2,202,244 attended rural high schools. The school buildings to serve this large number of American youth are designed, on the whole, for small teaching units. In 1934, 64.9 per cent of all rural school buildings were of one-room; 11.4 per cent of two rooms. These small schools were attended by 43.8 per cent of all the school children in America. An examination of these governmental statistics reveals that rural education in this country is still largely carried on in small teaching units.

This book has been written for those who teach or will teach in these small schools, and problems here attacked are those which make teaching in the small school different and difficult. Solutions presented have emanated in techniques developed from a modern philosophy of education and from experiences in the practical application of these techniques to actual class room situations.

This book has been made possible through the coöperation of many friends of rural life whose wisdom and practical knowledge have in great measure inspired its pages. The thirty coöperating rural critics of the State Teachers College at Buffalo have assisted the author from the inception of the book until its completion. They have suggested its contents, have criticised its development, have tested its theories. My debt to them is a large one.

Colleagues on the faculty have been equally helpful. Miss Grace A. Allen, Assistant Director of Training, Miss Irene Hirsch of the Child Development Department, and Miss Muriel Bardwell, Teacher in the Summer Demonstration School, have not only read the manuscript, but have given freely of constructive criticisms and of their time in conference. Miss Bardwell has also contributed the suggested daily programs and the minimum list of equipment found in the Appendix. Mrs. Hertha Ganey has generously contributed time and skill in the proof reading of the manuscript. The interest of the President of the College, Dr. Harry W. Rockwell, in the field of rural education and his encouragement in the writing of this book have been a source of constant inspiration to the author. His unfailing support and the assistance of my colleagues on the faculty of the State Teachers College at Buffalo have my sincere appreciation and thanks.

Dr. J. Cayce Morrison, Assistant Commissioner of Education, and Miss Helen Hay Heyl of the State Department of Education, Albany New York, have also read the entire manuscript, and the text has greatly profited from their experience and wisdom. To them are due hearty thanks.

Two former teachers, Professor Fannie W. Dunn and Professor Mabel Carney, of Teachers College, Columbia, have encouraged the author by their indorsement of the book. To Professor Dunn my obligation is great. Her philosophy of education, her interest in the small school, and her zeal in its improvement have been a strong influence, evidence of which appears in every chapter of the book. The text, itself, is in reality an expansion of a magazine article written by Professor Dunn in 1936.

To my sister Azile I am always in debt.

Indebtedness is also acknowledged for permission to quote copyrighted materials from many sources. These sources are too numerous to mention here but acknowledgment is made for each in footnotes throughout the book.

KATE V. WOFFORD

BUFFALO, N. Y.
May, 1938

is in reality an expansion of a magazine article written by
Professor Dunn in 1936.

To my sister Azile I am always in debt.

Indebtedness is also acknowledged for permission to quote
copyrighted materials from many sources. These sources
are too numerous to mention here but acknowledgment is
made for each in footnotes throughout the book.

KATE V. WOFFORD

Buffalo, N.Y.
May, 1938

CONTENTS

PART I

AN INTRODUCTION TO THE RURAL SCHOOL, THE RURAL TEACHER, AND THE RURAL CHILD

PART II

ORGANIZATION OF THE SCHOOL FOR TEACHING, LEARNING, AND LIVING

PART III

EDUCATIONAL CONTROLS OF THE SMALL SCHOOL

PART IV

ENVIRONMENTAL FACTORS WHICH AFFECT EDUCATION

APPENDIX A

APPENDIX B

APPENDIX C

APPENDIX D

APPENDIX E

APPENDIX F

APPENDIX G

APPENDIX H

PART I

AN
INTRODUCTION TO
THE RURAL SCHOOL,
THE RURAL TEACHER,
AND
THE RURAL CHILD

CHAPTER I

MODERN EDUCATION IN THE SMALL RURAL SCHOOL: AN INTRODUCTION

THE SMALLNESS OF THE AMERICAN PUBLIC SCHOOL

ELEMENTARY education to the average layman, and unfortunately to many educators, is usually envisioned in units of large, well-equipped, closely graded elementary schools. If thought on this subject goes further, a teacher in charge of each grade, a principal supervising the group, and the school itself located in a city block, in a village, or, if a consolidated school, in the open country, complete the picture. True such schools exist in large numbers, but they exist, so far as numbers are concerned, in the imagination rather than in fact. Indeed, the typical school attended by the elementary school children of America is a small one, and not only does this statement hold true for elementary schools, but for high schools as well.

The latest available statistics are for 1934–1936.[1] In 1934 the United States Office of Education reported 213,484 rural school buildings in the entire country. Of this number 138,542 were one-teacher, and 24,411 were two-teacher buildings. In other words there were in 1934–1936, 162,953 rural school buildings in the United States, built for one and two teachers. Seventy-four per cent of all the rural schools and three-fifths of all of the schools in the United States were taught in buildings containing less than three rooms. The size of the enrollment further witnesses to the fact that the median elementary school is a small one. According to the 1931–1932 Biennial Report

[1] *Biennial Survey of Education, 1934–1936.* Chap. V, United States Office of Education, Washington, D. C.

of the United States Office of Education the average size of the school in terms of pupil enrollment was 485 for urban schools, 58 for rural schools. The one-teacher enrollment was even less, averaging for the United States as a whole slightly less than twenty pupils. A recent study of the one-teacher school defines the enrollment and size further. According to an estimate of W. H. Gaumnitz, Senior Specialist in Educational Problems, United States Office of Education, there was in this country in 1930 a total of 18,638 schools with an average daily attendance of seven pupils or fewer; 60,325 with an attendance of twelve pupils or fewer; and 99,750 with an attendance of seventeen pupils or fewer.[1] The same study reveals also the smallness of the American high school. According to Mr. Gaumnitz approximately one-third of all American high schools have an attendance not exceeding fifty pupils each and more than two-thirds of the schools of the United States have an attendance of fewer than one hundred pupils each.

THE RURALNESS OF THE SMALL SCHOOL

Not only is the average school in the United States small; it is located in rural areas. It is not easy to determine when an area ceases to be rural and becomes urban, nor are the differentiating characteristics easy of definition. However, for the purposes of this book the definition of the term rural as agreed upon by the United States Census and the United States Office of Education will be used. These two governmental agencies define the urban areas as those incorporated places having a population of 2,500 or more, and the remainder of the United States as rural. According to this delimitation of rural areas by the census of 1930, there were that year living in the urban areas 15,685,345 youths between the ages of five and seventeen years; at the same time there were living in the rural areas 15,885,977 youths within the same age span. Kolb and Brunner

---

[1] *Economies Through the Elimination of Very Small Schools.* United States Office of Education Bulletin, 1934, No. 3, pp. 20–23 (Dept. of the Interior), Government Printing Office, Washington, D. C.

in their recent book, *A Study of Rural Society*, estimated that 49 per cent of the twenty-six million school pupils in the United States were rural children. Said they further:

90 per cent of our 256,000 grade schools and 78 per cent of our 18,000 high schools are rural; so also are 53 per cent of our 63,348 public school teachers.[1]

Rural education, in both elementary and high school units, thus becomes, by the light of these facts, the major responsibility of the American system of schools. The fact that the equivalent of graduation from an elementary school is required in all states as a common basis for citizenship in a democracy brings this responsibility into sharp focus and gives it large significance.

THE INHERENT EDUCATIONAL PROBLEMS OF THE SMALL SCHOOL

For many years the problems of the small rural schools have been among the knottiest in the whole field of education. They fall, generally, into six large groupings:

1. The educational and sociological problems attendant upon a society which has shifted from rural to urban within the short space of seventy-five years.

2. The problems of the rural child affected by this society, particularly in the resources offered by the modern rural community for his development.

3. The problems of organization within the small school to the end that children of different grades, interests, and experiences may become functioning members of the same educational group.

4. The need for differentiations in the curricula to meet the peculiar organization of the small school.

5. The lack of books and other equipment considered essential in modern education.

6. The rural teacher and her relationships to the school and the community.

[1] Kolb, J. H. and Brunner, Edmund deS. *A Study of Rural Society*, p. 396, Houghton Mifflin Co., 1935.

Critics emphasize that any one of these problems is sufficient to cripple the efficiency of a school, and that the combination of the six creates a situation which makes modern education impossible of achievement. This would be a very gloomy picture indeed, were it a true one, but the assumption is contrary to the facts. The best proof, of course, that such a program is possible in the present and in the future lies in the fact that it has been successfully demonstrated in the past.

DEMONSTRATIONS OF MODERN EDUCATION IN SMALL RURAL SCHOOLS

In the early years of the twentieth century, Mrs. Marie Turner Harvey of the North East Missouri State Teachers College, Kirksville, Mo., successfully demonstrated what are now commonly accepted practices in modern education. Not only was she one of the pioneers in the movement later to be called "progressive," but her demonstration was in that most difficult of situations—the one-room rural school. Of later date was the demonstration of the Quaker Grove school. This four-year experimental school under the supervision of Professor Fannie W. Dunn, Columbia University, was taught by Miss Marcia Everett, now a helping teacher of New Jersey. The report of the demonstration entitled *Four Years in a Country School* indicates that modern education is possible and highly desirable in the small school. It is a record of teacher and children sharing the happy, coöperative experience of living and learning in the Quaker Grove school, an achievement which ranks high in the history of educational experiments in the United States.

These are examples of isolated demonstration schools, but there is further testimony in the modern program of rural schools in certain progressive states, notably California, New Jersey, New York, and Vermont. In these states, under the intelligent leadership of progressive State Departments of Education, the introduction of modern education in small rural schools is reaching state-wide proportions.

WHAT IS MODERN EDUCATION?

Since this book deals with modern education in the small school, it seems only fair to define the term, at least the conception of it expressed in subsequent chapters. Such a definition is more difficult than at first appears. The difficulty arises in the misconception of the term "modern," in the confusion of terminology with which the term is beset, and in the dual nature of what the schools and the public expect of the educational process.

To many people the term "modern" immediately suggests the philosophy of John Dewey, and he in turn suggests the progressive movement in education. While Professor Dewey is generally recognized as the originator of the progressive educational movement in America, the ancestry of the philosophy underlying it has an ancient history. It is heir of the Golden Age of Greece as well as of the eighteenth century. Progressive education is modern only in the sense that it is a protest against modern educational conditions. But so was the philosophy of Plato a protest against the evils of the fifth century B.C. and Rousseau's *Emile* against the low estate into which education had fallen in the eighteenth century. "Modern" when applied to education is a relative term, and designates in every age the group who suggest new ways of doing old things.

The progressive education movement usually conjures up the terms "activities," "units of work," "project method," "centers of interest," "map of values," "emerging curriculum," and other terms which connote methods of procedure within the school system. Confusion often follows the use of these terms, arising from the tendency to think indiscriminately of modern education as a philosophy, a form of curriculum organization, a technique of teaching, or a way of learning when, in truth, it includes all four. The activity unit, for example, is at one and the same time the result of a definite philosophy of education, a specific type of curriculum organization, the exemplification of a teaching procedure, and a way of child learning. Modern education in this book is presented as an integrated educational process which includes (1) a philosophy of education, (2) an organization of curriculum materials, (3) a method of presentation of the materials, and (4) a way of learning. An effort will be made to integrate the four in this text as they are integrated in the practice of the best modern schools; that is, it will be difficult to determine where one begins and another ends, because all four are represented as integral parts of a suggested program for modern education in the small rural school.

CHARACTERISTICS OF THE MODERN SCHOOL

In spite of the confusion of terms and the lack of agreement in objectives, the modern school takes on definite and distinguishing characteristics. In general, it is not difficult to determine whether or not a school operates under the modern or the traditional point of view. The philosophy is reflected in many ways: (1) in the administration of the school revealed in the relationship of children and teacher; (2) in the curriculum, particularly in its organization; (3) in the technique of teaching; (4) in the relationship the community bears to the school and the school to the community; and (5) in the position occupied by children in the total educational situation.

Administratively, the modern school is conceived of as a democracy; and its organization, the relationships of the groups one to the other, reflects its democratic principles. This democratic pattern is traced to the philosophy of Professor Dewey as stated in his *Democracy and Education*. This is Professor Dewey's evaluation of our society with a clear pattern of what he conceives would be required in a democracy, if a system of education were now established *ab initio*. We do not educate children for a democracy, according to Professor Dewey, we educate them in a democracy.

It is not, of course, a question whether education should prepare for the future. If education is growth, it must progressively realize present possibilities, and thus make individuals better fitted to cope with later requirements. Growing is not something which is completed in odd moments; it is a continuous leading into the future. If the environment, in school and out, supplies conditions which utilize adequately the present capacities of the immature, the future which grows out of the present is surely taken care of. The mistake is not in attaching importance to preparation for future need, but in making it the mainspring of present effort. Because the need of preparation for a continually developing life is great, it is imperative that every energy should be bent to making the present experience as rich and significant as possible.[1]

The modern school practices this philosophy. Children and teachers work closely together in the problems of daily living. Fortunately the small rural school has many problems offering opportunities for education in practical citizenship in a democracy as, for example, problems in sanitation, keeping the school building warm, care of the school plant and grounds, and of pooling resources in a common enterprise.

The organization of curriculum materials in the modern school is different from that in the traditional school. The curriculum is built upon the nature and the needs of children. Professor Fannie W. Dunn, advocate of the newer conception of curriculum materials and pioneer in their organization, so well states the case for the new program that she is herewith quoted at length:

. . . Integration of subject matter is effected through large units of work developed around genuine life interests and experiences. Children are not classified in closely homogeneous groups on a basis of achievements in skills or factual knowledge, but work together, as people do in life outside the school, on enterprises of common interest in which each participates according to his ability. Some are clever with their fingers, others show peculiar ability in finding and bringing in interesting objects for group use, others contribute clippings and pictures, and others search the library and report what they have read. Some paint and draw, some contrive mechanical devices, some write poems

[1] Dewey, John. *Democracy and Education*, p. 65, Macmillan, 1916.

or plays, and still others take the lead in the organization and conduct of school clubs or group games.[1]

The way children learn is of much concern to the modern school. The process of learning need not be a disagreeable process, and under right conditions and with the right guidance normal children learn easily and happily. This is no new idea in education. Rousseau in the eighteenth century was equally concerned with the learning process of children. His concern was more sentimental and less scientific than that of the modern school, but he studied the child for his technique of teaching and made his way by the light which he had, dim as it was. From this study he put forth the following principle: Children learn through a series of satisfying experiences.[2] Professor Dewey makes a similar generalization: "Individuality develops through experiencing." This theory of learning is reflected in the technique of the modern school, which shows a variation from the old-type recitation with its emphasis upon question and answer. These recitations are used in the modern school but not as in the past to the exclusion of all other techniques. The modern teacher will provide opportunities for the necessary "experiencing" of children. He will be found promoting discussion groups, encouraging research, developing the technique of study, and assisting children to the independence of self-teaching and self-expression.

Where children have their experiences is also important in modern education. Consequently, modern schools are making progress in a new type of school architecture, in the beautification of grounds and buildings, and in the development of a school plant which, in the words of Pestalozzi, banishes "the ordinary school tone like a ghost."

Under this conception of education the community assumes new importance in the learning experiences of children. For a long time educators have been aware of the significance of the

[1] "Modern Education in Small Rural Schools," *Teachers College Record*, p. 413, Vol. 32 (Feb., 1931).

[2] Rousseau, Jacques. *Emile*, pp. 42–43.

interdependence of home and school, but it is only in recent years that a movement has developed to make the community, as well as the home, an integral part of teaching and learning. As a consequence, the modern school draws heavily upon the community for teaching materials and for teaching aids. In the best modern schools it is not unusual to find parents participating in all phases of school work. They may join in activities, they may observe, they may assist with the teaching.

At the heart of the modern school, however, is a sincere regard for the individuality of children; this, too, belongs to an older idealogy. Rousseau first, then Pestalozzi, indeed all of the great educational leaders of the nineteenth century, including Froebel and Herbart held to the fundamental principle that children in themselves are important. The development of the individual child is the foundation of Dewey's educational philosophy and from it the whole movement rises, finding expression in child-centered schools throughout the world. In the modern school, therefore, the personality of the child is respected in the same way that society respects the personality of an adult. His work is significant, his leisure important, the integration of the two a pleasure. School is a place to which children go with willing feet because they find there work that is challenging, leisure which is satisfying, and a social group which gives them a feeling of adequacy and security. In the modern school the well adjusted child is also at home. The California State Commission summarizes the differences between the traditional and modern school as follows:[1]

The Traditional School Is Characterized by:	The Modern School Is Characterized by:
Formal desks and seats screwed to the floor and arranged in fixed rows.	Informal tables and chairs arranged conveniently for group activity.

[1] *Teachers' Guide to Child Development in the Intermediate Grades*, p. XIII, California State Department of Education, Sacramento. 1936.

Space not occupied by fixed furniture limited.

Some open spaces unobstructed and arranged for such activities as dramatizations, rhythms.

More or less drab interior with blackboards on three sides and limited display space.

Colorful interiors with space on which to display interesting pictures and other material on a level with the child's eye.

The teacher is a taskmaster.

The teacher is a guide and counselor.

Silence on the part of children except during recitations. Each child expected to remain seated except by permission from the teacher. Whispering and other forbidden activity indulged in secretly.

A natural social situation in which children are free to move about and consult with others as they engage in a variety of worth-while activities without interfering with the welfare of others.

Meager equipment consisting largely of standard supplies.

A variety of equipment to meet the needs. Wood, clay, large rolls of paper, paint, tools, and visual aids.

A similar set of books for each child in a particular grade. Recreational reading material and supplementary texts at a minimum.

A variety of books, both texts and recreational, chosen to meet the needs of the individuals within the group. Books and other materials arranged attractively for effective use.

Rigid grade standards. Every child must master the standards for the grade before promotion.

Instruction adjusted to the individual needs and abilities regardless of grade. Children work and play in flexible social groupings.

Short recitations of the question and answer type in the separate subjects are scheduled throughout the day. Recitations consist of giving back to the teacher the statements in the text all have

Longer periods during which study, experimentation, and discussion of a significant worth-while central theme are participated in by the group guided by the teacher. References to many studied. Answers are correct if "That is what the book said."

authorities, exchange of ideas, and a scientific attitude characterize the period.

Acquisition of factual information, to be used in adult life.

Development of a happy, well adjusted, well rounded individual here and now, who has a life interest in his fact learning.

Casual parental contacts with school. Responsibilities of home and school widely separated.

Numerous parental contacts. Close coöperation given to insure better understanding of child.

Formal reports of child's achievement in subject matter according to grade standard.

Informal report of child's growth measured against his own previous record.

The inclusion of learning within the four walls of the classroom. School set apart in the community.

The use of educative resources within the community. Pertinent materials brought into the classroom by the children. School an integral part of community.

Conformity.

Creative self-expression.

ASSETS OF THE SMALL RURAL SCHOOL IN A MODERN PROGRAM OF EDUCATION

In order to bring the ideals of the modern school to fruition, certain characteristics of the school to be served are necessary. These are (1) groups of children small enough for the teacher to know each child intimately; (2) the opportunity for checking the tool subjects and individual instruction in them, if necessary; (3) rich community resources, especially in the natural sciences; (4) a school organization which provides opportunities for democratic living; (5) community programs which supplement the school program; (6) an adequate supply of books; (7) tools with which children work; (8) proximity to men and machines at work; (9) a teacher who thinks in terms of children as well as subject matter.

Of these nine prerequisites of what might be called the equipment of the modern school, the small rural school inherently has in it four of them. The smallness of the enrollment, long one of the points of administrative criticism, actually is considered an asset under a modern conception of education. Not only does the teacher in a small school have the opportunity of knowing each child intimately, but if he remains in the school long enough, he can also know his parents, often his grandparents, and much of his home and family background. Children are not promoted out of his room until they go to high school, and consequently his knowledge of the children year by year becomes richer and more subtle. The long study periods, necessitated by many grades, for which the teacher of an earlier period strove so diligently to provide busy work, have developed in modern education into something significant and worthwhile. The average rural community provides a "million dollar" laboratory for nature study, geology, astronomy, and the other natural sciences to which rural children can be scientifically introduced. Within the heterogeneous grouping of many grades, many ages, many interests, the modern teacher sees an opportunity for education in citizenship. This organization, considered for many years as a liability, in the hands of a skillful teacher becomes an asset. This text treats of the modern methods used in developing the assets and meeting the needs of the modern small rural school. The techniques have been developed from experiments with, and practices in, the coöperating rural practice schools of the State Teachers College at Buffalo, New York. The theories here presented have been tested in typical, small rural schools, and, whenever possible, case studies have been used to illuminate theory.

The book is divided into four parts. Part I is an introduction to those important factors which make up the whole of a school—the child, the teacher, and the nature of the social order which brings the two together. Part II deals with those problems which make teaching in rural schools different and difficult, the problems of organization for teaching, learning, and living. Part III examines and evaluates the educational controls of the small school; to wit, the curriculum, the use of books, modern aids in teaching, and the environmental controls as exemplified in school buildings and equipment. Part IV deals with the environmental factors important in a modern educational program—the community and those agencies of it which tend to make education rich and vital.

SUMMARY

The elementary schools of America have certain common characteristics which determine in a measure the problems discussed in this book. These are: (1) the smallness of the typical elementary schools; and (2) the ruralness of the schools. From these characteristics have developed inherent and persistent problems; namely, (1) the educational and sociological problems attendant upon a society which has shifted from rural to urban; (2) the problems of the rural child affected by this sociological shift; (3) the problem of organization within the small school so that teaching and learning can become efficient and effective; (4) the need for the differentiation of curricula to meet the special needs of the small school; (5) the lacks in the rural school and the community environment; (6) problems allied with the status and the special needs of rural teachers.

Because of these problems, the public in general and the educational profession in particular have assumed that a modern program of education is impossible of achievement in the small rural school of less than four teachers. This assumption has been refuted by successful demonstrations at The North East Missouri State Teachers College, Kirksville, Missouri and in the Quaker Grove experiment under the auspices of Teachers College, Columbia University. The latter experiment not only demonstrated that education of modern type can be achieved in a small school, but that it is highly desirable for the satisfactory development of children.

Modern education in this book is concerned with an educational process which offers maximum opportunities for child growth in right directions. From this point of view it is assumed that the educational process involves many educational experiences through which and by which children grow and which include those offered by both the school and the community. The home, the school, the community are thus viewed as integral parts of an educational whole.

This book further holds that to bring this ideal of growth to fruition in children certain characteristics should be present in the teaching situation. These are (1) groups of children small enough for the teacher to know each child well; (2) opportunity for checking the tool subjects and for individual instruction in them; (3) rich community resources, especially in the field of the natural sciences; (4) a school organization which provides opportunities for democratic living; (5) rich community programs which supplement the school program; (6) an adequate supply of books; (7) tools with which children work; (8) proximity to men and machines at work; (9) a teacher who thinks in terms of children as well as subject matter.

The small rural school inherently has in it four of these essentials for the adaptation of a modern program, and the other five are not impossibilities. The difficulties of the small school, from the traditional point of view, may under the modern conception become assets. This text, in its twenty chapters, makes an attempt to point out to prospective teachers in training, and to teachers in the field (a) the present problems in the school of less than four teachers; (b) the assets inherent in the organization of the small school and the community; and (c) the latest experiments by experts in the field to the end that these problems may be solved, and the inherent resources used with wisdom and efficiency.

SUGGESTED READINGS

Report of the United States Commissioner of Education, 1931–1932, Chap. I, United States Office of Education (Dept. of the Interior), Government Printing Office, Washington, D. C.

Bode, Henry H. *Modern Educational Theories*, Chaps. X–XI, Macmillan, New York, 1927.

Dewey, John. *Democracy and Education*, Chap. IV, Macmillan, New York, 1916.

Dewey, John. *School and Society*, Chaps. II, IV, McClure Phillips Co., New York, 1915.

Dunn, Fannie W. "Modern Education in Small Rural Schools," *Teachers College Record*, p. 411, Vol. 32, No. 5, 1931.

Kilpatrick, William H. *Foundations of Method*, Chap. XVI, Macmillan, New York, 1925.

Kolb, J. H. and Brunner, Edmund deS. *A Study of Rural Society*, Chap. XVI, Houghton Mifflin Co., Boston, 1935.

Melvin, A. Gordon. *The Technique of Progressive Teaching*, Chap. II, John Day Co., New York, 1932.

Porter, Martha Peck. *The Teacher in the New School*, Chap. II, World Book Co., Yonkers-on-Hudson, New York, 1930.

Rugg, Harold and Shumaker, Ann. *The Child-Centered School*, Chaps. I–II, IV–V, World Book Co., Yonkers-on-Hudson, New York, 1928.

CHAPTER II

OUR CHANGING SOCIETY—THE BACKGROUND OF THE PROBLEM

OUR AGRARIAN ORIGINS

THE settlement of the new world by the old was largely accomplished through the efforts of farmers. Whatever the reasons—economic, political, social or religious—which had originally motivated the immigration of the early settlers to America, free land occupied and held them after their arrival. As soon as shelter was provided, the pioneer cleared the surrounding ground and, the seasons permitting, planted crops. Food was always a pressing matter with the early settler; whether or not he wished it, he became first of all a tiller of the soil.

The type of farming followed by the settlers in the several sections of America greatly influenced the political philosophies, social patterns, and permanent institutions of those sections. Thus the Southern farm produced a Southern pattern of life different from that of New England, and later, divergent from the social pattern of the West. The tobacco farms, for example, of Virginia, Maryland, and the Carolinas required an abundance of cheap labor and first the indentured servant from England and later the slaves from Africa answered to this need, thus instituting a system of immigration which laid the foundation of the economic and social life of the South for the space of a century.

Likewise, the New England farm left its impress upon the national life. Of these New England farmers Wertenbaker says: "Agriculture in New England, for a new country where land was plentiful, was intensive in character, following somewhat the custom of the English manor, though with no vestige of a manor lord's monarchial control. In fact the land system of the New England towns affected their life profoundly, the agrarian bond rivaling the ecclesiastical in holding the community together.

. . . "The Northern farmer played a major part in the making of America. Upon his little parcels he expended his labor, seeking by intelligent management and hard work to compensate for the stubbornness of the glaciated soil and the shortness of the summer. It is safe to say that there was nothing in New England nor in the Middle colonies quite comparable to the wasteful system in vogue in Maryland, Virginia, and parts of the Carolinas. . . . Common possession of land and the problems involved in it gave the New England townsman a certain political training that was recognized as important in Revolutionary days."[1]

The early farmers of both East and South left their impress upon the national life and today politics, religion, economics, and education bear evidence of the shaping influences of their agrarian origins.

THE RURALNESS OF AMERICA

At the taking of the first census in 1790 the United States was composed of thirteen states bounded on the west by the Mississippi River, on the south by the Spanish Colony, and on the north by the Great Lakes and the St. Lawrence River. The gross area between these points comprised 820,377 square miles, of which only 29 per cent was settled. The country was predominantly rural.[2] In the settled areas there were only six cities with a population of over eight thousand; and with the exception of Charleston, South Carolina, all of these cities

[1] Wertenbaker, Thomas Jefferson. *The First Americans, 1607–1690*, pp. 55–59, Macmillan, 1927.

[2] *A Century of Population Growth from the First Census of the United States to the Twelfth, 1790–1900*, p. 17, Government Printing Office, Washington, D. C., 1919.

were in the northeastern part of the United States. The total population in the country, including the cities, was approximately four million but only 3.3 per cent of them lived in urban areas; and the urban areas of 1790 as compared with those of the present would be classified as country towns.[1] All of the land south of the Potomac was distinctly rural, as was the land west of the Allegheny Mountains. The marshall who supervised the making of the 1790 census in North Carolina accompanied his returns with a memorandum that in the large commonwealths under his supervision there was no community with a population exceeding two thousand persons.[2]

The greater part of the inhabitants of the United States— the Office of the Census estimated it at 90 per cent during the period covered by the years 1790–1890—not only lived in the country, but engaged in some form of agriculture. Agriculture was diversified. Horses, cattle, and swine were raised in all of the states and sheep in the New England and the Middle States. Tobacco was the staple crop of Virginia, the Carolinas, and Maryland, while rice was one of the principal crops of South Carolina. In such a diversity of products the newly developing nation gave promise of being a self-sufficient one; and, since its self-sufficiency came from the soil, it was destined, apparently, even from the beginning to become an agricultural country.

THE URBANIZATION MOVEMENT

The War between the States marked the close of a social and the beginning of an economic revolution in the United States. The latter was characterized by the transfer in industry from hand labor to machinery and the development of agriculture from a simple pioneer type of farming, largely self-supporting, into a complex business. A demographic characteristic also developing from this revolution was the tendency of people to

[1] *Ibid.* p. 15.
[2] *Ibid.* p. 12.

congregate in cities. In 1860, there were 141 towns with a population of eight thousand or more in the United States and in these towns lived 16.1 per cent of the total population. In 1890 the cities had expanded to 447 of eight thousand population or over, totaling 18,272,503 people—29 per cent of all the people living in the United States. In 1900 the percentage had increased to 40. Since 1900 there has been a constant and relative decrease in the rural population and a corresponding increase in urban areas for in 1930 at the taking of the last census only 43.8 per cent of the population of the United States were living in rural areas, while 56.2 per cent were living in the cities.[1]

REASONS FOR THE GROWTH OF INDUSTRY AND CITIES

The development of industries during the period of 1870–1900 was the result of many national and international forces. During the colonial period England had sought and had succeeded in keeping America rural and agricultural. At that time England was beginning her own period of industrial expansion, and it was obviously to her advantage to discourage manufacturing in the colonies in order that she might expand her own markets. No one can read the letters and the speeches of the statesmen composing the Council of the London Company without being made aware of the dominant purpose of their programs of colonization. It was to establish a rich source of supply for English manufacturing plants. "We are left in no doubt, then, as to what England expected of her colonies. British America was not to be a mercantile country in a general sense, or an agricultural country. It must not compete with England herself, must not duplicate her manufactures—her cloth and clothes, her household utensils, her metal ware, her furniture. But it was to produce—indeed it was founded chiefly for the purpose of producing—the raw materials which

[1] *Recent Social Trends in the United States. Report of President Hoover's Research Committee on Social Trends.* Vol. I, p. 8, McGraw-Hill Book Co., 1933.

the mother country sorely needed." [1] The American Revolution, however, threw the colonies upon their own resources with the result that, under pressure of necessity, farmers turned to manufacturing, and industrial plants sprang up at such a rate that the census of 1790 showed a doubling of the number of plants known to exist prior to the Revolution.

Very early the young government began its program of special privileges to manufacturing interests and under this benevolent protection industry expanded and grew strong. As early as 1807 the Embargo Act gave protection to the interests of the manufacturing cities and Europe, absorbed in the wars of Napoleon, provided an eager market for the expanding plants of the young industrial cities of America. The War of 1812 was both helpful and disastrous to the growth of industrial plants, in its sudden demand for uniforms, arms, and other materials for war. While the revolution in industry originated in forces at work in the eighteenth century, the real significance of these forces was not apparent until after the War between the States. It was in the nineteenth century that power and the steam engine were developed, canals opened, railways laid, the settlement of the West completed, and the frontier closed.

Other factors contributing to the evolution of an industrial civilization in the United States were (a) the rapid increase in population which provided an ever expanding home market for goods; (b) the protective tariff which succeeded in limiting the importation of foreign goods; (c) the rich natural resources, especially iron, oil, wood, and water power—sources which made power available; and (d) the network of railroads which brought the sections of the country closer together and made the transportation of materials and finished products quick and efficient.

While all of these factors were important in bringing about the urbanization and industrialization of the United States,

[1] Wertenbaker, Thomas Jefferson. *The First Americans, 1607-1690,* p. 18, Macmillan, 1927.

histories emphasize the significance of the rapid growth of means of communication, specifically the railroads. Of these Hacker and Kendrick speak as follows: "The story of America since the close of the Civil War is the story of its public lands, its growing wheat country, its immigrant hosts, its industrial cities and, not least in the array, its mighty railroads. If the generosity of the government made the expansion of the agricultural areas possible, the railroads brought the free lands their settlers; if the new industrialism exploited fresh mines, built countless mills and factories, and filled the land with thousands of flaming forges, the railroads joined the raw materials with the seats of fabrication, sought out the local centers of consumption, and reached the outlets to the sea so as to make foreign markets for America again a reality; if the ocean liners entered American ports with their hundreds of thousands of foreign laborers, the railroads quickly distributed them among the textile mills of New England, the steel and iron foundries of the Pittsburgh area, the sheep ranches of Wyoming, and the coal mines of Illinois and Kansas. The essential pattern of the rails was woven into the fabric of the American life." [1]

THE MEN WHO MADE THE CITIES

In order for cities to expand and industries to grow, men in large numbers were necessary. At the beginning of the industrial expansion there were two rich sources of man power, the overcrowded sections of Europe, particularly the southern countries, and the farmer group of the United States. It is the latter group which is our concern. A study of its treks to the industrial plants of the cities reveals one of the most interesting and significant migrations of peoples within our history. About 1890 there began a drift from the farm to the city which steadily mounted in numbers and acceleration until the economic

[1] Hacker, Louis M. and Kendrick, Benjamin B. *The United States since 1865*, p. 147, Crofts, 1932.

depression of 1930, when the drift was reversed. A study of the census reports during the four decades of 1890–1930 reveals a steady increase in the urban and a steady decrease in the rural populations, which reached the rate of 5.2 per cent per decade. An analysis of the census data for 1900, 1920, and 1930 has been made by J. M. Gillette and reveals the following facts concerning farm migration: between 1900–1910 approximately 3,500,000 people moved from rural to urban areas and between 1910–1920 the migration included 5,500,000 persons. Of the movement Gillette says if we add the amount of incorporation in each case, we find that practically 6,500,000 persons from territory that was rural in 1910 shifted to territory urban in 1920. This represents the population of a city as large as New York, that of more than two cities the size of Chicago, and that of ten cities the size of Pittsburgh or San Francisco.[1]

Many studies of this migration have been made by rural sociologists in an effort to determine (a) the reasons for it and (b) the type of people composing it. The reasons for the migration generally agreed upon are as follows: (a) the desire to secure better opportunities for work than were offered by the farm and the better wages attendant upon this work; (b) the withdrawal of many processes from the farm, such as the manufacture of butter, soap, and dress materials into the factories of the cities; (c) technological unemployment resulting from the introduction of farm machinery; (d) the relatively high birth rate of the rural areas, which necessitated the immigration to cities after all free lands were taken. The types of people who left the country for the city were usually, (a) the young who sought the advantages of superior wages, education, leisure time activities, and the cultural opportunities of the city; (b) women and girls who found protection as well as vocational opportunities in the city; and (c) the aged who found in the city and village protection, medical care, companionship, and leisure. In nearly every instance, as the studies

[1] *Publications, The American Sociological Society.* Vol. XIX, p. 141, University of Chicago Press.

indicate, the individuals who migrated from rural to urban areas did so for reasons satisfactory to themselves. There were those, however, even from the beginning who looked upon the drift as a menace to the body politic. Indeed it was the migration of country people at the turn of the century which centered national attention upon the rural areas and revealed the fact that serious social and educational problems existed, for which the city was partly responsible. Out of this concern grew the historic Roosevelt Country Life Commission and its study, both of which were destined to have significant influences in the field of rural education.[1]

THE EFFECT OF URBAN DEVELOPMENT UPON EDUCATION

Since the great body of the people of the United States prior to 1890 was living in the country, the great majority of the children were securing their education from country schools. These schools had been called by various names: free, dame, grammar, "old field," and district. The colonies newly transplanted from the older civilization of Europe, at first followed foreign policies in the founding of their schools and, until the rise of the common schools indigenous to America, they were, for the most part, subscription schools with free tuition, in some cases, for the deserving poor. Sometimes the schools were under the influence of a church and often under a voluntary organization of neighbors dependent upon neither the church nor the State for direction and support. The original pattern was that of a one-room building in which a single teacher taught all the grades. Nearly all subsequent educational advancement, so far as elementary education was concerned, began with the one-room country school pattern and departed from that point. The early country school was essentially a community school, small, locally supported and controlled. It was directly influenced by the fact that the system had its source in an agrarian social order.

[1] For a further discussion of the Commission see Chap. XI.

In the beginning schools, even in the few towns, were simple ones. As the towns grew, they retained the community idea resulting from the necessities of rural and pioneer conditions and, with practically no change, the district plan of control, originating in the country was absorbed in the growing towns. Massachusetts went so far as to perpetuate the local district control of schools with the law of 1879, a law which divided the town into separate, independent districts each with its own school. In the years following, constant efforts were made on the part of the city-school administrators to destroy the district system, which was devised and suited to thinly settled areas, but poorly adjusted to growing cities. As late as 1822, W. T. Harris reported the common and deplored habit of cities in maintaining rigid district levels; and, at a much later time, Horace Mann had been moved to denounce the practice as "the result of the most unfortunate law ever enacted." [1]

This principle of local autonomy and control, so vitally a part of the American school system, was destined to influence even to the present the whole question of the public school system in both urban and rural areas.

If the rural school system influenced the urban in the early development of a public school system, the urban system set the pace and fixed the pattern for practically all later educational progress. One feature of the urban school "early thrust upon the rural school" about which educational controversies developed was the closely graded system of the city schools, a problem discussed at length in chapter five.

Urban educational leadership was achieved through the development of the professionally trained Superintendent of Schools in urban areas and the addition of Supervisors to the Superintendent's Staff. It was this administrative combination of City Superintendent and Supervisor which developed the leadership of urban school systems, and gave to its educational programs a prestige never enjoyed by rural schools. The accumulation of wealth in cities plus the strength gained from

[1] *Massachusetts Annual Report of the Board of Education, 1847*, p. 30.

trained leadership tended to develop a system of schools superior to rural schools. Superiority was evidenced in (a) longer school terms; (b) higher professional and salary standards for teachers; (c) tenure; (d) better school buildings; and (e) richer curriculum offerings, all important factors in the development of an adequate educational system.

THE DEVELOPMENT OF INEQUALITIES OF EDUCATIONAL OPPORTUNITIES IN RURAL AREAS

Four years after the report of the Roosevelt Country Life Commission, Henry Suzzallo in the Introduction to the book, *The Development of Rural Schools*, made this criticism of what he called the "neglect of the rural school." "The rural schools are about to receive from educators the attention that they deserve. The modern industrial city with its peculiar pathological conditions, has commanded both public and professional interest, but the rural community and the rural school have been neglected. . . It must be apparent to those who have taken the trouble to look closely at the country school that it enjoys no such favor as the ward school of a large city. . . As a rule the poorly trained teachers are in the country; the best are in the city. The agricultural community is economically poor; the city is rich in taxable wealth. The country teacher is isolated culturally and professionally, while libraries, museums, theatres, concerts, reading-circles, lectures and professional meetings are accessible to the city teacher. . . Thus in more than one respect the rural school has not participated in the fruits of our educational progress." [1] Subsequent developments in the field of rural education fell far short of Suzzallo's prophecy. In 1931–1932 the small school in rural areas was still operating under a low financial status. In that year in spite of the fact that 90 per cent of the graded and 78 per cent of the high schools were rural and approximately half of the children of

[1] Cubberley, Ellwood P. *The Improvement of Rural Schools*, pp. V–VI, Houghton Mifflin Co., 1912.

the United States were therein enrolled, only two-fifths of the national expenditure for public schools were expended for them. This restricted expenditure suggested a restricted educational program and, since the restriction occurred in rural areas, it indicated an inequality of opportunity for rural children at many strategic points.

There are many ways of developing educational standards but the four criteria most often appearing are: (1) the length of the school term; (2) the estimated value of property per pupil enrolled; (3) the average yearly salary of the teacher; (4) the cost per pupil in daily attendance. The 1931–1932 Biennial Report of the United States Office of Education throws light upon these points. According to that report the average length of the urban school for 1931–1932 was 181.5 days, whereas the average length of the rural school was 159.9 days. The estimated value of property per pupil enrolled in an urban school was $353, whereas for rural pupils it was $143. The average yearly salary paid the urban teacher was $1,951, while the rural teacher received $930. Salaries for urban teachers were thus twice as large as those received by rural teachers. On a basis of a minimum salary of $1000 a year, the average salary for city teachers in all but two states equaled or exceeded this amount, but in only twenty-three states did the average salary of rural school teachers equal or exceed $1000. In twelve states the rural school salaries averaged less than $700 per year.[1] The salary of the teacher, plus other current expenditures, plus the capital outlay, made the cost per pupil in daily attendance in the city $108.93 as compared with an expenditure of $64.39 per pupil in the rural schools. By all the standards of measurement the rural schools in comparison with urban schools ranked low.

Educational inequalities created by inadequate financial support have always been characteristic of small schools located in the rural areas of the United States. A recent study covering

[1] *Biennial Survey of Education, 1931–1932*, pp. 42–43, United States Office of Education.

seventy years of educational history in rural areas contained this statement concerning one source of inequality of the rural school—the rural teacher. "Salaries remained consistently low throughout the study, ranging from an average of $180 in the early period of the study to $883 at the close of it. The rural teacher of 1930, like the rural teacher of 1860, was the youngest, the most inexperienced, the most unstable, the poorest trained, and the most poorly paid of any teacher in the profession." [1]

THE SMALL SCHOOL DURING THE DEPRESSION

Another way of measuring the strength of an institution is to gauge its ability to withstand the pressure of a national calamity. By such a measurement the small schools make a poor showing, as is revealed by a study of their reaction to the shock of the World War, and in recent years, by their low status during the years of the depression, 1930–1935. All of the schools of the United States suffered during the late depression, but the small rural schools suffered most. In 1933–34 the Joint Commission on the Emergency in Education of the National Education Association and the Department of Superintendence announced that more than a million rural school children in the United States were being denied educational opportunities. Nearly all of these children had been enrolled previously in small rural elementary schools. In 1933–1934, 110,800 school children in the United States were denied opportunity to attend any school; 35,750 children attended school less than three months; and 914,500 children had six months of schooling or less. All of these were children served by the small rural school. Mr. W. H. Gaumnitz of the United States Office of Education, estimated that approximately 29,000 rural schools were operated during this period with an abnormal lack of equipment and supplies and that about 27,000 buildings were lacking essential repairs.

[1] Wofford, Kate V. *An History of the Status and Training of Elementary Rural Teachers of the United States, 1860–1930*, p. 48, Siviter Press, Pittsburgh, 1935.

NATIONAL EFFORTS TO SOLVE THE PROBLEMS OF THE SMALL RURAL SCHOOL

Various sociological and educational efforts have been promulgated and advanced to relieve the rural problem at its most distressing points. These were in part: (a) a back-to-the-farm movement; (b) state educational surveys and campaigns which led in many instances to the passage of laws which brought about longer school terms, better attendance, and the building of more adequate school buildings; (c) definite standards set up for the rural school; (d) more centralized responsibility and professional administration and supervision; (e) more equitable distribution of funds and special aid for weak schools; (f) the consolidation of small schools into larger educational units; (g) requirements of specialized training for the rural teacher.

THE CONSOLIDATION MOVEMENT

The consolidation of small schools into large ones is the plan which has promised most, administratively at least, in the solution of the problems attendant upon the original one-room pattern of the American school. The consolidation of schools is accepted as a sound educational policy by leaders in the rural field and has been actively promoted by them since 1897, when the Report of the historic Committee of Twelve of the National Education Association urged it. In the period of reform following the report of the Roosevelt Country Life Commission the consolidation movement spread rapidly, and was hailed by many leaders in education as the one and only way to improve the small rural school. Consequently, the small schools rapidly disappeared under the consolidation movement, as is indicated by the following statistics: in 1919–1920 there were in the United States 189,000 one-room schools. In 1926, the number had diminished to 161,000, an annual average decrease of 4,600.[1]

[1] Covert, Timon. *Educational Achievements of One-Teacher and Large Schools*, p. 2, United States Office of Education, 1928.

Within another six years, in 1932, the one-room schools of the country had further decreased to 143,445, an annual decrease of approximately 2,800.

In spite of the impressive decrease of rural schools, one of the significant features of the consolidation movement has been the persistence of the small school. This fact, in addition to the actual decrease in the annual yearly consolidations from 4,500 to 2,800, gives weight to Professor Dunn's statement of 1931: "True, we have every year fewer and fewer one-teacher schools. In 1917 the Federal Bureau of Education estimated their number to be 195,000. Apparently 42,000 have been eliminated in eleven years. But at the rate of approximately 4,000 a year, it would be close to forty years before the present assumption of dodoism would be true. Of course nobody knows whether we shall maintain that rate. We may accelerate it with the increasing improvement of roads and of airplane transportation; we may decrease it with the increasing sparsity of farm population. What we do know, however, is that we now have at least as many rural children in one-teacher schools as in consolidated schools—indeed, probably more—and that so far as those particular children, or the vast majority of them, are concerned, the quality of their elementary education depends upon the quality of the instruction given in small rural schools." [1]

While the consolidation of the small schools will no doubt, and properly, continue, the indications are now that the movement will be slow and that the small school will persist. Kolb and Brunner in their recent study of rural social trends not only predict such persistence, but believe it inevitable. "It is estimated that because of low population density and topography it will be impossible to dispense with between 75,000 and 100,000 of one-room and two-room schools as long as people live in the areas these schools will serve." [2]

[1] "Modern Education in Small Rural Schools," *Teachers College Record*, p. 412, Vol. 32 (Feb., 1931).

[2] Kolb, J. H. and Brunner, Edmund deS. *A Study of Rural Society*, p. 410, Houghton Mifflin Co., 1935.

Whether or not the prediction of these two well-known sociologists will come true, it is impossible to escape the pressure of present facts. The fact that there exist at present 138,542 one-teacher schools and 24,411 two-teacher schools in the United States, representing the educational pattern of an agricultural era, creates special educational problems which challenge the attention of education, none the less because they persist in an industrial civilization.

SUMMARY

The development of America from an agricultural to an urban civilization within a century is one of the thrilling sagas of modern world history. The first census of 1790 revealed a nation of four million people, 3.3 per cent of which lived in the six cities which fringed the Atlantic seaboard. In 1930 the census showed that America had become more urban than rural. Of the 122,770,000 population, 56.2 per cent of it lived in cities. In between the taking of the first and the last census lies the history of the urbanization movement. Beginning approximately at the turn of the twentieth century, the movement spread rapidly, hurried to its destiny by the steady stream of immigration from Europe and the rural areas. This influx of peoples into urban areas resulted in the following conditions: (a) the development of industries which required an abundance of labor; (b) the desire of men to secure better educational and cultural opportunities; (c) the technological unemployment of the farm occasioned by the introduction of farm machinery; (d) the withdrawal of many processes from the farm and their reappearance in factories; (e) a large birthrate of the rural areas which it could not absorb.

The migration of country to city was the occasion of national alarm. Fear of social consequences led to the appointment of the historic Roosevelt Country Life Commission in 1908, the report of which was destined greatly to influence education. The drift of the United States from an agricultural to an industrial way of life had taken a heavy toll of the country, and especially of the institutions serving it. This toll had taken the form of inequalities in educational opportunities for rural youth, as evidenced by (a) the length of school terms; (b) the value of school property per pupil enrolled; (c) the average yearly salary paid the teacher; (d) the cost per pupil in daily attendance; (e) the professional training of teachers. By comparison with urban children the rural child and the rural school ranked low. This condition was true at the time of the Roosevelt study; it was also true in 1931–1932. Various national efforts were made to solve the problem as follows: (a) a back-to-the-farm movement; (b) school legislation which raised standards; (c) state-wide standards set up for rural schools; (d) the centralization of administration and supervision; (e) the institution of a system of state aid; (f) requirement of specialized training for rural teachers; and (g) the consolidation of small schools into larger educational units. It was the latter plan—the consolidation of small schools into larger areas—which apparently promised most for rural schools and the movement has been popular and rapid. Since 1917 it has proceeded with the elimination of approximately 4,000 small schools per year. In spite of this fact, however, there are certain factors which give the small school importance and significance. The small school is a persisting institution. This is evidenced by the fact that there are still remaining in the United States 138,542 one-teacher and 24,411 two-teacher schools, over 50 per cent of all the school buildings in the United States housing schools of less than three teachers. At the pre-depression consolidation rate of 4,000 schools a year, authorities estimate that forty years would have to elapse before all the small schools can be consolidated. Rural sociologists and educational authorities prophesy that such complete consolidation will never be possible in the United States as long as people live in the areas served by some 100,000 one-teacher and two-teacher schools which exist because of population density and topography. A consideration of these factors leads one to the conclusion that the original educational pattern of an agricultural era will probably persist in an industrial civilization. Since it seems destined to serve a large and significant number of American farm people, special study should be brought to bear upon its peculiar problems to the end that the democratic principle of equality of educational opportunity for all of the children of all of the people may become a reality rather than an idealistic dream.

SUGGESTED READINGS

Adams, James Truslow. *The Epic of America*, Chaps. I–II, Little Brown and Co., Boston, 1931.

Adams, James Truslow. *Provincial Society, 1690–1763*, Chaps. I–II, Macmillan, New York, 1927.

Commission on Country Life with an Introduction by Theodore Roosevelt, Sturgis and Walton, New York, 1917.

Gee, Wilson. *The Social Economics of Agriculture*, Chap. II, Macmillan, New York, 1932.

Hacker, Louis M. and Kendrick, Benjamin B. *The United States Since 1865*, Chap. VII, Crofts, 1932.

Kolb, J. H. and Brunner, Edmund deS. *A Study of Rural Society*, Chap. IX, Houghton Mifflin Co., Boston, 1935.

President's Research Committee. *Rural Social Trends in the United States*, Vol. I, Chap. I, McGraw-Hill Book Co., New York, 1933.

Sims, N. L. *The Rural Community: Ancient and Modern*, Chaps. I–II, Charles Scribner's Sons, New York, 1920.

Wertenbaker, Thomas Jefferson. *The First Americans, 1607–1690*, Chaps. II–III, Macmillan, New York, 1927.

Wofford, Kate V. *An History of the Status and Training of Elementary Rural Teachers of the United States, 1860–1930*, Chap. I, Siviter Press, Pittsburgh, Pa., 1935.

MATERIALS FOR DISCUSSION

Consider the following statements. What changes would make them more acceptable to you? What significant issues arise from their study?

1. The small rural school is an anachronism which is rapidly disappearing.

2. Inequalities in educational opportunity for the rural youth of America were the result of the shift from an agrarian to an industrial social order. These inequalities were administrative in nature, and can be remedied by administration.

3. A modern program of education is impossible of achievement in the small rural school. Therefore, emphasis in educational administration should be placed upon consolidation rather than upon the improvement and perpetuation of the small schools now in existence.

4. The ruralness of the pioneer life of America established agrarian patterns in politics, economics, religion and education. From the standpoint of the national welfare these have been desirable.

5. If the American government had been as benevolent to agriculture as it has been to industry, a balance in the equality of educational opportunities for all children would have been maintained.

CHAPTER III

THE STATUS OF THE RURAL CHILD

THE efficacy of an educational program is the result of four factors: the environmental controls, both at school and in the community; the curriculum; the teacher; and the child. Each of these factors has at one time, or another, dominated the field of education. Indeed, each has had a little educational history of its own, the usual outline of a cycle, beginning with a struggle for ascendency, rising gradually to authority, enjoying a period of domination, and then declining to the level occupied by the other three factors.

For example, the field of education has seen the rise to dominance of the printed word, whose authority was not questioned either by the teacher or by the learner until the period of scientific discovery caused men to question everything, even the instruments of discovery. In turn scientific experimentation, rather than the authority of books, came to dominate the field and education became pragmatic. Whether or not a theory worked became the magic sesame by which educational procedure entered the classroom. The child became the object of experimentation and was minutely examined, bit by bit so to speak. Scientific instruments were devised to measure his intelligence, his behavior, his emotions, and his reactions; and from these minutiae the psychologists constructed the whole with which the classroom teacher dealt. Likewise, the authority of the teacher has dominated the field. The statement that a great teacher like Mark Hopkins on one end of a log and a student on the other made a university, indicates the apogee reached by the domination of teacher resource and personality.

At the present time education appears to be in the ascending period of domination by the child. Never before in the history of education has the child occupied so important a place in educational procedure. The curriculum grows out of his needs, his interests, and his experiences. The results of child study bid fair to dominate even the architecture of school buildings. The dominating philosophies of modern educational leaders like Dewey, Kilpatrick, and Bode are in agreement that education should be centered in the child and that emphasis should be on his welfare. They hold that education can no longer content itself with the minutiae of child nature, but that the child must be dealt with as a whole. Thus, not only is the educational procedure concerned with the intellectual development of children, it emphasizes his physical and emotional welfare as well. Adjustment, happiness, stability, and achievement are a few of the key words to the modern conception of child welfare. Consequently, an understanding of the potential material with which the school works, that is, the child, is essential to any adequate understanding of a modern program of education.

THE CHILDREN'S CHARTER OF RIGHTS

The White House Conference on Child Health and Protection, called by President Hoover in 1930, exemplified the national concern and interest in American childhood, characteristic of the present generation. Thirty-five hundred men and women experienced in education, social welfare, and medicine made an exhaustive study of children and the factors which affect their development. Out of this study grew the *Children's Charter of Rights*, a statement so comprehensive that no discussion of modern youth can ignore it. This Charter [1] embodies nineteen points as follows:

1. For every child spiritual and moral training to help him stand firm under the pressure of life.

[1] "White House Conference on Child Health and Protection," *White House Conference*, pp. 46–48, Century Co., 1930.

2. For every child understanding and the guarding of his personality as his most precious right.

3. For every child a home and that love and security which a home provides; and for that child who must receive foster care, the nearest substitute for his own home.

4. For every child full preparation for his birth, his mother receiving prenatal, natal, and postnatal care and the establishment of such protective measures as will make child bearing safer.

5. For every child health protection from birth through adolescence including: periodical health examinations, and, where needed, care of specialists and hospital treatment; regular dental examinations and care of teeth; protective measures against communicable diseases; the insuring of pure food, pure milk, and pure water.

6. For every child from birth through adolescence, promotion of health; including health instruction, and a health program, wholesome physical and mental recreation with teachers and leaders adequately trained.

7. For every child a dwelling place safe, sanitary, and wholesome, with reasonable provision for privacy, free from conditions which tend to thwart his development; and a home environment harmonious and inviting.

8. For every child a school which is safe from hazards, sanitary, properly equipped, lighted, and ventilated. For younger children nursery schools and kindergartens to supplement home care.

9. For every child a community which recognizes and plans for his needs, protects him against physical dangers, moral hazards, and disease; provides him with safe and wholesome places for play and recreation; and makes provision for his cultural and social needs.

10. For every child an education which through the discovery and the development of his individual abilities, prepares him for life; and through training and vocational guidance prepares him for a living which will yield him a maximum of satisfaction.

11. For every child such teaching and training as will prepare him for successful parenthood, homemaking, and the rights of citizenship; and for parents, supplementary training to fit them to deal wisely with the problems of parenthood.

12. For every child education for safety and protection against accidents to which modern conditions subject him—those to which he is directly exposed and those which, through loss or maiming of his parents, affect him indirectly.

13. For every child who is blind, deaf, crippled, or otherwise physically handicapped, and for the child who is mentally handicapped such measures as will early discover and diagnose his handicap, provide care and treatment, and so train him that he may become an asset to society rather than a liability. Expenses of these services should be borne publicly where they cannot be privately met.

14. For every child who is in conflict with society the right to be dealt with intelligently as society's charge not society's outcast; with the home, the school, the church, the court, and the institution when needed, shaped to return him whenever possible to the normal stream of life.

15. For every child the right to grow up in a family with an adequate standard of living and the security of a stable income as the surest safeguard against social handicaps.

16. For every child protection against labor that stunts growth, either physical or mental, that limits education, that deprives children of the rights of comradeship, of play, and of joy.

17. For every rural child as satisfactory schooling and health services as for the city child and an extension to rural families of social, recreational, and cultural facilities.

18. To supplement the home and the school in the training of youth, and to return to them those interests of which modern life tends to cheat children.

19. To make everywhere available these minimum protections of the health and welfare of children, there should be a district, county, or community organization for health, education, and welfare, with full-time officials, coördinating with a state-wide program which will be responsive to a nation-wide source of general information, statistics and scientific research.

For EVERY child these rights, regardless of race, color, or situation, wherever he may live under the protection of the American flag.

THE SIGNIFICANCE OF THE RURAL CHILD

The rural child is significant for two reasons: (1) as an individual child, and (2) as related to the body politic.   In so far as numbers may be considered significant, rural children are more important to the national life than urban children. According to the census of 1930, 50.8 per cent of the children of the United States under 5 years of age, 51.6 per cent of those under 10 years, and 51.2 per cent of those under 15 are rural children.   As a member of his family group the rural child is also numerically important.   The 1930 census reports the average number of persons per family as 4.5 for the farm group as compared with 3.9 for the cities.   If the size of the farm family in 1930 were represented by 100, those in small towns would show an index of 86, those in cities 79, and those in metropolitan areas 66.   "Children are the most significant feature of rural families; in fact, they are the most distinguishing thing about rural society itself.   The country produces children; the city consumes them." [1]

THE INTELLIGENCE OF RURAL CHILDREN

One of the questions in education about which controversy has developed is whether rural children are less intelligent than urban children.   Many studies have failed to answer this question conclusively and opinions differ.   Generally it has been found that the intelligence of urban children is slightly higher than the intelligence of rural children.   The conclusions of the Iowa Welfare Research Station are fairly typical.   In a Report of that Station in 1931 it was said that children in one-room schools are inferior to children in consolidated schools and to children in urban schools in educational achievement, and in type of intelligence measured by groups.   The Report further concluded, however, that rural children are not at the start inferior to city children in intelligence as it is measured

[1] Kolb, J. H. and Brunner, Edmund deS.   *A Study of Rural Society*, p. 27, Houghton Mifflin Co., 1935.

by instruments now available.[1] This would indicate that the difference lies in nurture rather than in nature and that the learning environment of the two groups of children is the determining factor. If this be true, the fact has much significance for the making of educational programs, especially the curriculum. Professor Dunn made the same point in the *Thirtieth Yearbook* of the National Society for the Study of Education when she said: "Since certain of the differences, notably those in language, may be said to indicate definite mental malnutrition, clear implications for curriculum-making appear, because whether the condition is attributed to nature or nurture, the child who comes to school with a language deficiency is not equipped for content or rate of learning identical with the child of normal language abilities."[2] Upon this point the Iowa study concludes:

The facts concerning the mental ability of farm children in certain communities in Iowa suggest influences that shape the lives of these children. Differences in communities, largely expressed in the character of the schools, may have an effect upon mental development. Young children below school age are alike in different localities, but after a few years in school, children begin to differ in those abilities measured by verbal tests of intelligence. Apparently in linguistic abilities, development is not the same in various environments. Facility in expression plays a part in school progress and accordingly shows in the results of educational tests. Children in different communities, however, are much alike in capacities that are not expressed in language. Rural children also compare more favorably with city children on tests that do not demand the use of language.[3]

A state-wide survey of the intellectual and educational achievements of the children of Mississippi tends to corroborate the

[1] "Iowa Welfare Research Station Report," *Nation's Schools*, Vol. 7, No. 6, 1931, p. 76.
[2] "The Status of Rural Education," *Thirtieth Yearbook*, pp. 102–103. Public School Publishing Co., Bloomington, Illinois. Quoted by permission of the society.
[3] Baldwin, Bird T. and Others. *Farm Children*, p. 262. D. Appleton-Century Company, 1930.

findings of the Iowa research. It was found in that southern state that the rural children were inferior to city children from the kindergarten through the high school. A significant feature of the Mississippi findings was to the effect that children of less prosperous sections of the state were inferior in intelligence and in educational achievement to those of the more fortunate sections. A low economic status presages an impoverished educational program and the two apparently take heavy tolls in the lives of children. Studies in Kansas, Indiana, and other states add further evidence [1] to the findings of the Iowa Welfare Research Station. The range of difference in the mental ages of rural and urban children, as revealed by these studies, is from approximately three months to one year and six months. Sorokin and Zimmerman examined some thirty such studies in both England and the United States and their conclusions were:

the greater proportion of the tests place the rural children below the urban . . . all these studies agree that the intelligence of farmer-peasants and their children is lower than the urban average. [2]

None of these investigations, including the summarizing one of Sorokin and Zimmerman, accepts the findings without criticism. Each points out that the conclusions cannot be accepted at face value because of the factors of variability which enter into them.

DIFFERENCES DUE TO VARIOUS FACTORS OF VARIABILITY

It is generally agreed by all investigators that the usual type of intelligence test does not adequately measure the ability

[1] McIntosh, H. W. and Schrummel, H. E. "A Comparison of the Achievement of Eighth Grade Pupils in Rural Schools and in Graded Schools," *Elementary School Journal*, Vol. 31, p. 300.

Pressey, S. S. and Thomas, J. B. "A Study of Country Children in (1) A Good and (2) A Poor Farming District by Means of A Group Scale of Intelligence," *The Journal of Applied Psychology*, 1919, Vol. III, pp. 282–286.

[2] Sorokin, Pitirim and Zimmerman, Carl C. *Principles of Rural-Urban Sociology*, pp. 234–236, 261. Henry Holt and Co., 1929.

of rural children. The tests used in all of the studies were devised to measure the capacity of children for school success, especially in the fields of the languages and reading, two areas in which the deficiencies of rural children are well known. Further, the tests were expressed in terms of an urban verbal ability, since they employed the vocabulary of an urban environment. Myra E. Shimberg in an investigation of the validity of norms in urban-rural groups compared the scores of rural children on a standardized information test for urban children with the scores of urban children on a standardized information test for rural children and found the differences of inferiority on each test about similar. Her conclusions were that the investigation proved that neither group was superior to the other, only that the groups were different.[1]

Another variable factor is the mooted one of what intelligence is. While psychologists may disagree on the meaning of intelligence, there is general agreement that tests used to measure superiority in one field may not measure superiority in other fields. While inferiority may be present in one ability, it does not always follow that it is present in all others. Language disability need not necessarily accompany manual disability, nor does verbal disability forecast inability to cope with concrete situations. For these differences Clairette P. Armstrong points out in *A Study of the Intelligence of Rural-Urban Children* the need for performance tests and material more relevant to the environment of rural children, suggesting that the usual verbal tests involving the constant use of a pencil can scarcely be expected to give a total measure of ability in a community where the work is almost wholly manual.[2]

Another variable factor in the intelligence of rural and urban children may lie in the high correlation which exists between parental occupational groups and the intelligence of children. The studies of Collins, Pressey, Haggerty, and many others reveal that the higher ranges in the intelligence of children tend

---

[1] "An Investigation into the Validity of Norms with Special Reference to Urban-Rural Groups." New York, 1929. Reviewed in *Archives of Psychology*.

[2] *The Journal of Educational Sociology*, Vol. 4, p. 301.

to cluster around professional fathers, and that the children of unskilled laborers tend toward the lower levels. In the Armstrong Study, which equated findings on this level by using the Taussig classification of occupational classes, the following conclusion was reached:

Gradations of difference in central tendency between the occupational classes within each group are for the most part in accordance with other research with verbal situations. That is, the professional group always leads, with the business class second, and the skilled labor and semi-skilled labor classes always lower. With concrete situations occupational class differences are less consistent and less marked.[1]

Care should be taken, however, in a classification of the parental farm group to avoid too loose a grouping such as that made by the Taussig classification. The farm group cannot be loosely classified into skilled and unskilled laborers because land owners, comprising 57.63 per cent of the farmers in America, tend to resemble the owner and manager of a business, since land, buildings, and equipment represent invested capital. The high correlation of parental occupation and the intelligence of children does suggest, however, that before conclusions are drawn as to the comparative intelligence of rural and urban children, the groups should be segregated and equated as to occupational status, nationality, school opportunity, and various types of ability should be tested. So far, few investigations have differentiated and equated the two groups into such comparable divisions.

The best critics of these studies are those who have made them, and nearly all agree that a new type of test for rural children is needed and that the variable factors in the tests so far do much to lessen their validity. Armstrong illustrates the point of view of the investigators in the conclusions of her investigation. She says: . . . "Rural-village and urban children do not differ in intelligence, either verbal or concrete, if of American parentage, of equivalent occupational class, and of

[1] *Ibid.* p. 312.

equal school opportunity. Their 'understanding and invention'
are equally good and the rural-village is probably as beneficent
a milieu as the urban in which to bring up children." [1]

THE PHYSICAL WELFARE OF RURAL CHILDREN

To the uninformed, the country is a place where children
have the greatest opportunity for all-around complete development. The abundance of fresh air, sunshine, and play space to
be found in the country is presumptive proof that the rural
environment is, par excellence, adapted to happy, healthy,
well-adjusted childhood. For many years this point of view was
held by the average layman and by educators as well. Investigations, however, reveal that the natural assets of the country
do not avail, unless they are strengthened by the provisions of
modern discovery, such as the sanitary disposal of sewerage,
control of communicable diseases, and the positive benefits
which accrue from a good community health program. Apparently nature is most efficient when assisted by the scientific
and inventive achievements of man.

One of the first investigations of the physical status of rural
children to throw doubt on the general opinion of health in
rural areas was made in 1918 by Dr. T. D. Wood of Columbia
University. Dr. Wood compiled the data for more than 500,000
school children and in his comparisons of the physical status of
rural and urban children, the rural child showed up distressingly
low. For example, the percentage of rural children showing
defects as revealed by heart disease was .74 as compared with
.40 for urban children; lung defects in rural children was 1.25,
while urban children showed .32; malnutrition defects in the
rural areas, where food is supposedly cheap and abundant,
were startling, showing 16.6, while the urban areas had only
7.65. On every item the rural children had a low rating.

These findings, at the time of the investigations shook the
confidence of the public in the country as a healthful place to

[1] *Ibid.* p. 313.

rear children and focused the attention of the public upon this national problem. The findings, however, have been seriously questioned during the past few years by sociologists, notably Sorokin and Zimmerman. "These data," they said in 1929, "are so startling and so sensational, that it is not to be wondered that after their publication, they have been quoted in all corresponding textbooks and accepted as decisive evidence of the superiority of the urban children over the rural in health." [1]

These sociologists, in turn, collected data concerning 1,800,000 children and studied them carefully from two standpoints: first, the per cents of the urban and rural children defective generally; second, the defects predominating among the urban and rural children. Their conclusions were:

These data of almost 1,800,000 children examined do not permit any definite conclusion either in favor of the city or the country. . . . If from these data, we turn to numerous local studies, and to the kind and per cent of specific defects of urban and rural children, the conclusion is in no way unfavorable to the rural children. At the worst, they are to be recognized as healthy, at least, as the urban children.[2]

The White House Conference on Child Health and Protection in one of its reports gives evidence of the wide-spread need for programs of public health, both preventative and curative, for the childhood of America, urban and rural alike. From the investigations of 45,000,000 children this committee reported that 6,000,000 were improperly nourished, 1,000,000 had weak or damaged hearts, and 382,000 were tubercular. These findings are significant for any program of education, particularly for a program which weighs the assets and liabilities of child nature and child nurture.

A study was made for the conference under the direction of Dr. T. D. Wood, of the physical status of rural children in the following states: Maine, New York, Pennsylvania, North Carolina, Wisconsin, Nebraska, California, Minnesota, and Washing-

[1] Sorokin, Pitirim and Zimmerman, C. C. *Principles of Rural-Urban Sociology*, pp. 144–145, Henry Holt and Co., 1929.
[2] *Ibid.* p. 145.

ton. From the findings of the study the following conclusions were drawn.

1. That rural children lack proper nutrition, as evidenced by the absence of a balanced diet whose lacks included the very assets with which nature blesses rural people—milk, fruits, and vegetables.

2. That rural children need to develop regular habits of eating and sleeping.

3. That rural children do not show a proper annual gain in weight, presumably because of poor eating and sleeping habits.

4. That rural children do not develop proper posture and skeleton development.

5. That the teeth of rural children are so badly neglected that many cases of deafness, disorders of digestion, and general debility of adults can be traced to this neglect.[1]

All of these deficiencies are possible of remedy, and four of them easily so, were the natural assets of the rural environment properly used. Professor Fannie W. Dunn places the responsibility for this situation on the lack of intelligent effort. Says she in an introduction to a recent book on health:

It is in the application of intelligent effort that the crux of the matter lies. That rural homes and neighborhoods are not always wholesome places for human life comes, in very high degree, as a result of inadequate education for health. Here is the challenge to the rural school, and its opportunity and responsibility for utilizing to the fullest all the rich resources for healthful living which country life affords.[2]

PERSONAL AND EMOTIONAL CHARACTERISTICS OF RURAL CHILDREN

Research of the psychologists and the experience of the classroom teachers have revealed the fact that an unhappy,

[1] White House Conference on Child Health and Protection. *The School Health Program.* Report of the Committee on the School Child, p. 293, Century Co., 1932.

[2] Grout, Ruth E. *Handbook of Health Education,* p. VI, Doubleday, Doran and Co., 1936.

ill-adjusted child does not learn as easily nor as efficiently as one who is happy in his personal life and well-adjusted to his social group. Consequently, the study of the personal and emotional characteristics of children grows more important and significant both in preparation for teaching and in practical classroom procedure. Both theory and practice in child study are in agreement that every child has two fundamental needs which should be met for satisfactory emotional adjustment; namely, security and the opportunity for development. Three areas, all close to the child, are responsible for adequately meeting these needs. In the words of the Children's Charter, they are:

. . . A home and that love and security which a home provides . . . a school which is safe from hazards . . . which through the discovery and the development of his individual abilities prepares him for life . . . a community which recognizes and plans for his needs . . .

Unfortunately, information relative to the emotional development of children in rural areas is meager. Such studies as we have are too scattered and too limited for generalizations. However, they are suggestive, not only for the light they shed on rural children, but because they suggest the opportunity, as well as the need for further study and research.

GENERALIZED BEHAVIOR OF RURAL CHILDREN AS REVEALED BY STUDIES

The Witty-Lehman Study of Children's Interests

Adequate studies in the generalized behavior of rural children are lacking, and such studies as have been made are too limited for general statements. Consequently, the studies presented here are mainly those for which no generalization is possible. Witty and Lehman, long interested in the collecting activities of children, made through them in 1933 a study of the interests of town and country children. The general conclusions of this study follow.[1] 1. Country children collect many more objects

[1] Witty, Paul A. and Lehman, Harvey C. "The Collecting Interests of Town Children and Country Children," *Journal Educational Psychology*, Vol. 24 (Mar., 1933), p. 170.

than do city children. Amplifying this finding the study states: "Collecting is frequently an individualistic, competitive type of behavior. The child rarely engages in collecting as a member of a group or team . . . What effect this individualistic, competitive type of behavior is likely to have upon numerous attitudes of the rural child is a matter of conjecture. It seems plausible, however, in the light of the laws of habit-formation that the collecting endeavor of the rural child might make of him an individualistic adult. Today many assert that the American farmer is inclined to be individualistic in his outlook and in his attitudes—too individualistic for his own good. The charge is often brought that farmers are incapable of coöperating politically. Whether this charge be valid or not the data in this paper suggest that geographical isolation might well be a factor that makes for individualism.

"A foremost objective of the modern school is expressed by the single word 'Socialization.' This being the case, it seems plausible that, if interest in collections is a fair example of his generalized behavior, the rural child is in even greater need of a socialized school program than is the town child. The frontiersman, the pioneer and the farmer have doubtless lived in environments that made for individualistic outlook. Their children have also been subjected largely to similar influences. But if the modern child is to live his adult life in an urbanized environment, it is necessary that he learn coöperation." [1]
2. The largest number of collections for rural children took place at the age of eleven, and for the town children at the age of ten. This suggests to Witty and Lehman that the rural child matures more slowly than the city child, and this belief is given some substantiation by the fact that the typical rural child is likely to be slightly older than the city child of the same grade.
3. The articles selected by the rural child were, on the whole, botanical specimens, animal parts, insects, rocks, and minerals. The authors saw in this a naturally anticipated evidence that the rural child has closer contact and a better acquaintance with the

[1] *Ibid.* p. 182.

objects of nature and a greater interest in them than has the city child.

4. The study concludes that town life tends to suppress certain natural modes of behavior, specifically whistling and singing. These are participated in by rural children more freely and spontaneously than was evident in the town group. Said the study: "Although rural life seems to permit freer expression to certain natural modes of behavior, it affords less opportunity for participation in certain organized group activities." [1]

The Baldwin Study of Iowa Farm Children

The Baldwin Study reported from its observation of the farm children of Iowa that the outstanding characteristic of children in the small school is aloofness. [2] This reached the stage of positive timidity in beginners, some of whom refused to recite for days, or even weeks. The older children, while less reserved, showed embarrassment when addressed by a stranger and, a conversation once started, answered largely in monosyllables. This attitude suggests, as the Witty-Lehman study did, the need for socialization in the small rural school.

The Baldwin Study further revealed that, in spite of an occasional lowering of standards in personal conduct, the integrity, honesty, and sincerity of the adult farm family group was a potent influence in the lives of children. Occasional rumors of petty thievery and low conduct were to be heard, but family and community pride tended to minimize the guilt of such youthful offenders, indicating to the investigators a fact already well known; namely, the ability of the rural group to punish the misdemeanors of its own members by the powerful weapon of public opinion.

Studies of the Attitudes, Wishes, and Problems of Rural Youth

In 1926 Kirkpatrick printed the results of a study he had made of the attitudes and problems of farm youth. He reported that,

[1] *Ibid.* p. 183.

[2] Baldwin, Bird T. and others. *Farm Children*, D. Appleton and Co., 1930, p. 121.

while rural children want opportunities for group games and expressed the wish for recreational facilities more often than did city children, fewer opportunities were provided for meeting these desires and needs.[1]

The Baldwin Study reported the same lack of social contacts, giving as an indication of this need the behavior of the children observed. The study reported that children hurried through their home chores in order to arrive early at the school playground for a game of ball or tag. The same behavior was in evidence at recess, when children hurriedly ate lunch in order to play, many of them playing even as they ate. Morgan and Burt in their study of the "activity wishes" of Missouri young people also reported like findings. Of the 1,431 young people studied 56 per cent of the wishes expressed were recreational, but only 8 per cent of the total organizations found were available to meet these needs and only 7 per cent of the young people were members of such organizations.[2]

SUMMARY AND IMPLICATIONS FOR EDUCATION

One of the outstanding characteristics of modern education, as has been said, is the emphasis placed upon the child. The changing curriculum, school buildings, and the whole field of child development are outgrowths of the domination of the child in the educational program. A high point in this modern emphasis was reached in 1930 with the calling of the White House Conference on child health and protection by President Herbert Hoover. An investigation participated in by 3,500 people and lasting two years presented as the crowning achievement the Children's Charter of Rights. In nineteen principles, the Conference summarized and set forth what American childhood has a right to expect of modern civilization. The charter is ap-

[1] Kirkpatrick, E. L. *Attitudes and Problems of Farm Youth* (Mimeographed), United States Dept. of Agriculture, Washington, November, 1926.

[2] Morgan, E. L. and Burt, H. J. *Community Relations of Rural Young People*, Research Bulletin 110, p. 74, Missouri Agriculture Experiment Station, Columbia, Mo., 1927.

parently destined to have great influence upon the future programs which affect children.

According to the modern conception of education all children are important, but the rural child has special significance in American life for two reasons: (a) over half the children of America are reared in rural areas, and (b) the place occupied by the rural child is of supreme importance in the family group. In the available studies of rural children controversy has developed among psychologists and sociologists concerning their intelligence, their physical welfare, and their emotional development. Studies are few and the samplings limited; consequently there can be few generalizations. The studies, however, indicate the following:

1. The intelligence of rural school children is slightly lower than that of urban school children. This statement is not true at birth and indicates that its cause lies in nurture rather than in nature.

2. The health and physical well being of rural children are approximately the same as that of urban children.

3. The death rates of rural peoples are high from the communicable diseases now capable of control. This rate is possibly traceable to the fact that health-control standards are low.

4. In spite of the handicaps of (2) and (3) the health in rural areas is slightly better than the health in urban areas. This fact suggests (a) that the inherent conditions of rural areas are conducive to healthful living, and (b) with proper sanitary controls the country would prove a better place to rear children than urban areas.

Studies of the personal and emotional life of rural children indicate that the assets and deficiencies in their environment tend to develop in them the following characteristics: individualism, familiarity with the natural world, a feeling of personal security in their family groups, aloofness, conservatism, shyness, and high standards of personal conduct.

While it has been impossible in this chapter to achieve a clear-cut picture of the median rural child, the facts revealed in it are rich in implications for education. They suggest the following steps in the planning of a program which uses his resources and supplies his needs.

1. It is obviously the responsibility of the school and the community to provide rich reading experiences for rural children to the end that the lack of verbal ability revealed by intelligence tests be rectified.

2. Essential to the welfare of rural children and adults is the addition of proper sanitary controls in rural communities. The school as the community home should represent in sanitation and health the best that can be afforded. Health conditions further indicate the necessity for a functional health program in the school curriculum, taught in terms of local child needs, and developed to the end of healthful living every day.

3. The tendency to individualism, aloofness, and timidity suggests a program of socialization for rural children which begins with the organization of the school into larger groups than grades and extends to the community organizations which offer possibilities for social development and graces. It further suggests the organization of the school into a little democracy and the integration of the group to the point where the whole of living and learning becomes a joint and common enterprise.

These three points are another way of stating a long-accepted principle in education, only recently come into practice: in teaching we should begin with children where they are, using the resources at hand, and supplying the needs to the end that rural children develop to full stature, not only in their own environment, but in a larger one, which embraces the whole world.

SUGGESTED READINGS

Baldwin, Bird T. and Others. *Farm Children,* Chaps. VIII–X, D. Appleton and Co., New York, 1930.

Benedict, A. E. *Children at the Crossroads,* Chaps. I–II, Commonwealth Fund, Division of Publications, New York, 1930.

Brim, Orville G. *Rural Education,* Chap. VIII, Macmillan, New York, 1923.

Gee, Wilson. *The Social Economics of Agriculture*, Chap. XXI, Macmillan, New York, 1932.

Kirkpatrick, Ellis L. *The Farmer's Standard of Living*, Chap. IV, Century Co., New York, 1929.

Kolb, J. H. and Brunner, Edmund deS. *A Study of Rural Society*, Chap. II, Houghton Mifflin Co., Boston, 1935.

President's Research Committee. *Recent Social Trends in the United States*, Vol. II, Chap. XV, McGraw-Hill, New York, 1933.

Sims, N. L. *Elements of Rural Sociology*, Chaps. X–XI, XXI, Crowell Co., New York, 1928.

Sorokin, Pitirim and Zimmerman, C. C. *Principles of Rural-Urban Sociology*, Chaps. V, XI, XV, Henry Holt and Co., New York, 1929.

Taylor, Carl C. *Rural Sociology*, Rev. ed., Chap. XIII, Harper Brothers, New York, 1933.

MATERIALS FOR DISCUSSION

Consider the following statements. What changes would make them more acceptable to you? What significant issues arise from their study?

1. In spite of the fact that over fifty percent of the youth of America reside in the country, the national programs in recreation, education and culture are organized and promulgated in the interest of urban youth. This practice greatly influences the level of culture for the American people.

2. The country offers more opportunity than the city for the normal development of children in the following areas: health, mental growth, and emotional stability.

3. There is no conclusive evidence that rural children are lower in intelligence than urban children.

4. Since the rural child is an important economic factor in the home unit and is required to perform many farm tasks outside school hours, agriculture and farm mechanics should occupy an important place in the school program, and elementary education should emphasize these subjects.

5. The tendency to individualism, aloofness, and timidity characteristic of farm children suggests the necessity for a program of socialization in the home, the school and the community.

CHAPTER IV

THE TEACHER IN THE MODERN SCHOOL

STATUS OF THE TEACHER IN THE SMALL SCHOOL

CHAPTERS II and III have presented the problem of the small school in terms of children and the number of schools. The teacher in the small school presents another significant phase of the same problem. According to the 1934–1936 Report of the United States Commissioner of Education, there were in the United States in 1934, 138,542 teachers in one-room schools and 48,822 in two-room schools, making a total of 187,364 teachers, approximating one-third of all the elementary school teachers in the nation.[1] By sheer force of numbers this group of teachers is important, but of greater significance is the fact that approximately five million elementary school children of America are enrolled in their classrooms. The type of person composing this great army of teachers in the small rural schools is important because he is not only a determining factor in an educational program which seeks to meet the needs of children in modern schools, but is also, in many instances, a community leader who determines community programs. Fortunately, a recent study by the United States Office of Education reveals a rather clear picture of the individuals who make up this group.[2] In 1931 a study was made of 61,172 white teachers in schools of less than three teachers. This study represented areas well distrib-

[1] *Report of the United States Commissioner of Education 1934–1936.* Government Printing Office, Washington, D. C. Advance pages, Bulletin, 1937, No. 2, p. 8.

[2] *National Survey of the Education of Teachers*, p. 346, Vol. 5, United States Office of Education, 1933, Bulletin 10, Government Printing Office, Washington, D. C.

uted geographically in 48 states, and, according to Professor Mabel Carney who made it, gives a fair picture of the personnel serving the sampled areas. The results of the study were in accord with former studies and revealed the median teacher of the small school to be young, of the female sex, inexperienced, poorly paid, and poorly educated.

YOUTHFULNESS OF THE RURAL TEACHER

Twenty-five per cent of the group were twenty-two years of age or younger. The oldest fourth averaged only thirty-one years of age or older, while the middle fifty per cent of the entire group ranged in age from twenty-two to thirty-one years. Professor Carney compared these figures for the first quartile, the median, and the third quartile of the group with those of teachers in villages, in towns of less than 2,500, in towns from 2,500 to 10,000, and in cities ranging from 10,000 to 100,000. In each instance the teachers in the one-room and two-room schools were the youngest and the least mature. In the village situation the average was 23, 26, and 33 years; in the towns 24, 28, and 36 years; in the cities 26, 30, and 39 years, indicating a correlation between the size of communities and the ages of their teachers. Gaumnitz reported on a refinement of the data of the youngest fourth of the group teaching in the small rural school. He found 23.5 per cent of all the teachers of one-room schools to be twenty years of age or under. All of this leads to the conclusion that in 1931–32 the average age of teachers in the small rural school was only twenty-four years.

THE FEMININITY OF THE GROUP

Teaching in the elementary schools of the United States is done almost wholly by women. This fact not only holds true for the rural schools, but for the urban as well. According to the 1931 study by Professor Carney 87.8 per cent of all the elementary teachers in the open country and 95.7 per cent of those in the urban group were women. In the small rural schools the percentage of men teachers is higher than in the elementary schools located in towns and cities. According to Professor Carney, however, the proportion of men among rural elementary [1] teachers was 12.2 per cent, almost three times as great as was found in the urban elementary teachers, where it was but 4.3 per cent. In six states, Arkansas, Indiana, New Mexico, Ohio, Utah, and West Virginia, 30 per cent or more of the rural elementary schools were taught by men, while in Kentucky, Oklahoma, and Pennsylvania more than 20 per cent of all rural teachers were men. In spite of the large percentages of men in the above states, however, the median teacher of 1930–31 in the small elementary school was female as well as young.

THE MARITAL STATUS OF THE GROUP

Of the teachers composing the group for the small rural schools 81.4 per cent are unmarried. Indeed, marriage is one of the deterring factors in maintaining a long period of service for this group and explains in part the short tenure of the rural teacher. While the tendency in the past has been for the rural teacher to leave the profession upon the event of marriage, the present trend appears to be toward a continuation of teaching after marriage. In support of this trend Professor Carney reported that 18.6 per cent of the group studied were married and that ten states reported married women in a third, or more, of all the rural teaching positions. These states were: Arizona, California, Delaware, Florida, Nevada, New Jersey, New York, Oregon, Rhode Island, and South Carolina. The rural led the urban areas in the proportion of married women teachers, just as it did in the percentage of men teachers. Of the urban elementary teachers 16.5 per cent reported marriage. This tendency for married teachers to continue in the profession indicates a new trend in elementary education, however, the

[1] *Op. cit.* p. 345.

median teacher of 1931 was not only young and female—she was also unmarried.[1]

PROFESSIONAL PREPARATION

The professional preparation of the group teaching in the small rural schools was, by nearly all standards, low. Of the 61,299 teachers responding to the questionnaire, the survey revealed the following: 9 per cent of the group had a four-year high school education only; 33.6 per cent were four-year high school graduates with one year of college education; 28.7 per cent were graduates of four-year high schools plus two years of college background; 62.3 per cent were high school graduates with one or two years of normal school education; and 3 per cent were four-year college graduates. Of the group, 63.3 per cent reported that they had pursued courses related specifically to the problems of rural school teaching. While there is no agreement by authorities on the type of education best suited to preparation for teaching, there is rather general agreement that four years of education beyond the high school should be the minimum. To reach this standard the rural teacher must raise the average from two years of college preparation to four. Professor Carney sums up the median rural teacher as follows:

. . . The typical white teacher in the one- and two-room open country school in 1930–1931 was a young woman, unmarried, about twenty-four years of age, of farm or village background. Her education consisted of four years of high school and one year or more of professional preparation somewhat directed to rural school needs. The experience of this typical rural teacher was 4.6 years during which time she had taught in two different rural schools. Her median annual salary in the fall of 1930 was $788 but during the year she received a salary reduction of 10 per cent. She worked eight months out of twelve teaching twenty to twenty-five children through eight grades of elementary curriculum and performing, especially during the depression, a considerable number of community and welfare services as well.[2]

[1] *Ibid.* p. 346.
[2] *Ibid.* p. 356.

HOPEFUL ASPECT OF THE STATUS

The status of the rural teachers in small schools when compared with that of the teachers in the urban groups is low. However, an examination of the elements which compose the status reveals the following hopeful aspects: (a) historically, there has been a constant upgrading of standards in the rural group; (b) many of the characteristics of the rural teacher are considered assets in a modern program of education.

There have been three studies which throw light upon the upgrading of standards among rural teachers. One was made in 1910 by Lotus D. Coffman, who reported that the median teacher of the small rural school was then a young woman slightly over twenty-one years of age, whose teaching experience equaled two years and two months, whose education was three or four years beyond the elementary school, and whose salary totaled three hundred and sixty-six dollars per year.[1]

In 1912, two years later, Harold W. Foght reported similar findings to the Coffman Study but an increase in experience of the median teacher by approximately three years, and in professional preparation by one year of high school.

In 1935 a history of the status and preparation of rural teachers was published which covered the years 1860–1930.[2] The author concluded that, while low standards of education were a persisting characteristic of the seventy years covered by the study, there was evidence of a slow but steady improvement of standards for the group. This advancement began in 1880 and affected the age, the experience, the education, and the salaries of the group. Beginning in that year with elementary education only, the standards had increased by 1930 to six years beyond the elementary school. Evidence of upgrading in experience and maturity was also noted: In 1890 the rural teaching group was described as "school boys and girls;" by 1921 the maturity

[1] *Social Composition of the Teaching Population*, Contributions to Education #41, Teachers College, Columbia University.

[2] Wofford, Kate V. *An History of the Status and Training of Rural Teachers of the United States, 1860–1930*, Chap. 3.

of the group had increased to a median age of twenty-two years. While salaries remained consistently low, there was a gradual increase from $180 at the beginning to $883 at the close of the period covered by the study.

Professor Carney in her study summarized the advances as follows:

After a full half century of small laborious gains, open country teaching, peculiarly benefited and in some sense favored by the present economic depression with its resulting surplus of teachers, is at last on the threshold of professional standardization. Whether it now attains actual admission into the conclave of the elect will depend upon the wisdom with which necessary adjustments of the immediate future are shortly affected.[1]

Another hopeful aspect of the status of rural teachers lies in the fact that many of the characteristics of the group are considered desirable in a modern school program. Under a traditional program of education, authority in the person of the teacher was emphasized, and uncritical "respect for authority" was considered a virtue in children. The weight of authority rested in maturity, and youth was considered a liability which only time could remedy. Hence the youth of the rural teaching group was considered detrimental to a sound educational program, and leaders in the field of rural education deplored it. Modern psychological investigations, however, have revealed the fact that maturity does not always synchronize with chronological age. In one and the same person emotional maturity may be achieved at one time and chronological maturity at another. The adage concerning an "old head on young shoulders" may be psychologically true, and by the same token an irresponsible head may rest on old shoulders. Age is not always a criterion of wisdom.

The modern school, therefore, holds no special brief for chronological maturity. Indeed, it gives evidence of preference for young teachers who are emotionally mature. The combina-

[1] *National Survey of the Education of Teachers.* Vol. 5, Chap. II, p. 357, United States Office of Education, 1933, Bulletin 10.

tion of emotional stability and youth suggests an adaptable and adjustable personality, which is desirable in all teachers, but essential in those who teach in rural areas. In writing of these qualities in rural teachers Wayne Soper, Research Associate, State Education Department, Albany, New York, said:

For the obvious reason that the rural teacher must adapt herself to a variety of elements it is evident that she should possess that quality which enables her to make that adjustment. Her failure to adapt herself to one major element of the community, whether it be the younger pupils, the older ones, the parents, the "younger set," the religious group, or the farmers' union, may have a direct bearing upon her success as a teacher in the community. While city life is vastly more complex than country life, the urban teacher has no such variety of elements to adjust herself to *as a teacher*. She may even disregard many of these elements and suffer no ill effects so far as reappointment is concerned. She is rated by her superior officers on her ability to do a good piece of teaching. Her rural sister is rated by every element of the community on every aspect of life claiming attention in the community.

The unresourceful urban teacher may call upon her principal, her supervisor, her fellow teachers when need arises. The rural teacher has no such "ever present help in time of trouble." [1]

The social composition of the teaching group, described in Professor Mabel Carney's study, has in it elements considered valuable for modern education. These elements are found in the life-likeness of the group which includes a large percentage of married women and men. Leaders in thought, outside the field of education, have long pointed out the shortsightedness of a policy which selected teachers for the elementary schools from an isolated group of unmarried women. They suggested, and investigations have tended to corroborate their belief, that this policy has tended to set up an artificial situation from which children suffer. Marriage and parenthood are both enriching experiences and an individual is likely to be the better for them. If modern schools are to reflect life, it seems reasonable that

[1] "The Successful Rural Teacher," *New York State Education*, Vol. 18 (Nov. 1930), pp. 245–246.

the teachers in them be encouraged to pursue as normal a life outside of school as possible. Normality, insofar as our social order is now organized, includes marriage, the establishment of a home, and parenthood. The fact that 30 per cent of the rural teachers in 6 states are men and that in 10 states a third or more of the rural teaching positions are held by married women indicates a modern trend in educational practice which harmonizes with a modern philosophy of education.

Even the low educational standards of the rural group are not without their bright side. They suggest the desirability and—with rising certification standards—the necessity of further study. Courses in modern education are of recent addition to the curricula of normal schools and teachers' colleges. It is, therefore, these teachers of experience returning for additional work in summer schools and extension courses who are put in touch with, and profit from, the newer movements in education. Those teachers who have achieved minimum standards in educational requirements, and are therewith content, often become static and self-satisfied. The achievement of standards such as have been generally attained in the urban elementary teaching group may become a deterring factor to growth, just as the lack of them may encourage further achievement.

DESIRABLE PROFESSIONAL QUALITIES OF THE MODERN TEACHER

There is no agreement of authorities on the most desirable professional qualities for the modern rural teacher. Opinions differ because there has not yet been devised a satisfactory measurement of those intangible qualities which make for success in teaching. A canvass of all available literature, however, indicates a pattern of both the professional and personal qualities which writers in the field of education believe most often achieve success; namely, (a) a broad cultural education, which includes a rich knowledge of the social studies; (b) a functional knowledge of the natural world, especially in the fields of astronomy, geology, nature study, and agriculture;

(c) skill in the practical arts—carpentry, crafts, stage craft, etc.; (d) a rich knowledge of child psychology and 'development; (e) a knowledge of and skill in the new techniques, in addition to the old; (f) an acquaintance with the field of experimentation in methods of teaching reading, writing, and arithmetic.

(I) *The Encyclopedic Knowledge of the Rural Teacher.* The average teacher in the one-room schools of the United States teaches eight grades; the teacher in the two-room schools approximately one half the number; and the teacher in the three-room school an average of two and one half grades. This teaching load, characteristic of small schools, necessitates a broad, general education for the teacher. He must be able to teach among other subjects music, art, the social studies, science, mathematics, and literature. At the beginning of the school day he may participate in a discussion on tariffs and the gold standard; from this he may transfer to a recitation on Treasure Island; the next period he may teach a six-year-old child to read; and he may have to change from this to a unit on the geology of the neighborhood. A broad cultural education is desirable for all teachers, but it is a necessity for those who teach in small schools. This type of education becomes all the more essential in the light of the limited facilities of the average school library and of the fact that unless the teacher shifts from school to school he will teach the same children from year to year. There is no promotion of children from room to room; no relief which may come from special teachers of art, music, and health. The teacher in the small school is literally all things to all the children. He may not teach all subjects equally well, but he will find it necessary to attempt it. He cannot afford to be a specialist. He must indeed achieve an encyclopedic knowledge of the whole field of education. This goal is impossible to achieve in the two years of education beyond the high school, now the average attainment of the teacher in the small rural school. This suggests the necessity for the continued growth of rural teachers, the cultivation of an open, inquiring mind.

(II) *Functional Knowledge of the Natural Sciences Needed.* One of the fields in which the rural teacher should attempt mastery is that of the natural sciences. Essential to a modern program of education is the ability of the teacher to teach in terms of her environment. The environment of the rural school is closely allied with nature. Rural children, even before they enter school, are familiar with the functional aspects of their environment. The coming of seasons, the weather, the dependence of the farm group upon nature for its welfare are already a part of his life; indeed, familiarity with these phenomena may breed contempt for what his group may designate as "common things." Only a well-educated teacher whose text-book science functions in terms of "common things" can interpret to children the wonder of them. The soil and the earth-and-water formations of the neighborhood take on new meanings when scientific geology is presented by an enthusiastic teacher. So with the stars, the local birds, and the community flora and fauna. Success in teaching the natural environment of the rural school lies not so much in the identification of its flora and fauna as it does in the interpretation of natural phenomena to children. Emphasis should therefore be placed on nature projects, developed through activities in which children can participate. Not only will a functional knowledge of science stand the rural teacher in good stead for the teaching of the natural environment, it will also prove invaluable in other subjects. Every activity, if properly taught, at one time or another in its development draws upon the field of science for materials.

(III) *Knowledge of Child Development Necessary in a Modern Program of Education.* In addition to the encyclopedic fund of subject-matter necessary for the rural teacher, it is important that he have also a wholesome knowledge of, and respect for child development. It is no longer enough that teachers "get along well with children." They must bring to their tasks an understanding of how children learn, and a knowledge of the interests of children, at all levels, to which they respond and grow. These understandings include a knowledge of child

Photograph by William A. Thomas

Set in the midst of a "million dollar laboratory" the rural school offers rich opportunities for understanding the natural sciences.

nature, a respect for individual differences, and an acquaintance with the principles of modern dynamic psychology and of personality difficulties and adjustments. Personal interest in children has always been considered a characteristic of good teaching, but to this interest it is essential that the modern teacher add knowledge of how children develop—mentally, physically, and emotionally.

Closely allied with a knowledge of child development is acquaintanceship with current experimentation in the methods of teaching the tool subjects; specifically, reading, writing, and arithmetic. In these three elementary school subjects the largest number of experimentations have taken place in reading, and for good reasons. Investigations of retarded pupils have revealed the fact that more than 50 per cent of the first-grade children in rural schools fail of promotion each year. The subject in which these children fail most often is reading. Since reading is an essential by which children find their places in the organization of a rural school, this condition is serious. Fortunately, scientific investigations offer aid on this strategic subject. An example will illustrate the point. It is the custom for children in rural areas to enter school for the first time at the age of five, five and a half, or six. In addition, they may enter, except for a few controlled areas, at any time during the school year. At their entrance, since the small rural schools have no kindergartens, they are immediately set to reading, apparently before many of them are ready for the experience. Research studies and the practices of successful teachers indicate that children should not be introduced to reading until they reach the physical, social, emotional, and mental maturity of a child of six, or six-and-one-half, years. These states of development do not always synchronize and failure may follow. The ability of the teacher to recognize reading readiness in children might avoid the tragedy of failure for the immature six-year-old. To recognize reading readiness is a professional achievement. Scientific investigations are gradually giving light on all the learning problems of children, at all stages of their development. In order to utilize these findings the teacher will find it necessary to keep himself informed on them.[1]

(IV) *Essential Skills in the New Techniques.* The teacher in the modern school will need to develop skill in the old techniques of handling the assignment, hearing recitations, and holding examinations, but he will need also to add to his equipment skills in what are called the new techniques. Of these Professor Fannie W. Dunn says:

There is no question that the teacher who would successfully pursue a program of modern education in a rural school must be master of certain definite techniques. It is generally recognized that techniques are essential to any teacher. What has not been equally recognized is that certain special conditions of teaching require special techniques, and that the small rural school is one such special condition. Techniques appropriate for formal work in a graded school will fit very poorly, if at all. Techniques suitable for progressive work in a graded school come nearer fitting, but certain adaptations even of these are desirable.[2]

These adaptations are listed by Professor Dunn as follows:

One of the most important techniques required of the teacher for present-day education in the small rural school, and indeed in any school, is that of participating in group discussions as a member of a group, taking the lead only when or as the group's need for guidance requires, but surely taking it then. This technique most of us, wherever we teach, probably need to continue to perfect throughout all our teaching days.

A second technique of special importance to the teacher of the small rural school is that of handling a heterogeneous group of children as one class. I have seen skillful rural teachers do this again and again, but the ordinary training in class teaching will never develop the

[1] See the following:

Bigelow, Elizabeth B. "School Progress of Under-Age Children," *Elementary School Journal*, XXXV (Nov. 1934), pp. 186–192.

Harrison, M. Lucile. *Reading Readiness*, Chap. II, Houghton-Mifflin Co., 1936.

Morphett, Mabel Vogel and Washburne, Carleton. "When Should Children Begin to Read?" *Elementary School Journal*, XXXI (Mar. 1931), pp. 496–503.

[2] "Modern Education in Small Rural Schools," *Teachers College Record*, Vol. 32, No. 5 (Feb. 1931), p. 421.

technique. I recall a country teacher whom I watched as she conducted a geography lesson with all grades from fourth through eighth participating. They had a common problem, but pupils of differing advancement had different shares in its solution. The upper-grade pupils had used advanced geographies in preparation for the class discussion; the younger ones had used the first geography book. Some had read in supplementary geographical readers, others had found pictures in the *National Geographic Magazine* or the illustrated encyclopedia, and still others had referred to government bulletins. Sand-table work had been going on, also outlining and the making of booklets. Every child was participating, even—and as a matter of fact, especially—a dull and backward boy who had been classified as fourth grade solely on account of his size. "Harold found something for us in the Agricultural Atlas," the teacher would say, calling on her one eighth-grade pupil for his contribution. Or, "Fourth grade, you can tell us about this. You are helping to show it on your sand table."

A third important technique consists of the subordination of the so-called "recitation" to the independent study of the pupils. In the country school much of the pupils' study must go on at times when the teacher's attention is demanded for classwork with another group. Under these circumstances, class periods are too valuable to be wasted in mere recitation. Perhaps the city teacher can afford to spend them in this way, but the country teacher certainly cannot. There are too many other things needing to be done, if the study periods are to be profitably used. Selecting a group enterprise, formulating the purpose or the problem clearly, setting up plans for work, criticizing plans, distributing responsibilities, and reporting progress; practice under teacher oversight of desired habits of work to be later pursued unsupervised; guidance in the use of encyclopedia and dictionary, of indexes, tables of content, and of card catalogues; instruction in outlining and notebook work, or in the use of individual practice materials; introduction to tools and training in their use; discussion of school conduct and development by the pupils of plans and regulations for self-control and group control—these and many similar matters must be given right of way in the precious periods when teacher and pupil meet.

A fourth important technique is concerned with the organization of the school management in such a way as to make it definitely educative. In the care and beautification of school grounds, in the essential housekeeping duties and sanitary provisions, the responsibility for which in the small rural school devolves mainly upon the teacher and pupils, in organization of the play activities for all groups, in the school lunch, in the protective care of the smaller children, and in the government of the school, there are potentialities for genuinely progressive education, provided the teacher sees the opportunities and knows how to use them.

And a final technique involves recognition of times when individual instruction is more serviceable than class work on a common problem, and the provision as needed of a period or periods when each child is engaged in the work which is of most concern to him at the moment, while the teacher passes about the room, giving a word of advice here, a brief criticism there, sitting down by this child to help him over a difficult place, or calling these two or three to her for assistance on a point which is troubling them all.[1]

(V) *Skill in the Practical Arts.* One of the most obvious characteristics of the modern school is the participating of children in activities which involve the practical arts. In a room full of children some will be observed reciting, some reading, others may be using their hands in weaving a rug, painting at the easels, working on a frieze, or constructing a pioneer fort. Modern education makes use of both the head and the hand and places a high premium upon many forms of expression, including such media as the drama, the dance, art, and music. Consequently, the teacher in the modern school will find it to his advantage to develop skills in carpentry, stage craft, puppetry, and the like. The creative activities of children necessitate the activity of the teacher; therefore the ability to draw, to construct, to build, to weave, and to sew should be part of the equipment of every modern teacher.

DESIRABLE PERSONAL QUALITIES OF THE MODERN TEACHER

As with the professional qualities of the modern teacher, there is no agreement on the personal qualities which apparently make for success in teaching. Many studies have been made in an at-

[1] *Ibid.* pp. 421-423.

tempt to arrive at criteria for the measurement of such traits, the most comprehensive being the Commonwealth Teacher-Training Study. This study tabulated twenty-five traits in a master list ranked according to their importance for five groups of teachers; senior high school, junior high school, intermediate, primary, and rural. The following traits listed in their order of importance for rural teachers are as follows: adaptability, breadth of interests, considerateness, coöperation, good judgment, honesty, self-control, and leadership.

An examination of these traits shows them to be desirable for teachers in both traditional and modern rural schools. The latter schools, however, require, in addition, special differentiating traits. There is no agreement here, but a canvass of available opinions appears to rank the three following personal traits high: (a) the capacity for continuous growth; (b) a personal philosophy of education with not less emphasis on children than on subject matter; (c) a sincere regard for what is commonly called the "rural heritage."

(I) *Capacity for Growth.* The capacity for growth is the mainspring of the professional life of the modern teacher. Failure on the part of the teacher to grow is a contravention of the ideals set for the modern school, just as the failure of children in continuous all-round development indicts the whole system.

Education is a vital, growing, adventurous enterprise only as teachers participate in continuous growth. Life comes only from life; growth only from growth. The primary characteristic, then, of the master teacher is willingness, yes, eagerness to grow—to adventure boldly, to act compassionately, to live abundantly. If this imposes an obligation on the teacher, it bears its own rich reward. The growing teacher is repaid a hundred times over for her greater efforts; repaid in consciousness of accomplishment, in happiness in her work, in joy in useful living. There is comfort in routine, a certain appeal to the inertia in all of us; but in growth there is vibrant joy, the zest that makes life eminently worth while.[1]

[1] California State Department of Education. *Teachers' Guide to Child Development,* p. 9, California State Printing Office, 1930.

Capacity for growth connotes intellectual curiosity, courage to attempt the new, and willingness to put forth earnest effort in fresh experiences, by which adults as well as children learn. Growth does not necessarily mean promotion, or change in position or salary; though all three are likely to follow. Professional growth rather suggests an in-service development in the art and science of teaching. Graduation from college or normal school is only the initiation of a development in teaching which should continue throughout the period of professional activity. Adventures in learning are not in the prerogatives of children only; teachers, too, share in them, and so limitless are the possibilities for growth in teaching that for its apogee a lifetime is all too short.

(II) *A Philosophy of Education with Not Less Emphasis on Children than on Subject Matter.* William Boyd writing in *Progressive Education* for March 1931 says:

The difference between the old education and the new is not a matter of method at all, but of spirit and understanding. There is only one proper answer to give the teacher desiring to begin a new way of education, "Make a beginning with yourself." . . . The new education comes into being as soon as the teacher takes the right attitude toward the pupil. Kindness and humanity are the minimum essentials.[1]

The ability to think in terms of human values as well as in terms of subject matter is an attitude which should probably take precedence over all other attitudes in the teacher of the modern school. This is, of course, another way of saying a long-accepted truth in education; namely, that schools should be child-centered and the welfare of children placed first in all educational programs. While this theory has been accepted in the field of education, it has, unfortunately, not been put into general practice. The reasons for this slow development have been many.

In the first place, too many college teachers of education have exactly opposite attitudes in the treatment of teachers

[1] "Begin with the Teacher," *Progressive Education*, Vol. 8, p. 235.

in preparation. Their chief concern lies too often in the subject matter about education rather than in the development of individual students. The tendency to imitate is a well-known characteristic of the average student-teacher so that the attitudes of those who prepare him to teach are highly significant. Lip service to Dr. Dewey fails to make his philosophy function in the work of the student teacher and hence afterward. If this philosophy is divorced from practice by his college teachers, he is likely to imitate such procedures in his own teaching. He may state by pen and by word that he believes children are more important than subject matter; yet every movement he makes in his classroom may belie his statements.

Further, too many schools operate by a system of education which places undue emphasis upon rewards for a mastery of subject matter and too little upon satisfactory child development. This fact, unhappily, often hinders the teacher in the transference of his own attitudes toward children into practice. Discouraged, he may find himself slipping into old, accepted, and respectable ways of teaching subject matter instead of teaching children.[1] Paramount among the personal traits which make for success in modern teaching is that mental attitude which holds steadily in philosophy and in practice to the principle of child worth. Minus this philosophy, practice in dealing with children becomes merely "a sounding brass."

(III) *Regard for the Rural Heritage.* Another attitude highly desirable in rural teachers is respect for the inherent worth of what is commonly called "the rural heritage." Unfortunately, many rural teachers never recognize this unique asset. They are so busy gazing at deficiencies in the rural environment and bewailing what they discover that much of the fine quality of rural life is lost upon them. As has been suggested elsewhere in this book, there is no elementary school situation anywhere which offers such possibilities for the teaching of science as does the rural school. The rural environment is rich also in educa-

[1] Wofford, Kate V. "Significant Attitudes to be Developed in Rural Teachers," *Educational Method*, Vol. XXII No. 7 (Oct. 1936), p. 512.

tional possibilities for the teaching of art, music, history, and mathematics. There is no other organization in America which offers better natural opportunities for the teaching of civics and government at first hand than the meetings of the average rural community. Upon the attitude of the teacher depends in a large measure the rural child's attitude toward the glory and wonder of his rural heritage.

Another phase of this appreciation of the rural heritage which cannot be overlooked in the education of rural teachers is the acknowledgment of the place occupied in the nation by the American farmer. Politicians have appreciated this place, but the teaching profession has been slow to do so. The student of rural sociology and rural economics can scarcely avoid the facts concerning this important member of the social order. His record in the agrarian period of American life speaks for itself: he displayed energy, independence, self-reliance, loyalty, and devotion to democratic ideals. The new nation was literally a product of his labor and sweat, and into it went much of the fine idealism which characterized the early days of the Republic. With the change from an agricultural to an industrial social order the farmer suffered many losses. He not only suffered economically but sociologically and psychologically as well. In spite of these setbacks, however, the American farmer still remains one of the most independent men on earth. His courage, his long suffering, his ability to survive a depression which began ten years prior to the urban crisis of 1929 disclose a heroism and dependability rarely equaled. These qualities attest his nobility; they lengthen his shadow; they are worth preserving in the national life. It is important that he be exalted in the eyes of his own and his neighbor's children, not only because of his fine individual qualities, but also for his contribution to the welfare and happiness of the world. The teacher's attitude will likely find its reflection in the attitude of the children, and for better or ill in every professional, or social contact which he makes in the community.

TEACHING ACTIVITIES OF THE SMALL RURAL SCHOOL AS THEY AFFECT TEACHER QUALITIES

In 1929 Verne McGuffey made a study of the differences in the activities of teachers in rural one-teacher schools and of those of grade teachers in cities. His findings indicate that with respect to a large number of items that are associated with success the duties, responsibilities, and activities of the teacher in the one-room school differ from those of the grade teacher in the city. The activities involving the greatest difficulties for the teacher in the one-room school have to do with a comparatively small number of situations. These are "(1) problems involved in legal relations; (2) problems arising from managing all the grades together; (3) problems arising from the necessity of adjusting teaching methods to fit the rural situation; (4) problems arising from difficult living conditions to which the teacher is not accustomed; (5) problems arising from the necessity for assuming professional, social, and economic leadership in the community."[1]

An examination of these difficulties reveals that they fall into two groups: (a) those attendant upon the duties of a teacher; (b) those related to the duties of a principal. With the exception of the small school, there is no teaching situation which combines so completely the work of the teacher and principal. In the one-room school they are one and the same. The incumbent not only has the responsibilities of a teacher in a single grade, except that they are usually multiplied eight times, but, as a principal, he is responsible for the administration of the school itself; for making reports; for keeping records; for the satisfactory adjustment of the environmental controls of the school such as heat, water, light, or ventilation; for the administrative details of the daily program; for the adjustment of the courses of study; and for contact with the community and board of trustees. As a consequence of these dual respon-

[1] *Differences in the Activities of Teachers in One-Teacher Schools and of Grade Teachers in Cities,* Teachers College Contribution to Education No. 346, p. 58, Bureau of Publications, Teachers College, Columbia University.

sibilities, one of which is administrative, both the professional and personal traits of the teacher in the rural school should culminate in a superior quality of leadership.

SUMMARY

The teacher in the modern rural school, according to the latest available statistics, is a young woman, inexperienced, poorly paid, and poorly educated. These characteristics of rural teachers have been persistent throughout the history of education. There are, however, several hopeful aspects to the situation: (a) historically there has been a constant upgrading of standards in the rural group in all of the above named characteristics; (b) many of the characteristics are considered assets in a modern program of education. Specifically, these characteristics lie in the sociological composition of the group which contains large numbers of young married men and women, and in the lack of preparation which necessitates continued study while in service.

The status of the rural teaching group does not, however, tell the whole story of the modern teacher in the rural school. There are, apparently, special professional and personal characteristics which are desirable for the group. The desirable professional qualities suggested are (a) a broad cultural education which has in it encyclopedic characteristics; (b) a functional knowledge of the natural world, especially in the following fields: astronomy, geology, nature study, agriculture; (c) skill in the practical arts—carpentry, crafts, stage craft, etc.; (d) a rich knowledge of child psychology and development; (e) a knowledge of and skill in the new techniques, in addition to the old; (f) an acquaintanceship with the field of experimentation in the methods of teaching the tool subjects. In addition to the personal qualities agreed upon for the teacher in the traditional school, the modern teacher should also have: (a) the capacity for continuous growth; (b) a personal philosophy of education developed in the interest of children as well as subject matter; (c) a sincere regard for the "rural heritage."

All of these qualities culminate in the need for a superior type of leadership in small rural schools. Leadership is needed because of the dual nature of the task of the teacher in the small schools, which includes (a) the responsibilities of a regular classroom teacher and (b) the responsibilities of a principal. The teacher in a small rural school is faced with perhaps the most difficult task of any American teacher—a task requiring the best material our society can afford.

SUGGESTED READINGS

Carney, Mabel. "The Pre-Service Preparation of Rural Teachers," *Teachers College Record*, Vol. 34 (Nov. 1932), p. 110.

Cook, Katherine M. and Others. *Professional Preparation of Teachers for Rural Schools*, Bulletin No. 6, 1928, United States Office of Education (Dept. of the Interior), Government Printing Office, Washington, D. C.

Dunn, Fannie W. and Others. "Modern Education in Small Rural Schools," *Teachers College Record*, p. 411, Vol. 32, No. 5, Feb., 1931.

Gaumnitz, W. H. *Status of Teachers and Principals Employed in the Rural Schools of the United States*, Bulletin No. 3, 1932, United States Office of Education (Dept. of the Interior), Government Printing Office, Washington, D. C.

Heyl, Helen Hay. "Redirecting the Training Program for Teachers of Rural Children," *Proceedings of the National Education Association*, 1935, p. 413.

Lowth, Frank J. *Everyday Problems of the Country Teacher*, Rev. ed., Chaps. II–IV, Macmillan, New York, 1936.

McGuffey, Verne. *Differences in the Activities of Teachers in One-Teacher Schools and of Grade Teachers in Cities*, Chap. III, Contributions to Education, No. 346, Bureau of Publications, Teachers College, Columbia University, New York.

National Society for the Study of Education, Thirtieth Yearbook, *The Status of Rural Education*, Chap. VI, Public School Publishing Co., Bloomington, Ill., 1931.

National Survey of Education of Teachers. Vol. 5, Chap. II, United States Office of Education (Dept. of the Interior), 1933, Bulletin 10, Government Printing Office, Washington, D. C.

Washburne, Carleton. *Adjusting the School to the Child*, pp. 170–174, World Book Co., Yonkers-on-Hudson, New York, 1932.

MATERIALS FOR DISCUSSION

Consider the following statements. What changes would make them more acceptable to you? What significant issues arise from their study?

1. Potentially, rural teachers are the most significant force in public education in the United States. Comprising one-third of all elementary school teachers, they teach nearly fifty percent of American youth and assume at the same time large responsibilities for community leadership.

2. Contrary to the traditional conception of education, the distinguishing characteristics of the rural teacher—that is, youthfulness, the tendency to marriage, and the necessity for continued in-service education—are considered as assets in a modern program of education.

3. The rural teacher, more than any other, should have a broad cultural education of encyclopedic proportions.

4. The education of rural teachers should be differentiated in curriculum, in length of training, and in practice teaching from the education of those who teach in cities.

5. The capacity for growth is the mainspring of the professional life of the modern teacher.

PART II

ORGANIZATION OF THE SCHOOL FOR
TEACHING, LEARNING, AND LIVING

A play corner dedicated to the needs of five and six year olds is an essential feature of all modern rural schools.

CHAPTER V

MAKING THE PROGRAM

HISTORICAL BACKGROUND

THE teacher in the small school has always been faced with a problem of administration peculiar to his teaching environment. It involves the necessity of handling a group of children of different ages, abilities, interests, and stages of learning, so that they constitute an educational whole. This single administrative problem develops into many: the wise and economical use of the school day, the individual adjustments of children, and the skillful use of the curriculum in the learning process. These problems have always been present in small schools and have long pressed for answers. To meet them many devices have been employed.

The first was the grading of the schools, a practice adopted from its successful use in urban schools. The adoption of such a plan seemed inevitable. The teacher of the small school at the turn of the nineteenth century was faced with a teaching situation which had in it two annoying and wasteful deficiencies: the lack of classification of pupils and, accompanying this, the non-uniformity of textbooks. It was a common practice at that time for the children of the country schools to classify themselves according to their own textbooks, bringing those available at home without consulting the teacher or any other competent authority.[1] The use of many books under the direction of a trained teacher is desirable according to the philosophy of the progressives in education, but for the poorly qualified teacher of 1890 the multiplication of textbooks meant

[1] Wofford, Kate V. *An History of the Status and Training of the Elementary Rural Teachers of the United States, 1860–1930*, p. 59, Siviter Press, 1935.

a multiplication of classes, apparently to the bewilderment and confounding of both teacher and pupil. Children usually found their places in the school organization by reading ability and in answer to a question of location within the school system would reply: "I am in the third reader" rather than as now, "I am in the third grade." Much of the instruction was individual and pupils progressed, on the whole, at their own rate of speed. Teachers taught from early in the morning until late at night, but often at the close of the day had not "heard" all of the recitations. Under these conditions a uniform adoption of textbooks and a uniform system of grading children developed conterminously in the urban school, and the system was later adopted in toto into the rural schools.

While the grading system seemed well-suited to the administrative necessity of grouping large numbers of children in urban schools, it gave evidence from the very beginning, of being ill-formed for the small rural schools; but how ill, not even its critics could foresee. The grading of the rural schools could not be accomplished easily. Strong criticisms of the plan were voiced. Said W. T. Harris, at that time the distinguished Commissioner of Education for the United States, in his report of 1890–1891:

In my opinion there is no worse evil in the country school than the classification of pupils which is attempted in many states under the supposition that what has proved a good thing in the very large cities would be beneficial if practically adopted in the small schools of the rural districts.[1]

Later Dr. Harris, as Chairman of the subcommittee on Instruction and Discipline in Rural Schools of the Committee of Twelve of the National Education Association, reiterated his position and stated that the satisfactory grading of the rural school was not only undesirable, but impossible.

Dr. Harris had a strong ally in Henry Sabin, State Superintendent of Public Instruction in Iowa. In the 1891 annual

[1] *Report of the United States Commissioner of Education, 1890–1891.* Vol. 2, pp. 1054–1055, Government Printing Office.

report of the State Department of Public Instruction, Mr. Sabin declared that the educational forces were committing an error to force upon the small schools of the country and villages the standards of the graded school of the city. Said he:

These schools cannot be closely graded, fewer regulations and rules are necessary than in the larger places, and there is less need of close supervision.[1]

By 1910, despite the objections of educational leaders like Harris and Sabin, the rural teacher found himself not only teaching in a school graded after the manner of the city schools, but using a course of study made for urban situations. This course of study was usually planned for an eight-month, or a nine-month, school term and for a teacher with from one to two grades. Conditions which followed were inevitable. The teacher found himself struggling with a situation as difficult as the one prior to the grading of schools. He was attempting to use a course of study ill-suited to the needs of his school; he was teaching a group of children ranging in age from six to eighteen years and in learning from the A.B.C's to Caesar. His teaching day was divided into an average of forty recitation periods, each recitation averaging ten minutes in length. Under the drive of this multiplicity of classes, his day became a succession of hearing lessons, his teaching a deadly routine. It was the initiation of the school survey as a technique for determining the status of schools which revealed the sorry plight into which the rural schools had fallen. The early school surveys of North Carolina, Virginia, Maryland, Delaware, Indiana, New York, and South Dakota demonstrated that the small school presented a peculiar administrative problem to which educators needed to give attention. The problems of organization in the small school had not diminished under the graded system, but, as Dr. Harris had prophesied, had multiplied in number and increased in difficulty. Efforts to meet these difficulties took three directions: First, the ad-

[1] *Iowa Biennial Report of the State Department of Public Instruction, 1891*, p. 35.

ministrative plan to limit the number of grades to be taught in certain types of rural schools; second, increased attention to the remaking of the state courses of study in relation to rural life and their adaptation to the one-teacher and other small schools; and third, the development of plans or devices for the reduction of the number of grades and hence the number of classes in the small school.

The plan of limiting the grades to be taught in rural schools helped but did not solve the problem of too many grades and too many subjects. Moreover, the limiting of grades pre-supposed the centralization of schools and the transportation of children. Consequently, the plan could be used only in favored localities and under limited conditions. Two of the states leading in the movement to delimit the number of grades were Louisiana, which set the limit in 1913 to five grades for the one-room school; and North Carolina, which limited the one-teacher school to elementary grades only. The second plan of providing courses of study for the special needs of rural schools had wider use and results. This plan, however, will be discussed at length in Chapter XII of this book. The third plan; namely, the development of plans for the reduction of the number of grades and the number of classes in the small school is the concern of this chapter.

PLANS FOR THE REDUCTION OF GRADES AND CLASSES

The chief problem in the organization of the small school for efficient teaching and learning lies in the inherent difficulties found in the large numbers of classes and grades, the small number of children usually found in each class, and the wide difference represented by the group in age, experience, and interests. There have been many means devised for the meeting of these problems, but all have had the same goals: (a) to reduce the number of classes and recitation periods, (b) to extend the length of the class period with the teacher, (c) to enlarge the size of social groups. Chief among the plans devised to attain these goals have been: (a) the combination and alternation of grades, (b) the combination and the alternation of subjects, (c) the integration of subject matter into units of work.

The Combination and Alternation of Grades. One of the earliest plans developed for the reduction of the number of classes in small schools was what has come to be known as the "Combination and Alternation of Grades." Apparently, the idea originated in Illinois, where it was popularized by U. J. Hoffman, but it was quickly taken up by other states and spread rapidly. An indication of the popularity of the plan is revealed by a study made in 1922 by Charles M. Reinoehl, and printed by the United States Office of Education. Reinoehl discovered, after an examination of 44 State Courses of Study, that 73 per cent of the number recommended the use of the plan for the organization of small schools, and that most states made it mandatory.

Details for the combination of grades vary according to local needs. Usually the plan includes the combination of grades III and IV, V and VI, VII and VIII. In the South, because of its elementary school organization of seven grades, the combination usually includes grades II and III, IV and V, VI and VII. Because of its system of Regents Examinations, the State of New York recommends no combination in the grades VII and VIII. Many states do not recommend the combination of grades I and II except for classes other than the tool subjects. The combined grades are usually designated in the new organization by letters of the alphabet. "A" usually for grades VII and VIII, "B" for grades V and VI, "C" for grades III and IV, "D" for grades I and II. If grades I and II are combined, a school of eight grades becomes organized, under this plan, into four groups which meet as classes. The number of classes is thus reduced by half.

As a corollary to the reorganization of the program, a few states have organized their courses of study to fit the combination of grades. Generally, two outlines are furnished the schools for each group of classes: A, B, and C. Efforts are made to make the outlines as nearly agree in difficulty as possible, so that children can pursue either outline without being too seriously handicapped. The outlines—one for each year—are set up in terms of odd and even years, the children entering in the odd years pursuing the same outline of subject matter found in the regular order of the grades. It is only the children who enter school in the even years who take an indirect route through the grades, pursuing upper grade work before they complete the lower. Thus a child who enters school for the first time in September 1936 will take the following route: for the first two years of his school life he will remain in his normal grade; that is, for 1936–1937 he will be assigned to grade I, in 1937–1938 he will be located in grade II. In the fall of 1938 his route will become devious. He will be assigned to Group C and take fourth grade work; in 1939–1940 he will study third grade materials; in 1940–1941 he will skip to sixth grade; and in 1941–1942 will switch back to the outline for grade five; in 1942–1943 he will study and recite in the eighth grade level; and in 1943–1944 he will return for his seventh grade materials.

THE THREE-YEAR PLAN OF QUAKER GROVE

The experimental school at Quaker Grove, referred to in Chapter I, developed a different combination of grades, and since the plan is practical and is growing in favor an examination of it seems valuable at this point. One of the first problems attacked in the experiment was that of planning the daily program. Enrollment in the eight grades of the school ranged from forty to fifty children and obviously an efficient organization of the school day was immediate and pressing. It was soon realized, however, that the goal involved more than an organization of time since the necessity for grouping grades and children was also present. To meet this exigency the children were divided into three groups instead of the traditional four, or five, and the subject matter to fit these groups was organized into three cycles of X, Y, and Z years instead of the years designated as odd and even. One group consisted of the primary grades I, II, and III and was designated as Group C; a second grouping was accomplished by a combination of the intermediate grades IV and V into Group B; and the upper grades VI, VII, and VIII were combined into Group A. By such an organization the eight grades were thus reduced to three groups which fall easily into the framework of a daily program.

Grades VI, VII, and VIII worked together as Group A in all subjects except United States History, an exception necessitated to meet local state requirements. Grades IV and V were combined in all subjects as Group B. Grades I, II, and III were combined as a single class and worked together in all subjects except arithmetic and reading. Grade I was not scheduled for formal arithmetic, and had separate classes in reading and word study.

A rather helpful feature of the organization was the emphasis placed upon reading. This was accomplished as follows:

In addition to the regular organization of reading within the groups, i. e., Group A, Grades VI, VII, and VIII as one class; Group B, Grades IV and V as another; and Group C, Grades II and III as a third; there are two connecting classes, Grades III and IV as one and Grades V and VI as another. Thus each child, from second grade through sixth, has half his reading instruction with a grade below his own and half with a grade above his own. In each case, two combined grades read in texts suited in difficulty to the lower of the two grades comprising the group. Various types of reading exercises are used—book reports, audience reading, training lessons in silent reading for various ends, appreciative study of literary masterpieces, reading for oral expression, dramatization, etc. Individual practice exercises for comprehension and vocabulary development, and individual reading for recreation or information in connection with other studies, supplement the work of the reading classes.[1]

Ordinarily, under this plan, each group of pupils completes

[1] Dunn, Fannie W. and Everett, Marcia A. *Four Years in a Country School*, p. 4, Bureau of Publications, Teachers College, Columbia University, 1926.

the work in three years, and with the completion of the three groups is ready for entrance into the first year of a high school in the eight-four plan, and, with slight adjustments, the six-three-three system. However, the plan provides richly for individual differences. Indeed one of its strongest features is its flexibility. Highly superior children can complete the course in six or seven years instead of nine, while slow ones can pass from group to group at a slower rate of speed. This advantage is explained by the authors as follows:

Adjustments to individuals can be made in many ways. Ordinarily three years will be required to complete the work of Group C. Only a distinctly superior child may be expected to be ready for work of B-Group level at the end of two years. Children completing the whole course in eight years will divide the remaining five years variously. Some will spend two years in Group B and two years in Group A. Still others, after two years in Group B, working partly in Group A and partly in Group B, for a third year, will finish with two years more in Group A. Unless for some unforeseen reason there should be unusual slowing down of growth at the intermediate level, more pupils may be expected to spend two years in Group B and three in Group A than vice versa.[1]

The essential features of this plan have been incorporated into the New Jersey State Course in the Social Studies, used by the teachers of that state with considerable success. The plan has indeed much to commend it. By it the recitation period is increased beyond the time allowed by the grouping plans discussed in previous paragraphs. The social unit of pupil participation is enlarged and within the cycle of three years each child is given a unique opportunity for development. The first year a child enters a group, he is likely to be immature and exhibits little evidence of leadership. The second year, however, he stands between those who are younger and those who are older and from one group he can receive help and to the other he

[1] Dunn, Fannie W. and Bathurst, Effie G. *Guide and General Outline Social Studies for Rural Schools, A Tentative Three Year Plan for Combining Classes,* Dept. Rural Ed. and Institute of School Experimentation, Teachers College, Columbia University, 1932 (Manuscript) p. 5.

can give it. In the third year he is the "big boy," he is older, he knows more, and, presumably, he has developed leadership. In the meantime, the superior child has moved through the cycle in two years and may be ready at the end of them to assume his place in an upper group. In the process no one is failed, no one is retarded. Each child progresses at his own rate of speed and on his own steam, as it were. According to teachers who have used this plan it is a natural one, since it follows the natural psychological stages in child development. That is, Group C specializes in learning to use tools, Group B uses these tools in study, and Group A develops in the exploratory experiences of the junior high school. Leaders in rural education predict that the plan will grow in favor, particularly if courses of study are developed in cycles to correspond to the cycles of the organization. Experiments in such a curriculum organization are described in Chapter XII.

WEAKNESSES OF THE ALTERNATION PLANS

Weaknesses of these plans are obvious and criticism of them usually makes the following objections. (1) It is not always possible to arrange the material for a two- or three-year period with such even distribution as not to interfere at some points with the natural development of the child's ability. (2) To many teachers, and, more often to the layman, the step the child takes from Grade II to Grade IV and from Grade VI to Grade VIII seems excessive, while the step from Grade IV to III, and from Grade VIII to Grade VII seems slight and of little consequence. This difficulty is met by an adjustment to individual differences. Some teachers hold the advanced section of the class responsible for large assignments and for it require a higher standard of work. Others organize the subject matter material in the form of contracts or projects, requiring more work of the older and more advanced students. Many other teachers, however, out of their experience maintain that the steps are not excessive, and that the problem exists only in the preconceived mind-set of those who think in terms of a sequence of subject matter built upon grades. Professor Fannie W. Dunn writing on this point makes the succinct statement:

The fundamental difficulty in the situation, as has already been intimated, lies in the assumption of the grade as the irreducible and basal unit of organization in the one-teacher school, so that all plans for reducing the number of classes must proceed by combining and alternating *grades*. Now this means actually combining the *children* of two grades into one class, and alternating the already organized *subject matter* of one grade with the already organized subject matter of the other. This, in turn, seems to imply that the organization of subject matter, as it has been set up to fit the conditions in elementary schools of at least eight teachers, is the only and inevitable organization of that subject matter. And this is contrary to fact.

Subject matter may be organized in an indefinite number of ways. A history course may begin with primitive man or with Romulus and Remus, or with the discovery of America, or with the Civil War, or with innumerable other events according to the era with which the course is designed to deal. It may begin with the past and trace events chronologically to the present, or with the present and go back to seek its roots in the past. Geography may deal first with the globe, and the hemispheres, then with North America, the United States, South America, Europe, Asia, Africa, and Australia; or it may transport beginners in the subject first of all to Mesopotamia; or it may develop along other and quite different lines. Arithmetic may exhaustively treat addition before approaching subtraction, subtraction before multiplication, multiplication before division. Or, as in the Speer Arithmetics widely used during the last part of the nineteenth century, it may teach at one time the addition, subtraction, multiplication, division, and fraction aspects of any one number before proceeding to the next number. Long division usually precedes fractions in arithmetic texts and arithmetic courses. But it is possible to teach every fractional process before even introducing long division. That all these things can be done is uncontrovertibly proved by the fact that every one of them has been done. Moreover, we are yet without scientific proof of the superiority of any special organization.[1]

[1] Dunn, Fannie W. and others. *Organization of Curriculum for One-Teacher Schools*. Department of Rural Education of the National Education Association, Bulletin 1933, p. 10.

The other weaknesses, according to critics of the plans, are administrative; they are the problems involved in the transfer and promotion of pupils. The problems increase in difficulty in the areas surrounding large urban centers when the plan set up is at variance with the grading system used in cities. Criticism, in this instance, usually comes from urban administrators. When the population is mobile and there is frequent transfer from city to village to country, the plan may work an actual hardship on individual children. However, a study made in 1931 by Miss Helen Hay Heyl, State Supervisor of Rural Schools, Albany, New York, indicates that the problem is not so serious as it would at first appear. New York State has a large urban population and many rural schools are near metropolitan cities; yet Miss Heyl found the transfer of children from rural to urban schools in that state small. In Otsego County, Supervisory District No.3, 94 of the 124 children studied transferred in 1931 to the same type of school which they had left. Only 18 of the remainder or .08 per cent of the total enrollment represented any problem at all. The same trend held true in Supervisory District No.1, Clinton County, and Supervisory District No.1, Oneida County. In Clinton County 88 pupils out of a total enrollment of 2,985 were transferred within the year and 45 out of the 88 pupils were transferred to the same type of school. Only 8 pupils or .02 of 1 per cent of the total enrollment were affected by transfers from small to large schools. The same trends again held true for Douglas County, Nebraska, where only 16 out of 88 transferred pupils either changed the type of school or changed from one county to another. The Schools of Lucerne County, Pennsylvania, presented the following picture: (a) 265 pupils were transferred from one small-type school to another in 1931–1932; (b) 125 pupils transferred from a small-type school to a large-type school; (c) 100 pupils transferred from a large-type to a small-type school; (d) 40 pupils went from small-type schools to schools outside the county; (e) 45 pupils came from another county into the one- two- or three-teacher elementary schools of Lucerne.[1] Miss Heyl warned that the sampling in the study was too small for conclusions, but it indicates that transfers in rural areas tend toward schools of the same size and type and suggests that the problem is a local matter to be decided in the light of local conditions. Many schools are making such adjustments through objective tests and making each transfer and placement an individual matter to be decided on its own merit. Apparently this objection need not be taken too seriously.

ADVANTAGES OF THE COMBINATION AND ALTERNATION OF GRADES

The advantages of the plans have been pointed out in the presentation of the plans themselves, but a summary may be valuable at this point. (1) The plans make available to pupils more recitation time than under the old grading system. (2) The plans give greater opportunity for supervised study and for pupil-teacher conferences. (3) They enlarge the social unit for pupil participation. (4) They reduce the number of lesson preparations by the teacher. (5) They offer unique opportunity for child development. (6) They afford children the opportunity to pass through the grades at their own rates of speed. The early adoption of these plans, the imitation by nearly every one of the states in the Union, and the continued and successful use by thousands of rural schools throughout the country suggest that the combination and alternation of grades is one of the most helpful means yet devised for the organization of the small school.

The Combination of Subjects. The combination of subjects means the teaching of one subject in connection with another; in other words, making one class serve more than one purpose. In Reinoehl's study, 47 different combinations of two or more subjects were reported in an examination of 26 model programs.

[1] Dunn, Fannie W. and others. *Organization of Curriculum for One-Teacher Schools.* Bulletin 1932, Rural Education Department of National Education Association, pp. 26–27.

The combinations most often used include geography, history, and civics, designated as the social studies; reading and spelling; reading, English, and spelling; reading and history. Composition is often correlated with geography and history, or sometimes with reading. Under the influence of the progressive movement in education, there is a tendency to integrate much subject matter in many fields around common problems. For example, A Unit in Pioneer Life in America in the social studies for Group B might integrate all subjects studied by the group and for a long period of time. Such combination and correlation of subject matter are apparently on the increase in small schools. Not only does the practice seem desirable for the administration of the daily program, but, in a modern organization of curriculum materials, it appears essential for economical learning.

The Alternation of Subjects. The alternation of subjects has been a practice for many years in the effort to reduce the number of classes in the small schools. Alternation here means the provision in the program for the alternation of subjects by days, weeks, or school terms. In practice the chief alternations are: penmanship and art by days throughout the week, geography and history, geography and hygiene, civics and history. This plan, however, is losing favor to the newer movement to integrate curriculum materials, a technique which will be discussed somewhat at length in a later chapter. Under such integration art, for instance, would be taught as the need for it arose in the units; penmanship, save for remedial work of those failing to attain the standard, would be a part of all lessons; and health instruction would be integrated with the activities growing out of the problems of daily living in a group.

The Unit of Work as a Means of Reducing Classes. As has been suggested before, the Unit of Work is a modern device for the reduction of classes. While its primary purpose was to serve the ends of curriculum organization, teachers who have adopted it have declared that it meets two needs of the modern small school: it meets a problem in curriculum organization and it saves time. Our concern here is with its time-saving features. It is a time-saver because it is possible to combine one or two groups for a common project. Often it is desirable to combine all of the grades in the school on one unit of work, provided the project is one in which all the pupils are interested. Moreover, schools that employ the devices listed above can institute with ease such a perpendicular unit when the opportunity arises and interest is present. Because a perpendicular unit is adaptable to nearly all teaching situations, the organization features of the plan are presented here somewhat in detail.

A perpendicular unit is an organization of curriculum materials which extends downward through the grades, thus cutting across many levels of pupil achievement. It may be used in a one-teacher school of eight grades or in a system employing many teachers. One of its assets is its adaptability. The unit usually has the following characteristics. (1) For the unit, the school is organized as a whole. The children work on committees rather than by grades or by groups; in overstepping formal classification lines they become a part of a real school community project. (2) Each child participates in the unit on his own level of ability. For example, first grade children in an Indian unit might not be able to make the large wigwams of the village, especially if they necessitated the handling of poles and burlap, but they could make the paper decorations, which, pasted on, would beautify the tents. Second grade children would be interested in stories of Indian life, but not in the research involved in the reading of bulletins of historical associations. The eighth grade would assume that responsibility. (3) The unit presents a unified program for the whole school and many units, such as the Indian one, culminate in a program to which the community is invited. The unit usually lasts from six weeks to two months. The advantages of such a plan for the organization of the school program is obvious. It provides for the coöperation of large numbers of pupils and supplies a deficiency in the socialization of the small school. It plans for a combination of many classes, thus reducing the recitation periods and saving time. It is in harmony with the latest theories of progressive teaching. It simplifies the outside preparation of teachers.

OTHER PROBLEMS INVOLVED IN THE ORGANIZATION OF SMALL SCHOOLS

Limiting the number of classes, reducing the number of grades, and extending the recitation period, as valuable as these practices may be, do not solve the organization problems of the small school. There still remain for consideration many difficulties. To meet these difficulties there are guiding principles in program making which should be considered. (1) *The program should be planned so that each child and each group has an equitable distribution of the teacher's time.* It is not easy to arrange a time schedule which does justice to all members of the group. One of the questionable features of the daily program of many school organizations is the practice of distributing time unfairly. Often the unfairness takes the form of a neglect of the young children so that the upper-grade children profit. Reinoehl discovered in his study that the relatively fewer upper-grade children were favored with more recitation time and more class periods on the average program than were the more numerous primary children.[1] This is a fundamental weakness and no program which seeks to serve the needs of children should tolerate it. Reinoehl discovered that the first grade child in a one-teacher school received but 140 minutes a week of the teacher's time as compared with 275 minutes given to the seventh grade child. There is no surprise further to discover that approximately 50 per cent of the children in the first grade of one-teacher schools are repeaters the second year. This emphasis in the upper-grade division is often the result of community pressure in the form

[1] Reinoehl, Charles M. *Analytic Survey of State Courses of Study for Elementary Schools*, p. 29, United States Office of Education Bulletin, No. 42, 1922.

of state or county examinations, efforts on the part of children to enter high schools, and, in some states, college.

These practices actually work in a vicious circle because younger children in time become the older group on whom the teacher is frequently forced to spend the major portion of his attention. This need not have been necessary if the children had received proper attention in their earlier school years. Young children have their own special appeal in the organization of the small school and it lies largely in their inability to help themselves. Without care for the special needs of young children, it is possible and highly probable that wide differences may develop in the educational opportunities of children attending the same school and having the same teacher. There is general agreement that each child should contact the teacher at least once in each quarter of the day.

(2) *The organization of the school should be such that a fair allotment of time is made on a basis of subjects and subject matter.* Hollis Caswell says this distribution should be made in accordance with accepted standards. Unfortunately such accepted standards for rural schools are almost negligible.[1] Experiments in rural schools on time allotments have been surprisingly few. Often teacher preference for a particular subject results in an overemphasis upon that subject far out of proportion to its importance in the educational life of children. Reinoehl's study revealed that 60 per cent of the time on the programs examined was spent on arithmetic, reading, and language, thus making the tool subjects dominant and placing unfortunate emphasis upon the technical phases of teaching. The unit plan for the organization of curriculum materials promises release from this overemphasis of the mechanical features of a few favored subjects. The three R's are thus put in their proper places; they are treated as mediums through which children learn, rather than the ends of learning.

A safe principle to follow is to distribute time in accordance

[1] *Program Making in Small Elementary Schools.* p. 9, Field Studies No. 1. Division of Surveys and Field Studies, George Peabody College for Teachers, Nashville, Tennessee, 1930.

with the needs of the individual school. In many schools children are deficient in tool subjects; in that event, the distribution of time in the program should be weighted in favor of them. In other schools, children lack ability to express themselves clearly. The emphasis here should be placed on composition, art, music, and dramatics.

Just as there is no pattern to follow in the emphasis of subject matter, so there is none in the arrangement of subjects on the program. There is a general belief that the most difficult subjects should appear first in the morning when children are rested, but there is no scientific proof for this belief. Indeed, there is no agreement on the time of the day when children are best able physically and mentally to master difficult subject matter. Teacher preference often influences the arrangements of subjects on the program. Many prefer to teach reading in the morning and early afternoon in order to meet the needs of the young children who are dismissed early. For the same reason the social studies are often scheduled late in the afternoon so that the teacher, released from the responsibilities of the younger children, can give uninterrupted periods of attention to the older ones. There is a tendency in modern programs to block subject matter. This means that the program allows all children to engage in the same subject at the same time. Thus while Grade II is reciting arithmetic the other grades or groups are either studying the same subject or engaged in activities which involve it. The advantages in this plan are many. It saves time in the distribution and collection of materials, while one group recites the teacher may find it possible to handle the other groups as if they were participating in a supervised study period. This latter plan is especially advantageous in arithmetic and the social studies.

(3) *Every good program should provide for time to study and play as well as to recite.* Accompanying every daily program should be another, a study program, which cares for the time when the children are not with the teacher. This study program should be viewed as suggestive only, because one of the major

objectives in the modern rural school is the development in children of the habit of independent study. Independence in study not only involves a technique of studying, but also the wise and economical use of time. Consequently, children should be given, as early as they can accept it, the responsibility for budgeting their time of study. Often teachers merely write on the board after the morning conference, "Things Which Need to be Done," and allow children to make their own plans for when and how they are to be completed. Other teachers assist children in making their own study schedules. In many subjects the blocking of subjects suggests a guide for those who study as well as for those who recite.

(4) *It should always be kept in mind that the program is made to serve children, not to be served by them.* This is another way of stating an accepted principle in program making, especially for those programs used in modern schools. The program should be flexible, and should be possible of daily adjustment to meet the needs of children. There is nothing sacred about the order of the day's work and teachers and children should feel free to shift it as they are best served. A word of caution is, perhaps, timely here. Inexperienced teachers would find it best to adhere to the daily program until they gain confidence in manipulating it. Even they should feel free, however, to remake their programs until they reach a standard of service for their own individual schools.

Examples of teaching and study programs are given in the appendix. While they reflect the most modern principles of program making, they are suggestive only. There is no pattern for a model program. A model program is always the one which best serves the children.

As an aid to the inexperienced teacher a case study is herewith presented. It gives (a) the program by which the children of Lewiston District #2, New York worked, (b) the names of the children who made the program come alive, and (c) a description of one day of work within the life of the school.

CASE STUDY—I[1]

THE PROGRAM BY WHICH THE CHILDREN WORKED

PROGRAM A.M.

Time	Group D		Group B		
	Grade 1 Grade 2		Grade 5	Grade 7	Grade 8
9:00–9:20	*Opening Exercises*		*—All groups—*	*Planned by children part of the time*	
9:20–10:00	*Reading*		Preparation for reading or language	Project work previously planned OR library period	
10:00–10:05					
	Relaxation—all groups				
10:05–10:20	Seat work or stories read or told by some older child		*Reading and language alternating daily*	Study period for Reading—Language or Spelling	
10:20–10:35	Same as above		Preparation for spelling	*Reading and language alternating daily*	
10:35–10:50	*Recess—all groups*				
10:50–11:10	*Spelling—Mon. Wed. Fri.—Penmanship—Tues. Thurs. all groups*				
11:10–11:50	*Arithmetic—all groups* *Work to be partly individual and partly group instruction. All pupils except group D* are to work entire time. New work for different groups introduced on different days, other groups doing drill work.*				
11:50–12:00	*Arithmetic*		All other groups clear up difficulties		

* While other groups are busy with Arithmetic, Group D has a free period. If weather permits the children may play out-of-doors, otherwise they play quiet games or amuse themselves as they wish.

[1] Reported by Mrs. Roy Breckon, Lewiston District No. 2. Supervisory District No. 3, Niagara County, New York. Miss M. Gazelle Hoffman, District Superintendent of Schools.

CASE STUDY—I *(Continued)*

PROGRAM P.M.

Time	Group D	Group B		
	Grade 1 Grade 2	Grade 5	Grade 7	Grade 8
1:00–1:15	*Health or General Science—Alternating—all groups*			
1:15–1:35	*Reading*	Free period	Study period for history	
1:35–1:50	Reading, seat work or activity period	Do any work individual thinks necessary or study for social studies	History	
1:50–2:05				History
2:05–2:15	*Social studies Tues. Thurs. Language—Mon. Wed. Fri.*		Free Period	
2:15–2:30	*Music—All groups*			
2:30–2:45	*Recess—All Groups*			
2:45–3:20	Dismissed	*Social studies*	Study for geography	Do drill work in subjects in which pupil must take Regents Examinations.
3:20–4:00		Activity work or Library period	*Geography*	

NOTES: 1. All items in italics are periods in which the teacher is working with the children.
2. Free period means that the individual may do any work he thinks necessary.

THE CHILDREN WHO MADE THE PROGRAM COME TO LIFE

GROUP D	GROUP B
Mary Louise Freeman...Grade 1	Lucille Battles.........Grade 5
Joanne Sutherland......Grade 1	Harold Freeman.......Grade 5
Dorothy Widmer.......Grade 1	Stanley Juzwiak.......Grade 5
Virginia Scott..........Grade 1	
	James Scalzo.........Grade 7
Frank Scalzo...........Grade 2	Mary Juzwiak.........Grade 7
Stanley Scott ....Grade 2	Kenneth Sutherland....Grade 7
	Eva Scalzo...........Grade 8

THE PROGRAM IN ACTION

Promptly at 8:15 A.M., just fifteen minutes after the teacher arrived, the children began to come. James and Frank were the first comers. They watered the plants and the oats growing on the farm and then went out of doors to play. Eva came next. She put up the flag; it was her week to perform that duty. Kenneth, Joanne, Lucille, and Dorothy were the next arrivals. Kenneth brought several different kinds of seeds to put on the seed distribution chart. Mary, Stanley, Harold, and Mary Louise came together. Mary Louise brought a circus picture for the story Frank and Stanley were reading in second grade. Stanley Scott and his sister, Virginia, then appeared and immediately told the teacher of the guests from Pennsylvania they were expecting that day. Each child had a cheery "Good morning" for the teacher. Some of the children played outside and others played games inside or listened to "Cheerio" on the radio.

Promptly at nine o'clock school started. The children gave the "Flag salute" and sang "America," while Dorothy held the flag. Still standing, they repeated The Lord's Prayer. Health inspection followed. Harold spun the Health Wheel and the arrow pointed to "Did you clean your fingernails?" The teacher inspected each pair of chubby hands and stars were placed on the chart for those who had remembered.

Since it was Friday, each child was expected to give a current event. Stanley Juzwiak gave his first. He told that President Roosevelt was to visit Niagara Falls the next day and make a speech. James told of a little boy nine years old, of Lewiston Heights, who had won a prize for his log cabin made of matches at the D.A.R. exhibition at Syracuse. Lucille told of a farmer in East Aurora who had earned money by raising turtles for turtle soup. The teacher said that it was unusual to have three such interesting things happen so near home. Eva explained that Columbus Day could not be celebrated in Spain because of the war there. Mary told of the celebration held in Buffalo to commemorate Columbus Day. Kenneth related how the volcano near Tokyo had erupted and called the children's attention to its location on the world map. He said that the people carried umbrellas to keep off the falling ashes. Harold was not ready with his current event. The children decided that Harold did not read the newspaper or listen to the news on the radio.

Classes then began. The attention of the children was called to the assignment in general science written on the blackboard. Second grade were given their readers and told to re-read a story, so that they could read it well to the first grade. Fifth grade took out their English work books, (the children recited English that day instead of reading) and did an exercise on the use of "to," "too," and "two." Seventh and Eighth grades worked on their English work books and did an exercise in outline making and wrote a story to follow the outline made. This left the teacher free to work with the beginners.

The group of four, Mary Louise, Joanne, Dorothy, and Virginia joined the teacher at the front of the room and read from the chart. After matching cards with phrases and sentences on the chart, they gathered around the table and read from their pre-primers, carefully phrasing what they were reading. Mary Louise and Virginia were both anxious to help Dorothy with some sentences she could not read, but the teacher said, "Don't you think it would be better to let Dorothy get these herself if she can?" Mary Louise said, "She will remember them, then, won't she?" By looking at the pictures and at the chart Dorothy finally worked out her problem by herself and smiled triumphantly at the other girls. Before leaving the table, work books which accompany the pre-primer were given to the children and directions explained by the teacher. The children went to their seats and did the work by themselves.

Stanley Scott, and Frank then came to the table to read. Their story was "Playing Circus," and here Mary Louise proudly exhibited her picture, while both first and second grade discussed it. It was hung on the wall, and first grade went back to their work books, while second grade read. Stanley came to the word "tub" and did not know it. Frank said, "What does your mother wash in, Scott?" Stanley did not stop at that word again. After finishing their story they took their work books and read the directions to the teacher so that she was sure they understood them, and returned to their seats.

A lively setting-up exercise followed with two minutes for rest.

By this time first grade had finished their work. Eva checked it for them.

Fifth grade, with the teacher, then checked the work in their work book and did several other exercises using "to," "too," and "two" on the board.

Seventh and eighth grades then had their lesson in outlining and following the outline. All outlines and stories were read, and it was decided by the children that Mary's was best. Kenneth listed the reasons for this decision on the board, and each of the others decided where his could be made better. The teacher checked these individually and helped each child rewrite his first effort.

Recess followed. The day was bright and sunny, and the children played "Duck on the Rock." When the bell rang they came in with bright eyes and rosy cheeks from fifteen minutes in the crisp fall air.

It was now time for the final test of the week in spelling. Lucille and James were the only ones who had to spell, all others having had 100% on Wednesday. The teacher pronounced the words for them and they wrote them. Both succeeded in making a perfect score.

Assignments in arithmetic were then given out. Fifth grade was given drill work in long division; seventh grade, problems in percentage; and eighth grade, new work in finding volume of cylinders.

Before the teacher began work with the eighth grade she had each child in second grade pick out four words from his envelope containing "Words I cannot spell," tell what they were, use them orally in a sentence, and spell them while looking at them. They then wrote them ten times each in preparation for spelling.

First grade was at the easel, painting a house like the one they had built for their farm.

Lucille was having trouble with a long division problem. The teacher helped her with it and then proceeded to the new work in eighth grade arithmetic.

The teacher made sure that Eva knew exactly what a cylinder looked like, that the base was a circle, and that the volume was expressed in cubic measure. Attention was called to the formula "$V = $ area of base x altitude." Having already learned how to find the area of a circle, Eva easily followed the formula. Several problems of this nature were assigned to her.

Second grade were ready to spell by this time. They spelled their words orally and wrote them on the blackboard. Now they were ready to read the story they had studied earlier to the first grade gathered around them in a corner. This delighted them all and when Frank came to a word he did not know, he felt embarrassed.

The second grade then did a test in subtraction, while the teacher worked with the first grade. They were learning to write and recognize numbers. They used blocks and at the teacher's direction would bring her a certain number, five, for example, and write the number "5" on the board, thus connecting the symbol with the number of blocks.

The papers of the other grades were handed in to be checked and later corrected.

Dismissal for the lunch hour was then in order. All the children, with the exception of Eva, James, and Frank who live directly across the road from the school stayed for lunch.

Soup, the vegetables for which had been prepared by Mary and Lucille before the opening of school and added to a can of vegetable soup, was served by the children. All ate happily and then cleared the food away and washed the dishes. Since the group was small, each one helped with the work. When it was finished, the children went outside to play, while the teacher corrected the spelling and arithmetic papers. The fifth, seventh, and eighth grades were making graphs showing their marks in arithmetic. One by one they came to the teacher to find out their marks for the day and to record them on their respective graphs.

At one o'clock the afternoon session opened, with general science first on the program. The children discussed finishing their seed chart and proceeded to the discussion of plants without seeds. Some of these were named and listed on the board with the requirements for growth of such plants. Those which are of special use, yeast, for example, were given particular attention. Time did not permit finishing this, and the rest was left until the next science period.

Fifth, seventh, and eighth grades were asked to be ready to report on the trip they had taken the day before to Fort Niagara and other local places of interest. They were to outline the trip and report from the outline written, thus connecting the morning's English with the social studies. This was the climax of a unit in local history.

First and second grade then had a "phonic game" which was closely supervised by the teacher since it was a new experience for the beginners.

The first and second grades next came to the front of the

room where they could use the blackboard. They had planned to write more stories about the farm which they had built. They re-read the story already written and decided to write the story of "Our Barn."

Joanne suggested the first sentence, "We made our barn out of a box." The others agreed that this was good. Virginia said, "Joanne and Mary Louise painted the barn." This was accepted. Next they wanted to tell that the barn was red. Someone suggested that they write, "Mary Louise and Joanne painted it red." The teacher printed it on the board but helped the children to decide that it did not sound well to repeat the children's names and asked what we could say in place of Mary Louise and Joanne. Mary Louise said, "*Them* painted it red." Stanley immediately said, "No, that isn't right." Virginia finally said, "*They* painted it red." This was accepted. Frank suggested the next sentence, "We made the roof of cardboard." The teacher asked Dorothy to make a sentence. She said, "Stanley and Frank painted it brown." The story on the board was as follows:

OUR BARN

WE MADE OUR BARN OUT OF A BOX.
JOANNE AND MARY LOUISE PAINTED THE BARN.
THEY PAINTED IT RED.
WE MADE THE ROOF OF CARDBOARD.
STANLEY AND FRANK PAINTED IT BROWN.

We decided that the story was long enough. The children read it aloud. Certain words and phrases were selected and read, such as: "painted it"—"our barn"—"red"—"brown." After school the teacher printed the story on the chart which was to be part of the book entitled "Our Farm" and used for supplementary reading.

Music was next on the program. The children had great fun singing two farm songs they had learned; "The Farmer" and "Old McDonald had a farm." The choir sang the main parts and the chorus; all helped with the chorus.

Recess followed, and the first and second grades were dismissed.[1] The older children again played "Duck on the rock." This is one of their favorite games.

After recess the remainder of the day was spent with reports of the trip. These were very complete and served to summarize the unit. After reporting orally, criticizing, and correcting any false impressions, the children wrote reports for the booklets they had made on "Local History." The teacher gave help where it was needed and new words were added to the vocabulary list on one of the blackboards.

At four o'clock all were dismissed.

SUMMARY

The organization of the small school for teaching and learning, involves a knotty question, for some time a problem in the field of elementary education. It involves the necessity of a special organization for one-teacher schools and to somewhat the same extent for schools employing two and three teachers—an organization that will reduce the number of classes, increase the number of pupils in each, extend the recitation period, and eliminate small classes. It is indeed the crux of the problem in program making for the teacher in small schools of many grades. A teacher of eight grades who attempts to schedule four or five recitations per day for each grade finds himself responsible for forty recitation periods averaging ten minutes each, a practice which turns the school day into a dull and deadly routine. Even to the initiated the task appears formidable and impossible of solution. Experts in the educational field have given much thought to the problem. Various plans have been promulgated and advanced, chief of which are as follows: (a) the combination and alternation of grades, (b) the combination of subjects,

[1] If any of the children had been too young to walk home alone they should have gone to the play corner, here taken a nap for fifteen or twenty minutes, and then played quietly with dolls, books, and games until the older children had finished the work of the day.

(c) the alternation of subjects, (d) the integration of subject matter into units of work.

There are still other problems involved in an organization program to which the teacher should give heed. They are: (a) the distribution of recitation time, so that each pupil has an equitable amount of time to study and to recite; (b) provision for the special needs of young children; (c) an equitable distribution of time to different subjects, so that one does not overbalance the other. In the light of this discussion the following criteria are offered by which to judge the organization of the small elementary school:

1. Is the school organized so that the grades are combined into at the most four groups, and is the subject matter outlined so that the groups can be alternated in a two or a three year cycle?

2. Have all possible provisions been made for the correlation and integration of subject matter?

3. Does the organization provide for large perpendicular units of work?

4. In general, is there an opportunity for all children to come in daily contact with the teacher each quarter of the day?

5. Are the needs of young children cared for adequately? Are their recitation periods more frequent than those of children of the upper division? Are provisions made for their early dismissal?

6. Does the program provide for study and play as well as for recitations?

7. Is there provision for the program to become increasingly flexible?

8. Is the program arranged into subject matter blocks?

9. Is there evidence in the organization that the program is destined to serve the school rather than to be served by it?

By the use of these criteria and the above discussion it should be comparatively easy for the teacher to organize the school in the light of modern practices. Such a thoughtful approach to the problem seems more desirable than an attempt to make a model program. As a matter of fact, there is no model program, nor is it possible for supervisors and teacher-training institutions to put into the hands of teachers a pattern which can be followed in all situations. Every situation is different and presents local problems for which no standard method of procedure is possible. Principles rather than patterns should be followed in the organization of the small school for teaching and learning.[1]

SUGGESTED READINGS

Caswell, Hollis. *Program Making in Small Elementary Schools, Field Studies No. I,* Division of Surveys and Field Studies, George Peabody College for Teachers, Nashville, Tennessee, 1930.

Collings, Ellsworth. *An Experiment with a Project Curriculum,* Chaps. II–III, Macmillan, New York, 1923.

Dunn, Fannie W. and Everett, Marcia. *Four Years in a Country School,* pp. 12–25, Bureau of Publications, Teachers College, Columbia University, 1926.

Dunn, Fannie W. and Others. *Organization of Curriculum for One-Teacher Schools,* Bulletin of the Department of Rural Education, National Education Association, Washington, D. C., 1933.

Lane, Robert Hill. *A Teacher's Guidebook to the Activity Program,* Chaps. II–IV, Macmillan, New York, 1932.

Lathrop, Edith A. *The Organization of the One-Teacher School,* United States Office of Education, Rural School Leaflet No. 10 (Dept. of the Interior), Government Printing Office, Washington, D. C., 1923.

Lowth, Frank J. *Everyday Problems of the Country Teacher,* Rev. ed., Chap. IX, Macmillan, New York, 1936.

Reinoehl, Charles Myron. *Analytic Survey of State Courses of Study for Elementary Schools,* Chap. III, United States Office of Education, Bulletin No. 42 (Dept. of the Interior), United States Government Printing Office, Washington, D. C., 1922.

Rugg, Harold and Shumaker, Ann. *The Child Centered School,* Chap. VI, World Book Co., New York, 1928.

Stevens, Marion P. *The Activities Curriculum in the Primary Grades,* Chap. VI, Heath, New York, 1931.

[1] Plans for the organization of the small school are presented in the appendix. These are suggestive only.

MATERIALS FOR DISCUSSION

Consider the following statements. What changes would make them more acceptable to you? What significant issues arise from their study?

1. The grading of children in rural schools was one of the serious mistakes made in education. The rural school, unlike the city school, is not served by this administrative device, and, under a modern conception of education, is actually handicapped by it.

2. The organization of the rural school lends itself admirably to the alternation of grades and subjects, and there is no reason to believe that the best interests of children are not served thereby.

3. The most economical and efficient way of meeting the problems of organizing the small school is to consolidate it, so that the children can have the advantages of the graded system.

4. The younger children in the rural school are at all times the special responsibility of the teacher. Special consideration should, therefore, be given to them in the organization of the school for teaching and learning.

5. There is no pattern for the organization of the small school.

CHAPTER VI

INDIVIDUALIZED INSTRUCTION

INDIVIDUALIZED instruction has acquired specific educational meanings from practices developed in the Schools at Dalton, Massachusetts, and Winnetka, Illinois. To one unfamiliar with these practices the term might suggest a teacher for every pupil, but neither the plan nor the practice is so simple. The term has been recently defined as a number of pupils working at the same time, under the same teacher; but each child working for his own purposes, at his own rate of speed, by the method best suited to him, and on tasks which he needs to perform.[1] Thus it is seen that proponents of individualized instruction claim for it both individual and group participation in the life of the school.

This text has consistently held to the point of view that education should supply the deficiencies inherent in the environment of children and should develop the assets found there. The need for the socialization of rural children is a well established fact and recommendations for meeting this need are presented in several chapters throughout the book. In nearly every instance, the recommendations have emphasized for the small rural school: group decisions, group discussions, group participation —in short, group living. The small rural school lends itself admirably to such a normal, democratic type of organization and children apparently profit from it. However, teachers in these democratic institutions cannot afford to ignore the fact that the group is composed of individuals, each of whom is different. Experienced teachers have always known that a wide range of

[1] State of Michigan, Department of Public Instruction. *Instructional Guide for Elementary Schools*, Bulletin 301, p. 47, Lansing, Mich., 1936.

differences exist in a group of children of the same age and grade span. Some are tall, some short, some energetic, some lazy, some bright, some dull, some average, some poor in arithmetic, and some good in it and in nothing else. Scientific investigations have verified teacher experience and have revealed to what lengths variations frequently go.[1] For example, any so-called fourth grade will probably contain children of third, fourth, fifth, and sixth grade ability in any subject. An examination of all the other subjects in a school system would reveal a range equally as great and equally as disturbing. When these grade variations are multiplied many times, as in the small school of many grades, the problem achieves considerable magnitude.

HISTORICAL BACKGROUND OF THE PROBLEM

Historically, the small rural school has always been faced with the problem of individualizing instruction. The enrollment in the colonial system of schools consisted of itinerant pupils, here today and gone tomorrow.[2] Pupils attended school for a short time in the winter, dropped out in the spring to assist in the planting of crops, and returned for another short period in the summer or in the fall. Individualization of instruction was a necessity for these itinerants. It was not based upon scientific principles, but the plan was highly practical and its chief virtue, perhaps, lay in the fact that it worked. Each pupil entered school when he wished, proceeded at his own rate of speed, and dropped out as the circumstances of his life dictated. Upon his reëntry into school he merely resumed his work at the place where he had previously laid it down.

It was the development of an urban system of schools and its consequent organization by grades which first introduced the characteristics of the lock step into education. In the

[1] Washburne, Carleton. *Adjusting the School to the Child*, p. 1, World Book Co., 1932.
[2] Knight, Edgar W. *Education in the United States*, pp. 70–72, Ginn & Co., 1929.

organization of the "graded school," little recognition was given to the needs of individual children. Regimentation and standardization by the mechanical standards of age and grade were the predominating characteristics of the system. The rural school, quick to imitate the urban school, gradually acquired the same characteristics, so that it, too, lost touch with individual children.

EARLY ATTEMPTS TO BREAK THE LOCK STEP

If the urban school was the first to regiment children, it was also the first to attempt a program of individualized instruction. The first technique in this procedure was apparently developed in 1912 by Frederic Burk and Mary Ward of the San Francisco Normal School. The methods thus developed were enthusiastically adopted by their pupils and were taken into the schools of San Francisco, and later into schools scattered throughout the United States. The technique was simple and practical. It consisted of a plan to test and promote individually each child in every subject. In order to achieve this goal, self-measurement techniques were established, so that a child could measure and evaluate his own progress in the mastery of subject matter. Creative activities, however, were not ignored in the plan. These were developed through the social studies and English. A high premium, at the same time, was placed upon growth in citizenship.

Other attempts to break the lock step of class group instruction have been made at many places. Notable among these are the Dalton (Mass.) Plan, the Batavia (N. Y.) Plan, the Mount Vernon (N. Y.) Plan, the Gary (Ind.) Plan, the Ability Grouping (Detroit and Los Angeles) Plan, the Differentiated Assignments (University of Chicago and University of Wisconsin) Plan. Various viewpoints have been presented and varied characteristics stressed in these attempts at corrective systematization of schools. Some of the characteristics which have been injected into these schools are: the coaching of laggards, intensive study of problem cases, formation of ability groups within classes, maximum and minimum assignments, making the classroom a laboratory, and individual distribution of time.[1]

These several adjustments to the individual instruction of children took two directions. One plan made an attempt to break the lock step within the confines of the regular school organization, while the other maintained the usual organization of subject matter by grades, but ignored the time limit set by the school year. Leaders in education maintain that it is the latter plan which best suits the needs of children since it allows for a better adaptation of the school to the varying abilities of pupils.[2] The schools at Dalton, Massachusetts, and Winnetka, Illinois, have made considerable progress in the application of the principles involved in the second plan. Since a modification of their programs has been adopted by many small schools a brief outline of the plans of these two school systems is presented here.

THE DALTON PLAN

The Dalton Plan, frequently designated as the Dalton Laboratory Plan, is based upon the principle that children learn through self-directed experiences. School rooms are used as laboratories, and the major subjects are departmentalized. Assignment sheets are carefully constructed in each subject, and these in the hands of the children become "contracts" forming an agreement between learner and teacher. Frequently the "contracts" are developed on varying levels of achievements, so that a student in making a choice sets a goal which he believes he can reach. Once a goal is set, the student proceeds at his own rate, and whenever the contract is completed he takes up the next assignment. Schools using this plan of individualized instruction claim for it results in industry, independence in

[1] Taplin, Winn Lowell. *Relative Efficiency of Class vs. Individual Instruction in Graded and One-Teacher Schools, 1933–1934*, p. 10. Unpublished master's thesis, University of Vermont, 1935.

[2] *Ibid.* p. 11.

study and in thinking, coöperation, scholarship, honesty, and sincerity.[1]

THE PLAN USED AT WINNETKA

The plan for individualizing instruction at Winnetka, Illinois, is frequently referred to as the "Winnetka Plan" but this, says the Superintendent of the system, is a misnomer because the designation suggests the rigidity of a pattern when the school is in reality a laboratory where procedures are modified in the light of experimentations.[2] Founded upon the principles laid down by Frederic Burk and Mary Ward, the system has evolved its own procedures. One of the distinguishing techniques developed has been the division of all subject matter into two groups, and the individualization of each group. One group contains those tool subjects which every normal child should master: reading, arithmetic, language, and spelling. Superintendent Washburne holds that the individualization of these subjects is the only effective way in which children attain a common mastery in them. The second group of subjects contains those in which children may legitimately and desirably differ. These are the social studies, art, literature, creative work, and those subjects in which appreciations are developed. "By the term 'adaptation of schools to individual differences' we mean to signify not merely the techniques of teaching facts and skills on an individual basis, but also something of the technique of developing the individual's creativeness and social-mindedness and of helping him to an inner and social adjustment." [3]

A special technique of teaching has been developed which aims to achieve the goals of individual mastery in subject matter on the one hand and creativeness in the individual on the other. This technique consists of three steps. The first step is taken

[1] Parkhurst, Helen. *Education on the Dalton Plan*, E. P. Dutton & Co., 1922.
[2] Washburne, Carleton. *Adjusting the School to the Child*, p. V, World Book Co., 1922.
[3] *Ibid.* p. VI.

when the teacher decides exactly what every child is expected to master. These goals are not in outline form but in specific statements of what every child should master, and the standard to which mastery should reach. The details to which these specific statements go is revealed in the following: "We teachers as a class tend to think in generalities instead of in terms of specific needs and requirements. . . . It is much easier to say that every child shall know something about the discovery of America than to specify that every child shall know that it was Columbus who discovered America in 1492, that it was Queen Isabella who financed him, and that he was trying to find a short route to the Indies. Yet it is the latter type of statement in arithmetic, history, geography, spelling, formal language, and all other subjects dealing with definite content or skill, to be acquired by all children, that makes individual work possible." [1] The Rutland-Castleton-Fair Haven Supervisory Union of Vermont offers an excellent example of agreement on specific goals for individual progress. Below is an example of the achievement goals in arithmetic for children advanced to Grade III.

Counting to 10
Reading numbers to 10
Writing numbers to 10
Counting to 20
Reading numbers to 20
Writing numbers to 20
Largeness, etc.
16 addition facts
32 addition facts
48 addition facts
Meaning of signs
64 addition facts
Addition problems
Addition test
Review
80 addition facts

94 addition facts
100 addition facts
Addition problems
Counting by 2's
Roman Numerals
Telling time
Counting money
Simple measure
Meaning of signs
32 subtraction facts
64 subtraction facts
Subtraction problems
Subtraction: 35 to 50: (3 minutes)
Addition: 45 to 60: (3 minutes)
Multiplication to 20: by 2, 3, 4, 5
Standard tests in numbers

[1] *Ibid.* pp. 2–3.

The second step recommended is a complete diagnostic testing program to cover the objectives set up by the teacher. This program does not consist of the usual sampling test, common in school rooms, but makes use of tests constructed on small units of subject matter, and administered to individual children when each is ready for them. After the test each child begins to practice on his weak points. Under this plan of individualized instruction, tests are frequently substituted for the usual recitation. Washburne defends this practice on the ground that a complete, diagnostic test requires of each child everything he is supposed to learn, while a recitation gives the teacher a rough estimate of what the class as a whole knows.[1]

The third step is the making of self-instructive and self-corrective materials which children can easily and efficiently use. This, according to Washburne, is the most difficult of the three steps, and one which the average teacher is not prepared to take:

Obviously if teachers are going to permit children to progress at their own individual rates, they must be able to put in the children's hands material by which the children can to a considerable extent teach themselves. Furthermore, if they are going to abandon recitations in formal subjects, they must have some means for the children's correcting their own daily work.[2]

Help for the teacher in this difficulty is suggested in subsequent paragraphs.

INDIVIDUALIZED INSTRUCTION IN RURAL SCHOOLS

Modifications of the Dalton and Winnetka plans have been adopted, in part at least, in the rural schools of Connecticut, Illinois, Maine, Michigan, and Vermont. In 1926 the Illinois State Department of Education issued a bulletin which gave specific directions for individualizing instruction and urged the

[1] *Ibid.* p. 4.
[2] *Ibid.* p. 6.

teachers in rural schools to adopt the plan.[1] The purpose of this plan of school organization was expressed as follows:

To make it possible for the pupil to spend most of his time in study under the direction and assistance of the teacher, to give the teacher time to do real teaching, to help the pupil individually to learn.[2]

The recently published instructional guide for the elementary teachers in Michigan devotes an entire chapter to the problem of individualized instruction and commends it as a method for improving the program of the school:

No improved program can be created without a realization that learning goes on in a properly controlled learning environment and does not require a constant succession of recitations. In order to meet individual differences among pupils and promote independent habits of study, teachers will make use of individualized materials and methods.[3]

Vermont's search for a system of individualizing instruction is described in the following statement:

For years the schools of Vermont have been in want of a type of organization which would allow the teacher to use his time more efficiently. Revised time schedules for classes have been proposed; the doubling of successive grades in order to provide a smaller number of classes has been suggested; rotation of classes in certain subjects on successive days has been tried; pupil assistants to the teacher have been used; individual and special "adjustments" within the class were advocated; programs were modified and project teaching introduced.

None of these rearrangements within the class recitation plan of organization was successful in solving the time problem for the teacher

---

[1] Hoffman, U. J. *A Program of Study and Instruction in One-Teacher Schools,* Circular 210, Illinois, 1926.

[2] National Society for the Study of Education. The Twenty-Fourth Yearbook, Part II, *Adapting the Schools to Individual Differences,* p. 118, Public School Publishing Co., 1925. Quoted by permission of the Society.

[3] State of Michigan, Department of Public Instruction. *Instructional Guide for Elementary Schools,* Bulletin 301, p. 30, 1936.

to such an extent that it has been widely adopted. All had virtues, yet they did not furnish what was sought in practice.[1]

THE HOFFMAN PLAN

Through the leadership of U. J. Hoffman, Illinois developed a state-wide plan for the individualization of instruction in small schools. Under this plan it was recommended that the school day be divided into four sessions. Each session was devoted to a major subject when the pupil either recited or studied in that subject. For example, the first session of the school was devoted to reading, and lasted from nine until ten-thirty each morning. During this period the children in the first and second grades were engaged in class instruction. This was necessary because these young children must be taught how to read and, presumably, they acquired in these instructional periods the techniques for mastery in this important subject. The third and fourth grades were combined for reading, but recited to the teacher only twice a week. The remainder of the time in the first "session" was used by the children of these grades in reading easy books for pleasure. It was recommended that the children of the fifth and sixth grades, also combined, meet with the teacher for instruction only once a week. The remainder of their reading time was used for practice and for securing information. Children in the seventh and eighth grades engaged in class discussions once or twice a week; the major portion of their time went to reading the classics or in studying their assignments in nature study and the social sciences.

The second "session" was devoted to a study of arithmetic, a third to a consideration of language, and the fourth and last to the social studies. The procedure in each of these "sessions" was similar to that described in the reading "session," except that the older children received more class instruction than

[1] Taplin, Winn Lowell. *Relative Efficiency of Class vs. Individual Instruction in Graded and One-Teacher Schools, 1933–1934*, p. 1. Unpublished master's thesis, University of Vermont, 1935.

the younger. In the arithmetic "session," for instance, the children of the first and second grades did not engage in the study of arithmetic at all. Four arithmetic classes were recommended, and the "session" was divided among them. Twenty minutes at the beginning of the arithmetic "session" were devoted to individual instruction of these children not receiving class instruction. The next thirty minutes were devoted to the class instruction of the primary grades and apportioned to the needs of the children. The thirty-five remaining minutes of the "session" were assigned to class instruction for those classes that had not received individual instruction at the beginning of the session. Hoffman recommended that every class should receive the services of the teacher every day either in class or in individual instruction.[1] Michigan, however, recommends an alternation of types of work throughout the week:

It is convenient to alternate during the days of the week the types of work in any given subject. For example, a formally directed oral or silent reading may be conducted three days a week and two days may be used for self-directed silent reading followed by a brief test by the teacher.[2]

METHODS FOR INDIVIDUALIZING INSTRUCTION

The assigning of "sessions" to major subjects, described in the Hoffman plan, is similar to the blocking of subjects described in Chapter V of this text. Thus at first glance the programs for the individualized and the grouped schools appear the same. Differences, however, develop in the techniques of class instruction. Schools which feature the group instruction of children emphasize centers of interest for the entire class because they believe that the best maximum growth of the individual occurs as he contributes to the group. Consequently, there

[1] Hoffman, U. J. *A Program of Study and Instruction in One-Teacher Schools*, p. 12, Circular 210, Illinois, 1926.

[2] State of Michigan, Department of Public Instruction. *Instructional Course for Elementary Schools*, Bulletin 301, p. 30, Lansing, Michigan.

is present in this type of organization considerable emphasis upon group instruction. At the same time, the organization allows for a maximum of adaptations to the capacities, aptitudes, and abilities of individuals. These adaptations are usually procured through individual assignments, projects, and activities but related at the same time to the major group interest.

The teacher works closely with the group, and he, as well as the students, places high premium upon the time spent together in recitation. This is the time when the group meets to exchange opinions, to compare notes, to interchange views— all important activities for a genuine understanding of subject matter. Consequently, the school program is deliberately manipulated in order that children and teachers may spend together as much time as possible.

In schools where the individualization of instruction is featured, the contrary holds. Here emphasis is primarily upon the individual and secondarily upon the group. Techniques to attain individual efficiency in children have been developed in some detail at Winnetka, and in some sections they are recommended for rural schools. These consist of individual assignments in the light of prescribed subject matter goals, as stated above, individual conferences with the teacher, group conferences when the individuals are ready for them, and individual tests. Mr. Hoffman describes the work of the individual student as follows:

When the class period is omitted, the pupil has the whole session uninterrupted to do the work assigned. The teacher is free to help those who need help at the time they need it, when they are trying to do the work and fail. Most of the pupils have learned how in the class period. All they need is practice or time to complete the task. If any did not learn how in the class instruction period, the teacher shows them individually and does not waste the time of those who need not be shown. She encourages and guides the talented and skillful, but gives the slow and awkward the help which they need.[1]

[1] National Society for the Study of Education. The Twenty-Fourth Yearbook, Part II, *Adapting the Schools to Individual Differences*, p. 119, Public School Publishing Co., 1925. Quoted by permission of the Society.

MATERIALS FOR INDIVIDUALIZING INSTRUCTION

The essential characteristic of individual instruction, perhaps, lies in the fact that each child works at his own rate and on his own problems. Consequently, the school child spends much of his time alone and in study. While these two conditions are created by urban systems because they believe them desirable for children, both are inherently present in the small school of many grades. No matter how carefully the group program of the latter institution is constructed, there is always present the necessity for long study periods when children work alone. Consequently, an examination of the materials used for directing study is profitable for all rural teachers whether the organization is individualized or grouped. These materials usually include study guides, work books, tests and lesson sheets. These are described as follows:

Individualized materials, by which are meant study guides, work books, practice tests, lesson sheets, etc. provide one means through which teachers can adapt, especially in rate of learning, their teaching to the needs and abilities of individual pupils. Such materials are especially useful in rooms that include a span of two or more grades, because they make it possible to combine classes over several grades for part of their work and yet have each child work at his own level of development. The entire room of pupils can have at the same time the drill part of their arithmetic, or their spelling, or certain phases of their reading or language, but no two children may be working on precisely the same activities.[1]

MATERIALS FOR INDIVIDUALIZED STUDY

Workbooks. As pointed out by Washburne, one of the most difficult steps in an individualization program is the supplying of self-instructive and self-corrective materials to children. Fortunately, for the inexperienced teacher there are two sources for help in this difficulty. One source lies in the excellent com-

[1] State of Michigan, Department of Public Instruction, *Instructional Guide for Elementary Schools*. Bulletin 301, p. 46, Lansing, Michigan 1936.

mercial workbooks, designed to meet the study needs of children, and now available in every major subject matter field in the elementary school. The other source of help lies in the tendency of modern textbook writers to make the texts of the elementary school more like workbooks and less like textbooks. They have been constructed to meet the needs of children in a modern school. Many of these textbooks are highly individualized. They present problems, give directions, furnish practice exercises, and display other characteristics of good workbooks. Since there is a tendency to use an increasing number of workbooks in the elementary school various studies have been made to determine whether or not the results are beneficial to children. Miss Bess Goodykoontz of the United States Office of Education reviewed twelve of these studies [1] and reported that considerable evidence was present to indicate that the use of workbooks was beneficial to students. Such benefit was seen, as the results of tests, in outcomes of independence of study, "increase in power of self-direction," "helps in retention," "skill in fundamental processes," "reasoning ability," and "problem-solving ability."

Self-instructive materials assume the position of the teacher *in absentia*, in which case selection entails a considerable responsibility. Fortunately, a set of criteria is available for the measurement of workbooks.[2] If properly applied, the selection of workbooks is considerably simplified and the risk of mistakes materially lessened. The good workbook is one which:

1. Utilizes completely the findings of the scientific study of the learning process.

2. Utilizes as many as possible of the materials and opportunities for experience which are available.

3. Provides adequately for maximum growth on the part of all learners, no matter what their types or general levels of maturity.

[1] Goodykoontz, Bess. "Current Uses and Effects of Workbooks," *Curriculum Journal*, Vol. 6 (Apr. 22, 1935), pp. 30–40.

[2] Vreeland, Wendell. "The Rate of Instructional Aids in Teaching," *Curriculum Journal*, Vol. 6 (Apr. 22, 1935), p. 13.

4. Stimulates in wholesome ways the assumption of responsibility by the student for all aspects of his work.

5. Provides effective training in the technique of self-diagnosis.

6. Fosters an intimate personal contact between student and teacher.

The workbook is not a cure-all for the problems of individualized instruction, and the teacher placing her faith in its use is doomed to disappointment. It is merely a means to an end, and so used may serve both learner and teacher efficiently. Indiscriminately used, the workbook may become an unyielding instrument. The teacher unaccustomed to the use of workbooks would do well to introduce the practice slowly, perhaps beginning with a single subject like arithmetic. The Michigan Instructional Guide for Elementary Schools offers excellent advice on the use of workbooks.

Having chosen the books to be used, the teacher's next task is to become thoroughly acquainted with the book or series so that he knows just what it contains and how it is organized. Only then is he ready to plan its most effective use by pupils. Especially should he avoid the easy but not especially efficient method of having all children go through the material in the same sequence and at the same rate. The workbook makes possible individual adaptation of the rate and sequence of learning. This opportunity should not be lost. The diagnostic tests should be used to find out which of the activities should be carried through by each individual pupil.

. . . Time must be set aside for their use, usually the same time for the whole room in the same subject. Provision must be made for the checks and records of pupil progress. One difficulty of individualized work is that of keeping track of pupils when even those in the same grade are not all working at the same point at once. Good workbooks usually include a record form which the pupil himself keeps and from which the teacher may see his progress at a glance. Further, the teacher must realize that his teaching opportunities and responsibilities do not cease while the pupils are engaged on workbooks. After all, the chief purpose of these instructional aids is to free the teacher from some routine tasks in order that he may have time for genuine study and guidance of his pupils in the light of their needs.

During the workbook period the wise teacher goes about the room to give help as requested or to check progress and difficulties.[1]

Drill Cards. One of the most common devices for directing study and individualizing instruction is the use of drill cards. These cards, frequently constructed by the teacher or older children, are printed on oak tag and made available to children in the fields of arithmetic or reading. For example, the important words in primary reading may be printed on cards and used by children to drill each other. Likewise, the fundamental processes in arithmetic may be transferred to cards, and similarly used by children, either for individual or for group drills.

Lesson Sheets or Contracts. The use of lesson sheets or contracts is one of the most effective means of directing the study interests of children. There are many ways of devising such study guides but the most commonly used is the "contract", modeled after those in the Dalton Plan. This is usually a well-planned, well-written lesson sheet presented in such a form that each child can work in his own way, at his own rate of speed, and toward his own selected goal. The sheets may be duplicated on the typewriter, hectograph, mimeograph, or by using carbon paper and a well sharpened pencil. These are especially adapted to the rural school as they make in reality an extension of the short recitation period into the longer study period. On page 124 is presented an example of a contract developed in the Practice School, State Teachers College at Buffalo, by the teacher on the Life of Robert Louis Stevenson and given to students in the seventh grade. The contract is divided into three levels of achievement. Each child is required to complete Contract C, but those children more energetic and ambitious may complete Contract B and A. The contract follows: [2]

[1] State of Michigan, Department of Public Instruction. *Instructional Guide for Elementary Schools*, Bulletin 301, pp. 49–50, Lansing, Michigan, 1936.

[2] The Contract was written by Mrs. Hertha S. Ganey, English Teacher, School of Practice, State Teachers College at Buffalo, N. Y.

TREASURE ISLAND

by

Robert Louis Stevenson

PROJECT I   LIFE OF STEVENSON

Contract C

Write a short biographical account of the life of Robert Louis Stevenson in which you stress the following points:

1. Date and place of birth
2. Ancestry and parentage. What part do lighthouses play in Stevenson's family life?
3. Childhood. Health. Who was Cummie?
4. Education. For what professions did Stevenson train?
5. Travels. What countries did Stevenson visit? Why did he travel so extensively?
6. Literary accomplishments. What well-known book of poetry did he write for children? What is the title of his famous book for boys? What story tells of a man who could live as two different personalities?
7. Where did Stevenson spend the last days of his life? What did the people do when he died?

References: You will find material for the above contract in the following places:

1. Introduction and notes of your text, *Treasure Island*
2. Encyclopedias, such as, *The World Book, Book of Knowledge, Compton's,* or *The New International*
3. Overton, J. M. *The Life of Robert Louis Stevenson for Boys and Girls*
4. *Literature and Life—Book One,* pages 79–84

Contract B

Pretend that you are a newspaper reporter and have been sent to interview Stevenson for your paper. The occasion may be when he returned from the South Seas, or when he came to the United

States. Write up your article as you would want it to appear in print. Study some interviews in newspapers and magazines rather carefully before writing yours, so that you will catch the spirit and style of an interview.

Contract A

Stevenson always carried around with him a notebook into which he jotted ideas that he planned to use later on in writing his stories. Write out a few pages of such entries which he might have used in planning *Treasure Island*.

ADVANTAGES AND DISADVANTAGES OF INDIVIDUALIZED INSTRUCTION

Advantages of the Plan. Advocates of plans for individualizing instruction in small schools claim much for the system. It "establishes self-direction," "places emphasis upon the work of individual pupils," "serves each pupil according to his need," "removes the temptation to shabby work" and "allows children necessarily absent to make up work easily." [1] Moreover, individualization "frees the teacher for truly creative teaching of individual children," it takes care "of much of the routine of teaching," "many pupils may learn to direct their own study to a large degree" and "allow the teacher to become acquainted with the pupils and to help them with their individual difficulties." [2]

Under what may be termed average rural and graded school conditions individual instruction produced a suprisingly large increase in the efficiency of instruction when compared with the class recitation method. The summary of the results of the whole battery of tests . . . shows decisively that the individual method was superior to the class recitation method. . . The tendency toward improvement under individual instruction was greater in subjects involving reflective

[1] Hoffman, U. J. *A Program for Study and Instruction in One-Teacher Schools*, Circular 210, pp. 24–27, Illinois, 1926.

[2] State of Michigan, Department of Public Instruction. *Instructional Guide for Elementary Schools*, Bulletin 301, p. 46, 1936.

thinking than in subjects involving drill fixation. Even in the drill subjects the individual method tended to be superior however.[1]

These are impressive claims. Coming from such widely separated sources as Illinois, Michigan, and Vermont the accumulation of evidence necessarily carries great weight. It would appear that individualization as a method of school organization and as a technique of teaching might profitably be adapted speedily and *in toto* into the small rural school. However, there are educational leaders who warn of the dangers of such action. According to these leaders, a close scrutiny of the individualization of instruction reveals a prospect not altogether pleasing.

Disadvantages of the Plan. That the plan of individual instruction has its handicaps is evident, even to the uninstructed. To keep account of each individual child in each of the eight grades and in each of the subjects seems on the face of it an impossible task. The chief purpose of individualized instruction, as the Michigan Guide points out, is to free the teacher from routine to creative tasks. This is an ideal on which both advocates and critics of the plan agree, but the critics inquire practically at this point if the constant correction of work sheets and workbooks is not the most deadly of routine tasks. Yet the whole scheme of individualized instruction falls down unless the teacher is in close touch with pupils *via* their written work. Another weakness of the plan lies in the fact that many teachers are prone to believe that teaching responsibilities are met, so long as children are busy with their lesson sheets or workbooks. This tendency is a danger which cannot be lightly dismissed. It is a regression to the "busy work" of the first graded schools, and, ignored, tends to make the activity an end in itself. Brim criticises the Winnetka system on this very point:

[1] Taplin, Winn Lowell. *Relative Efficiency of Class vs. Individual Instruction in Graded and One-Teacher Schools, 1933-1934*, p. 73. Unpublished master's thesis, University of Vermont, 1935.

In the Winnetka Plan the child does not realize an intelligent appreciation of what this drill work is all for. In order to appreciate this, one must have in mind the formal nature of the textbooks used in the individualized work. The work for any grade in the individualized subjects is determined. Then it is carefully graded into lessons. A book for each lesson in each grade is prepared in such a way that the child will be able from the reading to understand what is to be done and be able to do it under his own direction. When this lesson is finished, he reports to his teacher for approval. Then he may go to his next lesson and the next until he has finished his grade in that subject. I asked a child who was coloring a certain design, what he was doing. The reply was that he was coloring that figure. When asked why he was doing that, he replied that that was a lesson. When further asked what he was going to do with it, he replied, "Nothing." When asked why he wished to do this particular piece of work, he said that it was necessary before he could go on to the next lesson. Now this may have been an exception. It is the writer's opinion that it is not so rare as one would wish, for the organization of the work is such that only the unusual child will ever look for any other meaning, relation, or reason for doing a task.[1]

Advocates of individualized instruction are aware of this difficulty and are the first to warn teachers against it. Upon this point the Michigan Instructional Guide for Elementary Schools makes this timely warning:

The workbook is a good servant but a bad master. . . Further, too many workbooks make "blank fillers" out of children. The workbook idea should generally not be used by a particular pupil in more than one or two subjects.[2]

All teachers who accept the principles of individualized instruction would do well to examine their practices from time to time to ascertain if in them they are exchanging the precious substance of teaching for its shadow.

In line with the criticism of Brim there is another danger inherent in the plan of individualized instruction. This fre-

[1] Brim, Orville G. "Rural Schools and the Winnetka Plan," *The Journal of Rural Education*, Vol. 4 (May–June 1925), pp. 401–402.
[2] State of Michigan, Department of Public Instruction. *Instructional Guide for Elementary Schools*, Bulletin 301, p. 50, Lansing, Michigan, 1936.

quently lies in the practice of teaching the facts without reference to use. Such practices are opposed to that philosophy of modern education which conceives of all education as functional. In the so-called "activity program," children are taught the multiplication table for example because they need to know this fundamental process for keeping store in a grocery unit. They are taught perspective in art because they need to give form and grace to the scenery for a group dramatization. Neither skill is taught because it is a prescribed goal, nor because children should know the answers. The skills are taught when and as children need them. Brim attacks this point also:

> In order that this "Plan" might be carried out, "essential" habits, facts, and skills have been carefully selected, carefully graded as to difficulty and painstakingly subdivided into digestible portions. These are presented to the child to be mastered without respect to his need for them. The arithmetic fundamentals, fractions, etc., are taught as a series of drill lessons without reference to use. They are not developed out of a meaningful situation in which they are needed. They do not enter into child life to make it more effective. The work in language is of similar nature. The essential language habits have been selected, graded and embodied in a series of exercises. Each of these the child does in turn. He may or may not have use for the particular skill embodied in this exercise. That is not in question. Attention is centered upon the rapid mastery of certain formal skills.[1]

THE PRACTICAL MIDDLE WAY

Students of rural education are aware that a combination of individualized instruction and group teaching is necessary in teaching small schools of several grades. There is in reality no choice between the points of view of those recommending group and those advocating individual activities. Some type of individualized instruction is a feature of all group organizations. Beginners, for example, are nearly always kept in separate classes and not grouped because it is considered essential that

[1] Brim, Orville G. "Rural Schools and the Winnetka Plan," *The Journal of Rural Education*, Vol. 4 (May–June 1925), p. 399.

each child acquire skill in reading before he finds his place in a group for the social studies, the language arts, or science. On the other hand, group instruction is an essential in all individualized teaching. It is necessary when a problem is presented, when the individuals need to exchange views, and when tests are surveyed. An examination of the policies of those who advocate "activity programs" reveals a unanimity of opinion that individualized teaching of the tool subjects is frequently desirable and necessary. Proponents of "individualized instruction" are equally agreed that "socialization" of the school program cannot be ignored. And so the two points of view become as one in a program which educates the individual to live in a social group.

This agreement has significant educational implications for the inexperienced teacher. It suggests that he would do well to take the best features of both programs and incorporate them into his program. He should, in other words, adapt the safety of the middle way. After his philosophy of education is mellowed with experience he may find it profitable to veer right or left to suit the exigencies of his own teaching situation.

SUMMARY

At the heart of the program of individualized teaching is the philosophy that children should be taught in terms of their own needs and abilities. From this philosophy has developed a well defined system of teaching techniques, best exemplified perhaps in the systems of schools located at Dalton, Massachusetts, and Winnetka, Illinois. Practices developed in these systems are: (a) the determination of specific subject matter goals on age and grade levels; (b) a complete diagnostic testing program to be given at the completion of each subject matter assignment; and (c) the development of teaching materials which assist children in the mastery of the specified goals. Many features of these practices are adaptable in small rural schools and five states have made considerable progress in the adaptations. These are: Connecticut, Illinois, Maine, Michigan, and Vermont. In 1926 the Illinois State Department of Education issued a bulletin which recommended a program for individualizing the small schools of the whole state. The plan was patterned after that of Winnetka and was modified to meet certain specific needs of the small school. The school day was divided into "sessions" devoted to major subjects. During these sessions the teacher conducted, for the most part, supervised study periods with certain designated periods reserved for group instruction and consultation. The methods of instruction were individual. They consisted of: (a) individual assignments, (b) individual conferences with the teacher, (c) group conferences, and (d) individual tests. Specific materials are also necessary for individualized instruction and these have been developed in the form of (a) workbooks, (b) study guides, (c) tests, and (d) lesson sheets or contracts. The use of each type of material is similar: to provide self instructive and self-corrective forms so that children may proceed at their own rate of speed in conquering their own difficulties. The most commonly used type of material in the rural school is the commercial workbook which frequently accompanys the textbook. While these have many good features to commend them, authorities warn against the tendency to make them ends rather than means to growth in children. This same caution should be observed in the use of all materials which attempt to substitute for teaching.

Advocates of the individualization of instruction claim much for the system. Some of the beneficent results claimed are: (a) self-direction in children, (b) independence in study habits, (c) responsibility in reaching standards, (d) easily administrated, (e) frees the teacher for creative teaching, and (f) allows the teacher to become better acquainted with the pupils. Critics of the plan, however, point out certain difficulties as follows: (a) the multiplicity of papers and other forms of written work, (b) the tendency of teachers to substitute workbooks for teaching, and (c) the practice of teaching facts without reference to use.

In spite of the differences in viewpoints of those who advocate "activity" programs and those who urge the individualization of instruction there can be no choice made of them in small rural schools. Practically, both plans are useful and both plans are necessary. Some type of individualized instruction is necessary in all small schools, and teaching in groups is essential to an adequate educational process. The teacher, inexperienced in modern education, is, therefore, urged to take the middle way using in his teaching the best offered by "activities" and by individualization. The lode-star of modern education is the child. He and not the "system" or "plan" is the important feature in all teaching.

A further discussion of the study problems of rural schools is presented in Chapter VII. This discussion, however, is based upon the work of the school group rather than, as here, upon the study activities of individual children.

SUGGESTED READINGS

Dewey, John. *Interest and Effort in Education*, Chap. II, Houghton Mifflin Co., New York, 1913.

Dunn, Fannie W. and Everett, Marcia. "An Experiment in a Rural School," *Teachers College Record*, Vol. XXIX, No. 8, pp. 675–683.

Hoffman, U. J. *A Program of Study and Instruction in One-Teacher Schools*, Circular 210, Illinois, 1926.

National Society for the Study of Education. The Twenty-fourth Yearbook, Part II, *Adapting the Schools to Individual Differences*, pp. 117–129, Public School Publishing Co., Bloomington, Ill., 1925.

National Society for the Study of Education. The Thirty-fourth Yearbook, *Educational Diagnosis*, Chap. VIII, Public School Publishing Co., Bloomington, Ill., 1935.

National Society for Study of Education. The Twenty-sixth Yearbook, *Foundations and Technique of Curriculum Construction*, Chap. XI, Part II, Public School Publishing Co., Bloomington, Ill., 1926.

Parkhurst, Helen. *Education on the Dalton Plan*, Chaps. II, III, IV, E. P. Dutton and Co., New York, 1922.

Tippett, James S. *Schools for a Growing Democracy*, Chap. V, Ginn and Co., New York, 1936.

Washburne, Carleton. *Adjusting the School to the Child,* Chap. I, World Book Co., Yonkers-on Hudson, New York, 1932.

Washburne, Carleton and Stearns, Myron. *Better Schools,* Chap. III, John Day Company, New York, 1928.

MATERIALS FOR DISCUSSION

Consider the following statements. What changes would make them more acceptable to you? What significant issues arise from their study?

1. It is impossible to adjust the school to the child and at the same time adjust the child to the group. One must be sacrificed for the other and the teacher is forced to a choice when he makes the daily program for the school.

2. Undue emphasis upon individual instruction tends to accentuate inherent difficulties of rural children—the tendencies toward aloofness and individualism.

3. There are no fundamental differences in the points of view of those who advocate "activity" programs and those who recommend a form of "individualized" instruction.

4. Both individualization of instruction and group teaching are necessary for a modern educational program in small rural schools.

5. Individualization of instruction tends toward drill upon isolated facts, toward formalization of learning, and the regimentation of the learner.

CHAPTER VII

PLANNING THE OUT-OF-RECITATION PERIOD

THE PROBLEM STATED

It is estimated that approximately 20 per cent of the time spent by a rural child in school is given to recitations, the remaining 80 per cent to out-of-recitation periods, in which the children, without the aid of the teacher, work alone. Dunn and Everett in their report of the Quaker Grove experiment were cognizant of this problem and stated it as follows:

In such a school [that is, the small rural school] no class can hope for much more than two hours a day of the teacher's time. For the remainder of the six-hour day pupils must occupy themselves unsupervised and largely, as it were, on their own steam, their periods of independent activity ranging from fifteen minutes to two hours or more in length. Stimulus motive, guidance, even correction must to a considerable extent inhere in the occupations available, else there will be enormous waste of time, idleness, listlessness, and what is in the beginning boredom, but in the end, for many pupils, relapse into satisfaction in inactivity, than which few mental states are more hopeless.[1]

These out-of-recitation periods usually include not only study periods but opening exercises, lunch periods, and recesses, involving important activities as well as important time.

THE TRADITIONAL METHOD OF MEETING THE PROBLEM OF THE OUT-OF-RECITATION PERIOD

There was suggested very early a method for the employment of the study periods in what was known as "educative seat-

[1] Dunn, Fannie W. and Everett, Marcia. *Four Years in A Country School*, p. 129, Bureau of Publications, Teachers College, Columbia University, 1926.

133

work." The very term used told much of the method, and earlier writers in the field of rural school-management emphasized it. The method, on the whole, was a teacher-planned and a teacher-imposed assignment, usually organized in the form of devices designed to keep children quiet and busy. Too often the seat work thus assigned had no connection either with the interest or the learning of children. Such connections as were present often existed only in loose directions such as "Go to your seat and study your arithmetic," "Read the next five pages in your geography," or "Get busy on your composition." Such directions were usually for the older children—those above the third grade—who had mastered the tools of learning. The younger children often fared even worse. Many spent their time writing numbers to one hundred, stringing small beads, memorizing the multiplication table, or sewing aimlessly on cards. Uneducational and time-wasting on the whole, these devices were in harmony with the traditional conception of education which emphasized passivity in children and placed a premium upon memorization and the accumulation of facts. Treatment of the other out-of-recitation periods was similar. The assembly period, that first period of the day rich with possibilities, usually consisted of the singing of a song, making the pledge to the flag, reading from a continued story by the teacher, or a recitation by a pupil. Like the seat work the program was nearly always teacher-planned and assigned with the children making a passive audience. The program thus presented, with slight variations from day to day, assumed characteristics of monotony and drabness which neither student nor teacher looked upon with enthusiasm.

THE MODERN CONCEPTION OF THE OUT-OF-RECITATION PERIODS

In planning the out-of-recitation periods the modern rural school is primarily concerned with child-participation and child-growth. Educational objectives are set up in terms of problems, and the method pursued is that of gathering data to solve them. Creative activities, from which school assemblies, study periods, and play programs develop, are normally expected to grow out of child interest, a felt need, and the research called for by each. The belief that growth takes place through all desirable experiences colors all school practices, not only when the teacher is "hearing" a lesson, but also when the child works alone and unsupervised. In the modern school program these periods are highly significant, are full of rich possibilities for child development, and are prized by teacher and student alike.

PLANNING THE STUDY PERIOD

The problem of planning the study period for the small rural school takes on a two-fold aspect: (a) the necessity for planning to meet the specific needs and problems of young children; and (b) provision for the special needs of the older children. The children from five to nine years compose the younger group and are at all times the special responsibility of the teacher. Within the span of this age group the foundations are laid for the development of the efficient use of the tool subjects, for helpful habits of study, and for desirable social attitudes. Once these foundations are laid, children who can read well and use the other tools efficiently can be trusted to work unaided; but younger children cannot well use the long study periods desirable for the upper grades. Their study periods will, therefore, be shorter and will require closer supervision. For these younger children there should be no compromise with worthless seat materials. Activities during study periods should grow out of the educational needs developed in the recitation periods. There should be provided, for instance, an abundance of easy supplementary reading materials centered about the current reading interests of the children. As with reading, so with the other tool subjects. Fortunately, there is an abundance of commercial material, much of it good, in the form of work books, exercises, etc., which are organized in terms of modern educational procedure. If used with discrimination, such material is helpful, especially if children like it. In these the acceptance of study responsibilities should be developed, but once these have been met, a free choice of activities should be possible. A sand table and a play corner offer many possibilities in creative effort, and the work may link closely with reading, the social studies, or the language arts. These activities, too, need guidance either at the hands of the teacher or through the assistance of the older children.

DIFFICULTIES IN PLANNING STUDY PERIODS FOR YOUNG CHILDREN

In the rural school it is as essential to teach children to use time well as it is to educate them in the technique of using tools and materials. The economical use of time is a habit of conduct and is built up slowly, as are all habits, through experiences in which the learner actually uses time well. In the development of this desirable habit the teacher will find it necessary to give as much time as possible to the guidance of individual children in the younger age group, because the sooner desirable study techniques become habits, the better. In the establishment of these study habits, however, the younger children and the teacher must successfully meet the following handicaps of the small rural school: (a) the long school day in which young children are likely to become tired and bored and (b) the limitation to quiet activities because of the presence of the older group of children who are studying. In order to meet the difficulties inherent in the long school day of young children, it is recommended that rest periods be provided for them, and that adjustments to their needs be secured through longer and more frequent recess periods. The necessity for quiet creates a conflict with the inherent tendency of young children toward such physical activities as jumping, running, dancing, talking, and singing. In reporting on these handicaps in the Quaker Grove experiment Dunn and Everett said:

Original tendencies, enormously important for education are multiform mental activity, multiform physical activity, and voice play. By nature the little child is continually in active motion, running, jumping, climbing, dancing; and continually chattering, asking questions, telling his simple adventures, carrying on dialogues with imaginary companions. In the rural school he must considerably repress the last two of these valuable tendencies for the sake of his fellows in more advanced grades. The first tendency is limited in its operation by the fact that the primary child is as yet unable to utilize printed symbols as a means of enlarging his experience and satisfying his curious mind, so that he is thrown back on concrete factors of his environment for stimuli to mental activity.   Moreover, he is so unskilled that in all matters where the habits he is forming are significant outcomes the products of his activities need frequently to be inspected for errors and false starts, and his concepts are so crude and his standards so low that he tends to complete an undertaking hurriedly and roughly, and finds himself then at a loss for something more to do.

It is therefore much more difficult with the primary than with the upper grade pupils to utilize with profit and without serious injury a considerable portion of each day in unsupervised occupation. The problem in their case is (1) to find materials and methods whereby in the time that is possible for the teacher to give them, sufficient stimulation, instruction, guidance, and criticism may be afforded to make possible their satisfactory performances of a desirable amount of work; and in addition (2) to provide conditions and materials for free play of types adapted to unavoidable schoolroom limitations, yet productive of such unspecialized growth as comes to a child from the quieter activities of a good home.[1]

THE STUDY PROBLEMS OF THE OLDER CHILDREN

With the older children the wise use of the study period is simpler. If habits and techniques have been established in the earlier years of school, the group can usually be trusted to handle its own study problems. This group in the rural schools is usually composed of students who take their work seriously. They are earnest about an education and appreciate the opportunities of long, uninterrupted periods for study. Often they feel that the study periods are not long enough to prepare

[1] *Ibid.* pp. 130–131.

assignments, to write compositions, and to read. At home, nearly every rural child has his chores which absorb his attention and strength, so that often he has no time or energy to prepare his school work after school hours. He comes, therefore, to look upon his day at school as an investment not lightly to be treated. To this serious student the school has certain responsibilities as follows: (a) a quiet, comfortable place for study and reading; (b) a work table with tools and materials for his activities; (c) sufficient conferences with his teacher and directions from him, so that the use of his study period is economical and efficient; and (d) a good library. Of these four, the last two are probably the most important. The problem of the school library is discussed at length elsewhere, but the planning period in preparation for study is herewith presented in the form of a case study.[1]

CASE STUDY—II

Our program attempts to provide a well organized "out-of-class" activity for each child. In so doing the child realizes his responsibility for, and the value of, time spent in school. Time, especially in a rural school, is one of our most valuable possessions, and we cannot afford to waste a minute of it.

The older children have studied budgets and understand the importance of the proper distribution of income into expenditures, savings, etc. We have attempted to use the same technique in budgeting time, for to us it is as precious as money. Each morning, after our opening exercises, the teacher and the pupils 10 years of age and older hold a conference period, when time, not spent with the teacher, is budgeted for the day. Each child makes his own "budget" after talking over with the teacher "the things which need to be done" and the "things which need to be learned." Not every child in a group needs to be doing the same thing at the same time during study periods, but it is essential that each child be busy at something which to him

[1] Reported by Mrs. Roy Breckon, Lewiston 2, Lewiston, New York. Miss M. Gazelle Hoffman, District Superintendent of Schools.

appears necessary and important. Consequently, every "budget" is personal, and acts as a study guide for each child throughout the school day. With this guide no child need sit, sunk into inertia, waiting for a suggestion from the teacher that he study his lessons. He knows what is to be done, and his chart gives his own decision regarding the best time for the accomplishment of his task. The budget is usually kept on his desk so that it may be referred to at any and all times.

The following are examples, selected at random, of time budgets. These were made by the children in the fifth, seventh and eighth grades:

5th Grade

9:20—I need to work in English.
> I will rewrite the sentences in my English work book.
> I need to reread my English book about using commas in a series. I must write sentences using the spelling words.

10:30—I need to drill in arithmetic.
> integers
> fractions
> The group will check each other in the reading corner.

1:15—I will help make boat we are building in our Transportation unit.

1:35—I will read from geography text and then work on report on "The Cotton Belt."

3:30—I will prepare a story which I expect to read in the opening exercises tomorrow.

7th Grade

9:20—Work in English
> verbs
> verb phrases
> check misspelled words of yesterday

9:50—Read about and prepare a report on Joan of Arc.

11:00—Arithmetic
    bank discount
    must have help here

1:15—Work with group on maps showing the Louisiana Purchase, Oregon Territory, expeditions of Pike, Lewis, and Clark. I must get materials ready for group.

1:50—Work on scrap-book for our Transportation unit.

2:45—Get ready for geography lesson.

8th Grade

9:20—English
    Work on assigned exercises in corrective English.

11:00—Algebra
    Solve equations and check work with the group.

1:15—Work on scrap-book for Transportation unit.

2:05—Read life of Edith Cavell and get report ready.

2:45—Check and read all sources on the unit, "The Industrial Revolution."

Not only is the system of time budgeting advantageous to the students, it is advantageous to the teacher as well. He can, by glancing at the room, tell whether or not the children are busy. By glancing at the budgets, he can tell whether or not the activity is educationally directed.

EVALUATION OF THE CASE STUDY

The outstanding characteristics of the group study activities, revealed by the case study, is that children make their own study plans. Another characteristic is that plans are made daily and are elastic. They are, therefore, subject to change as the needs of the children determine. Children also assume responsibilities for the successful culmination of study activities and for the economical use of time. Thus it is seen that through the experiences of purposing, planning and executing children move toward self-direction in study.

The plan, described by the case study, is a contribution to the individualized study plans described in Chapter VI. In the modified Dalton and Winnetka plans used in rural schools much of the responsibility for planning, executing and evaluating is assumed by the teacher instead of the children.

THE NOON HOUR

The school day in a rural school is nearly always a long one, usually extending to seven and sometimes eight hours. This is a long working day for an adult and when there is added to it the possibility of an hour of home chores before and after school, one does not wonder that fatigue is often a factor in the lives of rural children. The modern school program is concerned with all the hours of the twenty-four and their effect upon children. An effort is made therefore to coördinate the interests of the home and the school to the end that the best interests of children may be preserved. With careful planning and coöperation the hardships of the long school day can be met. The planning includes a program of rest, work, and play at school with a nourishing noon meal, good food at home, comfortable, simple clothing, and long hours of sleep at night. These will do much to maintain good health and normal mental attitudes in every child and will enable him to have a happy and successful school life.[1]

The noon hour at school is a period in the routine of the day which offers special opportunities for meeting the needs of rural children. It should be more than the traditional recess which witnessed a hasty eating of cold food from a lunch basket, or bucket, and a rush immediately afterwards to the playground. The modern teacher looks upon this period as an integral and important part of the school day and directs the activities of

[1] *The Noon Hour, A Social Hour in Central Rural Schools*, p. 5, University of the State of New York, Bulletin 1048, July 16, 1934.

it toward the meeting of definite educational objectives. These objectives have been set up by the New York State Department of Education as follows: (a) to provide rest for every child, (b) to give him a change from primarily mental activity to relaxing mental and relaxing physical activities, (c) to meet his needs for a midday meal.[1] To these ends the activities of the noon hour should be carefully organized and directed.

THE LUNCH PERIOD

The lunch of the average rural child consists of several cold sandwiches, a sweet, and perhaps a piece of fruit. In view of the fact that he eats an early breakfast and that he misses the principal meal of the farm day eaten at noon, nutrition specialists insist that rural children are likely to lack a balanced ration. They suggest the need of warm food at noon and a diet rich in vegetables and fruits. On this point, Miss Mary G. McCormick, State Supervisor of Health Teaching, State Education Department, New York, says:

Experiments have shown that the nutritive requirements of children are high. For each pound of weight the child's requirements are greater than the adult's: the total food requirement of an adolescent girl may exceed that of her mother and the total food requirement of an adolescent boy often surpasses that of his father.

Since the energy expenditure is a large factor in determining the total food requirement, those children whose energy expenditure is greater, other things being equal, will require a greater amount of food. The child who has manual tasks to perform at home, who walks a long distance to and from school, and after school again helps with the farm or home work obviously needs more food than does the child who has no duties at home and who either lives near his schoolhouse or has easy access to it by cars. Rural children, therefore, with their long and active day must necessarily have a relatively high food requirement. Three substantial meals a day should be supplied to satisfy their needs. Three substantial meals a day are

[1] *Ibid.* p. 6.

The noon day meal can serve children socially as well as physically.

an ideal difficult of accomplishment if the child is dependent on a box lunch for his noon meal.[1]

The addition of a hot dish to the cold lunch of the rural child is often designated as the "hot lunch period in the rural school." It may consist of hot soup, hot cocoa, creamed vegetables, soft custards, or other hot dishes, the variety of which is dependent upon the initiative, energy, and coöperation of children, teacher, and parents. It is one way of meeting the nutritive needs of the rural child and is recommended alike by teachers and health experts. As a school activity it has further assets in that it offers opportunities for (a) the promotion of good health habits and (b) the development of desirable social behavior. The health habits thus promoted are listed by Miss McCormick as follows:

(a) washing hands before preparing, serving, or eating food;
(b) rejecting food that has fallen to the floor;
(c) replacing at once by a clean one, any knife, fork, or spoon that has fallen to the floor;
(d) using individual cups, plates, forks, knives, spoons, and napkins as well as individual towels;
(e) sitting down to eat, relaxing, eating slowly, and enjoying lunch time;
(f) eating without protest the food that is served;
(g) drinking liquids only when there is no other food in the mouth;
(h) sitting in an erect easy position;
(i) sterilizing dishes that are used by a miscellaneous group;
(j) keeping cooking utensils in a state of immaculate cleanliness;
(k) keeping food supplies covered as a protection against dust and insects.

Desirable social behavior is likewise developed: (a) leadership, (b) followship, (c) coöperation, and (d) responsibility. Miss McCormick further suggests that a unique opportunity for the practice of good table manners is offered:

[1] *The Rural Hot Lunch as a Health and Social Activity.* p. 3, University of the State of New York, New York State Education Department, 1931.

(a) sitting down to eat together and remaining until everyone has finished;

(b) passing food to others;

(c) participating in conversation at table, using a low and distinct voice;

(d) talking only when the mouth is empty;

(e) keeping the lips closed while chewing food;

(f) chewing food and drinking liquids without making lip and tongue noises;

(g) using the fork and spoon and not the knife to convey food to the mouth;

(h) leaving the spoon in the saucer and not in the cup.[1]

There is also opportunity for learning about food values, preservation of foods, and skill in food preparation and service.

In a small school, the hot lunch, since the hot dish is often prepared in the classroom, requires careful planning. All sorts of adjustments frequently take place in order to provide the "kitchen." The "kitchen" of the experimental school at Quaker Grove was described as follows:

The kitchen of the school was merely the end of a long hall which extended across the front of the building. The other end of this hall was used as a cloakroom.[2]

This picture of the experimental school is fairly typical of all small rural schools. Sometimes the "kitchen" is in a cloakroom, often in a passageway; it may be in the basement, or merely the end of the classroom; space in the small school is precious and often every foot of it must be utilized. For the "kitchen" the equipment is simple and consists of the following:

1. A hot plate where electricity is available, or a three burner oil stove where it is not.

2. A shelf for holding the lunch boxes, and one for the staple groceries which should be placed in covered containers. A cup-

[1] *Ibid.* p. 4.

[2] Dunn, Fannie W. and Everett, Marcia. *Four Years in a Country School*, p. 110, Bureau of Publications, Teachers College, Columbia University, 1926.

board with doors is desirable and may, incidentally, provide interesting carpenter work for the older boys.

3. A kitchen table which may also result from a school activity.

4. The utensils usually recommended for preparing food are as follows:

1 saucepan	1 kitchen fork	1 spatula
1 double boiler	1 can opener	1 tray
1 measuring cup	2 tablespoons	2 dish pans
1 strainer	2 teaspoons	1 soap dish
1 egg beater	1 soup ladle	1 asbestos mat
1 paring knife	1 quart measure	dish towels and dish cloths

5. Each child should have as a minimum of equipment a large cup with a handle, a spoon, and a paper napkin. Either each child should furnish his own equipment, or the school should purchase these supplies as a part of the regular equipment. The latter plan is more desirable because the equipment is then uniform and lends itself to better care; every child is certain of proper equipment, and the equipment may be used for community meetings and the social hours of the meetings of the Parent-Teacher Association.[1]

Supplies for the hot dish are provided in many ways. There may be (a) contributions of vegetables, milk, fruit, and canned goods from the parents of individual children; (b) a cash contribution from the Parent-Teacher Association or the Board of Trustees; and (c) cash contributions from individual children or parents. Whatever the means of financing the activity, the teacher should take proper care that no child feels under obligation to another child for food or for services. The activity is essentially a coöperative one. The technique of the performance of the hot lunch activity is presented in the form of a case study submitted by a teacher of a one-room school.[2]

[1] McCormick, Mary G. *The Rural Hot Lunch as a Health and Social Activity*, p. 11, University of the State of New York, State Education Department, 1931.

[2] Reported by Mrs. Blanche Nichols, Clarence, New York. Mr. A. W. Harkness, District Superintendent of Schools.

CASE STUDY—III

At half-past eleven the two cooks appointed for the day arose quietly from their seats and went into the small anteroom used as a kitchen. The weekly menu indicated that a hot cocoa was to be served that day and the cooks extracted the recipe for it from an index file. This is the recipe they used:

Cocoa—¾ cup	Water—1 quart
Sugar —¾ cup	Milk —4 quarts
salt—1 teaspoonful	

The preparation of this hot drink did not require all of the thirty minutes allowed for the task, but the children laid out all of the materials, put the water on to boil, and returned to their seats and studied. A few minutes before twelve they again went to the kitchen to finish the cooking of the hot dish. When the children were dismissed for lunch they filed in orderly fashion to the back of the room to wash their hands. Water proved one of the greatest problems. There was no water on the ground and it had to be transported from the well of a nearby farmer. However, use was made of a large wash basin for washing hands, a slop pail for holding the soiled water, and paper towels. The teacher insisted that all hands be washed before handling food either in cooking or eating and the children gave fine coöperation in this. After washing their hands the children returned quickly to their seats where the food had been placed by two boys acting as the servers for the day. A square of oilcloth had been placed to protect the tops of the desks. The servers then returned to the kitchen where they helped serve the cocoa, pouring it from a pitcher into cups placed on trays. These were then carried into the schoolroom and a cup placed on each desk. Each child by that time had taken his lunch from his basket and was ready to eat. Before doing so, however, Mary took her seat at the piano and played the Grace which all sang to the tune of *Old Hundred*.

> We thank Thee for the morning light,
> For rest and shelter of the night,
> For health and food,
> For care and friends,
> For everything Thy goodness sends.

The children and the teacher sat quietly throughout the lunch talking and laughing naturally together. A second cup of cocoa was passed to those who wanted it. At the close of the lunch period the servers cleared the dishes, took the cups and spoons to the kitchen, put away the oilcloth squares and brushed up any crumbs that might have fallen to the floor. The cooks washed the dishes and as a consequence had little time left in which to play. However, work is divided so that they may play the next day when the others act as cooks, for tasks revolve and duties are distributed. In the meantime the other children have been out in the open air, playing on the school grounds.

EVALUATION OF THE CASE STUDY

An examination of this case study reveals several significant procedures. (1) The teacher did not dominate the activity. She advised, but the children assumed responsibility for planning the activity and for its completion. (2) The activity was coöperative, but the plan of procedure included a wise division of labor. (3) Boys as well as girls participated. (4) Evidence is given that health habits and habits of desirable social behavior were established.

THE PLAY PERIODS
THE NEED FOR PLAY IN RURAL SCHOOLS

In the Iowa study of farm children made by Bird T. Baldwin and others, one of the significant facts reported was the attitude of the child in the small rural school toward play. The study reported that while the play activities in these small schools were simple, they were considered of great importance by the children. This was revealed in two pieces of evidence presented by the report. The first was in the diaries kept by the children under observation in which they reported daily happenings at home and at school. For the most part the diaries were dull and uninteresting, presenting a picture of flat, monotonous days filled with chores at home and at school. While mention was made of the work in the schoolroom, usually the games at noon and the recess received the most attention, indicating where real interest lay. The other was the practice of the children in hurrying through the morning chores in order to conserve a little extra time to be spent on the playground before the duties of the schoolroom began. At the noon hour the children, eager for play, begrudged the time spent in eating their lunches. The report describes this latter procedure as follows:

By hastily swallowing the ample provisions of their lunch boxes, they had left the greater part of the noon hour for play. Playing and eating simultaneously was the more usual procedure and occurred at each intermission. The minute the morning or afternoon recess was announced there was a scramble for lunch boxes, and each pupil emerged to the playground carrying one or more sandwiches, or, more rarely, an apple. Games of "tag," "blindman's buff," "run sheep run," "hide and seek," and "fox and geese" were often played with the participants scarcely pausing in their scampering about for hasty bites from huge meat or jam sandwiches.[1]

This practice is an indictment of the lunch procedure as well as of the play period. Eagerness to play, even at the expense of physical hunger, shows how keenly the average rural child feels the isolation characteristic of his home life; and the opportunity for team play at school is, therefore, an essential for which the modern school should provide.

The Iowa study verifies an earlier one made by the American Country Life Association and reported by it in 1919.[2] A Committee on Recreation in Rural Areas came to the conclusion that, while farm work provides an abundance of physical exercise in the open air, young people need games for the development of

[1] Baldwin, Bird T. and Others. *Farm Children*, p. 141, D. Appleton Company, 1930.
[2] Proceedings of the American Country Life Association. *Rural Health*, p. 118, Chicago, 1919.

that physical symmetry, mental alertness, and neuro-muscular coördination which farm life in general fails to supply. The ordinary chores of the farm, as, for example, hoeing corn, taking care of horses, and splitting wood, tend to develop the large muscles, but they do not develop sufficiently the finer or accessory muscles which give grace and confidence to young children. If, as the report states, the vocation of farming inherently has in it deterrents to the satisfactory and symmetrical physical development, then the usual regimen of farm life should be supplemented with recreational activities which offset the deficiency. And, since organized education commands the major portion of a child's life, the responsibility for meeting his play deficiencies lies clearly within the province of the school.

PRACTICAL PROCEDURES IN MEETING PLAY DEFICIENCIES

In the usual program of the small school approximately one hour a day is available for play: fifteen minutes each day prior to and following the noon hour, often called by the children "little" recesses, and approximately thirty minutes after the noon meal. The traditional recess period followed a regular daily pattern as exemplified in realistic detail by the Iowa report:

Only a few of the one-room schools had playground equipment, although there was an occasional swing, teeter-totter board, or slide. But few of the teachers took part in the playground activities other than to maintain necessary discipline. When the children were left to their own devices, many playground periods deteriorated. The girls divided into small groups and wandered about arm in arm whispering harmless little "secrets" amidst much self-conscious laughter, while the boys pushed and wrestled among themselves, tumbling about as young animals play. . . . During rainy or severely cold weather the relaxation periods were necessarily spent within the schoolroom. The time was passed by the pupils in "foolin' 'round" unless the teacher was able to furnish music on cabinet organ or phonograph, that would keep the pupils marching up and down the aisles while windows and doors were opened for "an airing out."[1]

[1] Baldwin, Bird T. and Others. *Farm Children*, pp. 141–142, D. Appleton Company, 1930.

The description suggests the following difficulties typical of the mismanagement of recess periods in the average small school. (1) Apparently, there was no planning for play either by the children or by the teacher. Since there was no planning there was no group activity, except that hit upon by accident, and, while such accidental play may be desirable, results are not always certain. (2) The children received no training in accepting leadership for the promotion of group play, and, on the playground, as in life, everybody's business became nobody's business. Under a program of guidance and suggestion by the teacher, children may be encouraged to assume leadership and responsibility in organizing and conducting the activities of the playground. As the Iowa study showed, the felt need for play is always present in normal children and the responsibility of the teacher lies in the directing of activities to meeting these needs.

While there is no agreement, the opinion is held by some specialists in rural education that the usual plan of having two recess periods of fifteen minutes each and a period of one hour at noon is not desirable. A short rest period in the morning of, approximately, ten minutes; a noon hour of, perhaps, forty-five minutes; and a period of, perhaps, a half hour in length in the afternoon for a real physical education program has, apparently, many advantages.

Experience and experimentation have laid down the following principles:

1. All normal children should, weather permitting, have at least thirty minutes of organized play distributed among the three daily recesses. Out-of-door play is as necessary in winter as in summer; a program of regular exercises, plays, and games should be started in the fall and continued throughout the year. Such a program presupposes that the teacher, until proper leadership in children is developed, will play with the children.

2. With the exception of the very young children who should have their own play needs cared for, opportunities should be provided for group games which develop coöperation, team play, and sportsmanship.

3. Children should be encouraged and assisted in planning their

play activities and, as leadership develops, should assume responsibility for them.

4. Because of the rural child's need to develop skill and grace, care should be taken that activities be chosen which develop these qualities. Such activities involve games which allow the free use of the entire body, which require precision of action, which develop rhythm, and which are mentally exhilarating.

5. Children should be encouraged to develop an interest in, and a curiosity for, experimentation in play. In the modern program of education many units of work suggest activities which children naturally carry from the school to the playground. These should be encouraged, because the playground offers a laboratory where many things talked about in school may be experienced An article reporting on a physical education program in a progressive school gave records of such play activities developing from the interests of young children in a unit on the circus. "The circus as a unit of work or center of interest for the first grade has unlimited possibilities. The vivid imagination, the interest in dramatization, impersonation of animals, nature and people and the interest in activity for the sake of activity so characteristic of this age provided sources of never-ending interest. . . . Rhythm work linked up with dramatic activities was the chief source of interest. These children had had some work in rhythm; so when music of slow even tempo was played they were inspired to impersonate bears, elephants, camels, et cetera." [1]

Experimentation with folk dances and folk games should naturally follow an interest in foreign countries developed by social science units with older children. Creative play should be one of the goals set by the modern school.

OPENING EXERCISES

The time scheduled in the daily program for opening exercises is usually listed from 9 to 9:15, but in the modern school the period is elastic. It is also important, since it is one of the few times during the day when all the grades meet as one

[1] Schneider, Elsa. "Physical Education in a Progressive School," *The Journal of Health and Physical Education*, pp. 19–20, Vol. IV (Feb. 1933).

group. So stimulating should be the program that the school will anticipate it with pleasure. It is full of such possibilities as the following. (1) It can make vivid the high points of classroom recitation and study. Children in a modern school are constantly discovering things which they wish to share with others, and the period of the opening exercises offers opportunities for such sharing of experiences. Conversely, it offers audience experiences for those who listen, in which desirable social behavior may be developed. The social studies offer a rich field for creative expression in all the arts; dramatization, dancing, costuming, and story telling; and these as developed in the several groups may be shared with the school. (2) The opening exercises offer an interesting opportunity for envisioning the work of the day, or planning for such special interests as naturally develop in activities. Such a planning period lends itself well to a general principle in the making of programs for opening exercises, namely, that they should represent a coöperative effort on the part of the teacher and the pupils. An illustration of this procedure is reported by the experimental school at Quaker Grove:

The morning exercises were devoted to final plans for the evening. Ushers were chosen and a few final reminders of how much was expected of them were given by the teacher.[1]

(3) The opening exercises should also present worthwhile material in a stimulating way. Current events, in which children are interested, are an example of this type of material and easily available in nearly all schools, no matter how small. Another example of source material is the science exhibits which rural children often bring to school in the form of wasp's nests, cocoons, butterflies, live animals, and fossils. With encouragement, children provide their own materials for the opening exercises for the entire school session. (4) The opening exercises should also provide an opportunity for dealing with problems which are the concern of the whole school. A few

[1] Dunn, Fannie W. and Everett, Marcia. *Four Years in a Country School*, p. 40, Bureau of Publications, Teachers College, Columbia University, 1926.

of these are health, sanitation, school relationships, and the *esprit de corps* of the group.

These four general principles are suggestive only; put into practice they will suggest others, all of which should tend to vitalize the traditional fifteen minutes, with which the school day begins, into a period both stimulating and worthwhile.

SUMMARY

The out-of-recitation periods, namely, opening exercises, study periods, lunch periods, and recesses, persistent problems in rural schools, are developing in a modern program of education into rich and stimulating experiences. In all, they comprise approximately 80 per cent of the rural school day. The traditional method of dealing with these periods was to have them, in the matter of study periods and opening exercises at least, teacher-planned and assigned. Children accepted the program in the form of instructions and attempted to carry them out. The recesses and the lunch hour were usually neglected by the teacher, so that, without any direction or plan, children fumbled through to questionable results. The plan suggested by this chapter is a coöperative one in which children and teacher work together on problems challenging to both. It is suggested that the study period be treated as an opportunity for the development of children. The problem is attacked from two points; (a) efforts made to meet the specific needs of young children, provisions for which include shorter study periods, much activity, and opportunities for developing skill in the use of the tool subjects; (b) suggestions for meeting the problems of the older children. These include a quiet comfortable place in which to study, a well-equipped work table, a good library, sufficient conferences with the teacher for economy and efficiency in study, and training in the technique of study and research.

Likewise it is suggested that the opening exercises proceed on four general principles; (a) to make them an integral part of the work of the school; (b) to plan the work of the day or the special interests of the school; (c) to present worthwhile material in a stimulating way; and (d) to deal with problems which concern the whole group. The lunch hour and recess periods are also presented as coöperative activities in which children assume responsibility for their own requirements. This involves consideration for the difficulties attendant upon physical development as revealed by nutritional deficiencies, and the inherent needs of rural people for symmetrical physical development and neuro-muscular coördination.

The modern school recognizes the necessity of bending all effort toward a harmonious all-round development of child nature. In order to achieve this goal every hour of the school day, both in recitation and out, should be used to the highest educational advantage.

SUGGESTED READINGS

Baldwin, Bird T. and Others. *Farm Children*, Chap. IX, D. Appleton Co., New York, 1930.

California Curriculum Commission. *Teachers' Guide to Child Development in the Intermediate Grades*, Chap. II, California State Department of Education, Sacramento, California, 1936.

California Curriculum Commission. *Teachers' Guide to Child Development*, Chap. IV, California State Department of Education, Sacramento, California, 1930.

Dunn, Fannie W. and Everett, Marcia. *Four Years in A Country School*, pp. 104–116, Bureau of Publications, Teachers College, Columbia University, New York, 1926.

Lowth, Frank J. *Everyday Problems of the Country Teacher*, Rev. ed., Chap. XI, Macmillan, New York, 1936.

Monroe, W. S. and Streitz, Ruth. *Directing Learning in the Elementary School*, Chap. XIV, Doubleday, Doran and Co., Garden City, N. Y., 1932.

Mueller, A. D. *Progressive Trends in Rural Education*, Chaps. XIV–XV, Century Co., New York, 1926.

McCormick, M. G. *Rural Hot Lunch as a Health and Social Activity*, University of the State of New York, State Education Department, Albany, 1931. Pamphlet.

Ruediger, W. C. *Teaching Procedures*, Chap. XXIII, Houghton Mifflin Co., Boston, 1932.

Sandwick, R. L. *Study and Personality*, Chap. III, Heath, New York, 1929.

MATERIALS FOR DISCUSSION

Consider the following statements. What changes would make them more acceptable to you? What significant issues arise from their study?

1. Since 80 per cent of the day in the small rural school is spent without direct teacher supervision, it is essential that independent study habits be established in children as early as possible.

2. The school day of the rural teacher is too crowded, the demands upon her strength too many, to add to her duties responsibility for making the noon hour an integral part of the school day. It would be better for both children and teacher to use the hour for undirected relaxation and rest.

3. The necessity for play in rural schools is overemphasized. Children on the farm receive ample exercise in the performance of their daily chores, in their walks to and from school, and in the games which all normal children naturally play.

4. The opening exercises of the school should be the high spot of the day's work.

5. The out-of-recitation periods of the school day have more educational possibilities than the recitation time spent with the teacher. The modern teacher in the small school should make every effort to have these periods truly educational.

CHAPTER VIII

ORGANIZATION OF THE SCHOOL FOR DEMOCRATIC LIVING

. . . I believe that the school is primarily a social institution. Education being a social process, the school is simply that form of community life in which all those agencies are concentrated that will be most effective in bringing the child to share in the inherited resources of the race and to use his own powers for social ends. . . . Much of present education fails because it neglects this fundamental principle of the school as a form of community life. It conceives the school as a place where certain information is to be given, where certain lessons are to be learned, or where certain habits are to be formed. . . . The child should be stimulated and controlled in his work through the life of the community. Under existing conditions far too much of the stimulus and control proceeds from the teacher because of neglect of the idea of the school as a form of social life. The teacher's place and work in the school is to be interpreted from the same basis. The teacher is not in the school to impose certain ideas or to form certain habits in the child, but is there as a member of the community to select the influences which shall affect the child, and to assist him in properly responding to these influences. . . . The teacher's business is simply to determine on the basis of larger experience and riper wisdom, how the discipline of life shall come to the child.[1]

IN THE above statement of school organization Professor Dewey gives his personal creed, but at the same time he speaks for many teachers who are seeking through organization "to make schools like life." In America, group life is achieved through an organization designated as democratic, and modern

[1] Dewey, John. "My Pedagogic Creed," *Journal of National Education Association*, Vol. 18 (Dec. 1929), p. 292.

education seeks to prepare children for intelligent participation in it. This is achieved through procedures based upon the principle that children learn to be intelligent citizens for the future by achieving intelligent citizenship in the present, and since intelligent citizenship in a democracy is the end sought, democracy in school should become the means by which the end is attained. Under this conception, the school should become a democratic laboratory wherein children, through daily experiences, develop techniques for coöperative living. The modern school organization should, therefore, be essentially democratic in nature and in practice.

CHARACTERISTICS OF A DEMOCRATIC SCHOOL ORGANIZATION

The democratic school organization is characterized by practices which distinguish it from the organization of the traditional school: (1) Children participate in decisions which affect the group as a whole. (2) Children assume responsibilities which affect the welfare of the group. (3) Through school experiences children are offered opportunities in social adjustments. (4) Children are given opportunity for and freedom in choices. An examination of these characteristics reveals the outstanding differentiation in the organization of the modern school to be in the use of a large measure of freedom by children, a factor essential to the successful functioning of a democracy.

The organization of the school for experiences in democratic living is not easy of achievement. It involves a break with tradition for which many teachers lack courage, confidence, education, and experience. Usually, teachers themselves are the products of traditional schools where authority was centered in the person of the teacher, and the tendency to imitation of former experiences is strong. The traditional school was organized as a little autocracy in which the teacher was comparable to a benevolent despot. Under this dispensation school often developed into a continual warfare between students and teacher with little sportsmanship displayed on either side. The teacher sought to impose her authority by coercion and compulsion, while the children took what they considered their "rights" whenever and however they could get them. "Sniping" often developed behind the teacher's back in the throwing of erasers, in the avoiding of punishment, in doing as little work as possible, and in exercising deceit and cunning. While this picture was not true of all traditional schools, it was fairly typical. Ichabod Crane was no mythical figure. He existed in fact when Irving pictured him in fancy, and his descendants, multiplying, found their places in schools far beyond his day. Under their tutelage the school organization developed into an incongruous aristocratic organization which attempted to prepare children for later participation in a democratic social order. Under this system of divided aim and practice the results of citizenship training in the elementary schools have come to be seriously questioned. An example of such criticism is as follows:

Generally speaking the American people have not lacked conscience or devotion to democracy. They have seriously lacked both intelligence and skill. Through the revised curriculum the essential theory can be furnished. Its vitalized application can best come by group study and responsibility in the problems of the school community.

The coöperative skills through which group action is effected can be learned only by practise. For this reason the politicians big and little—particularly the little—are about the only group in the country skilled in getting results through community organization. Unless the schools face their fundamental duty of developing the intelligence and the skill necessary to salvage our badly shattered democracy both school and society may soon hail some American Hitler.[1]

The practicing of coöperative skills in group action necessitates the use of a large measure of freedom, and, since freedom is rarely overtly achieved, the process of achievement in schools is particularly susceptible to criticism. Thus, one of the most

[1] Lewis, William Dodge. "The School as a Democratic Institution," p. 416, *Fourteenth Yearbook*, Department of Elementary School Principals, Vol. 14.

frequent criticisms of the modern school is in this area; namely, that children in it tend to transform liberty into license. Unquestionably this criticism is often justified because overzealous teachers imbued with the philosophy of Dewey have misinterpreted his teachings to the point of believing that children released from restraint will of necessity grow in power to use freedom. This, however, is contrary to the facts. True, children achieve growth in the use of freedom through experiences which foster self-control and social coöperation; but young children cannot achieve complete freedom, nor is it possible for their school to attain the status of a complete democracy. Dunn and Everett in their report of the Quaker Grove experiment with student self-government made on this point the following comment:

Throughout this account, the government of the school has been referred to as a democracy. . . . Complete democracy is not possible in the elementary school. The children are not yet sufficiently mature or experienced to be left to bear the consequences of all their own mistakes. It is the teacher's province to relinquish to them the control of every matter which they can handle with ultimate beneficial effect on their own growth. It is equally her province to keep in her own hands those phases of the school government which are beyond the children's power to control with reasonable assurance of safety to the rights of all the members of the group.[1]

This position appears sound, particularly in the light of practices in the larger world outside the school. Activities there are never entirely free, but are restricted by laws, traditions, customs, and mores which have been developed by the group and presumably for its good. Somewhere between the practices of the ultra progressive and traditional schools there is a middle ground in school organization which offers many lifelike activities for pupil participation and many opportunities for growth in the technique of democratic living. The fact that these activities develop under teacher guidance and

[1] Dunn, Fannie W. and Everett, Marcia. *Four Years in a Country School*, p. 98, Bureau of Publications, Teachers College, Columbia University, 1926.

restrictions comparable to life outside make them none the
less realistic and valuable.

OBJECTIVES TO BE ATTAINED IN A DEMOCRATIC
SCHOOL ORGANIZATION

In a 1934 extension class at the State Teachers College,
Buffalo, an effort was made to set up objectives for a democratic
school organization toward which teachers and pupils might
purposefully work. Later, three members of this group experimented with such an organization in small rural schools and
since they found the objectives helpful they are given here:
(a) to make the school a better and happier place in which to
live and work; (b) to develop leadership and followship in
pupils; (c) to develop techniques through which democracy
functions; (d) to develop responsibility in children for personal
and group control; (e) to work steadily toward all the self-
government of which student groups are capable. In these
objectives the essentials of a democratic social order are suggested; namely, self-disciplined individuals who intelligently
work through proper channels toward a realization of ideals
which make group living happier and better.

THE PRACTICE OF SELF-GOVERNMENT

Self-government is a process of growth. Children attain
this growth slowly and it is a mistake for the teacher to attempt
quick results. Growth comes through participation in real
situations where the student makes choices in behavior, exercises initiative, uses his judgment, and rests on the consequences
of his decisions.

Since self-government is a process of growth, it should
be apparent, even to inexperienced teachers, that children
cannot assume the sole responsibility for the control of the
group. The teacher will, therefore, need to give wise and
discriminatory counsel to the organization at all times. The

place of the teacher in the democratic school is not easy of analysis, but the Quaker Grove experiment has given us guidance at this point:

The teacher's place in a scheme of school-government such as this, not yet completely democratic yet evolving toward a democracy, may be analyzed as follows:

1. The ideal of the democracy as it is to be, is the teacher's.

2. The realization of this ideal depends absolutely upon the strength of her desire and the degree of her ability to reach the goal. She must continually interpret her ideals. Her own conduct must set a good example. The youthful president must see and feel her insistence on obedience before he will do the same; he must see her thoughtful if he is to learn to think before he speaks; in short, the teacher must live her ideals for they determine the road the children will follow.

3. The teacher must be the recognized leader of the group. The members and officers of the club must all feel her strength protecting and encouraging them. Her final decision where she sees fit to render one, must mean law, for there are times when adult judgment is necessary for a fair and just decision.

4. At the same time, she must be democratic in spirit and in action. She must assume no authority merely for the enlargement of her own personality or the expression of her own importance, but only where the group is not strong or wise enough to guard its own interests and those of the individuals composing it. She must be one of the group, ready to acknowledge a mistake and apologize for it as freely as she would expect any of the children to do. She must be willing to explain the why's and wherefore's of many of her acts. She must play with the children and talk with them, in order that the artificial barriers which so often exist between teacher and pupil may be broken down.

5. When new situations arise, for which the children have no basis in experience, the teacher must guide the children into the formation of new habits or the extended application of old ones to fit the new demand made upon them.

6. Finally, the teacher must be the last resort for cases too difficult for the group to handle. Although public opinion is one of the strongest controlling forces in human society, child or adult, it

nevertheless is a fact that there are individuals who because of strong contrary motives within themselves cannot be controlled by this alone. These individuals are in many instances pathological cases, emotionally unstable, or inordinately self-centered. They are human misfits. As a result of deficient moral and social intelligence, or bad home conditions, past or present, they are a menace to society and to themselves as well.[1]

The principles thus laid down for teacher participation in pupil self-government lie almost wholly in the areas of counsel, encouragement, and guidance. The actual work of the democratic school should be handled by the children. Fortunately, the rural school offers opportunities for many activities which make the realization of the practice of self-government natural and effective.

STEPS IN THE ORGANIZATION OF THE SCHOOL CLUB

The organization of the school club is conditioned by the philosophy of the teacher. If he believes, and is willing to put his belief into practice, that children develop in the techniques of democracy through democratic experiences, the club will have an auspicious beginning. If his faith in children is supplemented by his willingness to experiment in democratic techniques, the club has an excellent chance for survival. He should be willing to assume the role of counselor, and to receive advice from the group as well as give advice to it. It is essential that all experiments be coöperative, and that the teacher be not too easily discouraged when blunders are made and when progress is slow.

The first step in the club organization is often taken during opening exercises, when the teacher is presiding and the work is being planned for the day. It may grow out of a direct suggestion from the teacher in a discussion of the assignment of housekeeping duties. It may develop from a discussion of group behavior. It may be as overt as the question from the

[1] Dunn, Fannie W. and Everett, Marcia. *Four Years in A Country School*, p. 100, Bureau of Publications, Teachers College, Columbia University, 1926.

teacher, "How do you think you would like to form a school club?" There is no pattern to follow in the initiation of the club, but there are certain desirable principles to keep in mind. These are: (1) The teacher should assume the initiative for the inauguration of the club and should act as sponsor for it after its organization. (2) The idea of the club should arise and be developed, if possible, from the normal work of the day. (3) Children should know as early as possible the types of problems the club can properly handle and those best left to the wisdom and experience of the teacher. Experience indicates that problems characteristic of and persistent in the group should be handled by the club, and specific ones affecting individuals should be a matter of conference and decision between the student and the teacher. This would invariably hold true in the area of school work. (4) Once officers have been elected and have accepted the honor, they should expect to assume the responsibilities of leadership. (5) Discussions on all questions at all times should be free, open, and unembarrassed.

After the officers are selected, a committee should be appointed to draw up the constitution and by-laws. In the committee's report the purpose of the club should be clearly and simply stated and the students should be encouraged to debate each article to which they cannot give unanimous consent. The writing of the Constitution could properly be an activity of the advanced group in social studies, who should be led to see that the procedure is similar to that of all democratic bodies. A copy of the constitution adopted by the South Wales School Club, Erie County, New York, is given in the appendix and may be used as suggestive of form and content in the organization of other school clubs.

THE SCHOOL CLUB: A MEANS OF ATTAINING A DEMOCRATIC ORGANIZATION

Inherently, the rural school is an embryonic democratic organization. No other type of school has the stage as naturally set for democratic living, and because of this, there is less danger of an organization's deteriorating into the spurious and artificial type of pupil participation with which many schools are beset. The sociological composition of the rural group is like a little community. The age levels within one room often range from five to sixteen years; both the strong and the weak of the community are represented there. The interest levels of the group are often at even greater variance, ranging from those of the self-willed, impetuous adolescent to those of the very young child who is making his first steps beyond the home circle. All the children of the community are usually in attendance at the small rural school, thus representing various levels of wealth, social backgrounds, and opportunities. The average rural school is indeed a cross section of the larger community of which it is a part and naturally lends itself to a democratic type of organization. To this end leaders in rural education have advocated for many years the formation of the school into a democratic organization. Earlier writers emphasized the desirability of such an organization because it offered training in parliamentary usage, in the conduct of a society, and in keeping minutes and records. In theory and in practice nearly all the activities of the club were justified upon the grounds of adult usefulness in future meetings of the school board or community in which erstwhile children, grown to manhood, would be participating members. The modern school, however, has a more comprehensive conception of a school organization. It considers parliamentary usage and the keeping of minutes and records important only because they are techniques by which the machinery of group living can be efficiently handled in the present. The chief concern of the club is the development of children in social control, which is interpreted (a) as that practice of self-government which best serves the individual and the group and (b) as the democratic administration of activities which normally develop from group living.

Social control is accomplished in the club through regularly elected officers: a president, vice-president, secretary, and treasurer. Standing committees continue the activities of the school throughout the time when the club is not in session.

Every child in the school may become a member of the club and have a voice and a vote in the management of its affairs, though practice usually limits membership to the children above the third grade. Many different names are assumed by school clubs, such as the "Good Citizenship Club," the "Health Club," "Student Council," "Student Government Association," "Hobby Club," "Current Events Club," and others too numerous to mention. The children in the Quaker Grove school called their club the "Young America Club" and stated in their constitution that it assumed the power:

(1) To make all laws for the control of the school. (2) To provide for punishment of those who break the laws.[1]

The emphasis of this club was clearly that of self-government, its purpose that of citizenship. A canvass of the thirty coöperating rural schools of the State Teachers College, Buffalo, revealed the existence of some fifteen clubs of different names, but all had been organized for the same purpose as that of the club of the Quaker Grove school. The purposes were unfailingly those of providing opportunities for the development of responsibility in and for citizenship. Clubs meet usually on Fridays during the first or the last period of the day.

The following report suggests the activities possible in citizenship clubs. It is compiled from stenographic reports of club meetings held in Newfane School District No. 7, Wheatfield No. 7, Niagara County, New York, and South Wales School, Erie County, New York:

1. Meeting called to order by the president.
2. Reading of minutes of last meeting and their adoption.
3. Treasurer's report.
4. Report of standing committees.

  a. *Hot Lunch Committee.* Gave menus for following week, assigned tasks, requested materials, presented plans for a mothers' tea to be held at the schoolhouse the following Friday. These were discussed at length, committees were appointed, and plans of committee approved.

[1] *Ibid.* p. 92.

b. *Committee on Ventilation.* Reported that committee had bought two screens for the windows for which they had paid 50¢ each. This in compliance with instructions given the committee in a previous meeting of the club.

c. *Playground Committee.* Reported that difficulty had arisen in the playground because of a dispute over the use of equipment. Both the younger and the older boys had insisted upon using the football at the same time. After discussion the children decided that each group should take turns playing with the ball, that the younger boys should have the use of it on Mondays and Wednesdays and the older boys on Tuesdays, Thursdays, and Fridays. Jimmie suggested that it would be helpful if the school had two balls, and he was appointed to interview the trustees and request the purchase of another one.

d. *Committee on Heating.* Reported that it had kept the temperature room chart every day and that the temperature had averaged 70 degrees for the week. Coöperation was asked of the ventilation committee.

e. *Committee on School Housekeeping.* Committee reported that children were careless about dropping papers on the floor and asked for coöperation, especially preceding the noon recess. This was discussed and a motion was made by Robert asking the committee to keep records of children persisting in this practice and report their names at the next meeting of the club. The committee reported that one of the goldfish had disappeared during the week. This had been discussed previously in the science class.

5. Under new business the teacher asked the coöperation of children for a Hallowe'en party to be held at the schoolhouse. Committees were appointed to make plans and report back to the club. The teacher also suggested that the club take up the matter of tardiness. This was discussed fully and the three children most often tardy, after a reprimand by the group, agreed to try to mend their ways.

6. Nancy, who had charge of current events for the week, made an interesting report and called the attention of the school to the bulletin board for which she had been responsible.

7. The meeting was adjourned.

An analysis of this report reveals that the activities of the club extended over many areas of group living—food, health, sanitation, recreation, discipline and the current news. These problems, however, were not peculiar to particular situations in these schools. They are present in all schools and at nearly all times. The significant thing about the report lies rather in the way the problems were handled—by children through their own democratic organization, and under the guidance of sympathetic teachers. Experience suggests that the committees of children responsible for those problems in group living should be changed frequently, sometimes as often as once a week. This frequent change shifts responsibilities which might become irksome if carried too long; it provides for sharing duties on a basis of equality, and gives everyone the opportunity of participating in all the community activities. The committees are organized along regular lines, with a chairman who delegates duties, but assumes responsibility for the whole undertaking. Often the committees and their membership are conspicuously posted on the bulletin board, so that children can check themselves from time to time.

ACTIVITIES OF THE CLUB WHICH GIVE TRAINING IN GROUP LIVING AND SELF-GOVERNMENT

The small rural school admirably lends itself to activities which develop efficiency in group living. These fall generally into four major headings as follows: (1) Activities of the group which deal with problems of social control, as discussed elsewhere in this chapter. (2) Activities related to the health of the group, commonly known as housekeeping duties such as ventilation, sweeping, heating, dusting, hot lunches, etc. (3) Civic activities which deal with the beautification of school buildings and grounds, care of library, visual materials, etc. (4) Recreational activities developed by the students.

ACTIVITIES RELATED TO HEALTH

The belief is generally held by administrative experts that lack of janitorial service in the small rural school is part of its handicap. They suggest that work in preparing the hot lunch, in ventilation, heating, and cleaning the building are not properly the work of children and that they suffer from the necessity of the performance of such duties. This belief would be difficult of proof because the results thus achieved by children are more often good than bad. Instead of suffering ill effects from such manual labor children actually appear to profit from it.

Indeed the whole situation has definite educational possibilities; namely, the opportunity to teach the laws of sanitation and health, and the additional opportunity to demonstrate that in democratic community living each person, so far as health is concerned, is literally "his brother's keeper." If the committee responsible for heating the room fails in its duty, the whole group may develop colds. If the student designated by the group to check ventilation is careless, all the children may have headaches before the noon recess. If the committee responsible for cleaning and dusting is remiss, serious health conditions may follow. The schoolhouse is the community home of the group, and each child should feel a personal responsibility in seeing that it is sanitary, comfortable, and attractive. The rural community has exactly the same problems, save that they are larger, involve more people, and are scattered over a wider area. Future citizenship in a democratic community may well have its beginning in the acceptance by children in school of individual responsibility for the welfare and happiness of the whole group.

CIVIC ACTIVITIES

Every democratic group has the responsibility, not only for keeping the community sanitary and healthful, but also for making the place of abode beautiful. This is the characteristic designated in the group as civic pride. As communities accept the responsibilities necessary to the attainment of such an ideal, so the school, organized for democratic living, strives toward the same end. Many desirable activities develop from this ideal and are promoted by the school club. These include (a) keeping the school building and grounds neat and tidy and (b) a program of improvement and beautification. Both are essential, but the latter activities are sorely needed. There is little that is attractive in the appearance of the small rural school building. The familiar rectangular frame building, set in its bare plot of ground, leaves much to be desired; yet the school building is the place where children spend much of their time during formative years and where they receive many of their standards of beauty and good taste.

An ideal rural school is a school *home*. Can you see the difference between a large building, housing hundreds of school children, with many teachers and supervisors, and a small one-room building with from seven to fifteen children and one adult in charge? If we make the rural school a school home we can capitalize this situation.[1]

The fact that the rural school building is a home which belongs to all the children makes its care and beautification both a personal and a joint responsibility. If this idea is implanted in the minds of children, civic pride and responsibility of a high quality will be developed. With proper guidance and through the channel of coöperative endeavor numerous rural schools in America already witness to the civic pride of young people.

Beautiful school grounds and beautiful school buildings arouse pride in the youthful citizen-to-be. I know a school in which five years ago the morale was so low that boys abused the building until it was almost impossible to recognize it as such. It was difficult to keep the windows properly fitted with panes because many of the twelve-year-olds liked to hear the glass tinkle when hit with a stone. Even the door was kicked open by the ruthless feet of the older ones to save time in opening it. It would be extravagant to say that a

[1] Heyl, Helen Hay. *New York State Education*, Vol. XVIII (Mar., 1931), p. 692.

concerted community effort on the part of both parents and children to beautify the school brought about a magic change, but it did help. . . . Today after five years the children in this school honor and protect the school property in a way inspiring to others; they have a flower garden planted from their yards at home and tended with all the passionate devotion of adolescent youth.

A flower garden on a portion of the school grounds is not impossible, particularly where land is cheap. Neither is such a garden impractical. In addition to the more subtle training in citizenship and in character the grounds put to such a use may be made a laboratory of nature study. Children who so easily learn the names of a dozen makes of automobiles and a like number of moving picture actresses should be given the opportunity of recognizing an equal number of flowers by sight and naming a dozen birds by their songs.

If the teacher is wise, the garden will soon develop into a haven for birds. At Landford School in South Carolina, in a county where the County Superintendent of Schools inaugurated a county-wide effort for the beautification of school grounds, just such a happy gathering place for birds has come about. The children named their garden "The Birds' Palace," because the birds use it so much. The classes in advanced mathematics laid off the garden in formal design, and the younger children provided birdhouses made by themselves. Not content with providing houses, the children went further and built a bird bath ornamental and useful and later a bird feeding station, so that their feathered visitors might feel entirely welcome.[1]

The rural school abounds in opportunities for civic activities, and children should not be denied these experiences. Often it is practical for the children to coöperate with Parent-Teacher Associations and through joint committees work on a long term program in the care and beautification of school buildings and grounds.

RECREATIONAL ACTIVITIES

Children should be encouraged to assume many responsibilities of the recreational program of the school. They should assist in planning their games, directing them, and administering

[1] Wofford, Kate V. "Beauty Goes to School," *Journal National Education Association*, Vol. 20 (Apr. 1931), p. 123.

the rules. School excursions, as suggested elsewhere in this book, should likewise be pupil-planned and executed. School parties and community meetings for which the school is responsible should be the result of student coöperation. Not only does such participation tend to relieve the teacher of many irksome details, but it offers opportunities for social experiences which inevitably result in pupil growth. All of these activities may properly be conducted through the coöperative efforts of the school club.

A case study to clarify the philosophy in the above paragraphs is given below:

CASE STUDY—IV [1]

We have made an attempt to provide an environment that will stimulate right conduct. Ours is the traditional one-room, box-car type of school. About fifteen years ago it was remodeled. All the windows were placed on the south side. Rooms were built in the front corners for coats and chemical toilets. This left the remaining room very small. With no basement it is necessary for the big drum type of furnace to be in the corner of the main room. Our first step was to remove all unused seats. These are of the single stationary style that followed the double seat in rural schools. We have gradually added supply cupboards, two round tables, chairs, open book shelves, a table and a floor lamp, piano, and victrola. An aquarium, plants, pictures, pottery, curtains, a rug, and books have helped to add to the home-like appearance of the room. India prints, candles, and prism curtain pulls add touches of color that help to make our room more cheerful. Two metal cupboards are used for dishes and lunches. The children have made and painted bookshelves, small chairs, book racks, and easels for their own use.

[1] Submitted by Mrs. Blanche Crossman, teacher in Newfane District #7, Niagara County, New York. Miss M. Gazelle Hoffman, District Superintendent of Schools.

THE SCHOOL CLUB

Each year the children organize a club. The teacher usually presides at the first meeting, where officers are elected by ballot. The name and object of the club vary from year to year. Indirectly the object is to develop leadership and a sense of responsibility, and to make the group partially self-governing.

The club membership includes all the children of the school. To earn money for their treasury, the members do the janitorial work during warm weather, spring and fall. With this money they buy equipment and furnishings for the school. Their purchases have included lawn seats, a basket ball outfit, material for see-saws, a swing, two lamps, scales, gold fish, stage curtains, dishes, and hot lunch equipment, a rug, and pickets for a fence. Committees for the janitor work are changed each week.

Each year a girl is chosen to act as hostess to greet callers, assist them with their wraps, and find seats for them. The pupils of the school occasionally entertain their mothers. In June they gave a tea, having a pet show and a doll show on the lawn at the same time. Tea was served to the mothers from a table in the house, while the children had lemonade and cookies in a shady corner of the lawn.

THE LUNCHEON HOUR

The noon luncheon hour is a most enjoyable time. Each child has his own luncheon mat made of dull-finished oilcloth. Paper napkins are passed and the lunches are brought in by the boys while the girls are washing. After the boys have washed, everyone is ready to eat.

During cold weather all sandwiches are toasted in a big toaster over the coal fire. There is always rivalry over the honor of being toaster for the day. Potatoes are baked in the furnace. Individual jars of food are heated in a large kettle of hot water on the top of the furnace. Three days a week cocoa is made and served by the children. Milk is furnished by the children and teacher. Occasionally, special dishes are cooked on the hot plate and served by the children. Italian spaghetti was popular while we were studying Italy. It was quite correctly eaten with spoon and fork.

Guessing games are popular during the luncheon hour. In the late spring and early fall we eat on our shady lawn. With our lawn seats, chairs, and a roughly built table the hour is so happy a time that no one has to be reminded to eat more slowly!

SCHOOL PARTIES

When a party is being planned, committees are appointed at a club meeting. These committees take charge of games, decorations, and refreshments. Sometimes an impromptu program takes the place of games. Usually one group is the audience, the other stages the program. One child is the announcer and another has charge of the curtains, chairs, etc. These are without doubt our happiest hours. Impromptu songs, speeches, dances, and imitations put the children at their ease and everyone enters into the spirit of the occasion. If parents could only see these school parties instead of our formal, rehearsed programs; but the very suggestion would put the children in the old traditional mood of giving an entertainment.

Having our party refreshments at noon seems much wiser than breaking the children's meal routine by serving in the middle of the afternoon. We try to avoid elaborate refreshments. Mothers frequently send in a treat such as home-made cookies, or pop-corn balls. Apples, doughnuts, and cider fresh from the Tompkin's press are our traditional Hallowe'en treat. Apple cookies, or big slices of apple sprinkled with sugar and cinnamon, are perpetual favorites. Each table has its host and hostess, who not only see that everyone is served, but learn to take the responsibility of seeing that all goes well and that everyone in the group is happy. They also take special responsibilities before and after lunch.

ENGLISH

Note writing takes on a new interest when we find that neighbors are celebrating a wedding anniversary and that we may write them a note of congratulation. Later, when death comes to the home of friends the children are just as anxious to send them a note of sympathy. Very solemnly they tell Nancy, their secretary, what they want to say, and a message, very simple and direct, but expressing what they feel deeply, goes to the home across the road. Many notes of thanks are written. Letters to friends and business firms bring replies that are filed in the school file.

Our school newspaper, the *Corwin News*, publishes accounts of our trips, our school activities, and community news, as well as our attempts at original stories and poems. Our last year's staff consisted of Nancy and Mary Kathryn, Editor and Assistant; Milton and Jack, business manager and assistant. Advertisements were solicited at stores in Newfane, the rates being ten cents an inch or fifteen cents for two inches. The children made a profit and gained much valuable experience.

Oral English furnishes an opportunity for social training. Aside from the usual reports, introductions, and other social forms are dramatized during this hour.

PLAYTIME

At playtime our games are quite as often directed by one of the children as by the teacher. We have found it to be a good plan to have a game chart hanging beside the door. Under an attractive picture are listed the out-door games and the indoor games that we know. It is always easy to choose a game and leaders at the beginning of the play period. This leaves no opportunity for arguments. No play time is wasted, and a happy spirit of coöperation is assured. Our play equipment though very simple is adequate, consisting of sand pile, basket ball outfit, slide, and swing, so that we learn many games during a year. In stormy weather we have to play in the school room.

Mary Alice plays the piano for many of our games. Charades are very popular. The children often prefer to use a part of their playtime for stories. Sometimes the boys use their tools and the girls sew, continuing the work of the activity period.

The school is a happy place where children are given the opportunity for new experiences, all as lifelike as possible and all directed to the development of those techniques which enable people to live together with the least friction. It has been our experience that the best medium for achieving these objectives lies in the organization of the school into a Good Citizenship Club.

SUMMARY

The modern school is a form of community life where children in it are given opportunities for the development of techniques in group living. Group living in the United States is achieved through a democracy, and this fact should affect all programs designed to prepare children for citizenship. It is held, therefore, that one of the most effective ways to achieve this goal is to give children in school an opportunity to participate intelligently in democratic living. To this end the modern school attempts an organization which is essentially democratic in nature and in practice.

This democratic school organization is characterized by (a) the participation of children in all decisions which affect the group; (b) the assumption of responsibilities affecting the welfare of the group; (c) natural opportunities for social adjustments; (d) freedom in choices. Such an organization is difficult of attainment, chiefly because the average teacher lacks courage, confidence, education, and the experience necessary to initiate it. The practicing of coöperative skills in group action always necessitates a large measure of freedom, and children unaccustomed to its proper use frequently turn it into license. This has brought upon the democratic school organization much unfavorable criticism. Freedom is rarely overtly achieved.

It is earned and children grow in power to use it through experience in its use. Consequently, the process of developing the school into a miniature democracy is a slow one, involving years of trial and effort, of many backslidings and spurts of achievement. It requires wisdom and patience on the part of the teacher; open-mindedness, tolerance, and coöperation on the part of the children. Self-government in school, as in life, is no miracle. It is achieved through a long, slow, and often discouraging, process of growth on the part of individuals who make up the group.

Experienced teachers who have attempted to establish democratic school organizations have set up objectives toward which pupils and teachers work. These are: (a) to make the school a better and happier place in which to live and work; (b) to develop leadership and followship in students; (c) to develop techniques through which democracy can function; (d) to develop responsibility in children to the point of personal and group control; (e) to work steadily toward all the self-government of which groups are capable.

One of the most effective means of meeting these objectives is through the organization of the school into a club which assumes responsibility for the problems involved in group living. These activities are similar to those in life outside, and usually include: (1) Activities of the group which deal with problems of social control. (2) Activities related to the health of the group, such as the preparation and serving of hot lunch, care and handling of lunch boxes, ventilation, heating, cleaning, dusting, etc. (3) Civic activities including the beautification of schoolhouse and grounds, etc. (4) Activities in recreation under which are listed the proper use of the recess periods, school parties, etc. The successful handling by children of these daily problems in group living offer many opportunities for education in citizenship and character. Children can thus learn the necessity of individual responsibility for the welfare of the group and experience the satisfaction of coöperative endeavor for the good of the community.

SUGGESTED READINGS

Brown, Edwin J. *Everyday Problems in Classroom Management*, Chap. II, Houghton Mifflin Co., Boston, 1933.

Department Elementary School Principals. Fourteenth Yearbook, *The School as a Democratic Institution*, p. 415, National Education Association, Washington, D. C.

Dewey, John. "My Pedagogic Creed," *Journal of the National Education Association*, Vol. 18 (Dec., 1929), p. 291.

Dunn, Fannie W. and Everett, Marcia. *Four Years in a Country School*, pp. 47–104, Bureau of Publications, Teachers College, Columbia University, 1926.

Eells, Harry L., Moeller, Hugh C., and Swain, Carl C. *Rural School Management*, Chap. XV, Chas. Scribner's Sons, New York, 1924.

Heyl, Helen Hay. "That Ideal School," *New York State Education*, Vol. XVIII (Mar., 1931), p. 692.

Lowth, Frank J. *Everyday Problems of the Country Teacher*, Rev. ed., Chap. XXIII, Macmillan, New York, 1936.

Lowth, Frank J. *The Country Teacher at Work*, Chap. XII, Macmillan, New York, 1930.

Strayer, George Drayton, Frasier, George Willard, and Armentrout, Winfield Dockery. *Principles of Teaching*, Chap. IV, American Book Co., New York, 1936.

Yoakam, Gerald Allan and Simpson, Robert Gilkey. *An Introduction to Teaching and Learning*, Chap. II, Macmillan, New York, 1934.

MATERIALS FOR DISCUSSION

Consider the following statements. What changes would make them more acceptable to you? What significant issues arise from their study?

1. Education is a social process, and the school is primarily a social institution. Consequently, all of the educational processes should be directed to social ends.

2. The organization of the school for democratic living is an idealistic dream. Children by nature and by experience are incapable of making individual decisions which are good for the group. This difficulty is further enhanced by the fact that the individual desires of the immature are nearly always in conflict with the welfare of others.

3. The mainspring of democracy lies in the coöperative efforts of self disciplined individuals who work intelligently toward a realization of ideals which make group living happier and better.

4. The responsibilities for the development of techniques for group living rests wholly in children. The function of the teacher in the democratic school is that of guide and counselor.

5. Because the small rural school is a cross section of a larger community life it lends itself, better than any other school unit, to an organization of children for democratic living.

CHAPTER IX

RECORD KEEPING—A TECHNIQUE IN UNDERSTANDING CHILDREN

INTEREST in children, it goes without saying, is an essential to good teaching and leads to the understanding which comes only through knowledge gained by the daily observation of children under many conditions.

Obviously, it is impossible for the teacher to carry the data of these observations in his mind. For this purpose records must be kept, and, once the data is assembled, it must have functional possibilities. In the above statement lie the two chief characteristics of modern record keeping: (a) school records are an assembling of significant data about children and (b) the data should function in a program, the purpose of which is to understand and counsel children.

Once the record is made, it should interpret the individual child to many people: first of all, to himself and to his parents; second, to his teacher; third, to subsequent teachers; and fourth, to all people interested in his welfare. The people to be served by these records, in a measure, determine the types of them to be kept, hence the selection and installation of a modern system would appear to be a simple procedure. However, the contrary is true. The whole question of school records is in a state of flux and uncertainty and there is a wide divergence of opinion on what records should be assembled, how they shall be organized, and how they should be used. How diversified the practice in school records is was revealed by a study made in 1925. The record forms of 131 cities in the United States were studied and it was discovered that they carried 1515 different items, 50% of which occurred only one time.[1] Out

[1] Heck, A. O. *A Study of Child Accounting Records*, Bureau of Educational Research, Monograph No. 2. p. 117, University Studies, Ohio State University, 1925.

of this conflict of opinion, definite philosophies and procedures are arising, but in order to understand these modern trends in school records it is well to take a look at past philosophies and procedures.

AN EXAMPLE OF A CENTURY OLD SCHOOL RECORD

"Elizabeth . . . . . . hath been engaged, during her attendance at this school in storing her memory, that strong and capricious store house of the mind, with useful ideas, lessons and information generally.

Pursuant to this end, she hath deposited in her memory for future use the multiplication and other arithmetical tables.

She hath repeated the principal divisions, oceans, islands, etc. and answered 109 questions on the map of the world.

She hath recited the principal divisions, lakes, rivers, bays, gulfs, etc. and answered 41 questions on the map of North America.

She hath defined the boundaries of 12 of the United States and repeated 95 of the chief towns and 33 of the principal rivers belonging to these 12 states and answered 86 questions corresponding to the geography of that fine country.

On the map of South America she hath committed to memory the different countries belonging to that great peninsula and repeated 58 chief towns and 33 of the principal rivers and answered 39 questions corresponding with its geography.

Let no one say, hereafter that females cannot learn for that is an assertion without foundation. Elizabeth is a living proof to the contrary and she merits the approbation and encouragement of her parents and friends." [1]

The above account is more than a century-old record of the scholastic standing of a child. It reveals at the same time a philosophy of education which magnified mental accomplishments and ignored the other two significant areas in child development—growth in body and in personality. As in every

[1] From a certificate issued in 1826. *Progressive Education*, Vol. 13 (Jan. 1936), p. 26.

age, this school record, reflects the accomplishment which education wished to have remembered. For example, an examination of the records of the first rural schools reveals that they were as meagre as the curriculum and that in many instances no records were kept at all. This lack of records was a matter of grave concern to the state superintendents of schools, as many of their early reports reveal. Their concern, however, lay not so much in the harm done to the children as to the system, and indeed practices in record keeping must have been confusing. For example, frequently, upon the entrance of a new teacher into the district school, the children proceeded to classify themselves, so that often precious weeks of the short term were lost in the efforts of the teacher to bring properly classified groups together.[1] The enactment of compulsory attendance laws also revealed the confusion existing in the field of child accounting, and the state departments of education were hard pressed to enact a law for which no accounting within the legal age limits was available. Reforms for these conditions came through the installation of the school register and monthly report cards, and in many rural schools this system holds unto this day. Each supplemented the other and met the chief administrative difficulty of record keeping in that succeeding teachers were able to find enough records to give a semblance of order to a disorganized system. Children, however, were little better served. Both the monthly report card and the register represented a uniformity of treatment and an authority of opinion which frequently acted as an actual deterrent in the development of the average child. The register at school told a meagre story of grades and attendance; the report card, which the child took home to his parents, merely stated that he was "poor," "average," or "superior" in subject matter and deportment.

"Superior" rating was frequently a painful point of debate. It represented a composite of many ratings but was, in reality, the teacher's opinion of the ability of the student to conform

[1] Wofford, Kate V. *An History of the Status and Training of Elementary Rural Teachers of the United States 1860–1930*, p. 59.

to the pattern of the school. Both academic standing and deportment of students were determined by a system of subjective comparisons by the teacher of one student with another, and with the group. Under this system the average and below-the-average student tended to develop feelings of inferiority. His superior class-mate on the other hand, needed to be an individual of strong character in order to maintain a sane perspective under the flattery of a report card which always placed him above his fellows. Reforms in this system have been slow, but at the same time they have been so persistent that an overview of them gives us a pattern of trends in this important phase of recording child development.

MODERN TRENDS IN RECORD KEEPING

An examination of the many studies of modern methods of record keeping reveals six significant trends.[1]

First, the modern school record is individual, continuous, and cumulative. It is individual because a record is made for each child, continuous because recordings take place at all times, cumulative in that the record continues year after year and is handed on from teacher to teacher. Of this modern trend Ruth Strang says:

A true and useful picture of a pupil's development can be obtained only from a study of his growth along many lines over a period of years. This kind of a record is called a cumulative record. It shows

[1] For helpful discussions of child recording see:

Giles, H. H. "Record-Making in an Experimental School," *Progressive Education*, Vol. 12, p. 473, Nov., 1935.

Hansen, Rowna. *Report Cards for Kindergarten and Elementary Grades*, Leaflet No. 41 (1931) Office of Education (Dept. of the Interior), Government Printing Office.

Progressive Education. *Evaluation in the Eighth Year Study*, "Anecdotal Records," Bulletin No. I, Sept., 1935.

"Interpretation of Data," Bulletin No. III, Oct., 1935, Ohio State University.

Strang, Ruth, *Every Teacher's Records*, Bureau of Publications, Teachers College, Columbia University, 1936.

trends in the child's school work, interests, home conditions, recreation, and the like.[1]

As emphasized by Miss Strang modern education is conceived as a process of growth, and, since growth is individual and continuous, any system of recording the process would of necessity reflect the same characteristics. As soon as the child enters school, therefore, an individual folder is prepared for him and into it go, so long as he remains in school, those records which best interpret his growth. The record need not call for an ambitious expenditure of money. Indeed it seems best that the system be kept simple; a manila folder 8" × 12" marked with the child's name serves nicely, and, if no file is available, the folders can be filed in a plain packing case or wooden box. They should always be readily available since they form the bases for the report to parents, interviews with those interested in the child's welfare, and directions for counseling and advice. All three of these uses of the records should be based upon reliable data, recorded at various stages of maturation and under many conditions. Records of individual behavior cannot be considered reliable unless they are accurately and continuously kept; nor can they be considered useful unless they are accessible and easily interpreted. The contents of the folder will be discussed in subsequent paragraphs.

Second, modern school records give a complete picture of the child. While traditional records give only one picture of the child, modern accounting gives many. In addition to achievement in subject matter, the child's physical growth and progress in personality development are recorded. These newer evidences of growth require a different type of recording than do the records for achievement in subject matter alone. Examples of them can be seen in the appendix.

Third, in modern records the child is compared with himself as well as with others, and the first comparison is considered more important for child growth than the second. It is impossible to escape, at any stage of growth, the fact that we are constantly

[1] Strang, Ruth, *op. cit.* p. 13.

measured and adjudged. The acceptance of criticism as a means of growth, is, therefore, essential to proper emotional development, and functional school records should make this development easier for children. Rowna Hansen writing on this subject made the following statement:

The report card if properly functioning should build in the child a sense of security. His accomplishment, although apparently small, should be recognized. One success is the basis for building further successes just as one failure too often results in a sequence of failures. Since a life situation at any age level is rated by individuals or public opinion, the earlier a child learns to accept criticism or evaluation, the better he is equipped for living. That this receptive attitude be constructively established, the necessity for fair evaluation is obvious.[1]

In modern education evaluation is fair because growth in children is measured (a) from a point of previous maturation and (b) as a point of departure toward the highest possible future achievement of the individual.

Fourth, record keeping is a coöperative enterprise. Many rural teachers faced with the manifold duties of the small school have hesitated to initiate a modern system of records. Their hesitancy has resulted from the belief that the system required too much time and too much clerical work. Under an older conception of education which guarded school grades and made the recording of them a secret, this fear might have been well-founded. The teacher then did all the work himself. In a coöperative procedure he has many assistants. Parents will help with the contents of the cumulative record, as will children. From these two groups will come important facts about the personal life and history of the student. Usually these are secured from the autobiography written by the student himself, or from the questionnaire answered by parents, or from personal interviews. In addition to this assistance, older pupils may assume much of the responsibility of keeping their own records

[1] Hansen, Rowna. *Report Cards for Kindergarten and Elementary Grades.* Leaflet No. 41, p. 19, Office of Education (Dept. of Interior), Government Printing Office, 1931.

up to date, as well as assisting with the younger ones who cannot assume the task. Under proper guidance students can profitably keep records, not only of individual achievements but of group accomplishments as well, and experience indicates that they take much pride in the task.

Fifth, home report cards are frequently supplemented by conferences between teacher and parents. The rural teacher, with his small enrollment and large families, has an advantage over the average urban teacher. It is well to encourage parents to come to the school for conference periods, since the individual records are there. If this is not possible, the teacher will find it profitable to pay personal calls at each home represented in his school, and at stated intervals. Not only will he find the average parent approachable on the subject of his child, but he will find him also appreciative and coöperative. At the same time that he is interpreting the work of the school to parents, the teacher also has the opportunity of collecting further valuable information about the environment in which children spend their out-of-school-hours.

Finally, modern records are functional. Many people need to consult the records of pupils. Consequently, all recorded data should be significant and written in a vocabulary easy of interpretation. In other words, the cumulative record should be considered as a means to an understanding of children. It exists to serve children, that is, to interpret them and the school of which they are a part to their parents or others and in turn their parents to the school and its teacher. The records should form the basis for all teacher conferences with the home, for much curriculum guidance, and for counseling and advice to students. Patterns from the lives of children can be seen in properly recorded data and herein for the teacher rest a responsibility and a challenge.

WHAT RECORDS SHALL BE KEPT

A question at this point seems pertinent. What are the best records assembling data for the understanding of children?

The answer to this question can be obtained in part by a study of the modern trends in education and these records which report them. This examination reveals significant patterns of procedures, which divide themselves into two large groups. First, there are those records which attempt to assemble information about individual children. These generally include data on (a) the mental characteristics and achievements of children, (b) information about physical maturation, and (c) data which give light on personality development. The second large group of records are those concerned with the achievements of groups of individuals and the proper recording of them.

RECORDS WHICH CHRONICLE THE INDIVIDUAL DEVELOPMENT OF CHILDREN

The Autobiography. One of the most significant records in modern child accounting is the contribution made by the child himself. This record form is designated by the term "autobiography" and it is what it states itself to be—personal data written by the student himself. This usually includes information about his ancestry, his family, his home, and other environmental factors. It also includes data of the previous education of the student, his interests, his group contacts, and his ambitions for his adult years. While the autobiographical form is completed by the older student in person, the younger children frequently dictate the information to the teacher or to an older student. Sometimes the blanks are filled in by parents. For the inexperienced teacher a suggested form is included in the appendix. An additional form should be filled in each year by individual students giving further facts, bringing the questionnaire up to date. Over a period of years this record may develop into a rich repository for the understanding and counseling of children.

Records of Scholastic Achievement. This record is familiar to all experienced teachers and comprises an accumulation of grades in subject matter and attendance for each child. This information, frequently required by law, can be found in the school register, usually furnished by the district or county school superintendent and kept by the teacher. While the reliability of teachers' marks has been for some time in question, they are one index to the judgment of children, and their importance in the rural school cannot be minimized. Frequently they are the only records available to a new teacher, and a study of them is recommended. Perhaps the clearest picture of child development to be obtained through the grades is secured from a cumulative scholastic record. An example of such a record is likewise given in the appendix.

Indications of Capacity to Learn. As previously suggested, a knowledge of the ability of the child to learn is perhaps as important to the teacher as a knowledge of what he has learned, and, if possible, this information should become a part of the record of every school. The individual differences of children have long been taken for granted, and recent psychological investigations in this field have verified the assumption. Intelligence tests have resulted from these investigations, and teachers using them have found that they predict with a fair degree of accuracy what may be expected of learners. Because of the importance of this technique in the study of children nearly all colleges educating teachers have included courses in tests and measurements in their curricula. These tests are of two kinds: group and individual. All teachers educated since the adoption of the modern technique in testing can administer achievement tests in subject matter. Not all feel so competent, however, in the ability to test the intelligence of children. If a teacher lacks this technique and doubts his ability to administer intelligence tests, perhaps it is the part of wisdom not to attempt them. However, the technique is not difficult to acquire and every teacher should attain this skill as early as possible. In the meantime, there are, as Professor Strang points out, certain simple ways of accumulating evidence of the capacity of pupils to learn.[1] She presents these techniques so clearly that she is quoted here somewhat in detail:

[1] *Ibid.* p. 21.

One of the best evidences a teacher has of a pupil's capacity to learn is the record of that pupil's past achievement studied in relation to his school attendance. If a child has always had a good attendance record and has been marked high in effort and deportment by his teachers and yet shows a persistent and consistently poor achievement in his school work, the chances are that he is lacking in scholastic aptitude—the capacity to succeed in the more or less abstract school subjects. One or two or more years' retardation together with a good attendance record is usually an indication of low scholastic aptitude.

Another evidence of a pupil's scholastic aptitude is his present attack on the work of his grade. Direct observation of children at work and at play gives indications of their unique mental abilities that are not revealed by standardized tests. One child may have a special ability to see relationships in social situations; another may have an almost uncanny skill in solving mechanical problems; still another may show unusual interest and persistence in accomplishing the academic work of the school. . . .

The teacher may attain a still more precise idea of the mental ability of the children in a class by giving them the Goodenough Test.[1] This test of mental ability is exceedingly easy to give. The teacher simply says to the children, "Draw a picture of a man." No additional directions or suggestions should be given. And, of course, no model or picture from which the children could copy should be in sight. The teacher should also be sure that the children do not see one another's drawings. Nothing could be simpler than the administration of this unique test of mental ability. The interpretation of the drawings, however, is so difficult that it should be done by a trained psychologist. It may be possible, however, for teachers to send their pupils' drawings of a man, carefully labeled with the child's name and date of birth to the psychology department of a near-by university or the psychologist of a city system or state department. The expert, after scoring this test, would return the papers to the teacher with an estimate of the child's mental age that should correspond fairly closely to the estimate obtained from a standardized individual test of intelligence. . . .

The teacher with some psychological background may further check his estimate of his pupils' general level of mental ability by noting the

[1] Goodenough, Florence L. *Measurement of Intelligence by Drawings*, pp. XI and 177, World Book Co., 1926.

kind of things they can do. The pupil's vocabulary is one sign of his mental capacity. . . . Ability to see similarity and differences and other relationships among things, and ability to solve arithmetic problems difficult for children of his age are likewise signs of scholastic aptitude.

Records of Accomplishments. Samples of the work of students kept over a period of time are somewhat revealing of scholastic abilities and needs. Composition work done at the end of the school year, for example, should show improvement over that done at the beginning. Contributions in all subjects can be assembled for the record: a poem, an interesting report of a school journey, a record of books read during the year, and other accomplishments. Children are frequently made responsible for this folder and take pride in its care. A refinement of the contents of the folder has many possibilities: a record of misspelled words and progress in conquering them, and persistent mistakes in grammar and their correction are but two of the many possible activities in self-checking and testing in which children may profitably engage.

Anecdotal Records. One excellent method of studying children is to observe them in spontaneous, unsupervised action. The record of this type of observation is usually known as an anecdote. It has been defined as follows:

. . . The anecdote is a record of some significant item of conduct, a record of an episode in the life of the student, a word picture of the student in action; the teacher's best effort at taking a word snapshot at the moment of the incident; any narrative of events in which the student takes such a part as to reveal something which may be significant about his personality.[1]

Not all behavior of children has significance; the teacher must develop discrimination in evaluating what he observes. This type of record is usually of behavior and personality and includes the following items: bravery, truthfulness, unselfishness,

[1] Randall, J. A. "An Anecdotal Behavior Journal," *Progressive Education*, Vol. 13 (Jan. 1936), p. 22.

leadership, self-control, coöperation, ability to accept criticism, dependability, and the ability to assume responsibility. The Winnetka School faculty has developed an excellent scale for rating school behavior and attitudes; an examination of it is recommended.[1] Enlightening comment on this scale is also available in the pamphlet by Professor Strang, referred to in previous paragraphs.

Health Records. Essential to proper mental and personality development is physical health. Records of this important phase of child development are, therefore, fundamental if we are to secure workable data for understanding children. Every child should have an annual physical examination and the records of its results should be used to direct remedial measures and to insure proper education in health. Many states make the keeping of health records mandatory and prescribe the form on which they are made and recorded. Inexperienced teachers should consult their superintendents on this point and procure directions for assembling these data. If no record forms are recommended, an appeal to the State Department of Health will doubtless bring assistance in the selection of an adequate recording sheet.

RECORDS OF GROUP ACHIEVEMENT

Records of group achievements are usually coöperative and are participated in by teacher and pupils. This record may be the result of activity in committees, in groups, or in grades. Whatever the group, the teacher should bear in mind that individual children compose it and that records are kept for the purpose of reporting not only group achievement but also individual contributions to it. There are many reasons for an adequate reporting of group achievements in rural schools. It is an excellent record for new teachers, since it furnishes an outline of the work accomplished in past years. It supplements

[1] Van Alystyne, Dorothy, and the Winnetka Public School Faculty. *Winnetka Scale for Rating School Behavior and Attitudes,* Winnetka Educational Press, 1935.

the course of study and tells what has been accomplished. It is a faithful accounting of the extra-curricular experience of rural children.

Records of Work Performed by Grades or Groups. A record, compiled by grades or groups, is kept from year to year. It is really the record of the progress of children through the grades and may at their graduation tell their complete history, so far as subject matter is concerned. Children and teachers alike share in the assembling of the material which tells the story. Children made responsible for this record are interested in listing their accomplishments, and the results are often surprisingly good. For example, a request from a group of rural teachers to their students for a report on the topic "What we have accomplished this year" brought forth full and enthusiastic reports in each subject covered. The reports were considered theme assignments, so that teachers merely edited them and placed them in a permanent file. A perusal of these reports at the beginning of a new school year should give valuable information to both pupils and teachers. In the small rural school, where teacher turn-over is frequent and there is no principal to consult, such a record is invaluable.

The above example of a record of a group reports the work of the school year, but there are also important records for shorter periods of time and for shorter items of subject matter. These are records kept of the progress and achievements of teaching units covering a period of from six weeks to two months. A record form was developed by one of the coöperating rural critics of the State Teachers College at Buffalo for reporting such a unit of work. It is so simple and practical that it is herewith given below.[1] This form is suggestive only. It may be adapted to any sort of unit and the items may be expanded indefinitely. The original form as well as its recording was exceedingly simple. The record was kept on a large sheet of brown wrapping paper tacked to the wall and each child recorded

[1] Reported by Mrs. Margaret Tower James, Porter District No. 8, Niagara County, New York. Miss M. Gazelle Hoffman, District Supt. of Schools.

his own data as he contributed to the achievement of the group.
After the completion of the unit each child may copy his in-

REPORT OF UNIT............BEGAN...........COMPLETED.............

Name of Child	Things Brought from Home for the Unit	Books Read	Things Con- structed	Research	Field Trip	Oral Reports	Written Reports

dividual data and place them in his folder. Frequently the
data accompanies his monthly report card home. A copy of the
complete record might be included in the permanent file of work
accomplished during the year.

Record of Work Performed by Committees. As was pointed out
in Chapter VIII, much of the life of the small rural school
functions through the work of committees. It is reasonable
then to expect children in school, as in life outside, to report
on work accomplished to the group which appointed them.
Consequently, it is recommended that such reports be made
and that they become a part of the permanent file of the school.
In that event, there would be available for both children and
teacher a complete resumé of the experiences in coöperative
living. For example, in a coöperative school excursion, such
as is recommended in Chapter XIV, the committee on arrangements might profitably make a report for the permanent
file as well as to the group. There would thus be gradually
accumulated information about expenses, transportation, food,

etc. which would make subsequent excursions easier to plan and manage. Through the records all school committees stand on the shoulders, so to speak, of those who have previously served in the same capacity.

REPORTS WHICH CHILDREN TAKE HOME

The report card has been accepted as a device for acquainting the home with the progress of children in school. It, too, like the records kept in school has reflected modern changes in educational philosophy and practice. Investigations, however, reveal that changes in this card have come slowly and that the most rapid improvements have taken place since 1932.[1] An examination of these improvements indicates that they are in harmony with the modern trends in record keeping listed in previous paragraphs. Thus a committee of the New York State Teachers Association at work on the reports which children take home listed the following practices which reveal a harmonization of reporting and modern education:

(1) Report cards list behavior ratings instead of the single complex term of deportment.

(2) An evaluation is made of the formation and development of desirable individual and social habits.

(3) Health ratings are made in terms of behavior rather than a knowledge about health.

(4) Printed messages to parents are included which invite coöperation on specific terms and invite the parent to visit the school and confer with the teacher. An explanation of the report is also given.[2]

A 1936 report of a study on report cards under the auspices of the United States Office of Education discloses similar

[1] See Hansen, Rowna. *Report Cards for Kindergarten and Elementary Grades*, Leaflet 41 (1931) United States Office of Education (Dept. of the Interior) Government Printing Office.

"Report of Committee on Reporting Progress in Kindergarten and Elementary Schools" *New York State Education*, Vol. 23, Dec. 1935, p. 233.

[2] *Ibid.* pp. 1–20.

trends on a national scale.[1] These trends were indicated as taking three directions. First, school systems were reported as abandoning all report cards and substituting therefor informal notes to parents, or individual conferences with parents in which the progress of the pupil was discussed. A good case for this type of substitution is presented by Mabel Rossman in the fifteenth Yearbook of the Department of Elementary School Principals of the National Education Association. While this innovation took place in a large city school system it would not be difficult to transfer the technique to small rural schools, provided parents understood the procedure and approved of it. The procedure was simple. After securing the promise of parent coöperation the formal reporting system was abandoned. In its place, each teacher obligated himself to contact every parent whose child was not making the progress in school of which he was capable. This contact was made by a mimeographed or a personal letter in which the teacher asked the parent to agree upon a time in which the two might discuss the individual child. The notices were sent home only when the child was not making satisfactory progress. Otherwise parents assumed that the child's progress reached acceptable standards.

The results claimed for this practice were impressive:

(1) Under this system parents and teachers studied individual children more scientifically and thoroughly than under the system of the home report card.

(2) There was an increased interest shown by parents in education and in the school.

(3) The school tended, under the plan, to adjust the curriculum to the needs of individual children.

(4) Teachers were released from an excessive emphasis upon fact learning destined to assist children in passing tests and piling up credible marks.[2]

[1] Davis, Mary Dabney. *Report Cards of Pupil Progress Recently Constructed for Elementary Grades*, Circular 169 (1936), United States Office of Education (Dept. of the Interior), Government Printing Office.

[2] Rossman, Mabel. "An Experiment in Reporting Pupil Progress to Parents," National Education Association, *Department of Elementary School Principals*, Vol. 15, 1935, p. 365.

Another group of schools, according to the national study referred to above, has listed both general and specific teaching goals in their progress reports and have left space for the teachers to describe the individual achievements and needs of their pupils. An example of this type of report is listed in the appendix.

Still a third group is described as developing detailed reports:

Many of these reports carry subheads under the curriculum subjects and character traits which help the teacher analyze the pupils' specific abilities and which also draw the parents' attention to what the school is attempting to do for their children. Many of these detailed reports also list school objectives and provide space for statements of height, weight and physical health records, for summaries of standardized test results, for home reports of the pupil's out-of-school activities and for a direct appeal to parents for coöperation in aiding their children's progress. It is interesting to note that in many instances some of these changes in the periodic reports are being incorporated in the permanent central office records.[1]

An example of this type of report is also presented in the appendix.

The above study indicates that practice is divided on the type of report which the child in the modern school takes home to his parents. However, the study also gives evidence of an equanimity of opinion among school leaders that the traditional type of report card does not serve the needs of modern youth. The reporting system which would meet these needs, therefore, should adjust its procedures to a conception of education which concerns itself with the satisfactory growth of individual children.

THE TEST OF A MODERN PROGRAM OF SCHOOL RECORDS

The practicability of a modern program of school records depends upon the ability of the average rural teacher to put it

[1] Davis, Mary Dabney. *Report Cards of Pupil Progress Recently Constructed for Elementary Grades*, p. 1.

to use. How this was accomplished by a teacher in a one-room
school in Erie County, New York, is herewith presented in the
form of a case study.

CASE STUDY—V [1]

When I began teaching, many years ago, my chief interest
was that every child learn his 3 R's. Of the 3 R's my main
concern was with reading, and I insisted that every child read
Book One his first year in school, the second book the next year
and so on into the eighth grade, when he was carefully drilled
for the Regents examination. This was my technique of teaching until approximately seven years ago.

About this time I received a contract to teach in a small,
traditional rural school. The school was located in a settlement
of church, store, and factory with a few houses sandwiched in
between. Fifteen children attended the school, all of whom
came from homes of strong religious influences. This, I dis-
cerned later, was an asset because parents were coöperative
in a program which looked toward character building and personality development. In the meantime, I was attending
classes at the State Teachers College, Buffalo, and became
interested in the new philosophy of education which taught
that we teach children as well as subject matter. In the psychology classes I discovered that one had the opportunity of
practicing in the classroom with children the theory about
children which I had learned from books. The year I made
these important discoveries I had no group to prepare for the
Regents examination so I began to use my extra time in studying
the children I taught. As I studied the children, each soon
became an individual to me, and every child took on significance
in terms of his abilities, his needs, and his capacities. I soon
found that I must record in some way the valuable information
I was securing from my daily contact with the children, and so
I began my own system of making permanent these precious

[1] Reported by Mrs. Helene M. Holmes, Springbrook School, Erie County,
New York. Mr. W. R. Buell, District Superintendent of Schools.

insights into the lives of my school group. I did not progress so far as I wished because after three years I changed schools, and thus left the group which by now I called affectionately "My Family Circle."

In my next school I had many more children to teach, but undaunted, I decided I would try to institute and complete the system of records begun in the first school. My district superintendent was sympathetic and offered his help. His advice gave me courage. I began with assembling records of group achievements. Achievement tests were easy to administer and gave me an insight into the scholastic achievement of my new children as experience had given me information of the children in the other school. In spite of the fact that my school was double in size to the one in which I had originally become interested in children, I was able to start individual studies of every child the first year. Now, four years later, I have a somewhat complete and detailed study of every child in the room. Not only do I know where my children now are in their mental, physical, and character development, but I know how they have improved in the past four years. The record is all before me and tells me with some degree of certainty the achievements and failures of individuals who make up our school group.

If every teacher were a little less concerned with subject matter and a little more concerned with child development, I believe that our whole educational program would be improved. In order to study children one must keep records, and out of my experience I should like to list the ones which have proven most helpful to me and to the children.

Records Kept by the Children. (a) *Individual folders of scholastic achievements.* These folders are ordinary manila ones which have been decorated by the children, and as a consequence are beautiful as well as useful. This is one of their art projects and the results show considerable initiative, originality, and artistry. At the end of each month the teacher and the children have a conference over the contents in their folders. Their weaknesses are checked and improvements noted. All papers are graded on a scale to which are assigned honor points. Each child records his total honor points inside his folder and each month attempts to better his score. No comparison of scores is made between children, but each child, as in golf, plays against his own score. The children take their folders home each month to their parents.

(b) *Monthly spelling chart.* This chart, too, is a product of the children. They make it, decorate it, and keep it up to date. Marks are recorded every day and the results of weekly tests are also kept. Thus a year's record in spelling can be easily checked.

(c) *Drawing folder.* All art work for a semester is filed in a portfolio, also an art project. These too are taken home at the end of the semester to be discussed with parents and friends.

Records Kept by the Teacher. (a) *Individual personality cards.* On these cards are listed the name, age, grade, parentage, financial conditions, environment at home, work habits, study and play habits, and personal characteristics and disposition. Each year additions are made to these cards. Changes in children are noted and thus there is a double check placed upon me, their teacher. I can always ask myself two questions: has the child improved, and what have I done to help him?

(b) *Weekly survey of children.* This is a summary of the accomplishment of children weekly—especially those of outstanding significance. These are recorded in my plan book, checked frequently and used often.

Required Records. (a) *Permanent record cards.* These cards contain an excellent picture of the child in regard to health— the school physician's report is included—, results of achievement tests, results of intelligence tests, school attendance, and extra-curricular activities. These records are required in our supervisory districts and must be left in the school for succeeding teachers. New teachers can secure from these required records valuable information about the children.

(b) *Registers and report cards.* These are features of our required records. The former is a book furnished by the State

Education Department and is used to keep the records of school attendance, and form the bases of the monthly reports to district superintendents. The report cards are these reports which children take home monthly to parents. These are more than the usual card which reports marks and deportment. These attempt to reveal to parents effort and achievement in health habits and character development as well.

Records of Group Achievements. (*a*) *Library chart.* This is a chart which children keep and on which are reported the books read and the simplest possible report of their contents.

(*b*) *Compiled record of a unit of work.* This is a complete record of the activities and achievement of each child participating in a unit. Here is a sample of one boy's record taken from the record of the group.

Name	Group	What I Want to Do	What I Made	Books I Have Read	Reports Made	Committees on Which I Worked	What I Most Enjoyed
Tom	B	paint, read	movie frieze		oral on modern transportation	Research movie	Painting

This record can be made on unprinted newspaper, lettered in black, and placed on unused wall space. The teacher can readily see what each child does and check on the way he meets his responsibility to himself and to the group.

Uses of These Records. (*a*) *Conferences with parents.* The records furnish a basis for all conferences with parents. In any problem which arises there is objective evidence available with which to attack it. Hence, better home and school coöperation is secured.

(*b*) *Basis for report cards.* Report cards to parents are easily assembled from this cumulative record system. In addition to the monthly report cards other reports accompany children home, as, for example, the art folder mentioned above.

(c) *Transfers to other schools.* This function of records is very important particularly in the light of the usual practice of transferring children from small rural schools to near-by junior high schools. Reports stressing strong and weak points, of my children accompany them when they enter high school. The superintendent of this high school reports that these rural children are easily and quickly adjusted into the school, and that the records they bring assist in this period of adjustment.

(d) *Conferences with pupils.* Individual, cumulative records are essential for conferences with pupils and children respect evidence when it is produced. Conferences are held frequently, not only to assist in overcoming weaknesses, but to commend abilities and achievements.

(e) *District superintendent.* Our district superintendent uses these records specifically in comparing individuals, grades, and schools. They are especially helpful at examination time, and sometimes they check teachers as well as pupils, revealing both strengths and weaknesses.

AN EVALUATION OF THE CASE STUDY

An examination of the case study reveals several significant items:

1. The system of school records described here grew out of a felt need of the teacher to put into practice the theory that good teaching is enhanced by a rich knowledge of child nature. A study of child nature requires records, and the system developed from this need.

2. The system meets all the criteria of modern trends in record keeping: it is individual, continuous, and cumulative; it gives a complete picture of the child; children are compared with themselves as well as with others in records of achievement; the keeping of the records is coöperative; and the records are supplemented with conferences.

3. The system is functional in the highest sense. It is used by the teacher, by the district superintendent, by parents, and by children. Thus it meets the fundamental test of whether or not a system is valuable.

4. The system of record keeping advocated in this chapter is practical and can be instituted in the average small school and under typical conditions found there. In spite of the fact that the teacher taught all of the grades in a one-room school, she yet found time to keep an adequate and functional system of records. Indeed it was the system of records which materially assisted her in the regular tasks of the teacher, giving vitality to her teaching because she taught both children and subject matter.

SUMMARY

Every age has left in records those accomplishments which it wished to have remembered. School records reflect this same *desideratum*. The first records of rural schools reflected the narrow curriculum of the pioneer period, and frequently no records were kept at all. It was the latter practice which called for the first reforms in record keeping, and, while the system was simple, it told the story of what education considered important. The first records, therefore, were of mental accomplishments within the range of a traditional system of education.

With the entrance of a modern philosophy of education well-defined trends in child accounting have developed; in general they are faithful to the modern ideal of the child-centered school. These trends are: (a) that the school record should be individual, continuous, and cumulative; (b) that records give a complete picture of the child; (c) that the child be compared with himself as well as with the group, the first comparison, considered more important than the second; (d) that record keeping be a coöperative enterprise; (e) that home report cards be frequently supplemented by conferences between parents and teachers; and (f) that modern records be functional.

There is no agreement of educational authorities on the type, the number, and the kind of records which are essential to the understanding and counseling of children. On the whole, however, a modern system of records is divided into two large groups: first, those records which assemble information about individual children, often including data on mental characteristics, information about physical maturation, and data which gives light on personality development; second, those records concerned with the recording of achievements of groups of children. The record forms for recording the individual growth of children are: the autobiography, records of scholastic achievement, records of indications of capacity to learn, records of accomplishments, anecdotal records, and health records. Records for group achievements should include these accomplishments made by groups, grades, and committees. That these records are possible, practical, and helpful in the average rural school is indicated by a case study submitted by a teacher of a one-room school in Erie County, New York.

SUGGESTED READINGS

Bain, Winifred E. *Parents Look at Modern Education*, Chap. X, D. Appleton-Century Co., New York, 1935.

Davis, Mary Dabney. *Report Cards of Pupil Progress Recently Constructed for Elementary Grades*, U. S. Office of Education, Circular 169 (Dept. of the Interior), Government Printing Office, Washington, D. C., 1936.

Dougherty, James Henry; Gorman, Frank Herman; and Phillips, Claude A. *Elementary School Organization and Management*, Chap. XIV, Macmillan, New York, 1936.

Giles, H. H. "Record-Making in an Experimental School," *Progressive Education*, Vol. 12 (Nov., 1935), p. 473.

Hansen, Rowna C. *Report Cards for Kindergarten and Elementary Grades*, Office of Education, Leaflet No. 41 (Dept. of the Interior), Government Printing Office, Washington, D. C., 1931.

Hatcher, O. Latham. *Guiding Rural Boys and Girls*, Chap. II, McGraw-Hill Book Co., New York, 1930.

Lowth, Frank J. *Everyday Problems of the Country Teacher*, Rev. ed., Chap. XXV, Macmillan, New York, 1936.

Minor, Ruby. *Early Childhood Education, Its Principles and Practices*, Chap. XX, D. Appleton-Century Co., New York, 1937.

Pugsley, Chester A. "Do Schools Report to Parents in Terms of School Objectives?" *Educational Method*, Vol. 15 (Oct., 1935), p. 15.

Strang, Ruth. *Every Teacher's Records*, Bureau of Publications, Teachers College, Columbia University, New York, 1936.

MATERIALS FOR DISCUSSION

Consider the following statements. What changes would make them more acceptable to you? What significant issues arise from their study?

1. In every age, school records have reflected the accomplishments which education wished to have remembered. A study of school records should reveal, therefore, a clear picture of the historical development of educational philosophy and practices.

2. The cumulative records of individual children are of questionable value. Teachers receiving the folders tend to accept the opinions of previous teachers there recorded. This uncritical acceptance of previous judgments tends to defeat the purpose of the system—the study of individual children.

3. Children are too immature in judgment to assist in keeping their school records. Record keeping as a coöperative enterprise is an idealistic suggestion too difficult to put into practice.

4. The reports which children take home to parents should reflect the objectives of the school. If the school is traditional the report card should assume a traditional form. If the school is modern the report should reflect these modern trends present, and no more.

5. It would appear desirable for parents, the child, and the school to abandon formal report cards and to substitute therefor the home-school conference.

CHAPTER X

THE EXCEPTIONAL CHILD IN THE SMALL SCHOOL

THE atypical or exceptional child is defined, at least for the purposes of this chapter, as the child who deviates from the normal. The White House Conference classified such children under eight major divisions: (a) the crippled; (b) the deaf and the hard of hearing; (c) the blind and the partially seeing; (d) the speech defective; (e) children of lowered vitality; (f) the mentally retarded; (g) the mentally gifted; (h) children presenting serious behavior problems. These classifications represent the threefold aspects of human nature: (a) the physical, under which the first five fall; (b) the mental, which covers the next two disabilities; and (c) the emotional, under which comes the last grouping.

AN HISTORICAL STATEMENT

The problems involved in meeting the needs of these exceptional children have for sometime engaged the attention of leaders concerned with their welfare. The state led the way, usually through the media of residential schools called institutions for the blind, the deaf, the feeble-minded, the tubercular, and so on. From the beginning, however, these institutions—with certain notable exceptions—were confused in their objectives, and their programs and policies reflected the confusion. Established as schools, it is only in recent years that they have been placed under the supervision of State Departments of Education and have adopted modern methods of teaching based upon the principles of modern psychology. Of the movement to make these institutions truly educational there is general approval:

It is unquestionably true that the problem of the handicapped child has its physical, its medical, its sociological, its psychological phases as well as its educational aspects. But so also has the problem of the normal child, and those who advocate the inclusion of special residential schools under general state educational supervision point out that adequate educational provision for all children involves consideration of health and remedial physical or medical measures wherever such are needed; that the primary need of the handicapped child is just such a comprehensive educational program adjusted to his special needs; that only in so far as his handicap requires should he be separated from the normal experiences of normal children; and that all efforts made in his behalf—whether in State residential schools or in the city day schools—should be centralized under one form of control.[1]

These state schools give further evidence of gradually evolving into institutions which care for extreme disabilities only, thus placing upon the local school and local communities responsibilities heretofore carried by state institutions. This has been necessitated by the fact that the institutions have become overcrowded, and the handicapped desiring admission too numerous. Augmenting this condition is the growing conviction that the handicapped, except for extreme cases, are best served locally in their own homes and communities. On this point the Superintendent of the Walter Fernald School of Massachusetts makes this statement:

We no longer see the necessity for institutional care for more than 10 per cent of the feeble-minded, 90 per cent . . . should be recognized and provided for by the community in its school program.[2]

Of this statement Elise H. Martens, Senior Specialist in the Education of Exceptional Children, United States Office of Education, says:

[1] Report of the United States Commissioner of Education, 1928–1930, Vol. I; pp. 385–386, Government Printing Office.

[2] Greene, Ransom A. "Progress in Understanding and Control of the Feeble-Minded," The Annals of the American Academy of Political and Social Science, Vol. 151 (Sep. 1930), p. 136.

This principle which holds for the mentally retarded and for the hard-of-hearing child is applicable also to the child with defective eyesight, yet not so blind that he needs institutional care; to the child who is anaemic, malnourished with a tendency to tubercular infection, yet not sick enough to find admission to a hospital; to the child who is crippled, yet who can learn to help himself in many ways in the ordinary school environment; to the child who presents a behavior problem, yet not so serious that he needs to be segregated. Segregation in State residential institutions is thus primarily reserved for those disabilities which force themselves upon the attention of society through utter incapacity to cope with the demands of the social group.[1]

Under the compulsion of public opinion and the advice of educators the community care of mentally retarded children, for example, increased between the years 1922–1927 125 per cent while inmates in institutions increased only 25 per cent. Inevitably the movement tends to place upon local communities the responsibility for exceptional children, and local school systems are being forced more and more to adjust their program to meet the special needs of these unfortunates with special care. Such provisions are in harmony with our democratic conception of "Education of all the children of all the people" and our progressive viewpoint that "Education should be adjusted to meet individual needs."

THE SCOPE OF THE PROBLEM

The White House Conference on Child Health and Protection made an exhaustive study of the exceptional child in the United States and made public its findings in a special report.[2] The numbers of such children, revealed by the study were startling. There are one-half million children in the elementary schools so mentally retarded that they require individualized instruction; three million have defective hearing; there are 300,000 crippled

[1] *Report of the United States Commissioner of Education, 1928–1930*, p. 388, Government Printing Office.
[2] White House Conference on Child Health and Protection, Section III. *Education and Training: Special Education.*

children; 50,000 children have impaired vision; three-quarters of a million children are definite behavior problems; from six to eight million children of school age suffer from malnutrition; one million children have speech defects; and there are approximately one million children of exceptional mental ability. Translated into percentages of the whole, the children in need of special attention are as follows: mentally deficient, 2 per cent; mentally gifted, 6 per cent; blind and partially seeing, 0.2 per cent; deaf and hard of hearing, 2 per cent; speech defectives, 4 per cent; behavior problems, 3 per cent; malnourished, cardiac, and tubercular, approximately 20 per cent. These are figures and percentages of the nation as a whole. Martens estimates that about half of the total live in rural areas. She says:

The most recent estimates indicate that of the 25,000,000 or more of children between the ages of 6 and 18 attending school approximately 12,000,000 are in rural areas and that 3,000,000 more of the same ages are living in rural areas, but are not attending school. If we assume that the percentages of exceptional children are about the same in city and country it seems safe to say that approximately one half of the millions of handicapped children estimated for the Nation at large live in rural districts where conditions are most unfavorable for any special consideration of their needs.[1]

The reasons for unfavorable conditions in dealing with exceptional children are apparent to the student of rural education. The smallness of the rural schools forbids the employment of special teachers, and the lack of funds in the average small district is a deterrent to the gathering together of groups of children large enough to warrant a special class. Urban areas have met their responsibility to the exceptional child by forming special classes, and even establishing special schools where equipment, buildings, teaching, and supervision are all modified to meet the needs of the group. Obviously, the small rural school cannot establish such an ambitious program for the care

[1] *Report of the United States Commissioner of Education, 1928–1930*, p. 395, Government Printing Office.

of exceptional children, but the large numbers of these children in rural areas is a clear indication of the responsibility which education bears to them. What, then, should be the steps taken by the rural teacher to meet this responsibility?

MEETING THE NEEDS OF EXCEPTIONAL CHILDREN IN SMALL SCHOOLS

In the states where provision is made for exceptional children the teacher in the small school should direct such children into the various channels established for their special needs. His responsibility in that instance would be advisory and coöperative. On the other hand, parents may prefer, even with available county and state programs, to keep their handicapped children at home and in attendance at the local school. There is much, indeed, to be said for this point of view, as a braille supervisor points out:

. . . Our day school children from the beginning develop the concept that they are primarily citizens of the school or of the community and only secondarily, blind, in contra-distinction to the concept now held by so many blind people, that they are, primarily, blind individuals, and secondarily, members of the greater whole. As a bit of social philosophy, these two concepts have a far-reaching effect, not only upon the blind people themselves in their efforts to earn a livelihood, but in the part which society is expected to play in furnishing means of support. Needless to say, these points of view form the basis for happiness or unhappiness in the normal life contacts of the individual, determining as they do the question as to whether the blind individual will seek his happiness and inspiration from the sighted friends about him, or whether merely tolerating these associations, he puts them aside whenever possible for contacts with other blind people.[1]

While it is not likely that children with a total disability of blindness will attend a small rural school, this conception of the braille supervisor holds true also for those children with partial vision and other handicaps. Annette Bennett in an article on

[1] White House Conference on Child Health and Protection. Section III, *Education and Training: Special Education*, p. 247, Century Co., 1932.

The Retarded Child in the Rural School makes a like observation of children with low intelligence. She said:

Many educators who have been in close touch with the problem are of the opinion that in non-centralized rural schools subnormal children with I Q's above 60 and probably some of an even lower grade of intelligence can best be provided for in the regular classroom.[1]

The necessities for teaching handicapped children in the small rural school are further enhanced by the fact that there are only 26 states which make legislative authorization for special education and only 16 of that number provide special financial aid. The teacher in the small rural school having such responsibilities thrust upon him is faced with the practical question of how he, with his manifold duties, can meet them.

There appear to be three responsibilities which devolve here upon the classroom teacher: (a) a study of individual children and a recognition of those who deviate from normal in the classifications listed by the White House Conference; (b) meeting the needs of those who can be served by the local school; (c) the securing of aid from the national, state, and local agencies organized in the interest of exceptional children.

MEETING THE NEEDS OF CHILDREN WHO CAN BE SERVED BY THE LOCAL SCHOOL

The Physically Handicapped. Once the exceptional child has been found—the law of averages admits of but few cases in the average small school—and his case diagnosed, the program of adjustment follows. For the physically handicapped child the task is somewhat simplified. It will consist largely of adjustment in equipment and methodology. A child with defective eyesight, for example, will be given special concessions in the matter of lighting, large chalk will be used, books in large print will be provided, written work will be kept at a minimum, and

[1] Bennett, Annette "The Retarded Child in the Rural School." *Mental Hygiene*, Vol. 17 (July 1933), p. 467.

nearly all directions will be verbal. The hard-of-hearing child will also have methods and equipment adjusted to his special needs. Emphasis here would probably be placed on written rather than verbal work, and the child would find much satisfaction in reading and homework. A general principle to follow is to develop eye-mindedness in children with defective hearing, and ear-mindedness in children with defective sight. The United States Office of Education, since 1933, has been issuing excellent pamphlets with suggestions for adapting classroom procedure to exceptional children. The following extract taken from one, suggests methods adapted to the special needs of partially seeing children: [1]

SUGGESTIONS FOR TEACHING PARTIALLY SEEING CHILDREN

A. *In Reading*

1. Secure large-type readers for the sight-defective child as basic material for use in developing his reading ability.

2. Limit his reading to the informational type and let reading for pleasure be minimized until improvement of eye condition takes place.

3. Use much oral reading of stories both by the teacher and by normally seeing pupils in class.

4. Encourage parents, brothers, and sisters to read aloud at home.

5. Substitute other activities to take the place of his desire for reading such as dramatics, garden work, and games.

B. *In Writing*

1. Require large, round letters with all superfluous lines omitted. Manuscript writing has been found helpful for children just learning to write.

2. Be sure that your own writing on the blackboard and on any papers read by the pupils is large and legible.

[1] McLeod, Beatrice. *Teachers' Problems with Exceptional Children,* Pamphlet No. 40, pp. 21–23, United States Office of Education.

3. Let the writing on the board be at the level of the child's eyes with words and letters well spaced.

4. Do not use lines on the blackboard, since they sometimes cause eye fatigue.

5. Avoid formal writing lessons except in the lower grades.

6. Use blunt pens, black ink (preferably India ink or a half-and-half mixture), heavy lead.

7. If it is at all possible, let the sight-defective child use a typewriter with enlarged type and heavily inked ribbon, since this aids greatly in saving sight.

C. *In Arithmetic*

1. Do not permit the child to strain his eyes trying to read the problems out of an ordinary text.

2. Since the arithmetic texts printed in large type are expensive, it is wise to copy the problems on the board or on paper with a heavy lead pencil or India ink.

3. Use much oral arithmetic.

D. *In Handwork*

1. Use the sand table for working out many projects which otherwise would require close eye work. Especially is this device useful for primary children.

2. Avoid fine detailed work in any form of manual activities.

E. *In Social Studies*

1. Do not expect the sight-defective child to use the ordinary type of wall map or globe. They are usually made with too much detail and in colors that do not show sufficient contrast. They may be greatly improved in these respects by inking the continents with India ink and by showing the land masses in strong color.

2. Do not expect the child to draw maps. Rather provide stenciled outlines on dark paper on which he may note simple features in connection with work in history or geography.

F. *In Music*

1. Do not expect the child to read musical notes of the ordinary type.

2. Confine his musical activities to rote singing and musical appreciation, but give him all the pleasure he can get out of this phase of his school work.

G. In Physical Education and Hygiene

1. Watch the child's posture. Postural defects are sometimes caused by visual defects, and should, of course, be guarded against.

2. Give frequent periods in which the eyes will have rest from near vision. Do not permit two consecutive periods of close eye work.

3. Teach the child to save his eyes in every way possible. Help him to face his limitations sensibly without growing discouraged or morbid. Follow the oculist's directions as to necessary restrictions.

Likewise the program for the undernourished child should be modified and adjusted. In spite of the fact that rural children live in the country where food is supposedly cheap and abundant, it is estimated that there are approximately from two and a half to three millions of undernourished rural children now attending school. It is impossible for small schools to provide enclosed porches, or glass cubicles, such as are provided in many urban schools; but the small school can make adjustments in the school program for children of lowered vitality. The most practical and the least difficult of these adjustments are concerned with rest and with food to supplement the lunches brought from home. A folding cot, such as is used by Boy Scouts for camping, will probably meet the needs of the average small school. The cot can be set up in the back of the classroom, in a hallway, or in a cloakroom, and rest periods should be observed regularly. In fair weather children can rest out of doors on rugs which they can make for themselves. Somewhat the same program can be followed for cardiac cases, since much of their difficulty can be met with the right kind of rest. A hot dish should supplement the cold lunches of all children, and the undernourished should have, in addition, a mid-morning and mid-afternoon portion of milk. The matter of the hot lunch is discussed at some length in Chapter VII of this text and many teachers meet this problem of nutrition in the small school by methods described there.

The Mentally Handicapped. According to the White House Conference approximately 2 per cent of the whole elementary school population is so mentally retarded that they require special consideration. Practically no provision is made either by the state or the local communities to care for the mentally handicapped in rural areas; and, since their numbers approach 225,000 children, the problem assumes rather serious proportions. In these small schools the mentally retarded are required to pursue, along with normal children, a single course of study usually taught by the traditional method of memorization of facts. Under this program the retarded child becomes more and more bewildered, resentful, and unhappy. The cruel picture of a child in a dunce cap belongs to generations ago, but the continued neglect of his special needs is a serious indictment of education in and for a democracy. Inevitably, social and economic repercussions must follow.

This lack of adequate education of subnormal children in rural districts is general throughout the country. There are many accounts of what ought to be done, but no account of satisfactory work or anything approaching it. Discussing the situation in this New Jersey State Educational Survey, Dr. Edgar Doll writes: . . . Some districts actually exclude certain types of handicapped children without any feeling of responsibility for seeing that such children receive the benefits of special educational opportunity even when it is provided elsewhere. This is particularly true of the low grade feeble-minded who are frankly excluded from school in certain districts without legal warrant for such exclusion.[1]

Modification of an educational program to meet the needs of the child deviating from mentally normal is not simple. The issue seems to be considerably confused by the lack of clarity

[1] White House Conference on Child Health and Protection. Section III, *Education and Training: Special Education*, p. 445, Century Co., 1932.

in objectives of what constitute a suitable educational program for mentally retarded children. The Superintendent of the Wrentham State School of Massachusetts has laid down principles upon which there is apparently much agreement. These are as follows:

In educating mental defectives, academic training, hand training, and social training should be well-correlated and emphasized in accordance with the needs presented by the individual child. It will be noticed that hand training is bolstered on one side by academic training, and on the other by social training. Hand training is of great importance, because a child who is retarded mentally to the extent of being classified in the mentally defective group will never be able to earn a livelihood by any other means than by the use of his hands. However, while giving this hand training, the importance of academic work should not be minimized. The child should have academic work to the extent indicated by his mental level, because he has a right to it. His academic education up to his mental level enables him to enjoy life more and to conduct himself on a higher plane. Academic training should not be attempted above his mental ability—in the first place, because he cannot absorb it; in the second place, because it is likely to confuse and embarrass him and make him unhappy. This is likely to induce in him antisocial traits. In the third place, it is a waste of effort and money to attempt to train the mentally deficient academically above his mental levels. The social training is more important than either or both of the others because the individual who has acquired both academic training and hand training and has not gained social adaptation is sure to fail. If on the contrary he is properly adjusted socially, he will probably, without academic training or hand training, be able, after his school life, to acquire sufficient skill in hand work to support himself. Therefore, it is extremely important that the social training of mentally defective children be emphasized in every possible way. These children should be encouraged to take part in competitive games and play with normal children, for there are many mentally defective children who can compete in games on fairly equal terms with the normal. This will go a long way toward compensating for the sense of inferiority engendered by their not being able to compete with normal children in scholastic work.[1]

The Gifted Child. The term "gifted child" unfortunately is often misused or at least misunderstood. It does not always connote a talent for art, music, or the drama. Children gifted in the fine arts form a small portion of the whole group. The term is here used with the same connotation as in the White House Conference Report; it simply means a child with exceptional intelligence.

The intelligence of a people is found to follow what is known as the Normal Curve of distribution. That is to say, there is a large middle group of average intelligence. At the lower end there is a small group of low intelligence, and at the other end a small group of high intelligence. The children discussed here are those at the upper end of the scale and constitute about 6 per cent of the total.[2]

Nearly everyone is aware that the school program has been constructed for the average child who composes the great middle group on the normal curve. Consequently, it has never wholly met the needs of the gifted upper 6 per cent. Indeed such adjustments which have taken place have been in favor of the retarded rather than the gifted group. The retarded make their own special appeal, but the gifted child is often left to shift for himself on the presumption that he can be depended upon to turn in a good account for himself. The facts, however, often disprove this theory. Recent psychological investigations have revealed that the gifted child is likely to be more sensitive than the average, that he is likely to resent discipline, and that, because of an exceptional intelligence geared to an educational program constructed for the average child, he tends to use his

[1] *Report of the United States Commissioner of Education, 1928–1930,* p. 404, Government Printing Office.

[2] White House Conference on Child Health and Protection. Section III, *Education and Training: Special Education,* p. 538, Century Co., 1932.

"unused" time from lesson preparation to embroil himself in school quarrels and mischief-making. The "bad boy" is not necessarily the school dullard; he is as likely as not to be a bright child with bad habits and undesirable attitudes.

Two methods are used in meeting the special needs of the child of exceptional intelligence. One, the "enrichment method," modifies the curriculum to meet his requirements. The other gives him the advantage of rapid promotion. In urban schools, such children are usually placed in special classes and the program enriched for them. This plan has been criticized on the ground that it is undemocratic, that it tends to give children a feeling of superiority, and that it is an artificial arrangement at variance with life in the world outside of school. Be that as it may, the enrichment feature of the plan works and according to the White House Conference Report with "truly remarkable results."

The children work with an enthusiasm and persistence that is delightful to see. There is no problem of discipline as they are too busy to get into mischief and are easily led to adjust themselves to the needs and desires of the group. Not only is there no problem of discipline in the ordinary sense, but even children who already present behavior problems, become quickly adjusted in the less oppressive atmosphere of the gifted class. It is not generally appreciated that the gifted child is more sensitive than the child of average intelligence to unwise limitations, to activities such as are often imposed by so-called "good disciplinarians."[1]

This type of child finds himself in the greater freedom of the special class with the more stimulating curriculum and in the happiness of the new-ordered freedom becomes a highly satisfactory member of the group. Thus the children develop into good citizens, and at the same time follow the line of their own abilities. A further technique frequently employed is that of rapid promotion for the gifted child. This is most easily accomplished, and with less questionable results in the small rural school. In spite of the fact that the child skips grades,

[1] *Ibid.* p. 538.

he still remains with his social group for his out-of-recitation periods, and the adjustment problem of the younger child in an advanced grade is thus partly met.

This enrichment program, while superior to a program which ignores the gifted child, is not without its dangers, largely the result of the lack of clarity in objectives. The enrichment may resolve itself into a process of "more and more about what the child already knows most." In other words, in the old familiar circle of subject matter, enlarged from that organized for the average child, there may be too little opportunity for using initiative and creative energy, the characteristics which distinguish him and differentiate him into the exceptional group. Martens points out this difficulty when she says:

We need the means whereby the bright pupil may economize time; but we need also (even more) the means whereby he may reach out into fields untouched by the average child—explore, analyze, create as his capacity prompts him to do, and at all times secure a rich variety of contacts and experiences.[1]

OPPORTUNITIES OFFERED BY SMALL RURAL SCHOOLS FOR THE ADJUSTMENT TO SPECIAL NEEDS OF THE MENTALLY RETARDED AND THE MENTALLY GIFTED

Fortunately, the typical rural classroom is flexible enough to adapt itself both to the retarded and to the gifted child and in this regard is superior to the average urban classroom. In classrooms where a progressive program has been instituted group activities such as are suggested in Chapter V allow for easy adjustments to the individual needs of both retarded and gifted children. They can be easily and successfully shifted from group to group. The gifted child of Group C, for instance, may work in the social studies with Group B; he may be given contracts in English which allow him wide margins for initiative and creation. He may assist with the teaching of the smaller children, listen to their reading, check arithmetic papers, or direct

[1] *Report of the United States Commissioner of Education, 1928–1930*, p. 406. Government Printing Office.

the making of a map. If care is taken not to exploit gifted children—experienced teachers recommend that not more than 20 per cent of their time be thus used—they may assume the responsibilities of pupil assistants to the teacher with profit to all concerned. Martens has this to say of the rural school and the gifted child:

The small rural school in which several or even all grades are under the care of the same teacher offers much greater opportunity to provide for the bright pupil than many teachers think. The usual query is: Since I have so many grades, how can I find time to meet the needs of these intellectually superior children? Many grades offer the very opportunity that you need, for there the bright child can be given a wealth of experiences originating with any grade in the room. Perhaps he will do arithmetic with the fourth grade, read with the sixth grade, study geography and civics with the fifth, sing with the whole group and write and draw as the muses inspire him. The flexibility of individual pupils' programs is promoted rather than limited through the presence of several grades in the same room.

If the activity curriculum is in progress, then an outlet is provided for the talents of all children. The teacher who knows the technique of planning activity units will have no great difficulty in finding opportunities for enriching the experiences of the gifted child. Suppose the topic of study is "Shelter." That subject opens wide the door for historical research into the types of housing of ancient peoples. It provides the means for a geographic survey through the study of the homes of peoples of today. It gives an introduction into the realm of civics and sociology. It makes possible the application of arithmetic to concrete problems of construction. It leads the way to the writing of drama and fiction and poetry. Achievement in all these activities will be dependent upon the age and the ability of the pupil, and the gifted child should naturally find unlimited opportunities for expression. Relieved of the monotonous drill of which he has no need, he can spend his time in rich and varied experiences of research and exploration which will contribute to the product of the whole group.[1]

The rural school program is correspondingly kind to mentally retarded children. They, too, may be shifted from group to

[1] Martens, Elise H. *Teachers' Problems with Exceptional Children*, Vol. II, Pamphlet No. 41, pp. 22–23, United States Office of Education.

group. In some of the tool subjects such as arithmetic or reading they may find their place in slow-moving groups which are given special drill. In other subjects they may be so seriously retarded that individualized instruction is necessary. This, too, they may have. Mentally retarded children may also be served by appointing them as student helpers. Through this service they acquire confidence, poise, tact, and a feeling of responsibility. They also develop academically through the review and drill which come in the assistance to the younger children. Experienced teachers believe that mentally retarded children profit from classroom and pupil-helper responsibilities even more than do the gifted children.

NATIONAL, STATE, AND LOCAL AGENCIES ORGANIZED FOR MEETING NEEDS OF EXCEPTIONAL CHILDREN

National Aid. Aid for exceptional children is provided by a number of agencies, both public and private, in the nation, the state, and local communities. The teacher in the small school should make an inventory of such resources and use them. The United States Office of Education has a group of specialists whose primary concern is the welfare of exceptional children. Bulletins are often printed dealing with such children and these are available at low cost by addressing the United States Office of Education, Department of the Interior, Washington, D. C. The senior specialist in the education of exceptional children has said in a recent bulletin:

Help that comes from without can bring the earnest seeker substantial reënforcement of his own efforts. The resources of a whole nation may literally be called upon to help solve the problem of a single child tucked away somewhere in an inconspicuous country school district.[1]

Aid for many problems of exceptional children may be secured by writing to the National Health Council, 50 West 50th Street, New York City.

[1] *Ibid.* pp. 4–5.

State Aid. State agencies are close at home and should be of great help to the rural teacher, provided she will ask them for it. State Departments of Education in twenty-six states make efforts to assist in the promotion of work for exceptional children, through special bureaus and divisions within the departments. Services of the divisions vary but in general they are advisory, administrative, and coöperative. The State of New York, for example, has a state-wide program which seeks to aid in the education of all exceptional children.

STATE AID FOR EXCEPTIONAL CHILDREN EXEMPLIFIED BY NEW YORK

The state of New York has been one of the pioneer states in bringing aid to exceptional children. This is accomplished through the Bureau for Physically Handicapped Children, a part of the Division of Vocational and Extension Education. This Bureau is charged with responsibility for the organization and direction of the work for physically handicapped children in rural as well as urban areas. The needs of each child are considered individually and efforts are made to meet them through the various channels provided by the state. Contrary to the usual *laissez-faire* methods of many states, New York does not wait for a program to evolve in the local community for its exceptional children; if it seems expedient such children are taken to the program. This is sound educational philosophy and administration. Children cannot—not even the exceptional ones—afford to wait for an education.

New York State makes an effort to provide locally the special care needed for exceptional children. City and union free districts must provide locally for exceptional children when there are ten such cases or may provide for a less number. In rural areas county judges may order that exceptional children be provided with special care. If special, local care for exceptional children is not feasible, efforts are made to secure it for them elsewhere. These efforts may include (a) special home training; (b) transportation to a center where special care is provided; (c) maintenance in a special district. Even hospital care and medical attention are provided for those who otherwise could not afford them. The state provides specifically for physically handicapped children, but the mentally retarded also receive consideration. Special classes are made mandatory in cities and in union free school districts whenever there is a sufficient number to form a special class, and financial aid and supervision are provided. While the number of retarded cases in the average rural school is too small for the formation of special classes, no aid would be available under the law were a required number present, since the law is specifically designed to aid children in the city and union free school districts. Thus rural areas work under great handicaps in bringing aid to exceptional children.

The activities of the Bureau for Physically Handicapped Children, through which the work for exceptional children is directed, are largely advisory and administrative. These activities, which suggest the program of the bureau, are as follows:

1. To advise with other state departments to the end that a coördinated and coöperative program be set up to meet the needs of the state's physically handicapped children.

2. To advise with local authorities, specifically the judges of children's courts, and county officials concerning educational needs, social welfare, and the physical well-being of the children in their respective jurisdictions. The judge of the children's courts occupies a strategic place in the service. He is authorized to issue an order for child care and, if necessary, to charge the cost of it to the county.

3. To confer and advise with local school authorities on the proper care of handicapped children. To assist in planning for their needs through differentiating curriculums, special teachers, and special equipment.

4. To advise and coöperate with other agencies, public and private, interested in the care of handicapped children.

5. To advise with parents in the educational needs of handicapped children and, if necessary, to provide home teaching.

6. To maintain a complete register of all the physically handicapped children in the state.

OTHER PIONEER STATES IN EDUCATION FOR EXCEPTIONAL CHILDREN

The Report of the United States Commissioner of Education for 1928–1930 states that Wisconsin has also been a pioneer in providing for the special needs of handicapped children.

The State Department of Education provides State supervision of such exceptional children, transportation, and, if necessary, special maintenance. Approximately fifteen special classes for mental defectives in towns of less than five thousand have been established, and provision has been made for a state course of study to meet the special needs of the mentally handicapped. Other states which have worth while programs are: Ohio, Michigan, Massachusetts, Minnesota, Connecticut, California, New Jersey, Illinois, and Wyoming. The responsibility of the state for the care of exceptional children in the small rural school is well set forth by Martens:

Rural areas are the state's peculiar responsibility. State authorization, State support, and State supervision are indispensable to the progress of special education in small and isolated communities which are in no way able to assume the additional financial burden alone nor prepared to plan the educational procedure that should be followed. A rural district may not even see its needs or its opportunities until attention is called to them and possibilities are outlined. It is for the state to take the responsibility of pointing the way toward capitalizing its resources and realizing the maximum progress giving such assistance as will make possible a constructive program.[1]

For years, the state has accepted responsibility for the education of normal children in rural areas. This is evidenced by the persistent granting of state aid for education in local districts. It is increasingly evident that the state must also assist local rural districts in the care of exceptional children.

[1] *Report of the United States Commissioner of Education, 1928–1930*, p. 395, Government Printing Office.

OTHER METHODS FOUND PRACTICAL FOR MEETING NEEDS OF EXCEPTIONAL CHILDREN

The county, apparently, is one of the popular and efficient administrative units by which the needs of exceptional children are met. This plan meets the approval of those sections of the country—the south and west—where this administrative unit is in favor. It has proved satisfactory for educational and health programs, provided state aid is available, and there seems no reason why the needs of physically handicapped children cannot be thus efficiently met. Two counties which have accomplished outstanding work for crippled children are Belmont County, Ohio, and Marion County, Illinois. Here county-wide classes are organized in centrally located places to which children are transported and given the special instruction which the local district cannot provide.

Other provisions for the care of the exceptional child are accomplished through the transportation of rural children to a near-by city school where special classes are established, or through the provision of maintenance at one of these centers. A comprehensive development under the former plan has been undertaken in Wisconsin, where rural children who need the care of special classes are transported to them, as regular students who need high school opportunities are transported to them. Maintenance for children in a hospital or private or public school is provided in many sections of the United States— in five states according to the White House Conference Report. In New York State, for instance, crippled children from rural areas receive maintenance in reconstruction homes throughout the state. In Vermont, children from country districts are maintained at state expense at Ormsbee House, a small private school. On this point of maintenance the White House Conference Report makes this significant statement:

While taking the child from his home is not to be generally recommended it is found that in the case of the crippled child, removed from the narrow outlook of his home, and the emotional attitude of his family and given the companionship of children of his own age who are handicapped as he is, he ceases to be the household tyrant and develops rapidly in self-control and initiative. For these reasons, home teaching for children in country districts is advocated only as "a very poor substitute for class teaching" (Ohio) or "a last resort" (Wisconsin) or "when no other method is feasible" (California).[1]

SUMMARY

The exceptional child is the child who deviates from normal physically, mentally, emotionally. The special needs of these exceptional children were formerly met through special state institutions to care for them. Because these institutions have become overcrowded, and, because there is a growing belief that they should care for only the most severe cases, responsibility for the education of exceptional children is more and more devolving upon local communities and local schools. The magnitude of this task was revealed by the recent Report of the White House Conference on Child Health and Protection. The number of exceptional children needing special care totals into millions, about half of whom are located in rural areas where plans to serve their needs are beset with administrative and financial difficulties. The teacher in the small rural school must often attempt to meet within the classroom the special needs of the physically and mentally handicapped and of the gifted child. This is usually accomplished by an adjustment in equipment, materials, and methods. Fortunately, the rural school program is flexible enough to make such adjustments easy.

The classroom teacher should also become acquainted with the national, state, and local agencies established to aid in the education of exceptional children. When possible, aid should be secured from these agencies, and children needing help should be directed to them. The state and the county appear to be the

[1] White House Conference Report on Child Health and Protection, Section III, *Education and Training: Special Education*, pp. 57–58, Century Co., 1932.

administrative units which are destined to assume the responsibility for the education of exceptional children. Already twenty-six states through special legislative provisions are pioneering in the fields of special education. Aid for the exceptional child takes many forms: (a) financial assistance; (b) supervision; (c) supply of special books and materials; and (d) the provision of special courses of study. The regular teacher in the classroom, however, will, so far as rural children are concerned, continue to be the strategic person through whom aid is secured. And this aid will come through individual diagnosis and care. As we come to understand more about individual differences in children, we realize that all are individual. Under this conception the exceptional child is merely one who, more than the average, needs care of a special kind.

SUGGESTED READINGS

Bennett, Annette. "The Retarded Child in the Rural School," *Mental Hygiene*, Vol. 17 (July, 1933), p. 466.

Bulletin 1930, No. 11. *Education of Crippled Children*, United States Office of Education (Dept. of the Interior), Government Printing Office, Washington, D. C.

Bulletin 1931, No. 20. *Biennial Survey of Education in the United States 1928–1930*, Vol. I, Chap. XI, Office of Education (Dept. of the Interior), Government Printing Office, Washington, D. C.

Bulletin 1933, No. 7. *Group Activities for Mentally Retarded Children*, United States Office of Education (Dept. of the Interior), Government Printing Office, Washington, D. C.

Hollingsworth, Leta A. *Gifted Children: Their Nature and Nurture*, Chaps. III, XI, XII, Macmillan, New York, 1926.

Martens, Elise H. *Teachers' Problems with Exceptional Children*, Vol. II, *Gifted Children*, Pamphlet No. 41, United States Office of Education (Dept. of the Interior), Government Printing Office, Washington, D. C., 1933.

McLeod, Beatrice T. *Teachers' Problems with Exceptional Children*, Vol. I, *Blind and Partially Seeing Children*, Pamphlet No. 40, United States Office of Education (Dept. of the Interior), Government Printing Office, Washington, D. C., 1933.

Osburn, Worth James and Rohan, Benjamin J. *Enriching the Curriculum for Gifted Children*, Chaps. VI, VII, VIII, Macmillan, New York, 1931.

Wallace, George L. "Some Observations on the Requirements in a State Program for the Care of the Mentally Deficient," *Mental Hygiene*, Vol. 14 (Oct., 1930), pp. 914–915.

White House Conference on Child Health and Protection. *Education and Training: Special Education*, Sec. III, pp. 3, 55, 94, 164, Century Co., New York, 1932.

MATERIALS FOR DISCUSSION

Consider the following statements. What changes would make them more acceptable to you? What significant issues arise from their study?

1. The program of the small rural school is too crowded with the needs of the average child to allow for the teaching of the exceptional one. The teacher should not attempt it.

2. Handicapped children are best served in state institutions where special needs are met with special care. Here they meet children like themselves and soon find their places in their own social group to which, experience indicates, they speedily adjust themselves.

3. The program of the modern rural school is more easily adjusted to the special needs of exceptional children than that of the urban school. The grouping of children of many ages and interests within a single room affords an opportunity to make adjustments that will meet individual needs.

4. It is believed desirable by many educators that in non-centralized rural schools all children with an I.Q. over 60 should be educated in the local school and under as normal conditions as possible.

5. The enrichment program for the gifted child, now much in vogue, is open to criticism because it tends to develop in him a feeling of snobbishness and superiority.

PART III

EDUCATIONAL CONTROLS
OF THE
SMALL SCHOOL

PART III

EDUCATIONAL CONTROLS
OF THE
SMALL SCHOOL

CHAPTER XI

TRENDS IN CURRICULUM MAKING

It is rather generally agreed by leaders in education that the curriculum is the product of five essential factors: (a) the philosophy or guiding principles upon which it is based; (b) the student group for whom it is made; (c) the environmental controls which condition it; (d) the group responsible for its construction; and (e) the technique of its administration in the classroom. For the purposes of this chapter the curriculum will be discussed from the standpoint of the philosophy upon which the elementary school curriculum has been constructed, the group responsible for its construction, and the technique of its administration. The environmental controls and the student group for whom it has been constructed are discussed in other chapters in this book.

THE PHILOSOPHY OR GUIDING PRINCIPLES UPON WHICH THE CURRICULUM HAS BEEN BASED

The Period of the Three R's. The first organization of curriculum materials in America began in the pioneer school. It consisted almost wholly of the three R's—reading, writing, and arithmetic. It met the needs of a pioneer existence and fulfilled the expectations of the simple agricultural community for which it was designed. The pioneer farmer cherished no illusions about education; that passion for schooling, which later developed almost to the point of an American fetish, came with the crystalization of a political and social philosophy built on the assumption that all men are created free and equal. To the pioneers it was enough that the child learned to read, write,

229

and figure; and once the school had fulfilled this simple obligation it was felt that the main business of growing youth was to
assist in the conquering of a wilderness. As late as the eighteenth century, Benjamin Rush deplored the habit of children
loitering in school, especially in the questionable field of the
languages. "It is," he said, "like turning one's back on a gold
mine to chase butterflies." The objective of this pioneer school
was to give children the skills of literacy, to attain which a
single textbook for each subject was sufficient material. There
was no course of study save that organization furnished by the
textbook. This domination of the textbook continued many
years. In 1922, when every state in the Union had elementary
courses of study, Charles M. Reinoehl made an analytic study of
them and concluded there was greater uniformity in the slavish
following of textbooks than in the intelligent use of the course
of study. Caswell and Campbell say in their recent book
Curriculum Development, printed in 1935, that this traditional
concept of teaching is still the dominant means of determining
the scope of work in the American schools. The persistence in
the use of the textbook as the course of study was due to the
fact that the plan was logical and easy. It was easy for the
administrator because a simple typewritten sheet indicating
texts and pages to be covered year by year and grade by grade
was sufficient guide for the school; it was easy for the teacher
because little effort was necessary in the assignment, and practically no lesson-planning was required for teaching it. The
technique of presenting the material was memorization and
drill; and emphasis was placed on the subject matter to be
taught rather than upon the child to be developed. The pioneer
school was interested in children, not because they were considered valuable on their own level of achievement, but because
they were potential adults.

The Period of Supplementing Course and Materials. The
materials of the period of the three R's were so lacking in vitality
and the technique of teaching was so deadly that improvement
was inevitable. The improvement came, however, not in the

organization of materials, but in the addition of enriching features to the curriculum. The philosophy behind the curriculum remained practically the same. Schools were considered as institutions which prepared children for life and the curriculum as an instrument for this preparation. Emphasis on skills based on the three R's still dominated the school and was reflected in the course of study which served them.

Change for the better came in two ways: (a) new courses were added to enrich the three R's and (b) supplementary readings enriched the textbooks. Other readers called "supplementary" were added to the reading and teachers were urged to use them. Small libraries began to appear and parallel reading was required in nearly all subjects. Supplementary to drill and the question-and-answer method of teaching was the introduction of the discussion as a feature of class recitations. Pupils discovered in the parallel readings that opinions of authorities often differed, even on a point of fact; discussion naturally followed this discovery and this method of administering the curriculum did much to enliven the recitation of the second period of curriculum development. But the method of organizing the materials, enriched as they were, remained consistently text-dominated; such new courses as were added were outlined by the pages of an adopted textbook. The chief differences of this period lay in the fact that more subject matter was provided, and that the type of it changed the barren, narrow curriculum of the three R's to something more vital.

During this period of curriculum development there were three systems of book adoptions in use, and, since the curriculum was almost wholly text-dominated, the methods of adoption were important. The three systems were: local, county, and state. For the small rural school, local adoption predominated. Under our modern conception of education the choice of textbooks to fit local conditions seems desirable, but for the teacher in the small school who had no course of study, nor outlined curriculum, to guide him the task was intolerable. In the counties and states where book adoptions were made, organized courses of study, if available at all, predetermined the subject matter to be taught and gave the order for its teaching. No encouragement was given for organizing the materials of instruction in a manner differing from the textbook. Such courses were made almost entirely by administrators.

EFFORTS TO LINK EDUCATION WITH LIFE

In the latter years of the nineteenth century, there was a definite effort made to link education with life, and the curriculum faithfully reflected this philosophy. This movement was an outgrowth of John Dewey's experimental school in Chicago, established in 1896, and his increasing body of philosophic contributions to education. Opposed to the philosophy that education was to train children for life—and life began at 21—was the new philosophy which taught that children were important in their own right, at every achievement level, and that the best way to prepare them for adulthood was to give them opportunity for experiences vitally concerned with every stage of their development. Children were no longer considered as plastic materials to be moulded by adults at will, but active agents capable of self-direction and self-growth. Leaders in this new educational philosophy, soon calling themselves "progressive," further held that this self-direction and self-planning tended to develop what they called the "whole child," and in this point of view they had the support of biologists, who held to the organistic conception of physical growth, and of the Gestalt psychologists who believed and taught the principles of configuration in learning. Whereas, said the leaders, education in the past has been concerned only with the mental development of children, the new education proposes a wholeness in the educational program which concerns itself with the physical, mental, and emotional development of children. This departure represented a new trinity in the educational progress and was destined to have far-reaching consequences in the organization of curriculum materials.

As a result of this philosophy of linking education with life many subjects hitherto ignored by education were added to the curriculum such as physical training, health education, home economics, music, manual arts, agriculture, and other vocational subjects. These additions at first appeared to accomplish their purposes; namely, to make education life-like within the school and to strengthen its affinity to life outside. The addition of such courses, however, had little effect upon the curriculum organization. Practice, as usual, lagged behind philosophy. The organization of curriculum materials was almost wholly in the hands of administrators, superintendents of schools, principals, and supervisors—people removed from the classroom and children. The state texts and state courses of study to fit them, both written by state supervisors, were the order of the day. In progressive urban areas, city systems set up their own courses of study and laid the foundation for the reform in curriculum making which was to come later. The small elementary school in rural areas, however, was destined for many years to operate under an organization of teaching materials which amounted to a prescription narrowly conceived in terms of subject matter only. This was almost an insurmountable difficulty for the teachers who accepted the new philosophy in education and who sought ways to put it into practice. It was further complicated in the small schools because of an administrative difficulty. The state courses of study were almost invariably organized for the graded urban system. Not only was the organization of materials made for one grade only, but it was set up for the length of term in the local urban schools. This always exceeded the term of the small rural schools, sometimes by as much as four months. Consequently, the teacher in these small schools was confronted with a course of study often at variance with his philosophy of education, organized for an administrative system different from his own, and outlined for a term of teaching longer than he was allowed.

In spite of these difficulties, however, there were progressive teachers here and there who instituted modern methods of administering the curriculum materials in harmony with the modern educational philosophy of Dewey. School projects were begun in this period, clubs were organized, school papers started, and field trips undertaken. Methods as well as materials showed changes. The principle that "we learn to do by doing" was recognized and "activities" were introduced; the project method appeared; and to the techniques of question, answer, and discussion was added a third, the participation of children in activities. But these activities were called "extra-curricular" and the name denoted their function. They were in addition to the regular routine and consequently considered of secondary importance. Academic traditions prevailed and were so strong that academic skills retained their places of honor, forming almost the whole basis of promotion from one grade to another. The newer subjects only became respectable when they became formal enough to become dull. So practical and vital a subject as Health, for instance, deteriorated under such formality into a mere recital of facts, such as the listing of the bones of the body and the tracing of the alimentary canal. Apparently the responsibility of making the study of health a means to more abundant living was but slightly felt. Most of these newer subjects have never been taken seriously, a fact suggested by the ruthless curtailment of them during the late economic depression.

EFFORTS TO VOCATIONALIZE EDUCATION

The movement to link education with life was stimulated during the early years of the twentieth century by the effort to vocationalize education. Urban development, with its corresponding industrial expansion, was well under way at this time, and the new industries needed skilled and unskilled workmen for their factories. There was not time to develop an apprenticeship system, such as had obtained in European countries; consequently industry turned to the schools, requesting that courses be added to the curriculum which would train the youth of America to take their place in the rapidly expanding industrial system. The new social order demanded an army of workers, each for his particular field of work, prepared by the public school. Efforts to vocationalize the public schools were strongest in the high schools, but elementary education was also affected. In the cities manual training and shopwork were added to the elementary curriculum, and while these were considered as having educational value *per se*, there was back of the new program the philosophy that it was well to begin early in the training of young America to use its hands. A counterpoint of this movement in cities, was developed in rural areas—the effort to adjust the whole school curriculum to agricultural pursuits and to rural life in general. To understand this educational movement it is necessary to understand the economic and social developments of the rural areas at that time.

The rapid growth of cities characterizing the last years of the nineteenth and early years of the twentieth century was the result of (a) the immigration of large groups of Europeans to America, and (b) the migration of large numbers of farm peoples to cities. The latter was looked upon with distrust by many of the leaders in the national life. They felt this constant drift of American farm youth to the cities to be a menace to the welfare of the whole nation. Theodore Roosevelt, then President of the United States, was outspoken in his distrust of a movement which threatened the stability of rural life. In a letter to Professor Liberty Hyde Bailey of Cornell University, President Roosevelt clearly stated his philosophy of rural life. He believed that the permanent greatness of a nation rested upon the soil and upon the men who tilled it. He pointed out to Professor Bailey that history repeatedly teaches the same lesson —no nation can rise higher than the character of its rural population. He felt that the loss of this population to the industrial centers was a serious one, and urged a newly created commission to develop a plan to stop the drain of rural peoples to the city. It was this philosophy of rural life which led President Roosevelt to appoint the Country Life Commission which now bears his name. Among other requests, the President asked the Commission for a procedure which would build up in children a compelling desire to live on the farm.[1]

The redirection of "rural schools to the training of children for life on the farm" is one of the outcomes of the Report of the Commission. The Commission which reported in 1909, emphasized the economic hardship of the farmer, the inequalities of taxes, and the need for a redirected education for rural youth. Every part of the United States was in agreement, according to the Report, on the demand that education be related to living, that schools express life, and that, in rural districts, schools educate by means of agriculture and country-life subjects. The Commission held that the schools were responsible for ineffective farming, loss of ideals, and the drift to town. The chief concern of the Commission was with the welfare of adult society, both urban and rural, and its direction to the school was clear. In other words, the Commission held that the nation was best served by a stable rural population and that the proper way to stabilize it was to begin with the young, prospective farmers. Educational leaders lent willing ears to this doctrine, for soon state and county officials began calling upon the rural school for help in the indoctrinating process. Proceeding upon the assumption that rural life was indeed "the good life," leaders in the movement held that indoctrination should begin in the elementary school and that once indoctrinated the children of the high schools should be trained to use their heads and hands especially in the field of agriculture and home economics. The efforts to vocationalize education in the rural schools were carried to unreasonable lengths, and the whole course of study was planned in the interest of agriculture and rural life. A series of farm textbooks were developed, so that rural children received all of their education in terms of rural materials.

[1] For further information on the Roosevelt Country Life Commission see *Commission on Country Life with an Introduction by Theodore Roosevelt*, Sturgis and Walton Co., New York, 1911.

Their readers became "farm readers" and their arithmetic was based solely on the needs of farm accounting. Since the textbook organization was the course of study, farm children were being exposed solely to an indoctrination process set up for the purpose of predisposing them to the farm and of definitely preparing them for farm work.

This plan for the stabilization of farm life at the expense of farm youth was seriously questioned as early as 1916 and in 1921 the Rural Education Department of the National Education Association adopted a platform which declared that "the standard of the educational product is the same country and city." Later this statement was employed by the Department of Superintendence of the National Education Association in its *Third Yearbook, Research in Constructing the Elementary School Curriculum* as follows:

In rural districts, the objectives of elementary education are not different from those in the city, but the means of reaching them and materials available differ from those in large centers of population. . . . The ultimate purpose of elementary education is the same everywhere, but the content and method through which it is achieved varies.[1]

In 1931 Orville G. Brim in the Thirtieth Yearbook of the National Society for the Study of Education emphatically stated:

The general objectives of rural education do not differ from objectives of urban education on the same level. Both are concerned in realizing the maximal individual growth and self-expression and in promoting greater social well-being and progress through the on-coming generation. Its responsibilities are to the child and to society as a whole, not to the local group whose children it is educating.[2]

[1] *Research in Constructing the Elementary School Curriculum. Third Yearbook*, p. 23, Dept. of Superintendence, National Education Association, 1925.

[2] National Society for the Study of Education. *Status of Rural Education, Thirtieth Yearbook*, p. 260, Public School Publishing Co., 1931. Quoted by permission of the Society.

The profession generally accepts this point of view and the curriculum for the elementary schools of today, as a whole, is organized on this principle. However, Professor Fannie W. Dunn says that "the earlier position is still more or less an influential determiner of the curriculum in certain situations, whether because the conviction is explicitly held or because it persists as an uncritical mind-set."[1]

MODERN TRENDS IN CURRICULUM MAKING

Under the impetus of the new educational philosophy there began in American education a movement for a complete reorganization of the curriculum and for the past twenty-five years the reorganization has held the center of the educational stage. Much of the inquiry has been concerned with the selection of subject matter, choice of which, in general is based on (a) its importance in and relation to a general subject matter field; (b) the relationship of the selection to the interpretation of modern problems; (c) child interest and use of the subject matter; and (d) its use in after school years. As Caswell and Campbell point out, the first two of these bases are determined by tradition and the latter two by scientific study.[2] In each of the last two, honest and intensive efforts have been made to arrive at logical and psychologically correct conclusions upon which curricula can be constructed. The trends, characteristic of a modern program of curricula construction, are listed below.

First, there has been a trend toward centering the curriculum in the interests and purposes of children. In the program of reorganization, theoretically at least, the child was placed first. This, in part, explains the recent interest and activity in the field of child development. Studies have been made of the interests, the habits, the health, and the environmental opportunities of groups of children in different localities. The reading interests of children, their health as affected by different

[1] *Ibid.* p. 100.
[2] Caswell, Hollis L. and Campbell, Doak S. *Curriculum Development*, p. 255, American Book Company, 1935.

Photograph by M. G. Schneckenburger

Projects developed from a unit on farm life create interest in the wonder of "common things."

environments, their use of leisure time, and children's use of language have also been investigated in seeking bases for curriculum development. These studies are as yet too isolated, sporadic, and insufficient for generalization; but even so they give promise of essential help in building up a curriculum that will meet the needs and interests of the child. A study now in progress in Breathitt County, Kentucky, while so far only affecting the high school curriculum, illustrates the case in point. Sponsored by the Southern Women's Educational Alliance, the Carnegie Corporation, the United States Department of Agriculture, and the University of Kentucky, a five-year study of local children and local environment is being made. It was revealed, at the end of the first year of investigation, that ninety per cent of the children of the county had hookworm and that whole families lived in windowless shacks. As a result, curriculum changes designed to help children solve their own social problems, were decided upon. All foreign languages, all mathematics beyond elementary algebra, and all old-type courses in history were eliminated. In their stead were put courses in hygiene and physical education related to local health needs, intense practice in English, agriculture, home economics, and a social-studies course centered largely about regional economic conditions. Simultaneously textbooks yielded to radio broadcasts, or were supplemented by government reports and current newspapers. In another year the elementary school curriculum will undergo a like reorganization.

This isolated example of curricula construction for the modern school indicates the interest of education in meeting the needs of children in terms of their environment. It also exemplifies the concern of education for the all-round development of children. As in the past, the adequate mental development of children is an important responsibility of the school, but sharing honors with it is the obligation to see that the development flowers—physically, emotionally, and spiritually—into a harmonious and well-adjusted personality.

Second, there is a trend toward organizing curriculum materials into an integrated program grouped about "centers of interest" or "units of work." The unit of work represents a decided break with traditional methods of curriculum organization and is thus characterized: (a) the units are large major topics which may or may not represent a logical development of subject matter; (b) the units are usually outlined in segments of group culture; (c) pupil interests are considered in the selection of topics; (d) the units provide for flexibility in administration.

Under this conception of curriculum organization the old subject matter lines tend to disappear, only to reappear in the form of problems. The California Curriculum Commission in speaking of the place of the social studies in an integrated program thus illustrates the point:

For many years the separate subjects which are included in social studies have been taught. But it is no longer sufficient to teach only the factual material from these subjects; schools are charged with the responsibility of functional interpretation of these subjects. . . . The memorizing of the rivers of Japan or China would have little social value for a child, but the study of Pacific relations would be of inestimable value and have meaning to the child in the schools of California. An understanding of Pacific relations would involve the development of attitudes, an appreciation for the contributions made by Oriental civilizations, the implications of the policies of these Pacific neighbors, all of which would be essential to the active participation of citizens in California.[1]

The organization of curriculum materials into units of work is usually accompanied by a number of varied activities. A single textbook and the formal recitation suffice no longer for teaching and learning. In order for children to solve the problems set up by such a form of curriculum organization, it is necessary to dip into many subject-matter fields.

Units of work are organized around life situations and involve the use of many books, charts, maps, pictures, and innumerable other aids. Excursions are planned to give that reality and vitality to

[1] California State Curriculum Commission. *Teachers' Guide to Child Development in the Intermediate Grades*, pp. 14–15, California Dept. of Education, 1936.

learning which comes through first-hand experiences. Many related fields are brought together around one center of interest. Art, music, literature, history, geography, science have each a contribution to make to a complete understanding of any given cultural epoch or social function.[1]

Subject matter in the modern school is treated as a means rather than as an end in education; no longer reverenced for its own sake, the use of it is functional. Subject matter is related to life.

Third, the modern curriculum is more comprehensive in its scope than at any time in the past. It is conceived to be concerned with all of the experiences participated in by children. These may be in the school, the home, or the community.

The so-called "subjects" represent adult attempts to organize the environment so as to give added meaning to significant aspects of our general experiences. Modern education is not concerned with this subject matter as such, but with the child's total experience, his total learnings, his present and potential behavior. All learning is the outcome of things done, and is integrated and unified around wholesome living. It is through participation in living that attitudes and habits are formed, skills are acquired, valuable information is gained, and character is built. The only required or compulsory curriculum is then, after all, practice in living. This problem is as old as man; time and environment may change, human inventions come and go, but to learn to live one's daily life well is still of prime importance as the basic purpose of the educative process.[2]

Thus education seeks to know and interpret the environment of the child through the organization of materials which are a part of the modern scene.

Not only does the school look to the community for educational experiences, but it also draws from it curricula materials. This type of curriculum organization is technically known as the "social functions procedure" and is one of the newest techniques used in delineating the scope of subject matter. It represents

[1] *Ibid.* p. XI.
[2] *Ibid.* p. 3.

an effort on the part of the school to organize the curriculum so that what is learned in school is easily transferred to life situations. Indeed, it is an effort to introduce children to life situations, on the assumption that community life has certain major and universal problems about which minor problems tend to cluster. As in the units of work procedure in curriculum organization, the technique provides for the integration of all subjects in a common core. Efforts are made to develop the curriculum materials out of the interests of children. This trend in curriculum organization is exemplified by the 1934 course of study for the elementary schools of Virginia. The outline for Grade I reads in part:

The program of instruction can be made significantly interesting and educational by utilizing the vital experiences which the home and the school present daily in the form of challenging problems to young children. . . . The experiences provided in Grade I should lead children to accept and to discharge effectively their responsibilities as members of the home and school groups. This will be achieved as children develop desirable generalizations to guide their actions at home and school.

Aspects Selected for Emphasis

1. How do we protect and maintain life and health in our home and school?
2. How do the things we make and grow help us?
3. How does our family provide itself with food, clothing, and shelter?
4. How do members of our family travel from place to place?
5. How can we have an enjoyable time at home and school?
6. What can we do to make our home and school more beautiful and pleasant?[1]

Fourth, there is a tendency to adapt curriculum materials to the needs of the individual student. One of the most significant findings of modern psychologists is the establishment of the fact that each individual is unique and different. Parents and

[1] State Board of Education. *Virginia Elementary Schools, Grades I–VII*, p. 33.

teachers have long been aware of the individual differences in children, but modern psychology has validated this belief by establishing proof that children not only differ in nature, but that nurture develops variance in physical equipment, cultural background, and emotional stability. With these differences the curriculum must reckon. As a consequence, there is no longer an effort made to force every child through the same curriculum and at the same rate of speed. The high school curriculum adjusts itself to this philosophy by establishing elective courses of study. The modern elementary school adjusts itself to the needs of individual children within the framework of the regular curriculum materials. This adjustment presupposes, on the part of the teacher, a rich knowledge of each individual child, and a program of guidance based on an honest effort to proceed in the light of this knowledge. The advice of the California Curriculum Commission to the elementary teachers of that state aptly illustrates this point.

The great contribution of educational psychology to the science of teaching is irrefutable evidence that children differ widely in health and physical vigor; in physiological maturity; in sensory perception, particularly in seeing and hearing; in general intelligence; in emotional response; in interests; in out-of-school experiences; in attitudes toward school; in social maturity.

Individual differences make of every child a special problem.

One pupil may need to engage in basic perceptual experiencing, a second pupil may need additional drill, a third may need to be assigned learning exercises commensurate with his capacity to learn, a fourth may need an explanation or certain other remedial instruction, and so on. The needs of individual pupils are so varied that a list of types does not seem feasible except when dealing with a restricted subject-matter field.[1]

Fifth, the teacher is allowed a large measure of freedom in adapting the curriculum materials to the needs of her classroom. This trend in the administration of the curriculum is an es-

[1] California State Curriculum Commission. *Teachers' Guide to Child Development in the Intermediate Grades,* p. 10, California State Dept. of Education, 1936.

sential step in the development of a modern school. No matter how progressive the philosophy of the teacher, nor how modern her methods, the program with children suffers if she is circumscribed by a set course of study. This situation, however, is less likely to develop in the use of a modern course of study. State departments of education, as in the past, still print the courses of study used in rural schools, but with two important differentiations. Nearly always the modern course of study is the coöperative product of teachers in the field. It is, therefore, a development from the work of teachers themselves rather than a prescription handed down from the administration. The organization of curriculum materials by teachers close to children has had the salutary effect of giving both direction and freedom in their use. Further, in nearly every modern course of study, teachers in the field are urged to use the organization as suggestive only, and to adjust the subject matter to the needs of individual children. Consequently, the teacher need not wait until January to teach South America, if an important conference in Buenos Aires in October has stirred the interest of his children toward that distant city. By the light of this new measure of freedom each teacher, in a sense, makes his own course of study.

SUMMARY

The development in curriculum making may be roughly divided into three periods. The first period is known as the Period of the 3 R's. It was characterized by a simple curriculum pattern composed of reading, writing, and arithmetic. This pattern was dominated by the single textbook; there was no organization of subject matter save that offered by the adopted text. The method of teaching was almost wholly composed of the testing of materials which had been previously memorized. This simple pattern of organizing materials and of teaching them fitted well the educational philosophy of the period. The community required of the schools that children be made literate and that they achieve a measure of efficiency in the use of what we now call "the tool subjects."

The second period is designated as the Period of Supplementary Courses and Materials. No great improvement took place in this period except in the addition to the curriculum of supplementary courses and the enrichment of existing courses with parallel readings. Textbooks continued to dominate the organization of curriculum materials. To the technique of question and answer there was added the discussion method, a technique which naturally grew out of an enriched reading program. The philosophy of education in this period showed interesting variations from that of the earlier period. There were definite efforts to link education with life, evidenced by the addition to the curricula of many life processes hitherto ignored by education, specifically in the field of the vocations. In the rural areas the attempt at the vocationalization of education was taken to unreasonable lengths. An effort was made in the rural schools to direct the whole curriculum toward the promotion of farm life. This position was later repudiated by the profession.

The third and last period is designated as the Modern Period in Curriculum Construction. Much of the reorganization has centered in two areas: (a) the selection of the bases for delimiting subject matter—four in number were generally agreed upon. These were: (1) significance to an organized field of knowledge, (2) significance to an understanding of contemporary life, (3) adult use, and (4) child interest and use—and (b) the development of techniques to encompass these selected materials within the limits of an organization.

The period is further characterized by an intense interest in child study and by an effort to make the curriculum and school child-centered. This philosophy of the child-centered school has greatly influenced the methods of teaching. Children participate in the life of the school in a manner never tolerated before. A study of the modern scene reveals certain results achieved and trends in process. These are as follows:

1. There is a trend in curriculum making to organize subject matter in harmony with the new philosophy of education. The curriculum is becoming child-centered and child needs and interests are often the determining factors in the selection of materials and the administration of them.

2. Materials are organized in large subject-matter topics which may or may not be logical in development. Often the materials cut across many subject matter fields. There is a tendency to organize the curriculum into large problems for whose solutions many different fields of human knowledge must be canvassed.

3. There is a tendency to adapt curriculum materials to the needs of individual children, a trend in harmony with the discoveries of modern psychologists. Efforts are no longer made to force elementary school children through the same course of study and at the same rate of speed. Adjustments, through skillful guidance, take place within the framework of prescribed subject matter.

4. Evidence is present that the modern course of study allows much freedom for the administration in the classroom. There is little prescription. The teacher finds in the modern course of study real opportunities for creative teaching. Curriculum making has become a shared responsibility. No longer are courses of study determined solely by administrators and supervisors. Classroom teachers are participating in ever increasing numbers. Further, lay groups, as well as professional groups, are contributing to the modern organization of curriculum materials. This, too, is a part of the new philosophy of education.

5. The modern courses of study are the product of both the traditional philosophic approach to the organization of curriculum materials and the modern scientific analysis, which includes a study of the child and of adult society and represents an effort to determine the educational materials which best serve both.

SUGGESTED READINGS

Bagley, William C. *Education and Emergent Man*, Chap. X, Thomas Nelson and Sons, 1934.

California State Curriculum Commission. *Teachers' Guide to Child Development in the Intermediate Grades*, Chap. I, California Department of Education, Sacramento, California, 1936.

Caswell, Hollis L. and Campbell, Doaks. *Curriculum Development*, Chap. X, American Book Co., New York, 1935.

Counts, George S. *Social Foundations of Education*, Part III, Chap. III, Charles Scribners' Sons, New York, 1934.

Draper, Edgar Marion. *Principles and Techniques of Curriculum Making*, Chap. III, D. Appleton-Century Co., New York, 1936.

National Society for the Study of Education. Twenty-Sixth Year-book, Part I, *Curriculum Making Past and Present*, Chaps. VI, XXII, XXV, Public School Publishing Co., Bloomington, Illinois, 1926.

National Society for the Study of Education. Thirtieth Yearbook, Part I, *The Status of Rural Education* Chap. IV, Public School Publishing Co., Bloomington, Illinois, 1931.

University of the State of New York. *Cardinal Objectives in Education: Trends in Unit Teaching*, Chap. I, University of the State of New York Press, Albany, New York, 1934.

Norton, John K. and Norton, Margaret Alltucker. *Foundations of Curriculum Building*, Chap. XVII, Ginn and Co., New York, 1936.

Zirbes, Laura. *Curriculum Trends*, Association for Childhood Education, Washington, D. C., 1935. Pamphlet.

MATERIALS FOR DISCUSSION

Consider the following statements. What changes would make them more acceptable to you? What significant issues arise from their study?

1. The tendency to develop curriculum materials in terms of local needs is at variance with sound educational principles, and defeats the ends of education in a democracy.

2. "The general objectives of rural education do not differ from objectives of urban education on the same level. Both are concerned in recognizing maximal individual growth and self-expression, and in promoting greater social well-being and progress through the on-coming generation."

3. The effort to make the curriculum child-centered is a questionable procedure in education. The interests of children are transitory, have no educational value, and are not always best for the individual or the group.

4. The organization of curriculum materials into units of group culture is superior to the logical development usually employed in textbooks.

5. In the average elementary school it is impossible to introduce into practice the philosophy of individual differences. Were it possible, the procedure is open to serious criticism. The dominant purpose of the elementary school in a democracy is to synthesize rather than to individualize children.

. . .

CHAPTER XII

DIFFERENTIATIONS OF THE CURRICULUM TO MEET THE NEEDS OF THE SMALL RURAL SCHOOL

It was suggested in Chapter V that the outstanding difficulty of the small rural school lay in the form of organization. Eight grades and twenty-five children of varying ages and interest levels present to the average teacher in the small school a seemingly impossible task. This problem of organization has been a persistent one of long standing and many plans have been advanced for its solution. Important among these plans have been the following: (a) the consolidation of schools into larger units with a teacher for each grade; (b) the passage of laws bringing about longer school terms, better attendance, and the building of more adequate school plants; (c) laws to limit the number of grades to be offered by the small school; (d) definite standards set for the rural schools; and (e) the raising of standards for the professional training of teachers. While each of these administrative efforts has been, in a measure, helpful, none has been wholly successful.

Of recent years, leaders in the field of education have advanced the theory that the fundamental difficulty of the small school lies deeper than administration and organization in a negativistic attitude adopted by both the public and the profession toward the small school. Over a period of years this attitude has developed into a mind-set of studied neglect, which no administration can solve. These leaders further insist that, since administrative practices have failed and the small school persists in significant numbers, it becomes the part of wisdom to improve conditions within the school itself. Professor Fannie W. Dunn, Teachers College, Columbia University, one of the pioneers in the movement to improve the small school, and one of its most articulate leaders, makes the viewpoint clear in the following statement:

Although consolidation of schools is progressing today more rapidly than ever, there is growing, also, a clear realization of the necessity for parallel improvement of educational facilities in one-teacher schools in order that genuine educational opportunities may be available to all our rural children *now*, not forty years hence. In a number of states today, school terms of equal length for all types of schools are required; graduation from a two-year normal school is set by law as the minimum qualification for teachers in all types of schools; and standard buildings and modern equipment are increasingly provided for one-teacher schools.

Necessary as they are, such improvements have not brought the one-teacher school to the fullest realization of its possibilities. Ask any well-trained teacher in one of these better rural schools today, what her chief problems are, and she will tell you, "There are too many classes. Besides, I don't have time to use some of the newer methods of organizing material to meet the children's real needs and interests. If I try to combine my classes to make more time, the children cannot work together profitably because the subject-matter is not equally suitable for the different classes combined."

If we analyze the situation, we shall find that the underlying cause of the too-many-class condition is the absence of an adapted curriculum. An adapted curriculum is a facility almost universally lacking in rural schools at present.[1]

The difficulty of an organization in a school with many grades and few teachers, together with the plans used for meeting this problem, was presented in Chapters V and VI. These plans, however, provided only the skeleton and framework for the educational process. Concomitant with such plans, is the necessity for an organization of curriculum materials to fit the framework for the combination of subjects and the alternation of grades. Nearly all of the state departments of education

[1] Dunn, Fannie W. and Bathurst, Effie. *Social Studies for Rural Schools— Guide and General Outline*, p. 2, Dept. Rural Education, Teachers College, Columbia University, 1931.

recommend some sort of an organization for the grouping of classes, but few make any adjustments in curriculum materials to meet their own recommendations. The usual plan followed by the state course of study is to set up the curriculum organization for a nine months' term for a graded system of schools and then suggest that the small rural school make the necessary adjustments. This procedure amounts to the organization of the state course of study in terms of the local urban situation and an invitation to the rural school to make the most of it. Two weaknesses in this procedure are apparent.

In the first place, the term of the average rural school is materially shorter than the term of the urban school, and the average attendance of children is lower. According to the 1930–1932 Biennial Report of the United States Office of Education, this difference in school term amounts to approximately one school month per year. In many of the agricultural states, however, the difference is as much as three months. The average attendance of the two types of schools showed a difference of two months. While this difference in the length of the school term and the number of days of attendance may not seem great for one year, over the period of school life for the child the difference is considerable. Assuming that the child continues to live in the same community for twelve years the urban child's opportunity for attendance at school within these years would exceed the rural child's by 259.2 days. In line with these facts the Biennial Survey asks the following question:

The following arithmetical problem may be presented: If a school term of 181.5 days a year is needed in order for the city child to complete the regular 12 year public school course, how many years would it take for the rural child who has a school term of 159.9 days to complete the same course? Based on the number of day's schooling offered, the answer is 13.6 years.[1]

One way of meeting the curriculum problem in rural schools would be to extend the number of years required to complete it.

[1] *Biennial Survey of Education 1930–1932*, p. 40, United States Office of Education (Dept. of the Interior), Government Printing Office.

Obviously, however, this would be unfair to rural children, and would indeed amount to a penalty for attendance on a rural school. As unfair as it appears, there are a few states that proceed in this direction; they organize these courses for eight or nine months' terms and suggest to the schools of shorter terms that they either abbreviate the work or spread the yearly outline over two years.

OTHER PLANS REPORTED

In a study made in 1931,[1] there was reported the suggestion that the additional months necessary for the completion of the course be acquired by children (a) in the summer through prescribed courses in agriculture and home economics, or (b) reading circle work, or (c) by passing an examination. All of these plans work undue hardships upon children enrolled in the small school and have not been widely adopted. However, the usual plan of requiring a rural school of six months to cover the curriculum materials organized for a nine months term is equally unfair, though perhaps not so obviously.

The second weakness in the usual procedure of curriculum organization lies in the fact that the responsibility for the necessary adjustments is usually placed on the teacher. The following suggestion taken from a state course of study in a state having a large enrollment in the small rural school is typical:

There are many phases of English work that frequently may be continued to advantage in rural schools. A study of the several units in the different grades and acquaintance with the abilities and needs of the pupils will assist in effective combinations. Among these units which lend themselves to such procedures are letter writing, creative expression of various types, learning to use the dictionary, appreciation of poetry and prose literature. There should also be a close coöperation with the social studies.

[1] National Society for the Study of Education. *The Status of Rural Education, Thirtieth Yearbook*, p. 115, Public School Publishing Company, 1931. Quoted by permission of the Society.

These suggestions, while better than nothing, are a naïve way of dismissing a very difficult situation.

The truth of the matter is that the teacher in the small rural school is not prepared by education or experience to perform the technical task of reorganizing the curriculum materials provided in the average state course of study, and the state department of education that expects it of him is either ignorant of the facts or refuses to face them. The low professional status of the median teacher in the small school is well known. Recent studies have revealed this status over long periods of time and in great detail.[1]

All of them indicate that the confidence of state departments of education in the ability of the young rural teachers to manipulate curriculum materials is misplaced. Curriculum organization is a large task requiring expert guidance and the pooling of many abilities. Large city systems are aware of this truth, as their curriculum bureaus of experts bear witness.

Because of the weaknesses in the present practices of curriculum organization, there is a growing belief in the field of rural education that the best way to meet the curriculum needs of the small school is to make a course of study specifically for it. A few states have already made considerable progress toward accomplishing this end by issuing state courses of study made for the teacher in the small school. As in practically all plans for improvement in the field of rural education, the demonstration school has led the way.

THE COLLINGS EXPERIMENT

In 1923 Professor Ellsworth Collings of the University of Oklahoma reported an experiment in the curriculum organization of a one-room rural school, organized to answer the following self-imposed question:

Can the country school curriculum be selected directly from the

[1] Wofford, Kate V. *A History of the Status and Training of Elementary Rural Teachers in the United States, 1860–1930.*

purposes of boys and girls in real life? If so, to what extent, with what effect, and under what conditions? [1]

The schools selected for the experiment were located in McDonald County, Missouri. One was a typical one-room school of forty-one pupils.

At the beginning of the experiment, the schools had the usual organization of grades and used a typical curriculum outline. The experiment lasted four years and its contribution to curriculum making in the small school has been considerable. Dr. Collings disregarded all grade lines and grouped his children on what he called a natural basis. The mental, social, and interest characteristics of the children, were considered in the grouping, and efforts were made to have children of nearly equal abilities in the same groups. The children naturally found themselves in one of three groups: (a) the children from 6 to 8 years; (b) the children from 9 years to 11; and (c) the children from 12 years and upwards.

"The obvious advantage of such an organization," reported Professor Collings, "is the opportunity afforded pupils by means of the larger groups and longer work periods to engage actively in working out their purposes effectively. In addition, such an organization provides rich opportunity for natural expression of the social traits of children. For instance, it is possible for the 8-year-old pupils of the first group to assume leadership in the group's work, while the 6-year-old pupils might quite naturally be the followers in some phases of the work. Then, too, boys and girls find that coöperation, fair play, and initiative are functioning factors in realizing their purposes in such a democracy of childhood." [2]

In corresponding harmony with the grouping of children was the organization of the curriculum into four types of projects: (a) play purposes expressed in games, folk dancing, and dramatization; (b) excursions which consisted of the purposeful study

[1] Collings, Ellsworth. *An Experiment with a Project Curriculum*, p. 4, Macmillan, 1923.
[2] *Ibid.* p. 50.

of problems connected with environments and activities of people; (c) appreciation of the story, as told in words, songs, pictures, music; and (d) the expression of ideas in concrete form, constructing, drawing, and cooking. These subject groups are not radically different from other forms of subject organizations; their chief difference lies rather in the source of curriculum materials. These were developed from the day-by-day purposes and experiences of the pupils. Hence the curriculum was at all times a developing body of materials, rather than the printed course of study usually handed to the teacher. Opportunities for acquiring the skills and facts commonly accepted as the ends in elementary education developed out of the daily "purposes" of children. While learning under this type of organization appears incidental and undirected, the testing of children at the end of the experiment revealed that it had been effective. In every test the children in the experimental school outranked the children in the control schools. Dr. Collings reported on this feature of the experiment as follows:

An experience of four years with the school . . . indicates that children can set up their own purposes and can work these purposes out effectively under proper guidance. . . . They grow in qualities of initiative, judgment, and self-direction. . . .[1]

As valuable as the results to children were, the plan would be difficult to initiate into the average small school, chiefly because the teacher of the school is not properly educated to do it. The situation is further complicated by a lack in proper supervision, and the combination of these two difficulties practically prohibits the initiation of the plan into the average school. A different type of teacher education in the future, already in evidence in a few progressive institutions, may eliminate this difficulty of the present teacher. It is possible that the product may even be so excellent that no supervision will be needed. In that event there will be no reason why the plan might not be successfully used in any small elementary school.

[1] *Ibid.* p. 225.

The experiment, however, has demonstrated certain features which are practical and are possible of imitation now. It demonstrated the practicability of disregarding the traditional grading in small schools and the substitution there for the grouping of children into as few as three "natural" groups. The experiment seems to prove that the curriculum can be selected directly from the purposes and experiences of boys and girls and that they profit from the procedure. It suggests that the course of study in the future might properly include in its outline a wide variety of projects actually worked out by boys and girls.

THE EXPERIMENT AT QUAKER GROVE

The Quaker Grove experiment was begun in a one-room school in Warren County, New Jersey, at about the same time that Professor Collings began his experiment in Missouri. Supervised by Professor Fannie W. Dunn, under the auspices of the Rural Education Department of Teachers' College, Columbia University, the experiment was an attempt "to discover whether by an organization of the school suited to its essential conditions, its limitations might be overcome and its potentialities realized." [1]

Two questions set up at the beginning of the experiment suggest the limitations of the one-room school recognized by Professor Dunn and her assistants. These questions were: (1) Can groups of so wide a range as two or three grades work together so that better or more learning will accrue than resulted from the graded system? (2) What distribution of curriculum content is required to make possible steady progress of a pupil throughout his elementary school life? [2]

At the beginning of the experiment, the Quaker Grove School was organized into three groups, known as Group A, the advanced group; Group B, the intermediate group; Group C,

[1] Dunn, Fannie W. and Others. *Organization of Curriculum for One-Teacher Schools*, p. 13, Department of Rural Education, National Education Association, 1933.

[2] *Ibid.* p. 15.

the primary group. First grade reading classes were separate, but the first-year pupils formed part of the primary group in all other subjects except arithmetic. No formal work in that subject was offered for the first-year pupils. The formation of such groups indicated that the experimenters had in mind a rotation of curriculum materials as well as a rotation of grades. The curriculum organization effected from such planning is, perhaps, the outstanding achievement of the experiment. The organization of the children of the Quaker Grove School into groups was no novel procedure; many schools for years have used this plan. The curriculum organization to fit these groups, however, was a new departure, and Professor Dunn and her associates found it necessary to chart new seas to accomplish it. The curriculum organization had the following characteristics: (a) it provided for a rotation of subject matter over a period of three years; (b) a special organization in various fields of subject matter was devised for groups instead of grades; (c) the traditional sequence of grade subject matter was ignored. In arithmetic, for instance, the materials of the last three years of the curriculum were distributed during three rotating years, so that no one year was prerequisite for another.

Each year the first month or six weeks was given to a fundamental presentation of percentage. This was a new topic for pupils just promoted from Group B, and a review for those pupils who had already spent a year in Group A. The extent to which these latter participated in the percentage study depended upon their need for the review. For the remainder of the year, the whole group studied as one class the remaining topics assigned to that year. In one year these topics comprised denominate numbers; the investment applications of percentages, including dividends, stocks and bonds as investments, interest, and banking as related to interest and savings deposits; and taxes and bonds as means of financing the nation. In another year the course covered decimals; merchandising, applications of percentage, including discounts, profit and loss, payment by checks and drafts, bank deposits and loans, commission and fire insurance; and inventories. The other year of the rotating three was given to miscellaneous applications of percentage, mensuration, including circular measure, board feet, cord wood, square and cubic measure and square root; working drawings and graphs; ratio and proportion; and algebraic expressions and equations.[1]

The same procedure in general was followed in the organization of the materials of the social studies. A unique feature of this organization was the selection of central themes for each of the three rotary years, thus affording a common idea which integrated the work of the whole school. There was a Home year, a Farm year, a Community year. Each group also had a central theme, closely allied to the integrating school theme.

Thus in the Home year the central theme of the primary group is *The Home and Home Life*, of the intermediate group is *Homes in Early Times and Now*, and of the advanced group is *Our Changing World*. In the Farm year the central themes are on the three levels, *The Farm, How the World Gets Food*, and *The Place of Agriculture in World Civilization*. In the Community year they are *Community Life, Our Country's Manufactures and Trade*, and *Interdependence Among Nations*.[2]

Units of work which covered the fields of history, geography and civics were expected to develop out of these topics. Experience in using the units also indicated that the fields of English and the fine and industrial arts were also heavily drawn upon for the solution of various problems raised in the units.

The advantages of this type of group organization to the rural school is apparent. It solves, in part, the problem of alternation of grades, since it provides a like alternation of subject matter. Hence the alternation of grades may become a practical feature of the average small school. Classes under such a group plan as developed in Chapter V are reduced approximately to one half the number in use under the grading system, and these large groupings provide opportunities for needed socialization in the small rural school. The subject matter is organized specifically for the rural schools. This has large implications for the making of state courses of study,

[1] *Ibid.* p. 14.
[2] *Ibid.* p. 15.

since a state which has varying lengths of school terms can, under this plan, organize curriculum materials in terms of the needs of the rural school. The plan provides for an economy of the teacher's time, since he does not find it necessary to scatter his preparations over so many fields as is necessary in the traditional type of organization. The central themes not only integrate the work of children; they also integrate the work of the teacher. The central themes also offer a guide for the purchasing of books and materials, thus giving purpose and direction to the purchase of yearly supplies.

The results of this experimentation in the organization of the social studies have already influenced the making of courses of study for rural schools and give promise of further influence as the plan is better understood by the teaching profession. The State of New Jersey has led the way by incorporating many of the features of the plan in the recent issue of a *Handbook in Social Studies and Related Activities*.

DIFFERENTIATION IN THE CURRICULUM FOR THE SMALL SCHOOL AS EXEMPLIFIED BY THE STATE COURSES OF STUDY IN NORTH DAKOTA AND NEW YORK

The differentiation of the curriculum to meet the special needs of the small school is a new movement in education, as evidenced by the fact that the first differentiated course was issued in 1929. Pioneer states that have issued courses of study which adapt the organization of curriculum materials to the rural schools are: New York, New Jersey, Montana, North Dakota, Pennsylvania, and to some extent Missouri and Indiana.

North Dakota provides in its course of study for the alternation of six subjects as follows: Agriculture, sixth and seventh grades; geography, sixth and seventh, fourth and fifth grades; health, sixth and seventh, fourth and fifth; and literature, seventh and eighth. The subject matter in these subjects is so organized that no sequence develops, and each yearly organization is complete in itself, having no dependence upon any preceding year. For example, the geographic materials of the fourth year are organized around type studies as follows: A. *Hot moist lands;* B. *Hot dry lands;* C. *Cold lands of the far north;* D. *Mountain lands;* E. *Fishermen;* F. *Fertile plains in the lands of the four seasons.* This organization of materials taken by the fourth and fifth grades in the even years offers no conflict for the work of the odd years, which is organized around the geography of North America in the following units: *United States, Canada, Local areas,* and *Home state.* There is a similar organization of materials in the other alternating subjects.

The New York State Department of Education in its recently issued *Handbook for Rural Elementary Schools, Social Studies Group,* Curriculum Bulletin Number 2, recommends that the following organization of classes be used; Group D, six and seven year olds; Group C, eight and nine year olds; Group B, ten and eleven year olds. Upon the basis of this organization of children an organization of subject matter has been devised which alternates between odd and even years. In other words, there are two outlines of parallel subject matter for each group, one outline designed for use in the odd years, the other for use in the even years. They are approximately equal in difficulty and, like North Dakota's course of study, follow a sequence. The social studies include the state elementary syllabi in history, geography, and citizenship, with the units rearranged in the Handbook for use in one-teacher and two-teacher schools. It is apparent that efforts were made in the rearrangement to associate the units of these three subjects which naturally belong together. Units which have no established relationships are presented separately in each subject. The chief associations in the organization are:

1. The geography of home life is followed by a study of home life in early days (primitive man).
2. The geography of Egypt and the Nile (regional studies) is accompanied by a study of the early history of the Egyptians and their contributions to civilization.
3. Stories of early Mediterranean peoples—Hebrews, Greeks,

Romans—are presented in connection with the geography of the Mediterranean Sea and lands.

4. The geography of New York State and the activities of today are followed by a study of the State's history wherever relationships exist between the two.

5. Europe is studied at the time that the contributions which have come to us from early Europe are being considered.[1]

While the units are a correlation of the history, geography, and civics outlined in the elementary course of study, there is always the possibility of the inclusion in them of other subject matter, also a part of the elementary course.   Teachers in a group of one-room schools coöperating with the State Teachers' College, Buffalo, New York, experimented with the inclusion of such extra materials in the units outlined in the *Handbook*. The unit chosen for the experiment was on New York State, designated in the *Handbook* to Group B.   The result of this experimentation is presented by a case study.[2]

CASE STUDY—VI

In planning and using units as outlined in Bulletin 2 I have found it almost impossible not to include all the subjects in the curriculum in order to have a well-rounded unit.   To illustrate this I shall briefly review a unit on New York State.

All subject material used was found in the *Handbook for Elementary Schools*, Curriculum Bulletin Number 2, covering the geography and history of New York State.   In order for the pupils to find this material it was necessary to know how to use the encyclopedia, dictionary, and supplementary texts.   This, of course, is included in the English syllabus.   When gathering material, each child had to take intelligent notes in outline form. From these, both written and oral reports were made to the

[1] *Handbook for Rural Elementary Schools.* Curriculum Bulletin No. 2, Social Studies Group, p. 15, New York State Department of Education, 1933.

[2] Reported by Mrs. Ruth Slacer Muck, Lockport District No. 5. Supervisory District Number 2.   Niagara County, New York.   Miss Mabel Sarbaugh, District Superintendent of Schools.

class. Essays led directly to a study of correct composition including sentence structure, grammar, paragraphing, and margins. When a fellow pupil was absent, a letter was written telling what had been done in class that day. Here, again, study of correct letter form brought in our English work. Although spelling was not actually taught here, all words used had to be correctly spelled. Since most of the unfamiliar words used could be found in the reference books, this was not difficult. Incorrect outlines or compositions had to be corrected or rewritten, thus developing more careful work. After reading supplementary fiction for this unit, book reports were given either orally, or in writing. Some of the literature included were: (1) *Treasure in the Little Trunk* and *The Gold Lace Coat* by Helen Fuller Orton; (2) *Rip Van Winkle* and *The Legend of Sleepy Hollow* by Washington Irving; (3) *The Great Stone Face* by Nathaniel Hawthorne.

The first book gave occasion for a valuable study of the settling of our own community; the second, a history of Fort Niagara in story form; the third and fourth called particularly for a description of the Catskill region; and the fifth was a lead to the Hudson River rock formations. Some of the poems had to do with farming, the principal occupation of our community, and were used for appreciation. Included in these were: Trowbridge's *Evening at the Farm*, Longfellow's *Harvest Moon*, Thomas' *Frost Tonight*, Hardy's *The Oxen*, and Frost's *The Woodpile*.

Science, too, was held an important part of the unit. Much of this material was a direct out-of-doors study of our region. The geology of the Niagara Frontier led to fossils found about our school . . . A study of soil, also, was a very local one, since we seem to have most kinds. Glacial formations began with the Niagara Gorge and held over for rivers, lakes, and mountains of the entire state. Niagara Falls naturally led to a brief study of electricity. Birds, trees, flowers, and wild life entered into our study with emphasis on our local types.

In making our notebooks, mentioned in the English group,

and having them attractive as well as valuable we studied color combinations, page arrangement, and proper mounting of pictures. Here, it can be seen, we brought in art. This subject was continued in the making of illustrations of people and industries, and in the drawing of maps. We also had displays, such as Indian villages which needed the making of Indian figures, homes, canoes, etc. Here we used the manual arts, which also included the construction of salt and flour maps. These maps showed relief, industries, and products.

Arithmetic skills were not taught as a part of the unit, but arithmetic was necessarily used in map study, particularly for distances.

Since all written work had to be neat and legible, penmanship was carefully watched and attention called to letter formations and spacing.

Music was not taught as a part of this unit, but was included in many other units. Southern songs, for instance, were learned and enjoyed in connection with a unit on Southern States, as were cowboy songs for the West. For the entire work on the United States, American national songs were used such as, "America" and "America the Beautiful."

Since all of this material, or most of it, was essential, it can readily be seen that the social studies units are not complete unless the other subjects are used. When the required material for these subjects is included in the unit, I found it possible to combine the periods for, let us say, geography, history, civics, English, art, and science, thus making one class of interesting things to do and learn instead of many short periods of chopped-up subject matter, and I did not have to worry as to whether the class would stop on one particular minute. It surely relieved time tension for me.

THE PERPENDICULAR UNIT IN WHICH THE WHOLE SCHOOL ENGAGES

The perpendicular unit is an organization of subject matter which engages the attention and interest of the whole school.

Centered in a problem of common interest and including all group levels, it offers many advantages to the small school . . . It is as practicable in a school which has no alternation of grades and subject matter as it is in the school which provides for both. Several such units could be provided during the year with profit to both children and teacher. It meets at one and the same time two of the problems of the small school: it reduces classes for the period of the unit, as stated in Chapter V, and it offers opportunities for socialization. Twelve-year-old children work in their own group and on their own level, but they may also engage in activities involving six-year-olds, and *vice versa*.

Such integration of subject matter into perpendicular units may center about many points of common interests such as a school fair, the migration of birds, colonial life in America, and a problem in health or safety. All of these units have been developed in the coöperating one-room rural schools of the State Teachers College, Buffalo, New York. A Case Study illustrating the organization of curriculum materials in a perpendicular unit follows.[1]

CASE STUDY—VII

Perpendicular Unit. The whole school busied itself for approximately six weeks on a study of China. The subject matter was developed on age and interest levels but for certain activities all the school united and worked together as one group. The children all worked together, for instance, on a scrapbook, the bulletin board, and a Chinese village. The latter was the product of many children, and it included a part of the great wall, Chinese homes and people, house boat, sampan, temple, jinrickshas, and Chinese people. The older children carried the major share of the responsibility, but they shared it with the younger children. Indeed, they instructed the younger children in many activities, and in a sense and for the time being,

[1] Reported by Miss Laura Clark, teacher in School District #2, Orchard Park, New York. Mr. W. R. Buell, District Superintendent of Schools.

became assistants to the teacher. The period of the opening exercises was often given over to this unit, and nearly all of the children took part in them; giving reports, telling stories, dramatizing their work. One day a neighbor, who had formerly been a primary teacher in China, came and talked with us about the far-away land. Because of the varying ages and interests the groups specialized on different aspects of the common problem. The children in Group A studied the different phases of Chinese history and the geographic influence on this historical development. China's natural resources, her agricultural products, her climate, etc., were thus included in the unit. Group B was specifically interested in the homes, the modes of transportation, and the ways of living of the Chinese people. Group C found its greatest satisfaction in a study of the Chinese village and the people who lived in it. While the unit met the needs of the special interests of children through their own group study, it also possessed certain integrating features which drew the whole school together, united them for problem solving and activities, and gave them the satisfaction which comes from shared responsibilities in a common enterprise.

DIFFERENTIATIONS IN THE CURRICULUM FOR INDIVIDUAL DIFFERENCES

While the development of large groups of children and large activity units are desirable for the small school, the organization of curriculum materials should also properly include differentiations for the individual differences in children. This trend in curriculum making was pointed out in Chapter VI, and it appears wise to adapt it whenever possible in rural schools. The growth of the individual child to his highest possible development is the main objective of the modern school program. Differentiations in subject matter should be made in order that individual instruction may be possible, and individual instruction is necessary for several reasons. In the first place, many of the skills in what is termed the "individual essentials" are achieved individually. Beginners, for example, are nearly always kept in separate classes in reading and are not grouped because it is essential that each child acquire skills in reading before he finds his place in a group. It is usually recommended that children in the small school be kept in separate reading classes until they complete the third year. If at the end of that time, they are deficient in this skill they are then placed in a remedial class where they will receive individual instruction in it. Individual instruction is one way of achieving skill in a subject and individual drill is another. Both are helpful and both are often necessary. While drill in the tool subjects in the past has perhaps been overemphasized, it also has a place in the modern school. This is often achieved by the inclusion of a daily self-improvement period, during which time each child corrects, through practice, his own individual weaknesses. There are many good commercial work books, drill exercises, and silent readers on the market which meet the needs of this self-improvement period. While each child is busily at work meeting his own needs, the teacher moves quickly about the room, giving help and encouragement when and where he is needed. The Quaker Grove experiment gives us light here:

The curriculum employed in the Quaker Grove school is, in general, a combination of group and individual activities. Class topics arranged to provide for rotation or alternation of work by years are supplemented by individual assignments or practice exercises of the Dalton "contract" nature . . .

Individual practice exercises for comprehension and vocabulary development, and individual reading for recreation or information in connection with other studies, supplement the work of the reading classes.[1]

Both second and third grades have silent reading in textbooks for which check cards have been provided to test comprehension of the matter read. Cards for this purpose have been prepared for a primer, a first reader, and some second readers. These books are required reading. Pupils progress in them at their own rate. When a child

[1] Dunn, Fannie W. and Everett, Marcia A. *Four Years in a Country School*, pp. 3–4, Bureau of Publications, Teachers College, Columbia University, 1926.

finishes a story, he gets the question and answer cards which belong to it, and by matching questions and answers correctly, demonstrates his comprehension of what he has read. This work is checked by a pupil of the intermediate or advanced group, using a key check card to insure his own accuracy.[1]

In the second place, provision for individual instruction is necessary because it allows for the development of the interests and the abilities of individual children. Not only should the curriculum afford opportunities for correcting deficiencies, it should also allow for the encouragement of special gifts enjoyed by individuals. Opportunities here usually develop through the activities of the units, particularly through the curriculum materials of the fine and industrial arts. Many modern school programs provide periods, usually the last one of the day, for expression in these arts. Sometimes the period is combined with the self-improvement period, and, while some children are perfecting arithmetic, writing, or reading skills, other children with no deficiencies may be carving, painting, writing a play, editing the school paper, or enjoying a book in the library corner. Group work, if properly presented, nearly always stimulates exceptional children to individual as well as to group activity. There are things to construct, pictures to paint, research to be made, papers to be prepared, and reports to be outlined. These individual activities usually take care of themselves and need only supervision when the teacher is available for help and direction. The child is thus given the opportunity for developing confidence in his own ability to plan, project, and produce.

Individual instruction, further, offers opportunities for guidance and is valuable here for both teacher and children. Even with the combination of grades, the number of children in the groups, as a rule, is small. Hence the teacher in the small school has the opportunity of knowing the assets and deficiencies of his children in a more comprehensive way than the teacher of a crowded single grade in an urban school. Not only can he

[1] *Ibid.* pp. 139–140.

know the personality characteristics of each individual child, but he can know his assets in the creative arts, his interests, his experiences, and his dreams. Upon facts like these all programs of guidance are built, and this activity occupies an important and significant place in the program and curriculum of the modern school.[1]

SUMMARY

It has long been realized that one of the chief difficulties of the small rural school lay in its organization. Consequently, many plans, most of them administrative, have been advanced to meet this difficulty. The small school, however, continues to persist in large numbers and gives promise of persisting for many years. Consequently, leaders in the rural field have, during recent years, made efforts to improve the internal difficulties of the small schools. One of the most significant developments is the trend toward the organization of curriculum materials to meet the specific needs of the small school. Important experimental schools have greatly influenced these trends. Chief among these have been the Collings experiment of Missouri and the Quaker Grove experiment, sponsored by the Rural Education Department of Teachers' College, Columbia University. These experiments have demonstrated the following significant aspects in the differentiation of curriculum organization for the small school: (a) curriculum materials can be profitably selected from the day-by-day experiences of children; (b) an alternation of subject matter by years is possible, and is practical, for the grouping of children; (c) there is no necessity for the traditional sequence of subject matter; (d) subject matter can be profitably organized for the small rural school.

These experiments have already greatly influenced procedure in the making of state courses of study for the rural schools.

[1] For a further discussion on individualized instruction see Chap. VI of this text.

Pioneers in this procedure have been the states of New York, New Jersey, Montana, North Dakota and Pennsylvania. Each of these states has differentiated the curriculum materials to meet the problems in the small school. These differentiations include (a) the integration of subject matter into units, especially in the social studies, and (b) the alternation of subject matter by odd and even years.

The perpendicular unit is another form of subject matter organization recommended to small schools. It is an organization of curriculum materials which engages the attention of all the children; it is as practical in the school which alternates subject matter as it is in the school which holds to a traditional program.

While the development of large groups of children and large activity units is desirable, the modern organization of curriculum materials also provides for the individual differences of children, usually through individual instruction, through drill, and through the activities growing out of large units of work. The differentiation of curriculum materials for small schools is in complete harmony with the modern conception of education, namely, that schools exist for the development of children to their highest capacity. If the schools fail to meet this objective, then the school itself must adjust, even to the point of breaking with tradition and blazing new trails.

SUGGESTED READINGS

Brim, Orville G. "Making the Curriculum A Stimulus Rather than a Milestone to Educational Progress," *Journal Rural Education*, Vol. 5, No. 9–10 (May–June, 1926), pp. 385–394.

Brim, Orville G. "The Curriculum Problem in the Rural Elementary School," *Elementary School Journal*, Vol. 23 (Apr., 1923), pp. 586–600.

California State Curriculum Commission. *Teachers' Guide to Child Development in the Intermediate Grades*, California Department of Education, Sacramento, 1936.

Collings, Ellsworth. *An Experiment with a Project Curriculum*, Chaps. III, IV, VII, Macmillan, New York, 1923.

Dunn, Fannie W. and Others. *Organization of Curriculum for One-Teacher Schools*, Department of Rural Education, National Education Association, Bulletin (Feb., 1933), Washington, D. C.

Dunn, Fannie W. and Bathurst, Effie. *Guide and General Outline for Social Studies for Rural Schools*, Department of Rural Education, Teachers College, Columbia University, New York, 1932.

Heyl, Helen Hay. *Differentiation of Curriculum to Meet the Needs of Rural Children*, Bulletin No. 24, United States Office of Education (Dept. of the Interior), Government Printing Office, Washington, D. C., 1927.

Lowth, Frank J. *Everyday Problems of the Country Teacher*, Rev. ed., Chap. XX, Macmillan, New York, 1936.

National Society for the Study of Education. *The Status of Rural Education*. *Thirtieth Yearbook*, Part I, Chap. IV, Public School Publishing Co., Bloomington, Illinois.

New Jersey. *A Handbook in Social Studies and Related Activities for Primary Teachers*, State Department of Public Instruction, Trenton, 1932.

MATERIALS FOR DISCUSSION

Consider the following statements. What changes would make them more acceptable to you? What significant issues arise from their study?

1. Administrators in education have deliberately failed to meet the needs of the small school in order that the program of consolidation might thereby be furthered.

2. If State Departments of Education find it impossible to provide courses of study for both urban and rural school systems, it would be advisable to proceed contrary to the present practice, namely, to organize the curriculum materials for the latter and request the city teachers to make adjustments.

3. Sequence in subject matter is not essential either for learning or for progress in school.

4. The organization of curriculum materials into units of work is neither logical nor psychological, and is a phase in curriculum making which will soon be outdated.

5. The differentiation of curricula to meet the needs of the small school is well nigh impossible in the average rural school situation.

CHAPTER XIII

BOOKS AS TOOLS OF LEARNING

THE RÔLE OF BOOKS IN MODERN EDUCATION

In the past we have thought of the school as an organization of grades, each grade as broken into compartments of subjects, and each subject amplified by an adopted textbook. Teaching concerned itself almost wholly with the assignment of pages in textbooks, the memorization of the assignment and the testing of the pupils on the materials memorized. Under this system textbooks and the information contained therein became authorities, and a child felt that he had no surer ground in argument than to reply "But the book said so!" One of the most significant changes in modern education has been the reassignment of the place of books in the learning and teaching processes. Occupying no less important place than before, books have shifted to a new and different rôle. They have come to be regarded today as tools of learning, essential to the equipment of the school in the same way as globes, maps, blackboards, and laboratory equipment. Many books offer a diversified set of opinions by qualified persons rather than the Olympic pronouncements of teacher and author.

The organization of subject matter has also undergone a change. It is no longer limited to the short daily recitation, but is built up by units which extend over long periods of time. Units in turn are organized about problems for which no textbook can give all the answers. In order to solve such problems the children must consult many books. Consequently, they learn early that on nearly all questions there are divisions of opinion and that it is the part of wisdom to wait until all the evidence is in before forming an opinion. Under such an organization of subject matter and technique of teaching children tend to develop alertness, independent thinking, and discrimination.

Reading as a Function of Learning. We have known generally, and for some time, that easy access to books has a salutary effect on children. Two recent studies seem to strengthen this trend of thought. One study is reported by Sarah Byrd Askew of the New Jersey Public Library Commission, the other by Edith A. Lathrop in the 1928–1930 Biennial Survey of Education.

The first study was a test of reading comprehension in two New Jersey townships, one of which had provided library facilities for rural children while the other had not. A test was given to the seventh and eighth grade children on a list of new books the children had not seen. They were asked to read the books and afterwards were tested (a) on their ability to comprehend what they had read; (b) on their ability to assemble their findings in usable form; (c) on their ability to report on it orally or in writing. From these tests Miss Askew drew the following conclusion:

In the township where library service had long been established the children enjoyed the books, wrote compositions, and gave talks of average originality and ability. . . . Perhaps 3 per cent did not do the job passably well. . . . In the other township with children just as intelligent, but more remote and without any but the most sporadic library service, the story was different. Not one single child was able to comprehend, to assemble and to digest the ideas sufficiently to give even a passable original talk or write a passable original composition.[1]

In an effort to find the reading comprehension of the children in the township without library service, the reading levels of the books on which they were tested were dropped from the seventh to the sixth grade, but here too the children floundered.

[1] Askew, Sarah Byrd. "County Libraries and Rural Schools in New Jersey," *School and County Library Coöperation,* United States Government Pamphlet No. 11, June, 1930, p. 32.

It was not until the books had been lowered to the level of the fourth and fifth grades that all the children were able to pass the test.

To Interpret and Understand the Modern World. Another development which has influenced the place of the library in the modern school is the effort made in it to understand and interpret the activities of the modern world. Such a program demands magazines and newspapers, and those sources of information form a significant feature of the modern school. No longer are magazines and newspapers considered luxuries but necessities in a program of modern education, and schools are using them in increasing numbers. In a recent study of rural school libraries and practices Edith A. Lathrop of the United States Office of Education made the following statement:

Sometimes one was agreeably surprised at the use being made of such material, (that is, magazines, pamphlets, clippings, etc.) in small schools. On the bulletin board of a one-teacher school in an isolated and decadent oil settlement in Santa Barbara County, California, there was an interesting exhibit of newspaper and magazine clippings used in the development of a unit on transportation. In preparation for *tuning in on the Olympics at Lake Placid*, the advanced room in a two-teacher school in Albany County, New York, was exhibiting on the bulletin board clippings from the *New York Times*, pamphlets and books, advertising the events.[1]

Reading for Recreation. The tendency to use books for enjoyment, pleasure, and recreation is another factor that has influenced the status of the library in the modern elementary school. It is no longer considered a crime to be "caught" reading a book in school; children are encouraged to read widely. Modern technique in the teaching of reading has as its goal the mastery of the tools and mechanics of reading by the third grade, and after that, increasing experience in reading because

[1] *A Study of Rural School Library Practices and Services*, p. 75. United States Office of Education and The American Library Association, 1934.

the child likes it, because it meets a recreational need, or because he receives pleasure from the experience. Part of the recreational program, indeed one of its aims, is to give children discriminating tastes when a choice is to be made in reading. As long ago as 1876 Charles Francis Adams deplored the fact that the schools taught children how to read, but did not teach them what to read, thus neglecting what he termed "the great connecting link between school education and self-education." [1]

To Develop Discriminating Standards. Leaders in education have pointed out that it is not enough to develop a literate citizenship in a democracy, that, if democracy is to function efficiently, the tools of literacy must be accompanied with discriminating standards in reading, music, and the arts. In order to develop this discrimination in reading, children must have access to many books. Dean William F. Russell of Teachers' College, Columbia University, makes this significant statement concerning books, the tools of learning:

But it is believed that something new is in the process of creation. For the education of children we have schools. Into these we have introduced libraries. For the education of adults we have libraries. Into these we have introduced schools. This paper suggests that the time may come when there will be neither libraries in schools nor schools in libraries, but a new educational institution will emerge which will combine the best features of both. [2]

THE PROBLEM OF THE SMALL SCHOOL WITH NO SUPPLE-MENTARY LIBRARY AGENCIES

In Chapter XIX of this book, a survey is made of the plans now in operation in the United States which attempt to bring library facilities to rural areas. The survey of such plans was not wholly encouraging. The fact that 1,135 of the 3,065 counties in the United States have no library services of any

[1] *Report United States Commissioner of Education, 1928–1930*, p. 646. United States Office of Education, Government Printing Office.

[2] *School Library Yearbook No. 2*, p. 53, American Library Association, 1928.

kind gives food for thought and planning. This status of the rural library agencies means that for many years to come a teacher in a small rural school who wishes to use modern techniques of teaching and modern organization of subject matter must work out local problems in terms of the local community. He will find it necessary to add to the library from time to time as the community, the state, or some interested local group is able to provide the funds. It is often possible to enlist the interest and support of the local Parent-Teacher Association, and this, incidentally, offers an excellent outlet for the activities of that organization. At the same time, the teacher has an opportunity to interpret a program of modern education to the adult group of his community. The average classroom library in a small rural school offers a challenge to every energetic, wide-awake teacher who has visions of what books can do for children. The average rural teacher upon entering a small school with no supplementary library agencies will find a condition all too familiar to the teacher of experience. Miss Lathrop made a study of what would be found in such a situation and the facts were these: The teacher will find that the entire library of his school could be accommodated on one short shelf in the corner of the schoolroom. The chances are about equal that he will find a set of good reference books. His chances are good for finding a dictionary; seventy-five per cent of the schools investigated had at least one. The greatest need will be revealed in the library facilities for young children, particularly in the lack of picture books. The next greatest need will be for encyclopedias and other reference books. There will also be gaps in the books of biography, plays, travel, and poetry. Usually the smaller the school the worse the condition of the books.[1]

. . . You know as well as I what the average rural school library is like and I don't care whether it is in a one-room descendant of the "little

[1] *A Study of Rural School Library Practices and Services,* p. 71. United States Office of Education and The American Library Association, 1934.

red" or the most modern consolidated over in my county, says the superintendent in a little booklet called *The Superintendent Makes a Discovery*. They are all alike except for size. There's a worn-out Chambers or an old Britannica, a dilapidated Webster's Unabridged, a brand new set of *This Glorious Land*—by the way, did the *Glorious Land* hit you last year? The agent gave a set to the best known preacher over our way and got an endorsement that sold the thing to every school director in the district except one who's an atheist and won't take the preacher's recommendation on either literature or religion. Anyway, if it isn't the *Glorious Land* that all the district fund has gone into this year, it's a twin sister and the library shelves are like tree rings—they represent annual growth in terms of subscription sets. Of course there are some other items: the supplementary readers recommended in the state course of study, a few classic novels donated by the intelligensia, who have moved away or died, some Peter B. Kynes and Boy Scout series and a few really attractive volumes of travel and biography which were bought fresh and new last year by the P.T.A., but are mostly out of their covers by now.

Maybe one of the younger teachers fresh from a six weeks' library course at U.T.C. has tried to organize the collection. She's done a good job too, poor child, considering lack of time and equipment. But if she's that ambitious she's too good to stay. Next year she'll move on, and her nice little catalog will be muddled up by the volunteer pupil assistants and a bored teacher who will have the library thrust upon her because she is a failure at teaching history.[1]

While this picture of the small school library is fanciful, it is verified by recent investigations, notably in Miss Lathrop's Study of 262 libraries in 32 states. She found:

In the classrooms library books were found in various places—on window sills, tops of unused desks; organs, tables, and shelves particularly set apart for books and shelves where dinner pails shared space with books; and also in cupboards and bookcases. Those in storerooms were often mixed up with textbooks, empty chalk boxes, teaching material and bits of broken furniture.[2]

[1] Fargo, Lucile F. *The Superintendent Makes a Discovery*, pp. 4–5, Library Extension Board, American Library Association, 1931.

[2] *A Study of Rural School Practices and Services*, pp. 75–76. United States Office of Education and American Library Association, United States Government Printing Office, 1934.

Both these pictures, one fact and one fancy, suggest tasks to which the rural teacher will need to give attention; namely, (a) the reorganization of the present library into a workable unit; (b) the development of the library into an efficient unit.

THE REORGANIZATION OF THE LIBRARY INTO A WORKABLE UNIT

Miss Anna Kennedy, of the Library Extension Division of the New York State Education Department, has recently compiled directions for the organization of a rural school library, which may prove helpful here. The first step in Miss Kennedy's recommendations is the sorting of all materials into groups of those that are valuable to the school and those that are useless. To determine the usefulness of the books three criteria are suggested: (a) the curriculum needs of the school (if the teacher is inexperienced she should consult the various state curriculum bulletins for each subject taught in the school); (b) the interests and reading ability of the children in school and the adults in the community; (c) the date of the publication of the books, except for the classics. All useless books, those that are worn or soiled, should be discarded. The books set aside will then probably fall into three groups: (a) those in good condition; (b) those worth reading; (c) those worth rebinding.

PREPARING THE BOOKS FOR THE SHELVES

The books should next be prepared for the shelves. The assistance of the children could well be enlisted here, not only because it is a community responsibility to bring order out of disorder, but because of the educational possibilities which are inherent in the task. The children will learn much about the care of books, the technique of cataloging, and the order of a library system so perfect that, no matter how large the library, books are rarely lost. The preparation of the books for the shelves might even develop into a perpendicular activity in which all the children of the school are engaged. Here are possibilities for socialization and opportunities for children to work on committees, to assume leadership, to accept responsibility. The teacher may act as an executive, instructing in techniques and giving directions, but he will not, if he is wise and fair to children, assume all of the responsibility, and so all the work, of this community project. Not only should children assume most of the responsibility for organizing the library but for keeping it in standard condition after it has been organized. The task of reorganization for a small library is not a difficult one, and, once children understand the steps to be taken, they will be able to do a creditable job. Miss Kennedy lists the following steps in the preparation of books for the shelves: (a) open, (b) stamp, (c) paste in the proper slips, (d) accession the books, (e) make and arrange book cards, (f) wash old books, remove labels, etc., (g) shellac. These steps seem obvious, but for the benefit of the inexperienced teacher they are explained in detail in the appendix.

Before the books are placed on the shelves the teacher and children should determine upon some plan of classification. "A million books unorganized and without expert interpretation and personal service are no more effective than a mob of a million recruits before trained officers have organized and drilled them into the order and efficiency of an army." [1] The books may be organized by topics or subjects, alphabetically by author, by the grades which are to use the books, or by the Dewey Decimal System of classification, which is the most commonly used in large libraries, and simple enough to be adopted by the small rural schools. If the Dewey Decimal System is used, only ten main classifications need be employed. These are: 000 General works; 100 Philosophy; 200 Religion; 300 Social Sciences; 400 Languages; 500 Science; 600 Useful Arts; 700 Fine Arts; 800 Literature; 900 History, Geography,

[1] *University of the State of New York, Bulletin,* New York State Library 113th Annual Report, 1930, p. 6.

and Biography. The subject divisions most often used in school libraries are: Stories, Poetry, Plays, Art, Music, Biography, Mathematics, Aviation, Farming, Homemaking, Industries and Inventions, Handicraft, Health, Manners, Sports, Social Sciences, History, and Science.

IMPORTANT RECORDS FOR THE SCHOOL LIBRARY

The Accession Record. The Accession record is a consecutively numbered list of the books in a library and should contain the following items: (a) the author and the title of each book in the library; (b) information about its cost and the date it was received; (c) when the book was presumably withdrawn and why. With this information the accession record becomes the history of the library as well as its permanent bookkeeping record. By subtracting the number of books permanently withdrawn from the last accession number, it is possible to tell exactly how many books are contained in the library. An inexpensive notebook for the small library is sufficient for this record. Since the accession record is chronological, it is not possible to arrange the books by author, title, or grade.

The Shelf and Author Lists. Two other records are recommended for the small school: the shelf list and the author list. The shelf list consists of a card list of books as they stand on the shelves arranged by classes and, alphabetically, by author. The shelf list shows how many and what books there are on each subject and can be used in shelving the books. In taking an inventory the shelf list and the accession record are needed. Of the author list Miss Kennedy says:

An author list is a list of the books in the library arranged alphabetically by author's name. The information given on an author card consists of author's name, title, publisher, date of publication followed by last copyright date, and, if needed, the number of volumes or the name of the series. The subject heading is written at the lower left corner of the card so as to show where the book is shelved. Since the most accurate method of referring to a book is by author and title and since alphabetic arrangement is efficient and simple, the author alphabetic list is very practical.

The Catalog. The catalog is an important record for the large library and is desirable in a small library whenever it can be properly made and continued. On separate cards is listed the author, the title, and the subject upon which information may be found. The catalog bears to the library the same relation that an index bears to a book. However useful this catalog record may be, cataloging is a technical task and should not be undertaken in a small school, unless the teacher has had special training for it. This is no great loss, for in the small library it is possible for children and teacher to know thoroughly the collection of books. All records in the small library should be kept as simple and elementary as possible without surrendering the efficiency of a system.

DEVELOPMENT OF THE LIBRARY INTO AN EFFICIENT UNIT

The development of the small library into an efficient unit means in nearly every instance the addition of books to it. It is important, therefore, that teachers know the volumes considered essential in a school library. Practically all authorities on elementary school libraries are agreed that the book collection should contain a dictionary, an encyclopedia written for elementary grade children, and an up-to-date atlas. The collection should also include ready reference books, especially the World Almanac, and a book of quotations. Supplementary reading of literary value, adapted to the needs of the individual children, should be provided in abundance. These books give a basis for the development of discriminating tastes in reading and should be chosen with great care. Books of nature study, travel, and life in foreign countries, and individual biographies of great figures inspiring to youth and written especially for children should be included in every efficient library collection. Modern and classic fiction should also be made available.

Periodicals and magazines and, if possible, a daily newspaper should also be a part of the small library.

WHO SHOULD PURCHASE LIBRARY BOOKS IN THE SMALL SCHOOL?

Educational surveys indicate that money expended for school libraries is frequently wasted because books are purchased which children cannot use. This fact brings up the question of how and by whom the books for the small library should be selected. It appears to be the consensus of opinion of both the educators and the librarians that the teacher is the proper person to make the selection. Many considerations should modify and determine the choice of books. The special needs of the children in school is of primary importance and demand of the teacher a knowledge of their chronological ages, their reading ability, their family background, and their community needs and interests. A thorough knowledge of the course of study is likewise essential. If books are to be used as tools, they must be available according to local subject-matter needs. This is particularly important because of the trend in curriculum organization toward alternating subject matter, especially in the social studies, by units and by years. The use of books might be delayed a whole year, therefore, if the teacher made the error of ordering in an even year the supplementary reading materials for the odd years. The teacher should be familiar with sources which give advice on book selection. Nearly every state department of education provides such assistance through its library extension division. These aids come in the form of book lists assembled, usually, by grades, age, and the psychological interests of children. The book lists sent out by the library extension divisions of Maryland, Minnesota, New York, and Oregon are particularly well-selected and helpful. The advice of county and district superintendents of schools, rural supervisors, and school libraries is always available, and it is wise for the teacher in a small school to consult them before the book selection is made. There are other sources, also, which give help in this task. Two good book lists based on the interests of children are: Terman and Lima's *Children's Reading*, published by Appleton and the *Winnetka Graded Book List*, published by the American Library Association, Chicago. *The Children's Catalog*, published by H. W. Wilson Company and the *Basic Reference Books for an Elementary School Library*, published by the Pittsburg Carnegie Library, are also suggestive and helpful.

THE LIBRARY CORNER

A permanent place for this modern laboratory, the library, should be provided, no matter how small the room; and in nearly all of the modern plans for rural school buildings such space has been made available. In a few of the old rural school buildings a separate room or alcove was available for books, but, in general, the teacher and children have had to exercise their ingenuity in handling this problem. One of the most satisfactory solutions of the problem when no room or alcove is provided, has been to set apart one corner of a classroom as a "library corner." Many rural teachers make much of these little "centers of culture." Mr. Frank L. Tolman, Director of the Library Extension Division, New York State Department of Education has this to say of them:

Increased state aid to rural schools has offered the opportunity to develop classroom collections into real miniature libraries. These reading corners have a library table with magazines and picture books inviting attention. The "library" is no longer a collection representing solely the persuasive achievements of the book agent and the lapses of the trustee. Purged of its worthless books, strengthened by new purchases of books of proved value and appeal, organized and grouped by subjects and graded by age-suitability, placed on open hospitable shelves after long confinement in a locked cupboard, strengthened by a traveling library of children's books from the State Traveling Library, the "library corner" is indeed a delight to

Photograph by William A. Thomas

The library corner—"little centers of culture and learning that transform and often transfigure the learning process."

children, teacher and visitor alike . . . little centers of culture and learning that transform and often transfigure the learning process.[1]

Adequate equipment for the library corner can be secured at small cost. There should be book shelves low enough for the smallest child and a reading table and chairs for the use of primary children. A shaded lamp for dark days should be placed near the open shelves. These items plus a few attractive pictures and growing plants, can make the library corner a spot to which children and teacher turn with happy anticipation. Often children can build their own equipment, urgent need offering the opportunity for constructive activity. In one of the coöperating rural schools of the State Teachers' College at Buffalo, New York, the children did this work with admirable success. For their shelves they painted strong, even boards very white and placed them on low standards of brick, painted very red. The reading table was a strong kitchen table donated by a mother and painted by the children. An old-fashioned "recitation" bench painted by the boys, cushioned in cretonne by the girls, was used until the school could purchase chairs. A braided rug made in school by the older girls, together with potted plants and a colorful wall hanging, the work of the social-studies group, completed the equipment of "the corner" and made it the center of interest and attraction.

THE TECHNIQUE OF USING THE LIBRARY FOR INFORMATION

In addition to the selection of books for the classroom library, there are two other responsibilities devolving upon the teacher; namely, the instruction of children in the care of the library and the training of children in the technique of using books for information and for pleasure. Both are important.

Instruction in the care of the library should be given to every child, regardless of the grade to which he belongs. This

[1] "Essential Contributions of the School Library to School Activities," *New York State Education*, Vol. 18 (Jan. 1931), p. 457.

instruction will include such items as the proper way to open a book, enough information about the physical make-up of a book to interest the child in its care, the correct way to turn the leaves and to mark places in a book, the knack of replacing books on the shelf, the necessity for keeping a book clean, and simple lessons in the mending of books. The instruction of the older children might well include the proper shelving of books by matching the subject headings with the shelf labels and by alphabetizing the author's name. They can also assume most of the charging-out responsibilities of the school library.

The second responsibility, the education of children in the technique of using books, looms large in the successful administration of a small school of more than one grade. The technique is likewise invaluable in the life of the student and the adult, since much of our social heritage is found in books. An increasing number of state courses of study are recommending that such units be included in the English courses for both primary and elementary children. The State Department of Education of New York through its Curriculum Bulletin No. I, *Handbook for Rural Elementary Schools—The English Group*, recommends that children in the first grade be given training in the technique of using reading materials. One of the aims of the English work for Group E (Grade I) is "to develop skill in handling materials essential to reading activities and to form desirable work habits in young children." A few of the activities used by the New York teachers to attain this are: learning how to turn pages and how to hold books; learning the "clean hands" habit when using books; finding all work materials easily accessible; finding all materials neatly and systematically arranged by the teacher. The same Handbook further recommends that this technique continue on different levels of achievement throughout school life. In Group C (Grades III and IV) one of the aims in English classes is "To learn on the primary level to use books for reference." Activities used to reach the goal include: learning how to use a textbook, examining title page, date of publication, author's name, introduction, table of contents, index, appendices; learning to use properly the table of contents; and learning the first steps in the use of a dictionary. By the time a rural child in New York State reaches Group B, which includes all fifth, sixth, seventh, and eighth grade pupils who need special help in reading, he is supposed to be able to use effectively the mechanical features of a text, to use a dictionary, and to locate information quickly and correctly. Group B sets as one of its objectives, however, improvement in these skills. Children in this group are further trained to interpret diacritical marks; to select the most applicable definition; to locate materials found in such sources as the encyclopedia, atlas, bulletins, etc.; and to organize and use the information once it is compiled; and to read maps, charts, graphs, and cartoons. The teachers and children of New York State who take seriously the suggestions of the Handbook develop, over a period of years, an adequate technique in the handling of books as tools. Children thus equipped are not only able to use the small library corner with efficiency, but also possess the necessary equipment for a later use of the libraries of an adult world.

USING THE LIBRARY FOR PLEASURE

Instruction in the use of the library is poor indeed if it does not inspire children to read books for pleasure. Joy in fairy stories and folk tales, the inspiration that comes from biographies, and the dreams that take shape from books of travel should be the mental outfit of every child. Such books establish ideals, fashion character, and give direction to life as mere textbooks do not. And how shall the teacher in a small school prevail upon his children to enter into the heritage of books? The love of books is caught as well as taught so that the teacher who is enthusiastic about reading will naturally become a point of contagion; and, since knowledge begets enthusiasm, the teacher should know well the books in the library corner of his own school. He should know the quality and charm of individual books and appreciate the moving power in a story of high adventure, or the beauty hidden in a poem. He should know his children well enough to point out these values and meanings at the right moment so as to kindle their enthusiasm for further reading.

In addition, successful rural teachers have developed the following simple devices for the promotion of reading for pleasure.

1. The use of a reading table in a quiet corner on which to display a few attractive books. When lesson assignments are completed, children may find here entertainment that will also foster good taste.

2. The use of attractive bulletin board displays dealing with books. Illustrations and clippings may also be effectively used.

3. The organizing of a Book Lover's Club to read easy storybooks aloud on Friday afternoons at school and at the evening hour at home where there are several children in a family.

4. The setting apart of at least one library period a week when books may be talked over and borrowed for home reading.

5. Arranging on the program one or more study periods every day for each pupil as his library period when he may read stories or look at picture books.

6. Informal book chats between teacher and pupils and among pupils.

7. The reading of books with children and passing them around to others.

8. The reading of a part of a story to the children and allowing them to borrow the book to finish it.

9. Encouraging pupils to write to publishers and book dealers for "book jackets" to display in the room.

10. Having pupils make attractive book jackets for old books on the shelves to improve their looks, especially those bound in sets with unattractive covers but good content.

11. Keeping honor-roll lists of books read by each child.

12. Encouraging pupils to read for reading certificates.

13. Collecting illustrated advertising materials from publishers.

14. Making book plates and book markers.[1]

SUMMARY

In modern education, in contrast to the old regime, books are considered as tools for learning rather than as authorities. In harmony with the changing conception of education is the change in the technique of teaching and in the organization of subject matter. Studies in the field of reading seem to demonstrate the soundness of the new point of view. Now, if books are essential in modern education, the problem of the small school with no supplementary library agencies becomes acute. Since 1,135 counties of the 3,065 in the United States have no library facilities at all save those found in individual schools the problem is national. Studies reveal that such libraries as are found in these areas are not workable. They are, on the whole, unorganized; books essential to a modern program of education are missing; and many of the books available are useless. The teacher facing such conditions should recognize her responsibility for two tasks: (a) the reorganization of the library she finds into a workable unit; (b) the development of the library into an efficient unit.

The first task involves a separation of the good and the bad material, and the organization of the good into an efficient and usable library. This also involves classification and equipment, slight for the small school, but as essential as for the large school. The second task divides into smaller ones: (a) the addition of materials to the library in order to bring it to a minimum standard, (b) the development in children of the ability to use the library and books for gathering information,

[1] *Handbook for Rural Elementary Schools—The English Group*, p. 26. University of the State of New York.

and (c) the habit of using the library and books for pleasure. Providing an adequate library for the small school and educating children in the use of books as tools is one of the best investments the teacher can make. Such materials of instruction and techniques of study not only give pupils a mastery of tools invaluable in their student life, but also a priceless possession for their adult and mature years.

SUGGESTED READINGS

American Library Association. Library Extension Board, *Rural Public Library Service*, American Library Association, Chicago, 1928.

California Department of Education. *Effective Use of Library Facilities in Rural Schools*, Bulletin 11, The Department of Education, Sacramento, California, 1934.

Dougherty, J. H.; Gorman, F. H.; and Phillips, C. A. *Elementary School Organization and Management*, Chap. XVI, Macmillan, New York, 1936.

Fargo, Lucile F. *The Library in the School*, Chaps. VI, VII, American Library Association, Chicago, 1933.

Fargo, Lucile F. *The Superintendent Makes a Discovery*, Extension Board, American Library Association, Chicago, 1931.

Lathrop, Edith A. *Elementary School Library Service, as It Is and as It Should Be*, Bulletin, Vol. 26, pp. 436–441, American Library Association, 1932.

Lathrop, Edith A. *Country Library Service to Rural Schools*, Bulletin No. 20, United States Office of Education (Dept. of the Interior), Government Printing Office, Washington, D. C., 1930.

Lathrop, Edith A. *Aids in Book Selection for Elementary School Libraries*, Pamphlet No. 65, United States Office of Education (Dept. of the Interior), Government Printing Office, Washington, D. C., 1935.

National Education Association. Department of Rural Education, *Rural School Libraries*, Bulletin, 1936.

Otto, Henry J. *Elementary School Organization and Administration*, Chap. X, D. Appleton-Century Co., New York, 1934.

MATERIALS FOR DISCUSSION

Consider the following statements. What changes would make them more acceptable to you? What significant issues arise from their study?

1. The library of the average rural school is small, unorganized, and inefficient. The teacher wastes her time in an attempt to organize and develop it.

2. The most efficient way of meeting the problem of the rural school library is to develop a county system of traveling libraries.

3. The teacher will find it advantageous to use textbooks as common, integrating cores, and to supplement them with books suited to the individual needs of the children.

4. The objective of the reading program in the elementary school is two-fold: to master the techniques of the mechanical process, and to develop some measure of good taste in the selection of reading material.

5. Elementary school children are too young and inexperienced to assume the responsibilities for the organization and care of books. These are technical tasks for the performance of which special training is required.

CHAPTER XIV

MODERN AIDS IN TEACHING

For aids in teaching, modern education draws heavily upon many fields. Science, commerce, and the arts have contributed generously to the school in order that teachers might develop more vivid and vital teaching techniques. The teacher in the small, rural school cannot always draw upon these fields for help, but there are three modern aids in teaching which may be secured with little effort and at a reasonable cost. These are: (a) visual materials which tend to give reality to words; (b) school excursions which tend to substitute real for vicarious experiences; and (c) radio which vitalizes teaching and connects the remotest rural school with the most recent developments in a rapidly changing world. These three modern aids in teaching are considered in this chapter.

Visual Aids. The supplementing of verbal teaching and learning by what has come to be known in modern educational parlance as "visual aids" is almost as old as civilization itself. The use of pictures and objects in teaching extends far back into the history of the human race. Prehistoric men left records of their exploits in battle and the chase, not in words, but in pictures sketched upon the walls of caves. Primitive Chinese developed a written language of pictographs, and an old proverb of that race shows the esteem in which the picture was held. "A single picture," ran the proverb, "is equal to a thousand words." Teaching by pictures was and is an important device in all primitive education, indicating that primates instinctively used what we now use deliberately—a technique of learning through the senses. Psychology reveals that fundamentally the chief way by which the mind is developed is through the senses;

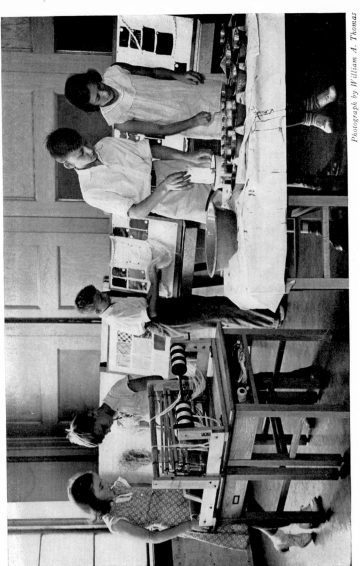

Photograph by William A. Thomas

"Learning resides in experiencing." At work on the activities of a textile unit.

that learning takes place only if and when the mind registers an impression and some reaction follows. The clearer and more forceful the impression on the mind of the learner the more positive his learning will be.

Apparently the eye is the sense organ by which man learns most quickly and easily:

Through it, aided by the telescope, the remotest material things are brought into consciousness. The microscope reveals the tiniest things of the universe known to mankind. The eye is the essential gateway through which these instruments bring the impressions to the mind. Concepts of intermediate things are largely brought to the mind through sight.

Visual appeals, by presenting objects, models, charts, photographs, stereographs, lantern slides, and motion pictures furnish the pupil with impressions for which language is simply a symbol. Whether we consider language in connection with literature, history, geography, or science, the foundation consists of sense impressions. Without numerous first-hand impressions, words are practically meaningless— hence the difficulty which pupils have in understanding the printed page.

We believe that slow progress in school work, and often failure, result from faulty presentation of fundamental impressions, which are essential to all study. The laborious efforts sometimes put forth in the school-room to draw out expressions from the pupils, suggest to us that teachers have failed to lay a foundation through clear impressions of those things they wish the children to discuss.

Visual instruction provides the concrete element for fundamental notions in educational work. The great field so essential for good school work is that of training the powers of observation, and developing the ability of interpreting correctly. To lead children literally *to see things* and to trace the relationship between causes and effects are two of the great basic ideas we should not forget. These thoughts are emphasized in visual instruction as in no other way.[1]

Visual Aids in Rural Schools. As in nearly all other modern teaching materials, the rural school is lacking in visual aids.

[1] National Education Association, Department National Elementary School Principals. *Thirteenth Yearbook*, 1933-1934, pp. 144-145, National Education Association.

City schools have partly solved the problem of providing these mediums for their teachers by the organization of centralized bureaus whose busines. it is to assemble and dispense motion picture films, projectors, stereoptican views, pictures, maps, exhibits, etc. The extent of the wealth of such aids was given for the city of Detroit in the Thirteenth Yearbook of the Department of Elementary School Principals, National Education Association, as follows:

At the present time there are 736 complete units of visual instruction equipment in the Detroit schools. This equipment includes 16 mm motion picture projectors, 35 mm motion picture projectors, stereopticans, combination opaque and slide projectors, micro-projectors, and micro-attachments. The visual education department services this equipment by daily inspection and repair. Teachers operate and use this equipment in classrooms and auditoriums.[1]

In contrast the average rural school teacher considers himself fortunate if he has a blackboard, a globe, and a set of maps. These, on the whole, constitute the equipment in visual aids found in small rural schools. The immediate problem is thus seen not in terms of the proper use of visual materials, but in how to secure them.

CONTRIBUTIONS WHICH TEACHERS AND CHILDREN CAN MAKE—PICTURE COLLECTIONS

One of the quickest and most effective methods for accumulating visual materials is in the collection of pictures and clippings to accompany units of subject matter. Many students in preparation for teaching begin such a file in their freshman year and continue it throughout their teaching life. It therefore accompanies the teacher to the rural school and supplements the file which may have already been assembled. The assembling of such a file in the rural school offers many learning possibilities for children and every rural teacher should initiate one, or add to the one he finds there.

[1] *Ibid.* pp. 188–190.

Such a picture file will consist of ephemeral and permanent materials, the latter consisting of those which may be used indefinitely, the former of those of transitory interest, such as clippings from newspapers. The filing of materials is important and children should receive instruction in the procedure. Marie E. Alexander in the Thirteenth Yearbook of the Department of Elementary School Principals of the National Education Association gives the following directions for this procedure:

A SIMPLIFIED SYSTEM OF FILING MOUNTED MATERIALS

(1) Classify the mounted materials under suitable headings. Try to get functional headings. To do this ask such questions as these: "What will the teacher call for when she needs this material?" Then give it that heading. A few suggested headings are listed here: Africa, Airplanes, Animals, Boats, Children of other lands, Designs for dishes, Indians, Meteors, Money, and Toys.

(2) Write on the back of each piece of material the heading under which it is classified and a number. For example *Toys* 1 would mean that the picture or article should be put in the envelope or folder marked *Toys* and that it should be the first piece of material in the front. Thus when a piece of material is taken out of the file it can be replaced quickly.

(3) Write each heading on a folder or a large envelope.

(4) Put the materials in their proper folders or envelopes according to names and numbers. All clippings and pictures on one topic will be together.

(5) The folders or envelopes prepared in this manner should be placed according to subject headings in a filing box or case behind alphabetical guide cards. For example, Africa, Airplanes, and Animals should be in the order indicated behind guide card A.

(6) If there is more material on a subject than one envelope will hold, make two or more envelopes for one subject and letter them as Animals A, Animals B, Animals C. *Then Animals B 3* on the back of a particular article would mean that it should be placed in the second folder or envelope on animals and it would be the third place in the folder or envelope.

(7) A card file of all materials which are in the large file should be kept. It enables one to find the materials more quickly.

a. Use a 3″ × 5″ filing card. In the middle of the top line write the subject heading under which the picture or article is filed.

b. On the second line, using about half that indentation, write the name of the picture or article, using lower case letters except for beginning the first word and for proper names. Skip a space below that line and write the number of the filing drawer or box, the name of the folder, and the number of the piece of material. *Drawer 3, Animal B 3* on a card would tell exactly where to locate the material.

(8) Colored filing cards may be used to distinguish clippings from pictures, as blue for pictures and yellow for clippings.

(9) File these 3″ × 5″ cards according to subjects behind alphabetical guide cards in a 3″ × 5″ filing box..

Provide a separate drawer for prints. They should not be mixed with ephemeral materials. Place the prints behind the guide cards made for the nationality of the artists. For example, write *English* on one guide card and place all prints of English artists' work behind this card. In the same way file the prints for other nationalities.

Make two 3″ × 5″ filing cards for each print. On the first, write the nationality of the artist on the top line for the subject heading, the name of the artist with his dates on the second line, and the name of the picture on the third line. Below this write the number of the drawer in which the print may be found. On the second card, write the topic with which the picture would be classified. For example, the picture, "Woman churning" by Millet could be used with a study of home life; therefore the subject "Home Life" would be written on the top line. The second line should contain the name of the artist with his nationality, and the third line the name of the picture. Below on the card the number of the drawer in which the print can be found and the name of the guide card behind which it is placed should be written.

File the first, 3″ × 5″ card in the filing box behind the guide card "Prints." File the second 3″×5″ card behind the guide card "Home Life." Thus, the picture could be found by looking under the nationality or if pictures are needed to use in a study of home life, it can be located by looking at the cards on that subject.[1]

[1] National Education Association, Department of Elementary School Principals, *Thirteenth Yearbook Aids to Teaching in the Elementary Schools*, 1933–1934, pp. 196–197, National Education Association.

The filing suggestions offered by Miss Alexander do not require expensive cabinets and equipment. Mounting board, construction paper, and tagboard can be obtained at reasonable prices. So with envelopes, and guide and filing cards. Filing boxes may be obtained from office supply houses at prices ranging from fifty cents to one dollar. When the school cannot or will not supply such cases orange crates or boxes made by a local carpenter prove acceptable substitutes.

The assembling and filing of materials should be made an activity for the children of the small rural school. They may also assume the responsibility for the daily distribution of materials and for the return of them to their proper places at the end of the day. These experiences may properly occupy children during the study periods of the day, and can be admirably handled by a committee from the school citizenship club.

EXHIBITS OF LOCAL PHENOMENA

All leaders in modern education are agreed that museums in art, history, and the natural sciences are important community adjuncts to the educational program of the school. Consequently, a visitor to any urban museum during the school year is likely to see groups of children with their teachers on tours to see the exhibits there. Except for the few rural schools near large cities this source of visual education, available for nearly all urban children, is for the average rural child, a closed avenue. However, there are a few enterprising teachers who have sought to remedy this deficiency by encouraging children to make their own museums from materials close at hand. The local environment may yield shells, fossils, rock crystals, Indian arrow heads, or examples of stratification. Nature is generous in her gifts to the rural child who accepts and respects them. Nearly any rural school can assemble an exhibit of birds' nests, wasps' nests, cocoons, butterflies, examples of seed dispersals, exhibits of leaves, grasses, woods, wild flowers, and parasitic growths. With encouragement, rural children will bring in enough materials to form the basis of all nature study work for the year, as well as assemble a creditable exhibit of concrete materials for further reference. Likewise, children can be encouraged to assemble historical materials; attics of many rural communities yield surprising results. Historic costumes, candle moulds, bed warmers, saddle bags, cooking utensils, and other relics of historical interest often take their place in school museums to the advantage and enlightenment of many children and adults.

The accumulation of free, commercial exhibits is not to be scorned in the assembling of visual materials. A collection of road maps, available at any standard filling station, will always prove helpful in the study of geography. Many manufacturing companies have assembled free exhibits of their product from its beginning, step by step to the finished product. Used with discrimination these exhibits are valuable in a program of visualization.

THE USE OF VISUAL MATERIALS IN THE CLASSROOM

While the accumulation of visual materials is desirable, the wise use of the materials is even more important. To many teachers pictures, maps and prints suggest only supplementary materials which enliven a lesson and give it interest. Visual materials are potentially more important than this and in the hands of a skilled teacher may become primary and vital. Like any other reference material, pictures may furnish primary information. [1] Children should be taught to look for information in pictures which textbooks do not give. Valuable information may thus be secured; for instance, concerning the customs and habits of peoples in lands different from our own. The best way to know and appreciate a foreign people is to live among them, but since this is possible for few children, the next best way to become acquainted is to visualize them through pictures.

[1] National Education Association, National Elementary School Principals, *Thirteenth Yearbook, 1933–1934*, p. 204, National Education Association.

In addition to providing primary and supplementary materials for learning, visual materials are also useful for the initiation of a unit, for tying up two units, and for a comparison of geographical concepts. In a study of the United States, for example, children might be introduced to a unit on the Southern States by pictures which graphically represent life in that area compared to life in the New England states. Differences in weather, industry, and agriculture, which have developed differences in habits and customs, would be made realistic by such an approach. In addition to the virtue which lies in the interest usually engendered by the visual approach, such use of pictures would also tend to make clear hazy geographical concepts.

A further use of pictures in the classroom is suggested by Miss Benita R. Blood in the *Thirteenth Yearbook* of the Department of Elementary School Principals of the National Education Association. She recommends pictures for testing children on their grasp of geographic concepts and on their ability to acquire landscape imagery in connection with the region studied and gives, to illustrate her point, the following examples:

(1) To test what the fourth-grade survey of typical regions of the world has given the child in the way of a concept of the effect of *latitude* on climate, native vegetation, and the life of man.

Directions to pupils:

Arrange Scenes 1 through 5 as one might see them in a southward trip across North America from Arctic Canada through Central America.

Scenes to be used with the above test—

1. Negroes at work in cotton field
2. A native village in the jungles of Guatemala
3. Prairie wheat field
4. Canadian trappers near home in forest
5. Eskimos with dog sled near igloo.

(2) For use at close of unit on the Rocky Mountains and Great Plains region.

Directions to pupils:

Use scene numbers to answer questions.

1. Select scenes which show two reasons why so small an area of this vast region is used for farming.
2. Select a scene belonging to the region of heaviest rainfall.
3. Which scene is in a very dry area?
4. Select scenes which show two natural obstacles men meet in constructing highways and railways in this region.
5. Which scene belongs to an irrigated section?
6. Which scene belongs to the Great Plains section?
7. Select four scenes which show the opportunities the mountains of this section offer for earning a living.
8. Arrange three scenes as you would probably see them in traveling from a low to a very high altitude in this region.

    (1) Ranch on Great Plains
    (2) Health resort in mountains
    (3) Power plant near falls in mountains
    (4) Heavily forested mountain side
    (5) Mining in mountains
    (6) Desert vegetation
    (7) Snow-capped mountain peak above timber line
    (8) Farm in mountain valley [1]

THE SCHOOL EXCURSION

The modern school emphasizes the necessity of identifying the child with the world in which he lives. The traditional school, however, often acts as a deterrent to this ideal. It tends to shut the world out, to shelter the child in a world of books, to turn his face toward the past. The modern school, on the other hand, attempts to link education with the problems of life existing today, and places the past in its proper per-

[1] *Ibid.* pp. 205–206.

spective, namely, as the background of the present. Many methods are employed in the modern school for the vitalizing of the child's learning, one of which is the school excursion. This is a type of activity embodying a basic ideal of reality in the educational process, and represents a ready vehicle for the transformation of the old education into the new. Like many methods it is of ancient vintage. Rousseau advocated it in his education of the young Emile. According to his plan, Emile could best establish his place in society and nature by journeying from place to place, learning as he went. Contemporary leaders in modern education have made wide use of the school excursion as a method of teaching and learning. For example, Collings in his experiment with the organization of curriculum materials for the small school, reported in previous chapters, made extensive use of the school excursion as a basis, indeed the very center, of his plan of curriculum organization.

As in many modern educational procedures, the school excursion originated in the kindergarten and was an attempt to bring the young child into direct contact with the objects of instruction. Usually the objects sought were specifically in the field of nature, or in the useful activities of workers in the child's community. Nearly always the journey utilized the instructional materials found in the child's environment.

A further characteristic of the school excursion is its international flavor. Both Germany and England make extensive use of it in the educational process. Every year ten full days are legally reserved in Germany for school journeys, and in many of the German secondary schools there has developed the custom of rounding out the high school course with a trip to a foreign country where the language, and the geographical, historical, agricultural, and scenic aspects of the country receive attention. As the curriculum of the modern elementary and high school becomes less pedagogical and more sociological, the school excursion both abroad and in America has come to be accepted as a desirable technique for making the educational concepts of children rich and valuable.

EXCURSIONS FOR THE SMALL SCHOOL

Rural schools, on the whole, have been tardy in adopting the school excursion as an aid in learning. The well known conservatism of many rural communities tends to discourage the practice. Parents do not understand the educational possibilities inherent in the excursion, and are disposed to look upon it as unnecessary and not concerned with education. The problem of transportation, unless there is an available school bus, is difficult in the rural school, since there are no street cars, subways, commercial cabs, and busses in the country. Private automobiles are therefore necessary, and, unless the community coöperates in making them available, the school is limited to its immediate environment for all excursions. Perhaps a word of caution is timely for the inexperienced teacher. Before a school excursion is taken in automobiles or busses the teacher should understand the legal liability in which he and the school board are held should an accident occur. The wise and safe procedure is to see that all conveyances, in which children are transported, are protected by adequate insurance. The varying ages and interest levels of children is another problem present in small schools. Not all children in a one-room or two-room school are interested in the same excursion, and if this difference exists, either the interested children must take the trip alone, or the group not interested must be dismissed from school for the day, both of which are disturbing to the school routine.

ASSETS OF THE RURAL SCHOOL FOR SUCCESSFUL EXCURSIONS

On the other hand, the small school has in it certain helpful aspects which, developed, should aid both children and teacher in making a success of the school excursion. The smallness of the number of children enrolled is one of these and the richness of the rural environment is another. Further, many rural families will be found to own either a car or a truck, and if parent coöperation is secured, cheap transportation is easily available.

In 1927, Charles A. McMurry listed five environmental sources for the teaching of geography by school excursions.[1] These were (a) local scenery and views, such as "the creek and pond," "valley and rock strata of Faribault, Minnesota," "View from Wheeling Hill;" (b) excursions to shops and factories, as for example "to a blacksmith shop," "planing mill," "the Warwick Pottery," "a grocery store," etc.; (c) commercial topics; "trip to Montgomery Ward building in Chicago," "The local town or village as a trade center," "a grain elevator," "a city market," etc.; (d) garden, farm and dairy; "local study of soils," "to the farm," "the dairy," "the hothouse," etc.; (e) government: "The city hall," "the fire department," "the gas works." Of these five, to which urban children must often be transported long distances, two are definitely within the environment of the rural child. On the other hand, many rural children can be transported short distances to observe shops and factories, commercial topics, and governmental agencies at work in nearby small towns and villages. The situation may be in miniature but the essentials are nearly always there. Thus the rural environment offers fine opportunities for linking theory and practice of education with life.

URBAN EXCURSIONS FOR RURAL CHILDREN

Education, however, is more than the utilization of a child's environment, and the school so limiting itself would be poor indeed. There is the definite responsibility of supplying what the child's environment lacks. This may be achieved in two ways: (a) through a use of that part of the social heritage found in books and records and (b) through contact with other environments remote from the learner. Concentrated within the urban area lie many of the educational resources lacking in the environment of the rural child. While music and art

[1] *Excursions and Lessons in Home Geography*, pp. vii–ix, Macmillan, 1927.

have gone to the country for much of their inspiration, the products of music and art are almost wholly concentrated in cities. Science and mathematics have been largely applied in urban areas. Historical remains and records have found permanent homes in museums. Even animals both domestic and foreign offer excellent opportunities for study when concentrated in a zoo. With such a concentration of teaching materials in the city, the rural teacher will find it profitable to take his children on educational journeys to the place of concentration.

Visits to art galleries and exhibits are necessary supplements to the teaching of art, no matter how closely art itself is related to nature. Opportunity to hear the transcription of a tone poem through the interpretation of an orchestra should, whenever possible, be a part of the education of the rural child. While a victrola or radio may be used for this experience, there is no thrill in these mediums comparable to the enthusiasms transmitted by a conductor to his orchestra, and thence to the audience. Recent social studies emphasize the fact that it is almost impossible to present concepts of man at work in the world, if children receive the ideas only from books, important as the written record may be. The work of the farmer is, to be sure, socially useful and necessary, but there are other workers whose labor is likewise essential and important, and rural children need first-hand contact with these workers.

DETERMINATION OF A PROGRAM OF EXCURSIONS

In order for the excursion to be educational, it should be intelligently planned. Three questions obtrude on the point: (a) what should be the basis for a program of school excursions? (b) how should the excursion be planned? and (c) what outcomes should be expected from them? Obviously these questions can be answered only in terms of educational objectives, curriculum materials, and the interests of children.

At the present, school excursions may develop from many

educational needs which are the outgrowths of many objectives. They may be initiated in order to stimulate or direct schoolroom activity in terms of textbook materials. The teacher may desire to vitalize traditional subject matter in history or geography or nature study by school excursions to a historical shrine, or the seacoast, or a nearby wood in the spring. All of these provide real learning situations and, since the school curriculum is not at present organized on the basis of vitalized child experiences, are highly desirable. Traditional subject matter thus becomes the point of departure and a basis for the selection of a program of excursions.

Or the school excursion may be decided upon the basis of immediate child interest. The maiden flight of the China Clipper, for example, might conceivably precipitate the interest of children into a study of airplanes, and an excursion to a nearby flying field or factory might develop from this interest. This criterion, like the first, however, is limiting in its scope and tends to develop a series of curriculum episodes rather than an integrated program of education. David A. Weaver, writing in the Thirteenth Yearbook of the Department of Elementary School Principals of the National Education Association lays down the following criterion for the selection and organization of an excursion program:

The acquaintance with those activities that are basic to the life of the community, and its interconnections with the outside world; sensitiveness to the social problems that emerge in the process of social living.[1]

Commenting on this criterion Mr. Weaver said:

It is by no means suggested that the children's interest should play no part in the selection of excursion projects. In fact, the project that is to be engaged in at any particular time is to conform to the children's interests and purposes at that time. The children's interests, however, are to be only one of the focuses of the excursion pro-

---

[1] National Education Association, Department of Elementary School Principals, *Thirteenth Yearbook, 1933–1934,* p. 291, National Education Association.

gram. The educational criterion above referred to should constitute the other focus. The teacher, as a member of the group, should as far as possible, guide the selection of the excursions and their conduct, so that for the most part they are calculated to the attainment of the objectives of social sensitiveness and social intelligence.

Furthermore, while it is here suggested that these values, and not traditional subject-matter be the selective principles in the organization of an excursion curriculum, it is by no means indicated that the excursion projects be insulated from such subject matter. On the contrary, it is advisable to utilize interests aroused in discussion of subject-matter in the decision of any particular project and, on the other hand, to employ experiences gained in the course of a trip to enrich other school work.[1]

PLANNING THE EXCURSIONS

The points of view presented in the previous paragraphs, namely, that the excursion may be a means of bridging the old and new education, that it should be based on child interest, and at the same time serve subject matter, has in it implications for the method which most often proves successful in the planning and conducting of them. In brief the method is this: children, no matter at what age and interest level, should purpose, plan, and execute their own school excursions.

This does not mean that the teacher stands inertly by while the planning, purposing, and execution go on. There are certain contributions which he will need to make to the success of the excursion. These appear to be three: (1) He should take the excursion himself first and thus be in readiness to give the children the benefit of his experience for their own planning. (2) He should build up a mind-set in children that an excursion is an important part of the regular school work, and that while it is to be enjoyed, it is not to be treated lightly. (3) He should insist upon high standards in all the decisions which children make. But while these teacher contributions are important, the real responsibility for the success of the ex-

[1] *Ibid.* pp. 291–292.

cursion should rest squarely with the children who plan to take it.

PUPIL PLANNING

Planning, apparently, can be best achieved in conference. These conferences, however, should be something more than a discussion of the destination, and the plan and cost of arriving there, necessary as these details are. It will also be necessary for the group to deal with other pertinent problems. (1) Children will need to agree on the standards of behavior for the trip. These will include attitudes and habits to be practiced, courtesy to one another and to strangers, safety regulations, laws, etc. (2) Children should set up in advance the questions which they hope to have answered. These will necessitate preliminary reading, research into the questions raised, and the organization of a bibliography. Here is considerable opportunity for the use of subject matter already learned in class, or for the acquisition of further information found in books, and the teacher as guide and counselor should participate at this point. (3) Once the objectives of the excursion are clear and the subject matter is organized, the materials for the trip should be assembled. These will be largely determined by the nature of the excursion itself: they may be notebooks, map-sketching materials, photographic supplies, or many other tools which children will need to use "on the ground."

EXCURSIONS AND CORRELATION OF SUBJECT MATTER

Excursions offer possibilities for the correlation of many school subjects. In one of the coöperating rural schools of the State Teachers College, Buffalo, an excursion was made in the Social Studies to a newspaper plant which involved the correlation of practically all elementary school subjects. Letters were written in the English period requesting permission to visit the plant, costs of the trip were computed in the arithmetic period, a P.W.A. project was visited en route which required investigation into the question of governmental participation and control, while drawings and illustrations of the reports upon their return motivated art for many days.

DESIRABLE OUTCOMES

It appears to be the concensus of opinion that school excursions should definitely contribute to the educational growth of children. Consequently, upon returning to the school-room, discussion should follow immediately. Here data should be organized, tabulated, and prepared in the form of reports. If specimens have been gathered for an exhibit, these should be classified, arranged, and put on exhibition. The questions listed prior to the excursion should be examined and answered in the light of the information gathered. Letters of thanks should be written, and further supplementary reading assigned if the teacher and children feel that this is necessary. Creative work usually follows an excursion and the teacher should encourage it. After the excursion referred to above, children wrote poems, developed riddles, created stories, and painted. So rich indeed was their creative work that enough material was available for an exhibit to which the community was invited.

Desirable outcomes of properly conducted school excursions are many. They usually include the following: (a) real and vital learning which links the theory found in books with the practice found in life; (b) a deeper interest in the topic under discussion; (c) practice in desirable behavior and safety habits; (d) growth in the technique of observation and research; (e) an appreciation of the child's environment; (f) the development toward a more complete knowledge of the social heritage not found in books; (g) inspiration for creative expression; and (h) orientation into different modes of life practiced by adults.

THE RADIO

While visual education and school excursions have come to be generally accepted as desirable teaching aids, the use of the radio in the class-room is as yet an experiment. Apparently there are two reasons for its tardy adoption. Education is naturally hesitant in the adoption of new devices not primarily of school origin. The development of the radio was initiated in the early years of the twentieth century by adventuresome amateurs, it was given impetus and purpose by the necessities of the World War, and it was adopted as an instrument of commercial advertising when the war was over. These agencies, alien to education, gave the new instrument little recommendation for its use in teaching. Indeed, they retarded the introduction of the radio into schools. True, a few educational leaders saw in the radio possibilities for supplementing the work of the classroom and did valuable pioneer work in the promotion of this modern educational aid. The very enthusiasm of the early pioneer group, however, tended to retard the progress of the program. Teachers were wary of this enthusiasm and of the instrument which inspired it. They feared the radio might be made a substitute for the classroom teacher and envisioned a single voice from the air directing large groups of children in widely separated sections of the United States. Developments in the field of music had given a basis for this fear. Teachers had witnessed the phenomena of highly skilled musicians being supplanted by "canned music" and saw in the losing fight of this group their own future struggle with instruments of a technological age. So retarding was this fear that in 1931 Dr. William John Cooper, then United States Commissioner of Education, was moved to an address of reassurance before the Institute for Education by Radio. He pointed out that the radio was only a supplementary agency in teaching and that it could never be a substitute for the personal contact of pupil and teacher, necessary for successful learning. He further suggested that the radio probably functioned best in a limited number of subjects which lent themselves to the ear rather than to the eye or hand. He listed such subjects as music appreciation, literature, history, sociology, and geography. He likewise questioned the advisability of teaching the sciences, art, and the tool subjects, and the actual performance in music through radio. [1]

PIONEER ATTEMPTS IN THE USE OF RADIO

As with many innovations in the field of materials, pioneer work was initiated in colleges and universities first, then in the city schools. The rural schools, as usual, lagged in the procession. The United States Office of Education announced in 1930 that 45 institutions of higher learning in the United States offered extension courses by means of radio during the years 1928 and 1929. These institutions were not localized but were situated in diverse regions: as far west as the University of California, as far south as the University of Texas, and as far east as the University of Vermont. It was estimated that the audiences totaled between three and four million students.

To the Haaren High School in New York City apparently belongs the honor of being the first public school to offer instruction by radio. In 1923 lessons in accounting were broadcast and transmitted by loud speakers to the various classrooms. So popular was the response to the experiment that by 1924 it was necessary to issue a 254 page pamphlet to meet the inquiries of educators and the public about it.[2] In the same year the State Department of Education of California broadcast talks to all the elementary schools in the geography and history of the State. These too were popular as evidenced by the fact that, coming at the beginning of the school day, they reduced the percentage of tardiness on all schools equipped with radio.

A year later, in 1924, the first attempt to reach the rural school specifically was made by the Sears-Roebuck Agricultural Foundation, which organized and sponsored a program known as the "Little Red Schoolhouse." This was a weekly radio program designed for the schools of Cook County, Illinois. Talks were

---

[1] Cooper, William John. "Educational Functions of Radio," *Education on the Air*, pp. 141–144, Ohio State University, 1931.

[2] *Report of United States Commission of Education, 1928–1930*, p. 628. United States Office of Education (Dept. of the Interior).

given on corn, dairying, birds, automobiles, and the achievement of boys and girls. Pupils as well as adults participated in the broadcasts, and efforts were made to make them definitely educational.[1]

The same type of program was initiated on a state-wide basis in 1926 by the Connecticut State Board of Education. Broadcasts here began to take educational forms, since lesson leaflets were distributed and preliminary work in the classroom for the broadcast was done with considerable thoroughness. N. S. Light, State Director of Rural Education was in charge of the radio course and estimated that the first lesson reached approximately 100,000 children and that the regular attendance was at least 25,000.[2]

The early pioneer efforts of radio teaching in college, city, and rural schools were localized and reached as a consequence a limited audience of students. Efforts to make use of the programs in teaching were unorganized and undirected. Students merely listened in; there was little direction in study, and practically no follow-up discussions.

NATIONAL SCHOOL BROADCASTS

It was natural that the development of teaching by radio should achieve national significance, once the plan had been successfully tested locally. Three important broadcasting systems were leaders in this national movement: (a) the *Radio Corporation of America*, (b) the *Columbia Broadcasting System*, and (c) the *Ohio School of the Air*. The chief contribution of the *Radio Corporation of America* was the institution in 1925 of a series of lessons in music appreciation under the tutelage of Walter Damrosch, known throughout the world as the Director of the New York Symphony Orchestra. These lessons were a success from the start, and the school audience has steadily increased. It is impossible to estimate with accuracy the actual

[1] *Ibid.* p. 629.
[2] *Ibid.* p. 631.

number of children who participate in Mr. Damrosch's music lesson, but it is believed that approximately six million children receive instruction from the Maestro every week of the school year. He has prepared a helpful instructor's manual which is used in connection with his broadcasts. But with all possible aids Mr. Damrosch insists that the teacher can never be supplanted in the teaching of music. In an address before the 1934 conference on *Radio and Education* Mr. Damrosch stated that the radio could bring orchestral music to young people and teach them the tone qualities of different instruments. It could teach the whole history of musical forms and engender love and enthusiasm for music, but the radio could never teach how to play the piano, how to sing, and how to compose music. These skills he held could be taught only by local teachers who worked individually with the learner. The teacher and the radio, in the words of Mr. Damrosch, work "hand in hand." [1]

The *Columbia Broadcasting System* inaugurated the American School of the Air, which gave one half-hour periods of instruction two days a week the first year, and a half hour every school day in 1930–1931. Programs included historical drama, nature study, vocational guidance, and a wide range of other topics designed to fit the needs of schools. Handbooks in these topics were issued at the beginning of the school-year. Like the Damrosch broadcast, the program reached a school audience estimated in the millions. [2]

The *Ohio School of the Air* represents, according to the United States Office of Education, the most extensive and thorough effort of any State Department of Education in the United States to supplement the regular work of the school by radio instruction. The programs are supported by a direct appropriation from the State Legislature and are broadcast one hour each school day. These include many subjects in the curricula

---

[1] "Radio and Education," *Proceedings of the Fourth Annual Assembly of the National Advisory Council on Radio in Education*, pp. 142–143, University of Chicago Press, 1934.

[2] *Report, United States Office of Education, 1928–1930*, p. 631. United States Office of Education (Dept. of the Interior).

of the grades and high schools. A wider coverage than Ohio is achieved through the courtesy of coöperating stations; in 1930 the programs were heard in 29 states.

E. D. Jarvis of Fort Recovery, Ohio, stated in 1929–1930 that the following were the objectives set up for school broadcasts; (a) to broaden the outlook or vision of the pupils; (b) to supplement classroom teaching; (c) to create, hold, and utilize interest; (d) to develop further intellectual culture; (e) to advance the cause of education; (f) to inspire the pupil; (g) to develop habits of concentration, thought, and listening; (h) to stimulate voluntary self-activity along desirable lines; (i) to stimulate the efforts of the teacher; (j) to supply certain needed recreational benefits; and (k) to allow the teacher to study individual differences.[1]

The Ohio School of the Air while not specifically designed for the rural school, apparently fills a need there. Said Mr. Jarvis:

. . . There is not the need for radio as a teaching device in the larger city schools that there is in the small village, the consolidated school, or the one-room rural school. In these smaller schools, library facilities, educational equipment, and instruction in general are likely to be limited, and any device useful in the enrichment of the curriculum is welcomed with delight.[2]

Commenting on the same point the United States Office of Education said:

Reports from all parts of Ohio show how the program of the Ohio School of the Air affects the individual schools. Rural teachers are able to obtain the assistance of the best teachers in the State through radio. When they prepare the pupils for the radio lessons in advance the interest of the classes usually is keen, and it leads to profitable discussions of the radio lesson at the end of the session. Also the teacher in the school learns from the radio teacher methods which she can profitably employ. The radio receiver brings music to schools

[1] Jarvis, E. D. "Teachers' Uses of the Ohio School of the Air," *Education on the Air*, pp. 162–163, Ohio State University, 1932.

[2] *Ibid.* p. 163.

which otherwise would have none. It places the pupils and teachers in direct contact with the leaders in many fields of thought.[1]

EXPERIMENTS IN THE USE OF RADIO IN SCHOOLS
TEACHERS COLLEGE, COLUMBIA UNIVERSITY

According to those most experienced in radio education the use of this modern teaching aid calls for special techniques in its use. In 1929, under a special grant from the Keith Fund, the Rural Education Department of Teachers College, Columbia, set up a research bureau to study the use and value of radios in rural schools, especially in schools of one room. Miss Margaret Harrison, who directed the research, stated that the investigators hoped to set up techniques by which the material on the air could be successfully adopted into the regular teaching day of the small school. Rural schools in New York, New Jersey, Connecticut, Delaware, Pennsylvania, and Maryland cooperated in the work. While the study was primarily concerned with the use of available radio programs, there was also an effort made to determine whether or not children profited from their use. Miss Harrison reported on two such objective tests, one of the Damrosch music hour, and the other in the field of nature study. Of the former Miss Harrison reported a decided growth of information. In the nature study test it was believed that (a) the interests of the children in animals and birds had increased about 30 per cent, and (b) there was a growth in specific information in which the average child grew from a score of 60 to a score of 74.9. Miss Harrison further concluded from her study the following: (a) that rural children receive new standards in speech from the radio; (b) that the radio increases the number and intensity of children's interests; (c) that it tends to increase the scope of the rural child's vicarious experiences; (d) that it offers material which the rural child could not otherwise receive; (e) that it is a means of carrying over the interests

[1] *Report, United States Commissioner of Education, 1928–1930*, p. 632. United States Office of Education (Dept. of the Interior).

of children from local to national and international fields; and (f) that it gives children varied points of view.[1]

THE MADDY EXPERIMENT

In 1930 Joseph E. Maddy of the University of Michigan experimented with the teaching of band music in the schools of small villages and towns throughout the state of Michigan. Each school participating was asked to appoint a local person who would agree to accept leadership in the group. These volunteer leaders were drawn from an interesting diversified group of vocations—teachers, janitors, ministers, and barbers. A handbook was provided for five lessons which were broadcast by the University band under the direction of Mr. Maddy. Between lessons the groups were visited by Mr. Maddy, who gave a twenty-minute lesson to the players and conferred with the leader for about ten. Mr. Maddy concluded that the experiment was successful, but expressed doubts as to how far the students could progress without personal instruction. The following conclusions were drawn: (a) that it is possible to secure close home coöperation in music broadcasts since parents often listened in; (b) that a fine development in tone quality might be expected since the class must play softly in order to hear the broadcast; and (c) that children received education in harmony from the studio band.

The success of the Maddy experiment is indicated by the following report of it in 1934:

The outstanding achievement of these radio courses will be best understood from a few illustrations. Arenac County, comprising the villages of Standish, Omer, Au Gres, Turner, Twinning, and Sterling, which has a population of eight thousand, had no music teacher and no school music prior to the first radio class in 1931. Every village school in the county organized radio classes in 1931 and thereafter was a regular participant. The county now has six full-time music teachers with more than one thousand regular music students—

[1] Harrison, Margaret. "The Teachers College Experiment," *Education on the Air*, pp. 215–217, Ohio State University, 1930.

children and adults. One school in this county purchased a used piano with 50 chickens.[1]

For small high schools and rural schools which cannot afford a band leader the plan promulgated by Mr. Maddy appears to have in it possibilities of considerable significance not only for immediate aid, but for future development.

THE USE OF RADIO IN CLASSROOMS

There is truth in the statement that children will continue to learn by radio, whether or not the schools do anything about it. In this the radio resembles the moving picture, except that its possibilities are perhaps even greater and its influence more powerful. Only rich, powerful school systems can afford moving picture apparatus but poor and small indeed is the school which cannot afford a radio. It is a piece of equipment which nearly all schools can afford to buy, and which few can afford to ignore. How to make effective use of it is probably the primary problem of the classroom teacher. E. D. Jarvis of Fort Recovery, Ohio, divides this problem into three and lists them as follows: (a) how to prepare a class for a broadcast; (b) how to use the lesson and make it effective; (c) how to obtain a measurement of its effectiveness.[2]

HOW TO PREPARE A CLASS FOR A BROADCAST

All those experimenting with radio in the field of education are agreed that the radio cannot be effectively used by hit-and-miss methods. To be effective the radio lessons must be presented to children who have been prepared for it. This is achieved in many ways and the broadcast station has coöperated in them. Thus there are manuals prepared for many radio

[1] Maddy, Joseph E. "Expanding Music Education in Michigan," *Education on the Air*, p. 98, Ohio State University, 1934.

[2] Jarvis, E. D. "Teachers' Uses of the Ohio School of the Air," *Education on the Air*, p. 167, Ohio State University, 1932.

series, mimeographed lesson outlines, booklets and various other organizations of materials designed to assist both teacher and pupil in preparation for the actual broadcast. These study helps should be used as any other reference material, as possible aids in solving problems. If the broadcast is of interest to the whole room, then the whole setting of it should be moved in that direction. Mr. Jarvis suggests the following procedure:

1. The room should be made into a visual laboratory to supplement the auditory stimuli upon which the radio lesson is based. If the broadcast is a typical lesson, pictures, charts, globes, maps, models, blackboards, and all other pertinent materials should be on display and ready for use.

2. The assignment covering the radio lesson should be as definite, as detailed, and as anticipatory of difficulties as are other assignments.

3. Provision should be made in the assignment for student activity to follow the broadcast.

4. The teacher should create a sense of expectancy, of intense interest, and of mental receptivity. He should develop in children the feeling that the broadcast is important because it will be helpful in solving some of their problems.

5. The habit of prompt readiness for the broadcast should be fixed. Children should have at hand all materials to be used, pencils, papers, reference and note books. Activities should cease and children should remain quietly seated once the broadcast has begun.[1]

HOW TO USE THE LESSON AND MAKE IT EFFECTIVE

There are, apparently, two sources of lesson materials on the air which can be successfully used by the schools; namely, the materials broadcast by the schools of the air, referred to above, and the program which is educational in its nature, but not specifically designated for schools. In general, the schools of the air follow the regular school curriculum and the programs

[1] Jarvis, E. D. "Teachers' Uses of the Ohio School of the Air," *Education on the Air*, pp. 168–169, Ohio State University, 1932.

are designed to supplement textbook materials. The "extra-school broadcasts" consist usually of current events, addresses of prominent men and women, and talks on books; they do not belong to a regular plan, but are to be used "catch as catch can." The use of the radio lesson, therefore, will depend some-what upon the choice of it. This presupposes a wide acquaint-ance, on the part of the teacher, with the materials available, and calls for planning, sometimes days in advance. Miss Harrison in her Teachers' College experiment felt that the teachers who were the most successful were those who used only the features which fitted into their programs.

One example of this is a Japanese program which was given as a cooking lesson, the real purpose being to give housewives recipes on Japanese food. Mixed with it was some music, to make it more interesting, and stories of methods of eating in Japan. We happened to have many schools in Connecticut which, in the Social Science periods were taking an imaginary trip to the Orient. Many of these students were supposed to be returning to the United States by way of Japan, and they were very enthusiastic about this radio program. Because they were studying Japan, it fitted into their curriculum; children are interested in eating; and they enjoyed the music. In a two-room school about forty miles from New York City two girls copied the recipes, and used them in giving the whole school a Japanese hot lunch the next day. That is education.[1]

Other uses to which the radio lesson can be put are suggested as follows:

(1) Nearly every radio broadcasting company in the country de-votes some of its time to a broadcast of current events and news. Children in the small rural school can thus keep abreast of the times as easily as children in the largest cities.

(2) Homemaking programs give much of their time to cooking classes. Children engaged in hot-lunch activities in the small schools might use these programs with profit.

(3) Famous people in the field of politics, art, letters, and music

[1] Harrison, Margaret. "The Teachers' College Experiment," *Education on the Air*, p. 215, Ohio State University, 1930.

frequently broadcast and these can be correlated with English, history, music, and art.

(4) Dramatization of standard literature offers a rich field for stimulating drama as a form of expression in the small school.

(5) Foreign broadcasts offer much possibility for the teaching of geographical material and the broadcast may properly be developed as a part of a social science unit.

(6) Listening to a broadcast is passive, but activities should follow it. Clever teachers and children are never at a loss in the use of materials obtained over the air.

There are many methods of utilizing these programs both for class study and individual work.

In one school the sixth, seventh and eighth grades used radio-news items in several ways. They wrote "Associated Press" articles for the school paper. To use the material for their articles, the children had to learn to take notes from the radio. They learned to file their notes for future reference. With their notes, they filed newspaper and magazine articles on the same subject. They learned to judge radio programs and to select materials. They read other mediums for further information. They wrote editorials for the school paper. They found that the radio frequently added information and interest to subjects they were already studying. Throughout the year, this use of radio-news items stimulated new activities and gave constant practice in composition, spelling, filing, note-taking, reading in the sciences and social studies.[1]

All sorts of school activities develop naturally from radio broadcasts. Musical programs offer opportunities for group work in rhythm. Handwork arises from programs to be directed toward sand tables, notebooks, and compositions. Creative writing, especially in the field of poetry and story telling often follows the broadcasting of a stimulating talk on art, music, or poetry.

The use of radio programs in teaching fits in admirably with the informal organization recommended for the small rural

[1] Harrison, Margaret. "Using Extra-School Broadcastings," *Education on the Air*, pp. 184–185, Ohio State University Press, 1931.

school. Children of all age levels listen to a program together, like a family, enjoying companionship in a common experience. Vicarious though the experience may be, it is apparently valuable as an instrument through which children may share the experiences of others and thus grow in understanding. The proper use of the programs necessitates close correlation with the regular work of the school, and each teacher should plan her work accordingly. If the teacher earnestly keeps in mind the primary purpose of the school and thinks in terms of educational objectives and child growth, the radio may become a powerful educational aid.

SUMMARY

Modern education draws heavily upon many fields for aids in teaching. The arts, science, and the commercial fields have all made contributions which make learning more meaningful and education richer. From the standpoint of the rural school there are three modern aids in teaching which have large significance. These are: (a) visual aids, (b) the school excursion, and (c) the radio.

In the matter of visual aids the chief problem of the small rural school is to assemble them. This may best be achieved through the activities of children, since the experience itself is educational and the results helpful in their further learning. Once the pictures are assembled, it is recommended that they be filed in so orderly a fashion that they are readily available. Such an assembled file, if kept up-to-date, becomes an invaluable source of reference material, especially in the fields of English and the social sciences. In addition, the visual materials motivate work, deepen learning impressions, and give color to classwork which otherwise might be drab and dull.

The school excursion is another aid in teaching employed by modern rural schools. It is a type of activity which makes learning realistic and helps to identify the child with his environment. The rural school environment is rich in assets for such excursions, and the modern teacher seeks to take advantage of them. However, the school excursion does more than interpret immediate environments to children. It also seeks to introduce to children the educational resources found in nearby cities. Visits to city museums, to art galleries, to libraries, to concerts and zoos (since much of the culture of the world is concentrated in cities) are recommended for rural children. To be educational the school excursion should be carefully selected and planned. On the whole, the program of excursions should be made on the basis of the leading community activities and their interconnections with the outside world. The planning should be accomplished by children with the guidance of teachers. In the planning, conclusions on the following seem essential: (a) an agreement on standards of behavior for the trip; (b) setting up of questions which the children hope to have answered by the excursion; (c) the assembling of the materials for the trip. The desirable outcomes which may properly be expected from a well-conducted school excursion are as follows: (a) real and vital learning which links the theory found in books with the practice found in life; (b) a deeper interest in the topic under discussion; (c) practice in desirable behavior and safety habits; (d) growth in the technique of observation and research; (e) an appreciation of the child's environment; (f) development toward a more complete knowledge of the social heritage not found in books; and (g) inspiration for creative expression.

The radio, a modern aid in teaching, is yet in the experimental stage, but gives promise even in experimentation of developing into a powerful aid in teaching, especially in the fields of music, the social sciences, and current events. Various experiments have pointed the way for the use of this aid, notably those of Teachers College, Columbia, in the field of the small rural school, and that of Joseph E. Maddy in the field of music. These, with such broadcasts as the Damrosch music hour, and those of the *Ohio School of the Air* testify to the value of the radio in teaching and give promise of the following results: (a) new standards in speech; (b) an increase in the number and intensity of the interests of children; (c) an increase in the scope of the vicarious experiences of children; (d) materials which children would otherwise not receive; (e) a widening of the local interests of children into national and international ones; (f) the attainment of varied points of view.

The use of the radio in the classroom resolves itself into three problems: (a) how to prepare a class for a broadcast; (b) how to use the lesson and make it effective; (c) how to obtain a measurement of its effectiveness. The radio lesson, like any other, must be carefully planned and thoughtfully presented. Poor results may be expected from the "hit-and-miss use" of the most modern of all teaching aids. The teacher and children should make as careful preparation for the lesson and as earnest an approach to it as in the use of any other reference materials. There are two chief sources of materials on the air available to the teacher. These are (a) organized curriculum materials such as is broadcast by the *Ohio School of the Air;* and (b) "extra curricular" activities secured from educational materials, not specifically ear-marked for schools.

The three modern teaching aids, discussed in this chapter, are available now for the energetic rural teacher of initiative and vision. They should be speedily introduced into all small schools, since trends indicate that teaching in the future will continue to use all mediums that make curriculum materials more interesting and the learning process more vital.

SUGGESTED READINGS

Bain, Winifred E. *Parents Look at Modern Education,* Chap. XII, D. Appleton-Century Co., New York, 1936.

Education on the Air. First Yearbook of the Institute for Education by Radio, p. 213, Ohio State University, Columbus, 1930.

Education on the Air. Second Yearbook of the Institute for Education by Radio, p. 182, Ohio State University, Columbus, 1931.

Education on the Air. Third Yearbook of the Institute for Education by Radio, p. 245, Ohio State University, Columbus, 1932.

Forman, Henry James. *Our Movie Made Children,* Chap. I, Macmillan, New York, 1933.

Israel, Marion L. "Picture Helps for Smaller Schools," *Proceedings of the National Education Association*, 1931, pp. 953–957, Washington, D. C.

Owen, Estelle. "Practical Aid to School Excursions," *Childhood Education*, Vol. 9 (Dec., 1932), pp. 146–148.

Peterson, A. G. "Adventures in Real Learning," *Progressive Education*, Vol. 10 (Mar., 1933), pp. 154–158.

Parker, Beryl, ed. *Studies of Environment*, Association for Childhood Education, Washington, D. C., 1931.

Thirteenth Yearbook. Department of Elementary School Principals. "Aids to Teaching in the Elementary School," Chaps. I, II, V, National Education Association, Washington, D. C., 1934.

MATERIALS FOR DISCUSSION

Consider the following statements. What changes would make them more acceptable to you? What significant issues arise from their study?

1. There is a tendency in the use of visual materials in the classroom to make them ends in themselves. Used as such they become detrimental in both the teaching and learning process.

2. The assembly and classification of visual materials in the rural schools is an educational experience in itself, and the time thus spent by children and teacher can be justified on this ground.

3. The concomitant learnings of a school excursion are often more important than those resulting from a planned program.

4. The radio has the possibility of developing into the most powerful educational instrument yet devised by man.

5. Many of the educational problems inherent in the small school can be met by the wise use of the three modern instruments of teaching listed in this chapter.

CHAPTER XV

ENVIRONMENTAL CONTROLS OF LEARNING— SCHOOL BUILDINGS AND EQUIPMENT

No ONE can thoughtfully observe the architecture of a country without being aware of the relationship which exists between a people and their art. The philosophy of social groups gives form to buildings; and the architecture of an age reflects the ideas and ideals of the society which produced it not less truthfully than literature mirrors the mind and heart of a nation. Architecture, therefore, is the flowering of a culture rooted firmly in the attitudes of men; the fact that we think of it in terms of style—Gothic, Tudor, Colonial, Modern—indicates that it is an expression of the composite soul of the period. These are terms which not only conjure up the picture of an architectural style, but conceptions of broad, national cultures. The architecture of the buildings in which the educational process has taken place is no exception to the general rule. It, too, reflects the educational philosophy of its time.

THE HISTORICAL BACKGROUND OF SCHOOL BUILDINGS

The first American school houses reflected the philosophy of the pioneer period as faithfully as did the curriculum. They were simple one-room "box-car" buildings constructed from the same materials that went into the first American homes, logs for the South and East, sod and adobe for the West. They were built with three ideals in mind: simplicity, economy, and a narrow program of learning. This narrow program provided for few activities, chief of which was reading. Consequently, the school equipment was simple, consisting largely of benches on which students sat and recited with narrow aisles through which they passed, military style, back and forth to class and out of doors.

The school building of this pioneer pattern continued meager and inadequate for many years. As late as 1900, while the average school building showed improvement over the log and sod buildings of the nineteenth century, the rural school houses were far below the standard set by the urban districts of the same period. In fact, it was not until after the educational revival of 1900 that the improvement was marked. Even then, the improvement was local until after 1910. A study made in 1910 by a Joint Commission of the National Council of Education and the American Medical Association, headed by Fletcher B. Dresslar, *Rural Schoolhouses and Grounds*, did much to give the problem national significance. The Report of the Commission was published as a government bulletin in 1914, and in a preface to it, the Hon. P. P. Claxton, then United States Commissioner of Education, said that most of the older schoolhouses in the rural districts were cheap, uncomfortable, badly ventilated, poorly heated and lighted, with no convenience for school work. The Commission gathered the data from eighteen states and its findings were that 58 per cent of the rural school buildings had inadequate play space, that 63 per cent of them were old, and that the great majority of the rural schools in 1910 were housed in one-room buildings inadequate for a sound educational program.

PLANS IN THE SCHOOL BUILDING REFORM

In the period of the reform following this Report and the Report of the subsequent Roosevelt Country Life Commission various state-wide plans were proposed in an effort to remedy mistakes and to prevent further ones. These plans were as follows: (a) consolidation of small school buildings into large ones and the provision of state building aid for them; (b) state aid for the improvement and building of the small schools; (c) the standardization of the small rural school through score cards and the setting up of standards of varying degrees; (d) the provision by legal enactment for the approval of all plans and the acceptance of school buildings by the state departments of education.

The consolidation of small schools nearly always necessitates the building of a new central building; and it has been almost the universal practice to build one conforming to the best type in current school architecture. According to the Biennial Survey of Education, 1930–1932 there were in the United States in 1932, 17,008 such consolidated school buildings. Twenty-seven states have made legal provisions for granting state aid to consolidated schools for buildings, transportation, or current expenses. Alabama, for example, granted $232,999 for these purposes in 1926 and Georgia $300,000 the same year.[1] This aid is usually granted when certain standards are met, and since these standards are relatively high, the plan has had a salutary effect on recent buildings in the consolidated areas. On the whole, these buildings compare favorably with the best modern elementary schools in urban areas.

Not only have states provided for building aid to consolidated schools, but there are various legal plans to aid in the improvement and building of the small school plant. The states having such plans are: Alabama, Arkansas, Delaware, Iowa, Maine, Minnesota, New York, North Dakota, Pennsylvania, South Carolina, South Dakota, Tennessee, Vermont, Virginia, West Virginia, and Wisconsin. As in the case of consolidated schools, the modern small school must also comply with specified building requirements before the aid is granted. Since these requirements are outlined in terms of sanitation, health, and learning procedure, the small schools have greatly profited.

Another plan widely used for improving the building and equipment of rural schools is the rating and standardization of them, in accordance with state rating scales set up by the

[1] *Outlook for Rural Education*, pp. 286–288, Research Bulletin, Vol. 9, 1931, National Education Association.

state departments of education. In 1930 the Bureau of Research of the National Education Association made a study of eleven of these score cards including the following states: Arkansas, Idaho, Kansas, Michigan, Mississippi, Nebraska, Ohio, Tennessee, Texas, Vermont, and West Virginia. All of them had many points in common suggesting that a good one-room school should have: correct construction, proper lighting, good housekeeping arrangements, proper ventilation and heating, and adequate floor space. Items of adequate equipment in the sampling included: single desks, special kindergarten and primary furniture, book cases, supply cupboards, teacher's desks, blackboards, supplementary books, globes, maps, musical instruments, and reference books. This plan nearly always resulted in the grouping of schools into classes A, B, C, D, and E, and schools of each division have striven through the raising of standards to attain the final rating of a Grade A school. It has given both school and community a systematic procedure for the improvement of the physical condition of the school and a reward, at various levels, for accomplishments.

State departments of education have also found it profitable to provide special divisions on school-building planning and the services of school building architects. Many states have instituted special drafting and planning bureaus in State departments of education. The newer types of rural schools, particularly the consolidated schools, show the results of their work, notably in the improvement of hygienic conditions, and in the provisions made for a modern program of education. Needless to say, both pupil and teacher have profited by the changed environment. In announcing the creation of such building services in 1928 the State of Mississippi announced that the program would be three-fold: (a) to foster the construction of hygienic and educationally efficient school plants; (b) to eliminate waste in planning and constructing the school plant; and (c) to foster the proper use and care of school buildings.

THE URBAN DEVELOPMENT OF SCHOOL BUILDINGS

Historically the urban school buildings have always fared better than the rural. With the concentration of people in cities, the school buildings serving the urban group improved in line with other educational facilities. They became larger, more comfortable and, with the increased knowledge brought to the urban field by professional leadership, more scientifically constructed. Here too, the improvements were almost wholly in the field of sanitation, health, and architecture. Reflecting the industrial ideals of the age, the buildings were large and factory-like, constructed on a standardized plan, and for the most part dreary and uninviting in appearance. Arthur B. Moehlman, Professor of School Administration, University of Michigan, stated in an article entitled *The Evolution of the School Plant* that from the opening of the Barstow Union School in 1850 to 1916 there was practically no development in elementary school interior planning except for the addition of the kindergarten.[1] The development after 1916 was still in terms of a traditional curriculum set in a factory environment. The building was usually of two stories with a basement, and in the latter was housed the new subjects of the curriculum which characterized that period: home economics, manual training, and physical training. The auditorium was above the gymnasium and the rest of the building was divided into classrooms, one for each grade. Education, even at this period, was narrow, hence the undeveloped buildings and the meager equipment. Teaching was largely drill and discipline. Children sat in formal rows of seats, giving back to teachers what was demanded of them. Later on Tudor fronts and Colonial doorways beautified the outside, but the inside, where the important work of education was in process, remained practically the same. A grade for a teacher in a standardized room was the goal in buildings and in education.

[1] *American School Board Journal.* Vol. 77 (Dec. 1928), p. 62.

MODERN PROGRESS IN SCHOOL BUILDING PLANNING

The modern conception of education presages great changes in the school architecture of the future. True, there is little evidence of such changes at present, except in the field of the modern private school; but, with such differences in points of view and curriculum as are now accepted, corresponding developments in school architecture will inevitably appear. Frank H. Wood, President of the Board of Education, Chatham, New York, speaking before a National Conference on School Planning called by the United States Office of Education in 1930 said:

We must start with the child in the center. We should begin with the school home of the child, interior rather than exterior.[1]

Contrasted with this point of view is the statement made at the same conference by the deputy superintendent of one of America's largest urban school systems. He places administration first and the educational program second:

The first job of the educational planner is to determine the type, size, and number of physical units required and so arrange these units as to conform to the demands of effective administration and proper building orientation. Having done this, his next step is to help the architect to plan a building which conforms to the educational standards set which is flexible and expansible and which lends itself to good architectural treatment without being over elaborate or extravagant in design.

The conflict in the two points of view of necessity affects the school building program and probably delays the movement to make the American school building as well as the program child-centered.

For some time the child has been made the subject of close study. Through scientific investigation and observation a body of information about children is gradually being accumulated.

[1] *National Advisory Council on School Building Problems.* United States Office of Education, Pamphlet No. 7, 1930, pp. 25–26.

There are certain characteristics, already determined, which appear to persist throughout school life and which apparently have significance for "the school home of the child, interior rather than exterior." These characteristics are: (a) the innate activity of all children, particularly those of the ages and interests of the elementary school; (b) the natural curiosity of children and their eagerness to learn, to explore, and to discover; (c) the persistent use of their hands in the urge to construct; and (d) the tendency of children to organize activities and to work and play in groups. No school building of the future concerned with serving the interests of children can ignore the implications of these findings.

Pioneers of school architecture are already providing for these persistent needs of childhood. New school buildings allow for much child activity. Rooms are larger, the furniture is movable, and there is much playground space. Opportunities for exploration, discovery, and construction in the large elementary schools take the form of special project, laboratory, and reading rooms. In the small schools these needs are telescoped into small spaces: a work table for art, a science shelf for experiments, the library corner for a quiet hour of reading, and a work bench for construction.

The striking feature of the modern school building, said Philip N. Youtz, is this tendency to give increasing space to such project rooms. The forward-looking architect may observe that, if this tendency continues, it will not be many years until the old routine classroom has disappeared and its place has been taken by inviting rooms where children may make discoveries for themselves instead of bending over books.[1]

THE PRESENT STATUS OF SMALL RURAL SCHOOL BUILDINGS

The school building constructed in terms of a modern program of education is an ideal. Actual features of the building now in

[1] "School Buildings That Educate," *Progressive Education*, Vol. 9, 1932, p. 191.

use in rural areas fall far below the ideal. The latest information concerning school property in the United States is available through the United States Survey of Education for 1930–1932. According to this Survey 57.8 per cent of all the school buildings in the United States are of one-room. They are not localized but are found in every state in the union, the range being from approximately 94 per cent in North Dakota to 12 per cent in Utah. Some other states with high percentages of one-room school buildings are: Nebraska, 84 per cent; Wisconsin, 80 per cent; Iowa, 79 per cent; and Minnesota, 77 per cent. It is not in the agricultural states alone that the percentage of one-room buildings is high. The state of New York, largely urban, has 63 per cent of its schools housed in buildings of this type, Illinois exceeds New York by 7 per cent and Michigan has 1 per cent less than Illinois.

In spite of the fact that nearly 60 per cent of the school buildings of the United States are located in rural areas, the estimated value of them is almost one half the value of those located in cities. Measured in terms of average daily attendance, the value is almost three times as great in urban schools as in rural. The expenditure in capital outlay per child for rural schools in 1930 amounted to $12.29 and for the urban group $29.51. The research Bulletin of the National Education Association entitled *The Outlook for Rural Education* on this feature of rural school buildings reads:

With this financial differential operating against the one-room school it is not surprising that in safety, comfort, health, sanitation, and attractiveness, educational fitness and equipment, the rural schoolhouse lags behind national standards.[1]

The value of school property, however, gives only one index to the measurement of a building and its fitness to serve education. The measuring device known as the building score card and the scientific survey of educational systems, both referred

[1] *The Outlook for Rural Education.* Research Bulletin, No. 9, 1931, p. 286, National Education Association.

to in a previous chapter, are valuable sources of information. Both analyze the status of school buildings and give a picture of conditions at the time the measurement is taken. The three score cards most often used in the scoring or rural school buildings are (a) *A Score Card for One- and Two-Teacher School Buildings*, by Julian E. Butterworth; (b) *Score Card for Village and Rural School Buildings of Four Teachers or Less* by George D. Strayer and N. L. Englehardt; and (c) *A Score Card for Rural School Buildings* by E. T. Ashbaugh and P. R. Stevenson. While these score cards are not designed to measure the small schools in terms of a modern program, they reveal the type, the condition, the equipment, and the adjustments for health and sanitation in such buildings. With these items of the picture at hand, it is possible to see more clearly the implication of the building as a controlling factor in the educational process.

A survey made in 1929 of 397 one-teacher school buildings in West Virginia, measured by the Butterworth score card, revealed that the median score of the buildings was 553 out of a possible total of 1000 points. They ranked low in provisions for adequate lighting, heating, and ventilation. Nearly all of them were of the square type of architecture with desks of the non-adjustable type. These and other items lead us to believe that the schools were constructed for a formal type of education whose program consisted of drill, memorization, and a passive acceptance of textbook materials. These buildings, in common with all other school buildings of this period, reflect the educational philosophy of the time.[1]

A survey in 78 one-room school buildings in Texas revealed that the median score was 594 out of a total possible score of 1000. Two-thirds of the buildings had less than the standard amount of window space; approximately 50 per cent had no playground equipment; one-third had no place for hats or cloaks when not in use so that they were left lying on desks and floors; one-third of the schools studied made no effort to shelve

[1] Holy, Thomas C. "School Buildings," *Survey of Education in West Virginia,* Vol. 3, p. 228, 1929.

library books; and four-fifths of the buildings had no ante-room at all.[1] An examination of the results of surveys in other states indicate that these examples are typical. The average school building in the rural areas is inadequate for either the traditional or modern school. On entering one of these buildings the modern teacher is faced with the necessity of harmonizing his philosophy of education with the actual conditions he finds. Fletcher B. Dresslar, specialist in schoolhouse planning, recognized the dilemma of the rural teacher after a national survey of rural areas in 1930 and said:

Everywhere young, well-trained, and enthusiastic teachers enter rural communities to work in school buildings which have no extra rooms such as work rooms, libraries, or teachers' rooms; nor such built-in features as bookcases, lunch cupboards, etc., about which they learned at the teachers' colleges.[2]

HARMONIZATION OF THE PRESENT STATUS OF SCHOOL BUILDINGS AND A MODERN PROGRAM OF EDUCATION

Modern education requires that the school become a laboratory, a home for children, and a community center for adults. The schoolroom and its equipment are thus an active educational agent which affects the teaching and learning process. The controlling features of the buildings, grounds, and equipment are important from the standpoint of the curriculum, and they affect child growth. It is essential for these factors to conform in so far as is possible to the program of education. Yet the teacher at work in one of these small buildings finds a traditional equipment with which she is expected to institute a modern type program. If it is a one-room building, it is nevertheless expected that all educational procedures will take place within its circumscribed space. If the building has two or three rooms,

[1] Works, George A. "Organization and Administration," *Texas Educational Survey*, Vol. I, Chap. 18, 1925.

[2] *Rural Schoolhouses, School Grounds and Their Equipment*, p. 2, United States Office of Education, Bulletin 21, 1930.

there is little difference in the set-up except that the conditions in the one-room have been multiplied by two or three, as the case may be. The difference lies in quantity and not quality.

The question here, of course, is the practical one of how a modern program of education can be instituted in a building constructed for a traditional one. Naturally, there are only two ways of meeting this situation: either the traditional school building must be replaced with a modern one designed to accommodate the needs of children and a modern program, or the old building must be adjusted to meet the new requirements. Obviously, it is not possible or practical to replace at one time all small, poorly constructed buildings with modern ones; consequently, the wisest program at the present appears to be one of adjustment. There are many evidences that such a program is in process in rural areas.

As was suggested above, authorities are apparently in agreement that the school building which best serves the modern program of education should have the following characteristics: (1) It should be a laboratory and a workshop for children. (2) It should be home-like. (3) It should be a community center for adults and children. These characteristics suggest modifications in the average school plant. All three, for instance, seem to require movable furniture. Such equipment is desirable to make the room homelike in appearance; it suggests possibilities and space for laboratory facilities; and with it the room can be quickly cleared for a community meeting. Too, such equipment offers opportunity for social development, it allows children to work in varied group activities, it is easy to use in individual instruction, and it assists in breaking down the caste attitude characteristic of the traditional arrangement of the schoolroom into "the little folks and big children's side of the house, with the teacher established in the front." For this modification, tables and chairs are usually used, or a unit of seat and desk arranged on an easily moved standard. If the purchase of new seats is not possible, and unhappily it often is not, the stationary units may be nailed to skids, four inches wide and the length of the unit desired, and the old desks will thus become in a sense movable. If tables and chairs can be provided for primary children, the situation will be much improved. If none of these modifications is possible, the teacher should not let the screwed down condition of the desks deter him from instituting an activity type of program. If desks are stationary, children need not be; at least they can move about the room. Two of the characteristics of the modern school, namely, the school as a workshop, and as the school home are discussed below. The third characteristic, the school as a community center, is presented at some length in a subsequent chapter entitled *The School and the Community*.

THE SCHOOL AS A WORKSHOP

Ideally, every child should have his own work space where he keeps his personal supplies. In many urban schools this space is provided by flat-topped, individual tables with chairs to match. Both chairs and tables are easily moved, and lend themselves to committee work, to conference, and to class discussion. Few rural schools have such modern equipment but the teacher can insist upon individual desks adjusted to the needs of children. Individual adjustment suggests that the desk should fit the growing body of each child, that the light should be good for him at all times during the day, and that his special needs in hearing and giving attention should be regarded. He should also have adequate space provided for reading, for constructing, for writing, and for drawing. Every school desk in itself should represent for children a place where tasks are accomplished without lost motion.

One or two work tables should be provided for the room, wide enough to hold charts and maps and low enough for children to use with comfort and efficiency. If the room is small and crowded, the table in the library corner can serve a double purpose. Such tables are almost essential for they give opportunities for construction, for painting, and for all sorts of activities which children like and naturally engage in. If no money is available, often the children can construct a table, and cheapness itself becomes a socially useful school project.

Every inch of space in the room is used by teachers and children engaged in an activity program. Spaces under windows are utilized for shelves to hold experiments and exhibits. In some rooms corners are fitted up for special uses, such as the science, the nature study, and the library corner. A work bench outfitted with simple tools for construction is nearly always in evidence. Cloak rooms are made to do double duty. Hooks for coats and hats and racks for overshoes are provided, and above these, rows of shelves may be built. These often reach to the ceiling and provide the storage space essential for supplies and work in progress. Work overflows into the entry, the basement, and the out-of-doors. The facilities of the small school must be developed to the point where they serve the functions of several rooms in larger schools.

Space, however, is not the only item to be considered in the making of the school into a workshop. Children should have tools with which to work, and in a modern program of education these consist of more than a textbook, a pencil, and paper. Materials should be supplied for various forms of expression. For expression in the arts, for example, there should be available, construction paper, paints, crayons, and at least one easel. One musical instrument is essential, many are desirable. Thus it is no longer considered extravagant for a rural school to own at one and the same time a piano, or organ, a victrola, and a radio; all three contribute to satisfactory modern living outside, and to learning inside the school. Soap for carving, clay for modeling, and wood for whittling are also important as media through which children of today find artistic expression.

For experiments in the sciences simple apparatus should be provided. Scales, a thermometer, a magnifying glass, a magnet, insect jars, cotton, field glasses, bottles, a spectroscope, a herbarium, an aquarium, a feeding station for birds, bird-houses, a syphon, and seed testing trays are a few of the tools which should be made available for rural children if we wish them to be earnest students in this world of science. A good collection of such apparatus may be assembled at low cost, particularly if the teacher has an inventive turn of mind. A spectroscope, for instance, may be constructed from a tin can, a light bulb, and a mirror. An aquarium may be fashioned out of a galvanized laundry tub painted with aluminum paint, or a five- or ten-gallon glass water bottle whose top has been cracked by heat. A glass bottle or a can makes an excellent substitute for an expensive herbarium. Rubber tubing makes a satisfactory syphon.[1]

For expression in the social sciences it is essential that the modern school be supplied with adequate reference materials and supplementary reading books. These, however, have been discussed somewhat at length in a previous chapter entitled *Books as Tools of Learning.*

THE SCHOOL AS A HOME

One of the very first steps in the institution of a modern program of education is to make the schoolroom into a small home. This process involves steps to deinstitutionalize the school by making the schoolroom attractive, homelike, and colorful. It is not difficult of achievement nor is it expensive. Any teacher with imagination and energy and with the help of the children can easily effect the transformation. The most unlikely schoolroom responds to light-colored draperies at the window, growing potted plants, a rug or two, a few pictures or prints, and an inviting library corner. Mrs. Belle Nichols, a teacher in a one-room school near Clarence, New York, demonstrated such a procedure for the State Teachers College at Buffalo, and her experience is offered here as a case study.

[1] Suggestions are given in the appendix for the substitution of inexpensive for expensive teaching materials and equipment. The inexperienced rural teachers will probably find these suggestions helpful. A minimum list of equipment for small schools may be found also in the appendix.

These data were assembled by practice teaching students assigned to the school for the school year of 1935–1936.[1]

CASE STUDY——VIII

When Mrs. Nichols arrived at the school in 1935, she found a small, square building of cement, built in 1860. It had been well-built—the walls were approximately twelve inches thick— and this fact, together with the presence of a jacketed stove, guaranteed comfort even in zero weather. The thickness of the wall and the consequent deep-set windows, eight in number, three on each side and two at the back of the room, were a solid prisonlike foundation, which made the windows themselves appear narrow and unattractive. At the front of the building there were two cloakrooms, ample in size, but apparently of no use except to hold discarded materials, which were piled to the ceiling with the accumulation of years: broken-down desks, old black-boards, and old books. There was no electricity. Water for drinking and washing purposes had to be carried from a neighboring house. Fortunately, the building was equipped with movable desks, but these, together with a piano and the teacher's desk and chairs, constituted the furniture of the school. The teaching equipment was meager, consisting of a globe, maps, and a few books. The toilets were out-of-doors, directly behind the schoolhouse. The school yard gave no evidence of care or attention, but was saved from utter dreariness by two old apple trees shading one side of the grounds, their presence a happy accident. Both the interior and exterior of the school building bespoke the institution; there was nothing homelike about either. They gave evidence of being designed for a formal program of education, since neither the building nor the equipment had any characteristics of a workshop or laboratory.

[1] Reported by practice students of the school taught by Mrs. Belle Nichols, Clarence, New York. Mr. Archie W. Harkness, District Superintendent of Schools, Erie County, New York.

An analysis of the situation presented to the mind of the teacher still other unpromising conditions with which she had to deal. The health problem of the school was particularly acute. The out-of-door toilet, the transfer of water from a neighboring well, and the lack of provision for a hot lunch—all were a menace to the health and happiness of the children. The schoolroom was unattractive, drab, and gloomy. It had no provision for any activity except reading, and for that there was no quiet spot to which a child might retreat. All in all, the outlook did not seem hopeful. The budget for the year had been voted upon in the spring and since the installation of indoor toilets and running water is expensive, such innovations were obviously an impossibility; any program of improvement would of necessity be a program of adjustment.

The first step taken by Mrs. Nichols was a wise one. She took the children of the school into her confidence and asked for their coöperation. She outlined the situation as she saw it and asked for suggestions. The children set up as an objective for the year the making of their school a sanitary and attractive place. They began their program with one of the cloakrooms, long unused, which they decided to make into a kitchen, thus meeting two of the needs of the school at one time. The children cleared out the debris, papered the walls, built a set of shelves reaching from floor to ceiling, and painted the inside door and window facings a soft green. Curtains blending with the wall paper were hung at the windows and over the shelves designed to hold kitchen supplies. A kerosene oil stove donated to the school and a table with two matching benches, constructed by the children, equipped the little room. It was singularly satisfactory, when completed, and its uses were many and varied. In it was prepared the daily hot dish for the school lunch described in Chapter VII. It served as a storage place for supplies; it was an attractive spot to which a group of children might go for conference and committee meetings. The other cloakroom was similarly treated except that the use to which it was put was different. An orderly system of keeping wraps and overshoes was agreed upon and the room used for this purpose, in addition to its use for drinking water and hand-washing facilities. Through coöperative efforts the main schoolroom itself began to take on the characteristics of a home and workshop. Curtains of soft but cheerful colors were used at the windows. These were drawn completely to the sides of the narrow windows in order to admit all possible light, and the drab walls took on color. Growing plants and vines added further charm and gaiety to the room. A library corner with its own delightful atmosphere was developed; a work table with a few tools for construction was added; and a shelf was set up for exhibits and simple scientific experiments. At the end of a year of work, even a casual visitor could see that the school was different, in appearance at least, from the average school. It was more convenient, more pleasing to the eye, full of activities, and the children were busy and happy.

AN ANALYSIS OF THE PROCEDURE

An analysis of this procedure of adjustment of environmental controls to a modern program of education reveals certain sound educational principles. (1) The adjustment was made in practical terms. There was no effort to attempt the impossible either in effort or in outlay. The teacher and the children delimited their problem into those aspects possible of solution at the present and those best postponed to some future time. This was the part of wisdom in both choices and procedures. (2) The program was planned in terms of objectives and the work to achieve them was systematic and orderly. First things came first, and, as each objective was achieved, children and teacher proceeded to the next one. (3) Criteria for harmonizing the room with a program of modern education were applied and efforts which did not achieve this goal were abandoned and others substituted for them. (4) Coöperation of teacher and pupils characterized the achievement of all objectives. Thus the very adjustment itself constituted an activity full of educational possibilities. Children worked on committees; they conferred with each other, with their teacher, and with local community people. They developed habits of coöperation and capacity for leadership. All of the activities in construction, painting, and sewing offered practice in applying the children's knowledge of arithmetic, English, art, and language. They measured; they calculated; they bought materials. They developed standards of taste in the choice and use of colors to obtain effects. The project was a coöperative one and all profited from the experience. Of such a coöperative activity Miss Helen Hay Heyl of the State Department of Education, Albany, New York, has this to say:

Socialization of the school atmosphere, through which a school home gradually emerges in place of the traditional schoolhouse, even where the building itself remains largely unchanged. The phases of this evolution are; first, introduction of the idea and practice of pupil participation, through the organization of committees of children to assist in school beautification and school housekeeping, school and playground management, and similar activities. This practice is gradually extended, as pupils gain power to manage their own affairs and to decorate and arrange their own school homes, until full responsibility is carried by the children with the teacher acting as assistant and guide. Second, extension of the same idea into the actual teaching and learning processes. Although traditional "lessons" are still being taught and recitations made, pupils are participating to some degree in planning the work. Gradually children are encouraged to assume larger responsibility for planning.[1]

Since there are no score cards available for measuring the building, grounds, and equipment in terms of an activity program, the theory classes at the State Teachers College at Buffalo, New York, adopted and used for this purpose the suggestions made by the California Teachers Guide to Child Development to make schools more pleasant places. These suggestions are:[2]

[1] National Society for the Study of Education. *The Activity Movement*, p. 114, Public School Publishing Co., 1934. Quoted by permission of the Society.
[2] *A Teachers' Guide to Child Development*, pp. 392–402, California State Department of Education, 1930.

1. Does the room present a pleasing appearance of simplicity and restfulness?

2. Is the room suitable for the children who are to live in it, in choice and arrangement of furnishings?

3. Is the room attractive from the viewpoint of the child, as well as from that of the adult? Is it the kind of room in which children enjoy staying?

4. Are there interesting materials in the room?
   (a) Has color been pleasingly used?
   (b) Are the adornments of the room suitable and attractive?
   (c) Do the children have things to work with?
   (d) Are there collections of visual materials?
   (e) Are there provisions for the enjoyment of nature?
   (f) Are there provisions for the enjoyment of music?
   (g) Are there adequate books and publications?

These criteria were used to check the results of the work of the children and teacher of this one-room school. In nearly every item the room was ranked high.

SUMMARY

School buildings, like all forms of architecture, reflect the philosophy of the period which built them. The first American school was built for a single curriculum which provided for few activities. Consequently, the first buildings were the "box car" pattern, unattractive, inadequate even for a traditional program, and limited and meager in their equipment. This pattern persisted for many years, reform in the rural field beginning after 1910. During the period of reform various plans were developed in an effort to remedy existing mistakes and prevent new ones. These plans were as follows: (a) consolidation of small schools with large ones and the provision of state building aid for them; (b) state aid for the improvement and building of the small school; (c) the standardization of the small rural school through score cards, and the setting up of standards of varying degrees; (d) the provision by legal enactment for the approval of all plans and the acceptance of school buildings by the state departments of education.

The modern program of education involves many changes in school architecture. While few changes in school buildings are evident as yet, the fundamental changes in philosophy and curriculum indicate that architecture will in time reflect both. In line with the new philosophy of the child-centered school, educational leaders have insisted that designers of new buildings take account of persisting outstanding characteristics of childhood. These are: (a) the innate activity of all children, particularly those of the elementary school ages and interests; (b) the natural curiosity of children, and their eagerness to learn, to explore, and to discover; (c) the persistent use of their hands and the urge for construction; and (d) the tendency of children to organize activities and to work and play in groups. Pioneers in modern school architecture are meeting these needs by (a) providing larger rooms; (b) creating special project rooms and laboratories; (c) creating houses of beauty as well as utility.

The present status of the small rural school building falls far below the ideal of the building constructed for a modern progressive program of education, as well as being inadequate for a traditional program. Knowledge of this status is derived (a) from the studies of the United States Office of Education; (b) by use of school score cards; (c) through school surveys. On entering one of these inadequate school buildings the modern teacher is faced with the necessity of harmonizing his philosophy of education and the actual conditions before him. Modern education requires that the school become a three-fold combination—a laboratory, a home for children, and a community center for adults. There are two procedures open in such a program of harmonization; (a) the schoolhouse built for a traditional curriculum must be replaced with one designed for modern needs; or (b) the old building must be adjusted to the modern program. The latter program seems more feasible and indeed is the procedure most often followed. There are many evidences of such adjustments being made in the field by progressive, wide-awake, energetic teachers. A case study of such a teacher and such an adjustment was presented in this chapter, as an example of how a sensitive teacher with the coöperation of the children can bring environmental conditions under control. Since an activity program is specifically sensitive to such controls, not only teachers but administrators should give this problem increasing attention.[1]

SUGGESTED READINGS

Baldwin, Bird T. and others. *Farm Children*, Chap. VI, D. Appleton and Co., New York, 1930.

Collings, Ellsworth. *An Experiment with a Project Curriculum*, Chap. VI, Macmillan, New York, 1927.

National Advisory Council on School Building Problems. United States Office of Education, Pamphlet No. 7, 1930 (Dept. of the Interior), Government Printing Office, Washington, D. C.

Dunn, Fannie W. and Everett, Marcia A. *Four Years in a Country School*, p. 129, Bureau of Publications, Teachers College, Columbia University, 1926.

EEls, Harry L., Moeller, Hugh C. and Swain, C. *Rural School Management*, Chap. VI, Charles Scribner's Sons, New York, 1924.

Lowth, Frank J. *Everyday Problems of the Country Teacher*, Rev. ed., Chap. VI, Macmillan, New York, 1936.

Mumford, Lewis. *Sticks and Stones, A Study of American Architecture and Civilization*, Chap. VIII, Boni-Liveright, New York, 1924.

National Education Association. *The Outlook for Rural Education*, Research Bulletin, Vol. 9, National Education Association, Washington, D. C., 1931.

Strayer, George Drayton, Frasier, George Willard, Armentrout, Winfield Dockery. *Principles of Teaching*, Chap. V, American Book Co., New York, 1936.

Tippett, James S. *Schools for a Growing Democracy*, Chaps. IV, VI, Ginn and Co., Boston, 1936.

[1] Copies of standard score cards for rating rural school buildings may be obtained from the World Book Company.

MATERIALS FOR DISCUSSION

Consider the following statements. What changes would make them more acceptable to you? What significant issues arise from their study?

1. School architecture, like all overt expressions of philosophy, lags behind theory. Many years will probably elapse before school buildings can be constructed to meet the ideals of a modern educational program.

2. The scientific scoring of school buildings has hindered rather than helped a building program keyed to modern educational needs. The construction of nearly all score cards has developed from a compilation of acceptable standards in building construction rather than from the psychological investigations of the needs and interests of children.

3. There are no unsurmountable obstacles to a modern program of education in the average traditional school building.

4. The school building and its equipment are powerful educational controls in the teaching and learning process. They vitally affect the curriculum, the technique of teaching, and the development of children.

5. The outstanding problem in administration at the present is the harmonization of the present status of school buildings and a modern program of education.

PART IV

ENVIRONMENTAL FACTORS
WHICH
AFFECT EDUCATION

CHAPTER XVI

THE SCHOOL AND THE COMMUNITY

HISTORICAL DEVELOPMENT OF SCHOOL—COMMUNITY RELATIONSHIPS

THE first American schools were closely connected with community interests—the outcome indeed of coöperative, neighborhood efforts. A group of friends and neighbors met, pooled their resources, and built a school. The teacher usually a man in the winter session and a woman in the summer term, "boarded around." The itinerant schoolmaster of those early days was often more than a schoolmaster, he was a friend bound with affectionate ties to the family groups of his community. While no one would advocate a return to these primitive ways, the efficacious results stemming from the close relationships of parents, teachers, and children were mutual understanding and coöperative effort. Moreover, that intimate knowledge of the child's tendencies and activities in his out-of-school time, which is considered important in modern education, and of which the teacher is often ignorant, had its advantages under the regime of the pioneer pedagogue who "boarded around."

The pioneer farm family coöperated with the school in yet another field which cannot be overlooked. It supplied many practical features, now a part of the regular school life. The teacher was left free to specialize in the essentials of education, the three R's. The home assumed responsibility for the vocational education of children and for much of their character education. In the old days it was under the tutelage of their fathers that boys were taught farming, blacksmithing, and tanning. Mothers gave to their daughters training in cooking, housekeeping, the care of children, and dressmaking. When the young people had finished the rudiments of learning at the neighborhood school, they had also acquired vocational mastery at home. Girls were then ready to establish their own homes, and the boys were prepared to support them. Thus home and school so supplemented each other in the pioneer educational process that it was difficult to tell where the responsibilities of one began and the other ended.

The second stage in the historical development of the school and community witnessed a widening between the interests of the two. The change came gradually, paralleling in a measure the transformation of the United States from a rural to an urban type of civilization. With the development of the urban school system there appeared a new kind of professional leadership exemplified in the superintendent and the principal. On the whole, these executives set themselves up as experts and assumed certain characteristics of the expert. One of these persisting characteristics was that they brooked no interference from laymen in professional matters. They delimited an area, called it education, and rarely moved out of it; at the same time they welcomed no one else into it. Indeed, there was a feeling that aloofness in community affairs, especially if concerned with politics or religion, added dignity and security to their position. During this period the usual contacts of the home and community were limited to the monthly report cards and occasional visits. Teaching was considered the chief responsibility of the teacher and the school superintendent encouraged no contacts with parents, save through isolated and carefully controlled conferences, held usually under his supervision. As a result, the home, the school, and the community drifted apart and lost much of the fine coöperation of the earlier period. Naturally the group most affected under this system was the one composed of the children.

Historically, the third stage in the development of the home, school, and community relationships has grown out of the philosophy of the progressive movement in education. The acceptance of this philosophy has been based on certain assumptions fundamental to the field of modern education. Chief among these is the doctrine that education is a continuous process and that it takes place both in and outside the school environment. In other words, there is no one institution which has the sole opportunity and responsibility for the education of children. The school is important in the educational process, but so also are the home, the moving picture, the church, the radio, the community organizations—indeed, all of the community agencies with which the child comes in contact. Education, therefore, becomes a coöperative rather than an individualistic enterprise.

WHAT IS THE PLACE OF THE SCHOOL IN THE COMMUNITY?

If education is a coöperative community enterprise, what then is the place of the school in it? This is one of the mooted questions in modern education upon which the teaching profession generally divides itself into three groups. One group holds that the school is the community center and the teacher is its leader ex officio. Another maintains that the primary and sole responsibility of the school is the teaching of children, and that community activities lie outside its province. A third believes that the school should be the center of the community, coördinating and harmonizing its forces, and that its chief contribution to community endeavor should be the development of leadership.

THE SCHOOL, THE COMMUNITY CENTER

The exponents of the belief that the school is the true community center maintain that all educational, social, and recreational activities should focus in the school and its staff. They advocate that the rural school serve as a medical dispensary, a library for adults, a gathering place for clubs, assemblies and drives—in short, that the school be in truth a community club house. Directing these activities is the rural teacher who acts as community leader, on call at all hours of the day and night if the people of his community need him. Those who conceive of rural community leadership in these terms would have school architecture conform to this philosophy. They envision school buildings, therefore, as community houses, so that both children and adults may be served at one and the same time. Teacherages on the school grounds or apartments in the school buildings guarantee the presence of the teacher whenever he is needed. Outstanding among the advocates of the rural school as a community center is Miss Elsie Ripley Clapp, formerly of the Rogers Ballard Memorial School, Louisville, Kentucky. On this point she makes the following statement:

A school in a rural district has a unique opportunity to function socially. In the country there is a community, a neighborhood, linked by common interests and by intimate relationships and informal friendly intercourse. A rural school shares those interests and enters into them. As the neutral and often largest place of the village or the countryside, the rural school is used for neighborhood gatherings of all kinds, for local clubs, sometimes for church services, for entertainments, lectures, and concerts. The school's own assemblies and suppers and meetings provide a community interest in a way unknown in cities. To the school in a rural community, families turn for help in time of sickness and trouble, at birth or death as well as for help in daily difficulties. They feel that the teacher will understand, they are sure she will care, and that she will help them.[1]

A teacher who undertakes this type of community program should be strong physically and should make few mental reservations about his personal life. He should believe firmly in the satisfaction which comes from the shared life and should approach his task with an enthusiasm which resembles missionary zeal. That these theories can be put into practice is evidenced by the fact that many rural teachers every year, in varying

[1] "A Rural Community School in Kentucky," *Progressive Education*, Vol. X (Mar. 1933), p. 123.

degrees of victorious achievement, do make their schools centers of community life.

THE SCHOOL—AN INSTITUTION ISOLATED FROM THE COMMUNITY

Again, there are those in the teaching profession who hold that the primary and sole responsibility of the teacher is the teaching of children. They maintain that rural teachers, especially those in small schools, find even in this primary responsibility an impossible task; that the handling of eight grades with approximately thirty daily classes leaves the teacher too exhausted for community leadership; and that he should not attempt it. They reason that, since one person cannot assume both teaching and community leadership, the teacher should devote his thinking and his energy to problems and tasks concerned with the immediate welfare of the children entrusted to his care.

They can find no good reason why rural teachers should board in the communities in which they teach. Indeed, they point out, modern trends in transportation are against this time-honored custom. Commuting by automobile is seen as a means of solving the boarding and social problems of the rural teacher which have plagued the rural community for two decades. Adherents of this point of view will, as a rule, be found living in villages from which they commute each day to nearby schools. Contacts with the community are infrequent, usually consisting of sporadic visits to farm homes and the semi-annual school entertainments to which the whole community is invited. Under these circumstances, more often than not, there is little social life present in the community, save that offered through the church, or other local organizations. The school assumes no responsibility for contributing to community activities, nor does it make any effort to foster community leadership. It assumes that it has accomplished its task when the educational needs of the children of the community have been met.

THE SCHOOL——A TRAINING CENTER FOR COMMUNITY
LEADERSHIP

Between the two points of view discussed above there is a third, advocates of which urge a middle course. They hold that the school occupies a strategic place in community work, since it is the one community institution in which the interests of all the people are centered; and that, with the school building always available for meetings, the school should assume certain responsibilities for community leadership. Unlike the first group, however, it does not believe that the teacher should assume such leadership, holding rather that the school should regard itself as a center for training in leadership. The teacher would, therefore, find his responsibilities diverging in two directions: (a) the development of leadership in children for whose formal education he is primarily responsible; (b) the education of adults to the point of ability to assume leadership.

Development of leadership, like the development of techniques for democratic living, is a long, slow, laborious process. It is achieved in children and adults alike through satisfactory group experiences in which individuals share the responsibilities of leadership. The conception of leadership in a democracy is different from that in other forms of government. Education in the United States should sense this difference and adjust the education of youth to it. Responsibility for leadership in a democracy rests with the many and not with one. Kilpatrick clarified this point when he said:

The leadership which promises best for long-run efficiency seems to arise from the fullest group sharing. This is so contrary to widely held views that we must consider the matter closely. Let us look at it first in the small. Suppose a dozen men about a table working at a matter of common concern. How does the process of shared search go on, and how does leadership function? All share in the discussion. What one says stimulates others to new and better thought. One proposes a plan. It is considered. Bearings are noted which the proposer had overlooked. The plan is amended. Still other bearings are noted, and still further amendments. If actual progress is made, interest will grow. All work with new zeal, each from his peculiar background and experience. Out of such variety comes discriminative criticism. So the men work together, now this one advancing the process, now that one. They seek a plan which shall integrate what all know and feel. A better plan should result than the best man acting alone could have produced. . . . The points most to be noted in this analysis are that leadership is many, not one, and that each leadership by its own step forward mutually brings the others into fuller being and action. . . . Leadership is essentially a group achievement.[1]

If education accepts this philosophy of leadership in a democracy, the procedure of the school in training leaders is considerably simplified. Techniques for developing this characteristic in children are suggested at some length in Chapter VIII, *Organization of the School for Democratic Living*. The problem of adult education in leadership, however, is somewhat complicated and the procedure handicapped because education has not yet devised a plan to make available to adults a systematic, meaningful program such as the school offers to children. Leadership experiences available for adults through the average school are nearly always incidental and seldom educational. If available at all, experiences usually consist of holding an occasional office in a local parent-teacher organization, or acting as sponsor for a 4-H Club. Education for leadership in rural areas is further complicated by the fact that the rural community has been for some time widening beyond the small local school district which formerly marked its boundary. As a consequence, the rural adult finds his social satisfaction in other centers than that represented by the rural school. In spite of widening community contacts, the farm family remains individualistic. Both of these factors seriously affect the social organization of the community and hence the development of leadership. Nearly all recent sociological studies in rural areas emphasize this fact. A 1936 study of farm townships

[1] Kilpatrick, William H. *Education and the Social Crisis*, pp. 33–36, Liveright, 1932.

in Illinois illustrates the point.[1] Among other conclusions the study comes to the following:

The problems facing leaders in rural communities are complex and perplexing. The business of farming, while less individualistic than it once was, still fosters a definitely individualistic point of view; and while this attitude of mind and the qualities associated with it are not undesirable in all their aspects, it is a force that rural leaders need to understand and reckon with. The farm family, even with the advent of better roads and communication, still retains much of its independence as a social and economic unit. Furthermore, when the farmer leaves his farm to do his trading or visiting, he often goes entirely out of what was once regarded as the bounds of the community in which his farm is located. As a result, community interests—particularly local trade enterprises and interests of a religious and social character—suffer from lack of support.

In order to meet these difficulties in the rural community it seems logical that the school assume its share of responsibility in the development of adult leadership. As an organization fostered by the school, the parent-teacher association, discussed somewhat fully in a subsequent chapter, lends itself admirably to such purposes. It is an organization whose *raison d'etre* is to act as an interpreting intermediary between the home and the school. Composed of the adult members of the community directly interested in the welfare of children, if offers large opportunities for the development of leadership and for the use of it in community development. Often in the organization of such a group no leadership is available. In that event, those who hold to the point of view that the school should develop leadership suggest that the teacher accept the responsibility, but only for the length of time necessary to develop a leader or leaders within the membership of the organization.

While the average rural school is somewhat limited in its op-

[1] Lindstrom, D. E. *Forces Affecting Participation of Farm People in Rural Organization*, p. 126, University of Illinois Agricultural Experiment Station, Bulletin 423, 1936.

portunities for training adult leaders, there are other agencies which have been more successful. It would, therefore, seem the part of wisdom for the rural school to coöperate with them. The strongest and perhaps the most outstanding of these agencies is that of the Agricultural Extension Service. It represents the coöperation of the United States Department of Agriculture, the State Agricultural Colleges, and county governments. The aim of the extension service is frankly practical. It is designed to assist the American farmer and his wife in reaching higher standards in farming and homemaking. The Extension Service functions in considerably over one-half the counties of the nation, and in 1936 the professional staff of leaders exclusive of Washington headquarters numbered 8527 persons. Locally, the service is represented by county agents, and, while leadership is somewhat centered in them, at the same time they offer many opportunities for the development of lay rural leadership. These opportunities come through local study groups, experimentations by local committees, farm and home demonstration clubs. The most significant feature of these local groups is the fact that the responsibility for their program is assumed almost entirely by volunteer leadership. Of this volunteer leadership Brunner and Lorge have this to say:

One of the most interesting aspects of this program of adult education in rural America is the large development in the use of volunteer local leaders who are given some training, assistance, and supervision; and who then carry the details of the local program. . . . These local leaders serve without pay, and bear their own expenses to training conferences. . . . The willingness of rural people so to volunteer is perhaps but a twentieth century equivalent of the neighborly coöperation at barn-raisings, corn-huskings, and the like in the nineteenth century.[1]

The program usually undertaken by the Extension Service has been, in the past at least, vocational. However, new

[1] Brunner, Edmund deS. and Lorge, Irving. *Rural Trends in Depression Years*, pp. 181–182, Columbia University Press, 1937.

trends in program making are appearing, and these, too, have significance for the development of local adult leadership. An examination of these new programs reveals that farmers and their wives are engaging in discussions on economics, child development, leisure time activities, current issues, modern literature, and art. Better still, out of these discussions are developing activities which foster leadership and give direction to the warm impulses of coöperative groups. Brunner and Lorge report on this development in their new book *Rural Trends in Depression Years*. They say in part:

The annual reports of the extension directors or extension rural sociologists present a vivid picture of the strength of the movement. In one small New England state, there are drama groups in 100 communities. Oregon, where the work is newer, already has 90. In Tennessee, rural men and women came from all over the state to 5 regional drama leadership training schools (each of which lasted four days) and returned home to assist local community leaders in their counties. In New York, 10 demonstration drama festivals and 20 county festivals were held, culminating in a state festival. . . . In some states, the drama work has been tied in with the public schools, either directly or by using 4-H Club groups.[1]

THE MODERN CONCEPTION OF SCHOOL-COMMUNITY RELATIONSHIPS

An assumption basic to a new program in community relationships is the acceptance on the part of the profession and the layman of the fact that the school and the teacher are an integral part of community life. This assumption holds large implications for the future. It assumes a redefining of the position of the school in the life of the community. The school can no longer, as in the past, hold itself aloof from the main currents of American life. The teacher must expect to function as a responsible citizen, actively identifying himself in the community group, accepting responsibilities for both leadership and followship when they come to him. In the redefining of

[1] *Ibid.* pp. 191–192.

the relationship of home and school, the community occupies an important place and that a redefinition is already in process is evidenced in the following developments: (a) an increasing number of rural community surveys are in progress, which broaden the horizons of teachers; (b) members of the community, particularly parents, are becoming participating members in the learning process; (c) children as well as teachers consciously have a share in the life of the community.

THE PURPOSE OF COMMUNITY SURVEYS

Many surveys in rural communities have been made in recent years, but these have been sociological rather than educational studies. The latter are an innovation. Practical outgrowths of the new philosophy in the field of home-school relationships, they are still largely experimental in nature. New Jersey, Michigan, and certain progressive sections of New York State have pioneered in this field. Usually initiated by teachers or supervisors, the procedure is often highly coöperative, involving teachers, adults, and children. The object of the survey is to assemble all local information pertinent to the educational program.

THE PATTERN OF THE SURVEY

The survey is important for teachers because it is a method for understanding the environmental background of children. Properly conducted a survey should reveal to the teacher: (a) the limitations of the community and the problems developed therefrom and (b) the resources of the community possible of use in the educational program. The survey is important for children because it is a means for making them aware of their environment, appreciative of the world in which they live, and sensitive to the needs revealed in community limitations. The survey is drawn from many socio-economic sources and is usually assembled in the following patterns:

A. *The Financial Status of the Community—the Economic*

Pattern. (1) Income; (2) uses to which income is put; (3) standards of living developing from the income.

B. *Sources of Income—the Occupational Pattern.* (1) Generalized services such as farming, fishing, and lumbering; (2) specialized services—creameries, canneries, store-keeping, etc.; (3) marketing and the problems therein involved.

C. *Natural Features of the Community—the Geographic Pattern.* (1) Weather and its influence upon the economic and occupational patterns; (2) types of soil and their sociological and educational influences; (3) natural resources and their uses; (4) agricultural assets, for example, a long growing season and difficulties such as pests, insects, etc.; (5) local flora and fauna; (6) county geological formations, specimens, and remains.

D. *The Personnel of the Community—the Sociological Pattern.* (1) Racial strains and their contributions to community life; (2) family histories which include characteristics of mental and physical health, temperament, standards of home life, size, etc.; (3) church affiliations.

E. *The History of the Community—the Historical Pattern.* (1) Significant developments in the pioneer period; (2) leaders contributing to state and national life; (3) local historical incidents which have influenced events; (4) community legends; (5) land marks; (6) historical materials such as pictures, kitchen and farm utensils, costumes, furniture, and all exhibits which help children to understand the life of various historical periods.

F. *Organization Life in the Community—the Civic Pattern.* (1) Types and numbers of organizations; (2) service programs for adults and youth; (3) political organizations; (4) religious organizations; (5) coöperatives and credit unions.

G. *Living Men and Women of Opportunity and Achievement.— The Achievement Pattern.* (1) Men and women who have traveled in the United States and abroad; (2) writers, artists, and other creative individuals; (3) leaders in social, political, educational, business, and religious fields; (4) master farmers and homemakers.

H. *Dominant Mores of the Community—the Traditional Pattern.* (1) Community prejudices in religion, politics, and other controversial subjects; (2) community cliques and their leaders; (3) community attitudes toward children and toward schools, and other educational programs affecting youth; (4) evidences of feelings of superiority and inferiority.

UTILIZATION OF THE INFORMATION REVEALED BY A SURVEY

The information secured through a community survey may be used in many ways. It should enable the teacher

(1) To understand the problems of children and to plan intelligently the work of the year for them.

(2) To organize the curriculum in terms of the environment.

An example of curriculum utilization is available through the work of an extension class in State Teachers College, Buffalo, of the winter session of 1935. A schedule of activities was developed from a survey directed by the group. The schedule is suggestive only, since activities will vary greatly with communities, and are conditioned by the interests, ages, and cultural backgrounds of children. The survey covered two districts in Niagara County, New York, and revealed rich teaching sources. All the work was performed by children. The following activities are a few of the many suggested.

1. A scientific exhibit of fossils and rock formations characteristic of the Niagara frontier.

2. An historical exhibit of costumes, household utensils, and farming implements.

3. A collection of flora and fauna indigenous to the region.

4. A unit in the social studies dealing with the story of Fort Niagara.

5. A unit in science organized around the development of the Niagara escarpment.

6. A unit of English on the Leatherstocking stories of James Fenimore Cooper, a native of New York State.

7. Maps of the following types: contours, historic, literary, forestry, and neighborhood.

8. An historical pageant, written, staged, and played by the whole community.[1]

PARENTS AS PARTICIPATING MEMBERS IN THE LIFE OF THE SCHOOL

The relationships of parents to the modern school are different from those of any other parents in the history of schools, although certain characteristics, reminiscent of the pioneer parent, exist especially in the coöperative effort to deal with school problems. However, the modern parent goes far beyond coöperation and enters into actual participation in the life of the school in a manner undreamed of in the pioneer period of American education. It is not unusual, for instance, to find a parent in a modern school teaching a group of children. Parents who have traveled in foreign countries are often pressed into service to assist with the teaching of the social studies, as was exampled in the case study in Chapter XII. Parents frequently assist in school excursions, acting as chaperones, guides, and lecturers. Mothers supervise hot lunches and often, when children cannot prepare them, do so for them. Where the traditional school sets aside a "visiting day" when all parents are invited to visit their children on exhibit, the modern school attempts to make the school life so vitally a coöperative enterprise that any and every day might properly be called "parents' day." Parents are accepted as a normal part of the school "fraternity." No one is surprised when they drop into the school, and no one thinks it odd when they assist children and teachers on problems vital to all.

An interesting picture of the participation of parents in the life of the school is presented by Miss Alice Thompson in an article entitled, "A Community-Centered School." She says in part:

---

[1] A community study and suggestions for its use are given in the appendix.

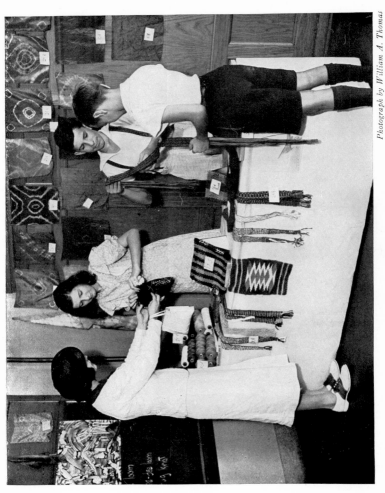

Photograph by William A. Thomas

The textile unit culminated in a school fair. Friends and relatives came to admire and to buy.

The painting began. Laborers ranged in age from twelve to fifty. Whole families stood upon the scaffold, working without distinction of sex or age; ability to wield a brush—the only qualification. From eleven in the morning till six at night, laughter and voices intermingled with the steady swishing of white paint going on over the dull gray cement. Cracks from winter shrinkage, ravages of cold weather all were taken in the stride of eager, volunteer workers. . . . Furniture was scrutinized and a call sent for more painters. As weary groups sat contemplating their handiwork at dusk, they planned a gardening workday when shrubs and vines would be brought from overflowing gardens for planting at school. . . .

This labor was a concrete manifestation of the acceptance by the parents of the school as an integral part of their lives, inseparable from the development of their children. It was evidence of their recognition that what in any way concerns the life preparation of children must be the adults' immediate concern. Not dutifully nor dolefully, but gladly and jointly they work out the problems that occur in their children's learning years, be they wall painting, or health programs, or richer library facilities, or personality kinks— problems worthy of their fullest and best efforts.[1]

THE PARTICIPATION OF CHILDREN IN THE COMMUNITY LIFE

Children in rural areas have always participated in many phases of community life. Many conditions inherent in the situation have tended to bring this about: the structure of the rural community is less complex than that of the urban; children nearly always accompany parents to community meetings, and not infrequently take part in the discussions of adults. The community status of the average rural child, like that of his home status, is different and at the same time more important than that of the average urban child. Just as he participates in the family councils at home, he is likely to participate in the community councils. A recent survey further amplifies this point of view:[2]

[1] *Progressive Education.* Vol. 9 (May 1932), p. 380.
[2] Hanna, Paul R. *Youth Serves the Community*, pp. 258–259, D. Appleton-Century Co., 1936.

The large number of projects carried on under the supervision of such groups as the 4-H Clubs or Future Farmers of America indicate that rural youth has more leadership and more opportunity for socially-useful work than has urban youth. This may be due to a number of causes; but, undoubtedly, it is chiefly due to the fact that the rural environment is more often owned or controlled by the adults who are directly concerned with its improvement. The urban environment is usually controlled by impersonal corporations, set in a complex economic and political milieu, which is so impregnable that youth cannot really have free access to it. When rural children undertake to improve the esthetic charm of their roads and their own farm home-yards, direct access may be had to the owners of the property, and usually that ownership resides under the same roof as the young. In such a manageable situation, the project is very likely to succeed.

The acceptance by youth of actual responsibility for community work directed toward the improvement of social conditions is of recent development. However, the movement is widespread. The survey referred to above revealed that thousands of children in urban as well as rural areas, in all sections of the United States, as well as in foreign countries, are engaged in projects directed toward community improvement. An illustration of such projects in a rural setting is herewith quoted in detail from the survey:

In 1920, the new principal of a consolidated rural school desired to direct the energies of her school to the creative task of improving the living in the community in as many phases as possible. As a first step, the principal discussed the strengths and shortcomings of the school, the neighborhood, and the wider community with her small staff of teachers and with the parents. Soon after the opening of school in the fall, the teachers talked with their pupils about the homes they lived in, the agricultural practices of the farmers, the recreational facilities of the environment, the health of the children, and a score of similar subjects with which the children were familiar so far as their own lives were concerned.

After considerable discussion, the pupils were led to undertake an inventory of the whole community from which the school drew pupils. The pupils in the school, grades one through nine, participated as individuals in amassing certain types of information from their own homes, and as members of committees in surveying public aspects of the larger area. Data were gathered on the farm homes regarding running water, bath, electricity, number of rooms, furniture and equipment, musical and recreational materials, reading matter, general comfort and sanitation. Facts were obtained concerning the farm practices in crop rotation, seed selection, fertilization, cultivation, harvesting, storing, and marketing; in the care and breeding of livestock; and in provision for orchard, garden, and general diversification of crop.

The survey also included the status of the community health and the provision for medical and dental care; the plant and equipment available for social gatherings of the adults, the young people, and the children; the frequency and availability of such social and cultural activities as lectures, concerts, and dramatizations; and many items of a similar nature that gave a picture of the level of material and spiritual living in this rural community.

These findings were then summarized by the children in their school classes, and conferences of pupils and teachers were held to plan a program of study and work. The parents were invited to the school for several evening conferences on the aim of the school and the type of coöperation from the homes which would be most beneficial. Eventually, the school selected an area of the community life which was evidently in great need of improvement, and this became the theme of the work of the several classrooms for the year. "How can we improve the health of our community?" was the question which directed every effort.

The year's study involved many types of activities. The pupils studied the food served at home and compared it with balanced diets which they found in health books; they went further and kept cages of white mice, to which they fed balanced and unbalanced diets and observed the results in changes of weight, lustre of eye, color of fur, and general bodily activity. When they became convinced that a change in diet at home would be beneficial to their own health, the the pupils invited the parents to visit the school and view the exhibits. Almost universally the parents were eager to learn, and wherever possible they changed the home practice to harmonize with the conclusions drawn from the evidence.

The pupils discovered that pure water is essential and must come from wells safeguarded from contamination by farm refuse. They learned that screens on windows and doors kept out infection-bearing flies and mosquitoes, and that homes equipped with modern baths and plumbing facilities contribute to proper health habits. The parents were given this information, and where possible, the children and parents moved the well farther from the barn, covered doors and windows with screens, and installed modern bathrooms.

The children found that the dental and medical services available to the community were far below any reasonable standard. They conducted a campaign for visiting the dentist regularly and calling the doctor when ill. They were instrumental in bringing a dentist into the community two days each week and in having a county nurse visit the school frequently. Medical books found their way into the meager home libraries, and to medicine cabinets were added supplies of a staple nature.

Toward the close of the spring term the children wrote and staged a pageant in which they dramatized their efforts to improve the health record of the community. The commencement exercises were centered around the year's achievement. The objective results were evident. The whole area was conscious of the values of health and of the means of raising its level on a community-wide scale.

Each year during the following decade, a major area of community living was chosen for study and improvement. Significant progress was made by the whole geographic area working coöperatively and consciously on the raising of the standard of living under the egis of the school. At the end of the decade, the children in the school again took an extensive inventory. They found a gratifying increase in such material equipment as bathtubs, electric lights in homes and farm buildings, pure water supply, screens on windows and doors; in such agricultural practices as would raise the yield of grain, meat, dairy, and poultry products; and in such cultural materials as daily and weekly newspapers, monthly farm journals, and magazines of controversy.

A donor had been persuaded to build a beautiful community church, with facilities for a varied social and educational program for all ages of the population. The farmers had formed buying and marketing coöperatives and were engaging in many activities jointly, to their mutual benefit. The survey provided ample proof that the children of this school, working with the adults, had made a significant contribution toward solving many of the problems which lay at the heart of the community's progress.[1]

This vital account of the participation of children in the life of a rural community reveals several unusual facts. In the first place, unlike the traditional school group, children were keenly sensitive to the problems present in their immediate environment. These problems were revealed to them through what they called an "inventory," a procedure similar to the survey recommended in previous paragraphs. In the second place, the findings were used. They were summarized and brought into the classroom, thus forming the basis for intelligent criticism and discussion. Discussions apparently led to a feeling of responsibility for community conditions because plans for solving them developed through study. In the improvement program the students acted with wisdom. They made it a coöperative parent-school enterprise. Results of this coöperation speak for themselves through increased standards in health, improved agricultural practices, and increased cultural and social advantages offered by the improved community.

SUMMARY

Historically, the development of home and school relationships has progressed by three stages. The first was characterized by the personalized relationships of teacher and parent during the period of the pioneer school-relationships brought about partly because of the nature of the pioneer school itself, and partly because of the custom of the teacher in "boarding around" with the several families of the neighborhood.

The next stage witnessed a widening difference in the interests of the home and the school. This change was influenced by the shifting of America from an agricultural to an industrial nation and by the development of professional leadership in education which paralleled the shift. These leaders believed that the school was best served when teachers withdrew from com-

[1] *Ibid.* pp. 260–264.

munity contacts and held themselves aloof, especially in matters of religion and politics. The monthly report card and carefully controlled conferences were the contacts that were approved and encouraged.

The third stage has grown out of the modern conception of the educational process held by progressives in education. Under this philosophy the relationships of school and community bid fair to develop into something powerful and vital. Education is recognized as a continuous process developing from experiences received from both within and without the school. It is a coöperative enterprise in which the school shares the responsibility with all the community forces which affect the child.

The place of the school in this coöperative enterprise is a mooted question, opinions falling also into three divisions. One group holds that the school is the community center and that the teacher naturally becomes the community leader. Another believes that the primary responsibility of the school is the teaching of children and that the duty of the teacher is achieved when this responsibility is met. A third takes a middle course and maintains that the chief community responsibility of the school is the integration of community efforts and the training of leadership for participation in them.

Modern education inclines to the latter view in school-community relationships. Indeed, there is evidence of a movement in education to redefine the whole question. This evidence manifests itself in the following ways: (a) there is an increasing number of community surveys in progress, from which teaching sources are being developed; (b) members of the communities, particularly parents, are participating actively in the teaching and learning processes of the school; (c) young people, in increasing numbers, are participating in the life of the community. These tendencies augur much for future home, school, and community relationships. They suggest a happy blending of interest and effort on the part of all the people toward making the educational process lifelike and vital, not only in the lives of children, but in the life of the community as well.

SUGGESTED READINGS

Dewey, Evelyn. *New Schools for Old*, Chap. V, E. P. Dutton Company, New York, 1919.

Department of Elementary School Principals. *Eleventh Yearbook. The Principal and His Community*, Chap. VI, National Education Association, Washington, D. C., 1932.

Kolb, J. H. and Brunner, Edmund DeS. *A Study of Rural Society*, Chap. XIX, Houghton Mifflin Co., Boston, 1935.

Kolb, J. H. and Wileden, A. F. *Special Interest Groups in Rural Society*, Research Bulletin 84, Dec., 1927, Agricultural Experiment Station, University of Wisconsin.

Pierce, Alice A. *Agencies Contributing to Rural Education*, Research Bulletin, Department of Rural Education of the National Education Association, Washington, D. C., Feb., 1932.

Smith, C. B. "4-H Club Work," *Journal of the National Education Association*, Vol. 19 (Mar., 1930), p. 95.

Stowell, Jay S. "Religious Training for Rural Youth," *Missionary Review of the World*, Vol. 54 (May, 1931), p. 349.

Warren, Gertrude L. "4-H Club Work with Rural Girls," *Journal of Home Economics*, Vol. 24 (Aug., 1932), p. 686.

West, James. "Character Education in Scouting," *Journal of the National Education Association*, Vol. 18 (Oct., 1929), p. 219.

Yearbook of Agriculture. *Report of Extension Work in Agriculture and Home Economics in the United States*, June, 1933, p. 64.

MATERIALS FOR DISCUSSION

Consider the following statements. What changes would make them more acceptable to you? What significant issues arise from their study?

1. The school in a rural district has a unique opportunity to function socially. Because the school is the house of all the people, it should serve as the center of community life, and the teacher, by the very nature of his position, should assume leadership for it.

2. The primary responsibility of teachers is the education of children After this duty is met the average teacher in a small rural school has neither the time, nor the strength to assume community leadership.

3. Unless teachers are native to the rural district in which they teach, it is not possible for them to function therein as responsible citizens. Their term of service is too short, and their social relationships too casual. Moreover, the conservatism of the average rural community discourages the participation of the teacher in its social and political life.

4. The community status of the average rural child, like that of his home status, is different and at the same time more important than that of the average urban child.

5. Responsibility for leadership in a democracy rests with the many and not with one. "The leadership which promises best for long-run efficiency seems to arise from the fullest group sharing."

CHAPTER XVII

COMMUNITY PROGRAMS WHICH AFFECT EDUCATION

THESE new community demands cannot be met by the present organization. The school, in particular, must be extended and assigned general and specific functions in terms of real community needs. The educative process is much larger than school activities and as control of the process grows the school becomes more important. The idea of school takes on new meanings if we add to the current concept of school—a controlled educational environment—meanings which make school synonymous with educative process. The educative process is coextensive with life and assumes importance as life activities assume importance.[1]

While the above is a philosophic statement of the place of the high school in the life of the community, it is applicable as well to the elementary school. As has been stated in previous chapters, modern education is an all-inclusive process concerned with the development of the whole child. This process includes all of the experiences of children whether acquired in school or elsewhere. In the light of this theory the modern teacher cannot afford to ignore the non-school forces of a community for sometimes they are even more significant than the school itself. It is, therefore, highly desirable that they become a part of the "controlled educational environment."

What then are the agencies which contribute to the education of modern rural youth? What contributions do they make in terms of human values? Do these contributions encourage desirable growth in right directions? Are the programs in-

[1] Everett, Samuel and Others. *A Challenge to Secondary Education*, p. 323, D. Appleton-Century Co., 1935.

tegrated, or do the several agencies compete for the time and interests of children? Is it possible or desirable to coördinate local programs in terms of child and community needs? In what ways and under what leadership may the community resources be better used for educational advancement than they now are? What contributions can the school make to the educational, social, or recreational life of the community that are directly contributory to the education of children?

THE LABYRINTH OF COMMUNITY LIFE IN CITIES

The community is composed of many groups different in their interests and having many programs which serve them. This statement is true for urban and rural communities alike, differences existing in the number and the kind of agencies serving the two types. In 1933 a committee from the faculty of Teachers College, Columbia University, listed the supplementary agencies responsible for educational work outside of the schools, in a metropolitan area like New York City. Forty-nine such agencies were listed, falling under the following heads: [1] (a) educational agencies, such as libraries, museums, radio, visual education, etc; (b) recreational and character building agencies such as the Boy and Girl Scouts; (c) agencies for the dependent and handicapped; (d) health agencies including such organizations as hospitals, visiting nurse associations; (e) agencies for adjustment and guidance, as, for example, vocational adjustment and mental hygiene clinics; (f) correctional agencies such as homes for juvenile delinquents, reformatories; (g) general adult education agencies; (h) parent education agencies; (i) religious agencies of churches and synagogues; (j) agencies for the education of workers; (k) special interest and propaganda agencies established for the promotion of peace, politics, and patriotism; (l) commercial and industrial

[1] Limbert, Paul M. *Educational Work Outside of School.* Adapted from a list compiled by a committee of the faculty of Teachers College, 1933 (in mimeographed form).

agencies with definite educational programs such as is promoted by life insurance companies, public utilities, and department stores. These examples present a labyrinthine picture of overlapping agencies, revealing in part the sociological complexities of very large cities.

IN RURAL AREAS

The structure of the smaller rural community, while less complex, is far from simple. Indeed, there is little simplicity about it. Miss Alice A. Pierce, Instructor in the Department of Education, State Normal School, Cortland, New York, made in 1931 a study of the educational agencies, other than schools, serving rural communities.[1]

The data were secured from twenty-four supervisory officers in nineteen states; namely, Arkansas, California, Connecticut, Indiana, Iowa, Kansas, Kentucky, Louisiana, Maine, Nebraska, New York, North Dakota, Ohio, Oklahoma, Pennsylvania, South Carolina, Tennessee, Texas, West Virginia. In this sampling of states, twenty-one agencies were discovered working with rural boys and girls of school age: The 4-H Club, Agriculture Extension, Parent-Teacher Association, Nursing Service, Boy Scouts, Library Association, The Church, Junior Red Cross, Y.M.C.A., Campfire Girls, Young Citizens' League, Anti-Tuberculosis Association, Girl Scouts, Y.W.C.A., Sunshine Club, Knighthood of Youth, Thrift Club, Girl Reserves, Social Service Workers and the Isaac Walton League. Of these twenty-one supplementary agencies, eight showed high frequencies in servicing the areas studied. The Parent-Teacher Association served twenty-one communities out of the twenty-four studied. The Library Association showed a like number, followed by the Boy Scouts which was active in eighteen communities. Nursing Service and Agriculture Extension ranked next, seventeen of the communities reporting services

[1] *Agencies Contributing to Rural Education. Bulletin of the Department of Rural Education.* National Education Association, Feb. 1932.

from each of these two agencies. Ranking high also in services rendered to the rural areas were the Junior Red Cross, Anti-Tuberculosis Society, and the 4-H Club.

A study in 1927 of five counties in central and southern Wisconsin further amplifies this picture of the rural community with its many interest groups. Three hundred and fifty-one organizations were listed, and, while some of them were functioning solely in the interests of adults, the majority of them could be definitely classed as affecting the education of children. As in Miss Pierce's study, the Parent-Teacher Association ranked first in the number of communities served, followed closely by farmers' clubs, community clubs, and 4-H clubs.[1]

Kolb and Brunner have pointed out in their book, *A Study of Rural Society*, that this penchant for many organizations is an American characteristic with its roots in pioneer days and that the "tendency to join hands in the prosecution of common interests is an essential part of a democratic society."[2] The characteristic is therefore significant and persistent.

In the earlier neighborhoods there were so many common interests that group organization could be quite simple, differentiations few, and practically everyone was included in the general plan. As has been shown in an earlier chapter, the more active neighborhoods of the present are characterized by activities, institutions, and special interests more than by locality, nearness of residence, or traditional ways of life. It must be said, however, that many of the newer forms of group alignment have sprung from the soil of the older neighborhoods.[3]

Very few studies have been made to evaluate community agencies, but the few initiated in rural areas, such as the one made by Miss Pierce, indicates, as suggested above, that the

[1] Kolb, H. J. and Wileden, A. F. *Special Interest Groups in Rural Society*, Research Bulletin 84, Dec., 1927, Agricultural Experiment Station, University of Wisconsin.

[2] Kolb, J. H. and Brunner, Edmund deS. *A Study of Rural Society*, p. 140, Houghton Mifflin Co., 1935.

[3] *Ibid.* p. 141.

following rank high in the education of children: the church, the health program, the library, the Parent-Teacher Association, the Boy and Girl Scouts, and the 4-H clubs. An attempt will be made in this chapter to examine the programs, as they affect rural children, of the following agencies: the church; the Boy and Girl Scout movement; and the youth organizations fostered by the Federal Government—the 4-H Clubs and the National Youth Administration. The Parent Teacher Association, the library, and health agencies will be treated more fully in separate and subsequent chapters.

THE CHURCH AND ITS YOUTH PROGRAM

Concerning the church Kolb and Brunner, make this significant statement:

> In terms of the number of units, of the total amount of current income and capital invested, of the number of people employed, population enlisted and attendance secured, the rural church outranks all other types of rural social organizations combined, with the single exception of the public school. In some communities the church is an even greater institution than the school.[1]

If this statement is true, the church and its program assumes large significance for the rural child.

In the development of an educational program the rural church is handicapped for leadership. The chief source of leadership lies in the rural minister, and, since in most cases he is available only for ministering on Sunday, the educational program of the church, so far as his leadership is concerned, is likely to suffer. According to a recent study, "less than one-tenth of the open country and only a few more than two-fifths of the village churches have full-time resident clergy." However, with volunteer leadership the rural church maintains a Sunday School with a program for the religious education of the community's youth. "Ninety-two per cent of the village and

[1] *Ibid.* p. 462.

eighty-six per cent of the open country churches maintain Sunday Schools enrolling an average of 127 and 66 students, respectively, and securing about two-thirds of the enrollment on any given Sunday." The program is, in the main, traditional and seeks to promote character training in the light of the Bible and Christian doctrine.[1]

Daily vacation Bible schools in rural communities, conducted from two to six weeks, are now promoted by one-fifth of the rural congregations in the United States. As the name suggests, these Bible schools are held during the summer vacation under the auspices of the local community church. Many rural school teachers participate in these schools, and worthwhile educational programs presented in accordance with modern techniques are being developed. In addition to the program of the Sunday school and daily vacation Bible school, "about seventy per cent of all rural churches possess an average of two-and-a-half subsidiary organizations each." These include women's organizations, young people's groups, and clubs similar to the Boy and Girl Scouts.[2] Lectures, concerts, and dramatics are activities that are being slowly included in the rural-church program. The same study reveals that three-tenths of the village and one-tenth of the country churches included such activities in their 1930 program, and some rural churches have a rather broad program of worship, preaching, religious education, group organization, and extensive community service which has won wide support.[3]

A recent extension movement of the rural church in promoting a program for character development augurs well for the future. This movement is an effort on the part of the church to bring religious instruction to rural children in school and presents new opportunities for coöperation between the two institutions. The plan, in brief, includes a traveling rural teacher of religion. The program of studies is broad and does not involve denomina-

[1] *Ibid.* p. 472.
[2] *Ibid.* p. 473.
[3] *Ibid.* pp. 473–474.

tional doctrine. An effort is made to present religion as a practical experience by which men live. The large objective is character development, and the establishment of those ethical standards by which individuals and nations have reached their highest development. The salary of the traveling teacher is usually paid through the coöperative efforts of the Protestant churches in the supervisory district, and the work is under the supervision of the local council of churches. Concerning this movement the Rev. Jay S. Stowell in 1931 made the following report:

A small but growing army of trained young women are today at work in rural areas on a new program which promises to revolutionize religious procedure for these districts. It holds out to the boys and girls in rural areas new and better opportunities in religious nurture than they have ever before had. The plan, if extended, will bring religious nurture to millions of youth attending rural public schools, but who for the most part have no regular contact with any church or Sunday school. . . . Rural teachers of religion are already at work in states as widely separated as New York, Pennsylvania, Arizona, Connecticut, Idaho, Kentucky, Maryland, Minnesota, Georgia, Illinois, Kansas, Michigan, Oregon, California, Montana, New Jersey, North Carolina, Ohio, Oklahoma, Tennessee, West Virginia, Wyoming, and probably other states for which no reports are at hand.[1]

The home, the church, and the school have been popularly conceived as a trinity which forms the cornerstone of American democracy. It is important that these three agencies understand one another, and that they coöperate and unify their efforts in setting up standards of personal behavior and in developing an adequate program of character training for American farm youth.

BOY AND GIRL SCOUTS

Boy and Girl Scout clubs are increasing in importance in the community program for rural children. Scout troops are

[1] "Religious Training for Rural Youth," *Missionary Review of the World*, Vol. 54 (May 1931), p. 349.

often adjuncts of church and public school programs and are closely allied to the life of the community. "The Boy Scout Movement," says James E. West, chief scout executive of the Boy Scouts of America, "is a program that is offered to religious, school, and civic institutions supplementing their other functions." [1]

Originally the Scout movement was an urban one and was organized in order to counteract in the lives of young people some of the undesirable influences of cities. The materials and inspiration for the program were drawn from the country, and it was inevitable that the movement, sooner or later, should make its appeal to rural youth. The following taken from a folder of the organization of the Boy Scouts of America warrants the above statement.

A scout! He enjoys a hike through the woods more than he does a walk over the city's streets. Over his camp fire, what a breakfast, dinner or supper he can prepare out there in the open. Does he enjoy the meal? Just watch him and compare his appetite with that of a boy who lounges at a lunch counter in a crowded city. . . . A scout can tie a knot, he can climb a tree, he can swim, he can pitch a tent, he can tell you what weeds are poisons, in the woods he knows the names of birds and animals, in the water he tells you the different varieties of fish.

This program is developed in terms of a rural child's environment, and many of the club activities are familiar to him. The advantage of scout training for the rural boy, however, lies in the fact that the materials of the program are systematic, accurate, and scientific. Opportunity for social adjustment is also one of the desirable characteristics of the training. Efforts are made in the troops to build up an *esprit de corps*, a feeling of group solidarity, and a sense of individual security. These are desirable for all children, but they are particularly desirable for rural children. The fact that the rural child has but few children of his own age to form his work and play groups is one

---

[1] "Character Education in Scouting," *Journal of the National Education Association*, Vol. 18 (Oct. 1929), p. 219.

of the distinctive problems in rural education. The modern rural teacher, therefore, welcomes for his children all the opportunities offered by Scout troops for development in desirable social habits and coöperative living.

The local unit of the Boy Scouts organization is known as a troop. It is composed of a small group, usually from twelve to fifteen boys of the same age, selected if possible from groups that have had similar experiences. Attached to each troop is an adult leader whose responsibility is to offer advice when needed, supervise the program, and give guidance as the need arises. The scout leader is in every sense a teacher, and the fact that his teaching takes place outside of school hours makes his teaching none the less important.

The Boy Scout movement has gradually spread to rural sections. Of the total 900,000 scouts and scout leaders in the United States 266,000 are in rural territory. The Boy Scout in the country has a wealth of projects closely related to rural life from which to choose in his advancement from "tenderfoot" to "eagle" rank. Of the 100 subjects of choice 42 of them apply directly to rural interests. These are as follows: Agriculture (as a life's work), cement, carpentry, dairying, farm home and its planning, farm layout and building arrangement, farm records and bookkeeping, first aid to farm animals, forestry, fruit culture, gardening, landscape architecture, masonry, nut tree planting, painting, personal health, physical development, plumbing, poultry keeping, and soil management. In the development of these projects 701,126 merit badges have been earned by boy scouts, during the first five years of rural work. The committee on Farm and Village Housing of the President's conference on Home Building and Home Ownership gives high praise to the work of the Boy Scout movement in a program of rural home development.

When the number of boys of scout age in a rural community is so small that no troop is possible, provisions are made for the lone scout, and what is known as the farm and home patrol. Programs for these isolated scouts are so organized that every boy may have the benefit of scout training if he wishes it. A plan for the small rural school growing in favor is the one encouraged by the Boy Scouts of America whereby a lone scout is trained and then becomes a demonstrator of Boy Scout principles and practices in his own school.

The Girl Scout movement is similar to that of the Boy Scouts. It emphasizes the recreational, physical, and personality development of its members. Like the Boy Scouts, it trains in out-of-door activities, and places special emphasis upon team work and responsibility for civic and community life. The Girl Scout is also trained for home activities and every effort is made to assist her in developing a superior personality, well-adjusted to life and useful in the home, the school, and the community. The rural teacher who is interested in forming or promoting a Boy or Girl Scout Troop should communicate with the nearest representative of the Scout movement and from him request information. This representative can usually be found in the nearest large city or town. Failing to secure such local contact, the teacher may obtain information from the two National Headquarters: Boy Scouts of America, Rural Scouting Department, Division of Operations, 2 Park Avenue, New York City; Girl Scouts, 14 West 49 Street, New York City.

4-H CLUBS

One of the chief sources of educational experiences for rural boys and girls is provided through the 4-H Club movement. This youth movement is important for rural teachers because of (a) the number of young people of school age enrolled in it, (b) the magnitude of the program offered, and (c) the large expenditure of funds to maintain the program. The movement is a part of the coöperative extension system of the United States Department of Agriculture and the several State Colleges of Agriculture. Apparently the movement began in the South and was initiated as a means of improving farm and home conditions through the interest and participation of young people in the agricultural activities of adults. The movement is modern, though it is difficult to date its origin. C. B. Smith, Chief, Coöperative Extension Work, United States Department of Agriculture, states that the movement began about 1899, but that the Smith-Lever Act in 1914 gave it impetus, provided federal funds for its support, and started it on its modern program.[1] Under the auspices of the Federal Government the movement spread rapidly. In 1927, 619,712 members were enrolled in 4-H Clubs in the United States. In 1930 this number had increased to 822,714; in 1933, approximately one million boys and girls had enrolled and were participating in the 4-H Club program.[2]

Leadership is provided for these members through agricultural agents, home demonstration agents, county club agents, and the state and Federal agricultural and home economics extension specialists. In addition to these paid and trained workers, the movement is further fostered by volunteer workers, usually farmers and their wives, rural teachers, ministers and other public-spirited local citizens. In 1930 there were about 2600 county agricultural agents; 1,300 home demonstration agents; 250 county club agents; 1100 specialists and 60,000 volunteer leaders assisting with the promotion and conduct of the 4-H club work for rural boys and girls.[3]

Paralleling this growth in membership and personnel have been the increasing appropriations in the local, state, and Federal governments for the support of the movement. In 1915, for instance, there was appropriated by the Federal Government the sum of $32,944.29 for the promotion of boys' and girls' clubs throughout the United States. By 1930 this

[1] "4-H Club Work," *Journal of the National Education Association*, Vol. 19 (Mar. 1930), p. 95.

[2] *Yearbook of Agriculture*, 1935, p. 745, Dept. of Agriculture, Government Printing Office.

[3] Smith, C. B. "4-H Club Work," *Journal of the National Education Association*, Vol. 19 (Mar. 1930), p. 95.

sum had increased to $557,633.89.[1] From the standpoints of membership, number of leaders, and the expenditure of funds the 4-H Club is, with the exception of the organized school, the most important single agency affecting the modern American farm youth.

The membership of the 4-H Club is composed of both boys and girls between the ages of ten and twenty years. The clubs are usually small, rarely exceeding fifteen members and the program is informal. There are no membership dues. The symbol of the club is the four-leaf clover, with the letter "H" on each leaf. Each "H" stands for points of attack in achieving the standards which the organization seeks to maintain. The club pledge explains their meaning, and somewhat suggests the program. "I pledge: my head to clearer thinking, my heart to greater loyalty, my hands to larger service; and my health to better living for my club, my community and my country.

Mr. C. B. Smith, of the United States Department of Agriculture, has recently set forth the aims of this modern youth movement in the following statement:

What does all this mean for the boy and girl? First, they learn to do something worthwhile in the best way. Their interest is aroused in the work because it is of importance to the family or the community. Their minds are interested. Here is something not out of books, but a part of life. There is competition and contest in it. It is a game not work.

Second, young folk at an impressionable age are brought into contact with outstanding farm men and women, with county agents, club agents, extension specialists, men and women with college training, with bankers, business men, fair officials, people who have achieved and whose success warrants emulation.

Third, through the club meetings, they early learn something of parliamentary law, how to preside at a meeting, how to appoint committees, how to make a report, how to work together to carry out a

[1] United States Dept. of Agriculture. *Report of Extension Work in Agriculture and Home Economics in the United States, 1932,* June, 1933, p. 64, Government Printing Office.

program. Here they get the beginnings of coöperation, one of the greatest needs of rural people.

Fourth, their outlook is broadened through: their attendance at county and regional club camps; the visit of many to the state college of agriculture, where they spend a week in instruction, sight-seeing, listening to inspirational talks; their attendance at county, state and national fairs, where many make exhibits; and the attendance of a select group at the National 4-H Club camp in Washington. All this stimulates ambition and interest and helps lift the vision.

Finally, the work reaches both boys and girls in school and boys and girls out of school. It teaches them that it is the trained men and women who succeed these days. It encourages them to go back to school if they have left it, and complete the high school work or go on to college, or take a vocational course. 4-H Club work is a strong supplement to school work and makes wide use of the native leadership found in every community if looked for and given a job.[1]

An examination of the aims as set forth by this national leader in the 4-H Club movement indicates that (a) the program is definitely vocational and cultural, (b) that it is organized for the development of the individual head, heart, and health, as set forth in the pledge, and (c) that the best interest of the community of which the member is a part is to be served. The program has further characteristics that are significant for education. It deals with interests closely linked with the child's immediate environment; participation in the program is voluntary; each child follows his particular bent; and the completion of a project is in terms of individual ability. The member does much of his work unsupervised, and, as a consequence, he is found to develop habits of independent thinking and action; his decisions are personal and, once they are made, he must abide by them. The very nature of the tasks set by the club program provides for valuable supplementary learnings for rural children. The aims of the 4-H Club program and the aims of the modern rural school are at many points the same.

In view of this fact, it is unfortunate that the interests of the

[1] "4-H Club Work," *Journal of the National Education Association*, Vol. 19 (Mar. 1930), p. 97.

two are seldom integrated. While a few states have taken steps toward an integration of agricultural extension work and the programs of the rural school, the administration of the two is, in general, separate. The public school system is administered by State Departments of Education which have a loose affiliation with the United States Office of Education. The Agricultural Extension Service is administered by the Department of Agriculture. For this state of affairs there are many reasons. Traditionally, education has always been slow to adopt new ideas. It is naturally conservative and tends to establish its program in terms of the *status quo*. The 4-H Club, on the other hand, almost from the beginning set as one of its aims the improvement and even the change of the *status quo* of the farmer and his family. Hence under the early traditional pattern of education, the philosophy of the 4-H Club and the philosophy of the school were at variance. The nature and number of the small local districts have also been a factor in separating the administrations of the school and the 4-H Club. In comparison with the needs of the field, the number of club leaders has always been small, and a single worker has been forced to cover a large territory, usually a county. Consequently, the small local district has not been financially able to sponsor a program which includes a club leader.

The personnel of the schools and the 4-H Clubs have not always been sympathetic and coöperative toward a joint program. At first the club leaders sought to work through the organized schools, but the program of the school at that time did not lend itself readily to club activities, and the local school officials resented the efforts of club leaders to force upon the system a program which teachers did not consider educational. In the beginning, the suspicions of the teaching profession were justified. The program of the 4-H Club was not educational, but narrowly vocational. The cultural and educational features are of recent development. This changing program of the 4-H Club movement has not been fully appreciated by the profession. On the other hand, the club leaders have not wholly grasped the fact that the rural school is changing also and that the programs of the two grow yearly more similar in functions, in practice, and in aims.

In view of this and the fact that promising attempts at correlation are now in progress, the American Country Life Association is at present considering the appointment of a "Coördinating Committee on Rural Education in the United States"; chief among its duties will be the consideration of this problem and the recommendations for its solution. The National Advisory Committee on Education has recommended that an interdepartmental council on education be established among the departments of the Federal Government to secure better correlation of educational activities. The National Society for the Study of Education and the Rural Education Department of the National Education Association have laid down the following guiding principles as desirable for the integration of all Boys' and Girls' Club work and the public schools. These principles have been generally accepted as desirable by the teaching profession:

While recognizing the general value of independent and competing programs and the distinctive contribution of club work, the writer holds that an indefinite continuance of this dual program for children is unsound and unjustified for two reasons: (a) it is inconsistent with the emphasis in education upon the development of an integrated personality and the belief in the principles of integrated learning and an integrated program; and (b) the fostering of the club program has drawn from the rural school many of its dynamic leaders, and has thus weakened and retarded seriously the service and improvement of this major educational agency.

As club work becomes truly educational, and as school work loses its formal, bookish, and abstract nature in favor of an experience-activity curriculum, the two programs become alike in purpose, organization, and method. To the extent to which they are kept apart, the club activities suffer for want of enriching and broadening contacts they might have if closely related to the history, geography, civics, and science of the school; the school program likewise suffers because it lacks sufficient contact with the vital problems, interests, and activities of the child's out-of-school life. The best educational results can be realized only when the child's out-of-school experiences and activities and his in-school contacts with the rich resources of our social heritage are integrated into a unified program and made to supplement each other. The life activities and experiences available in his environment are the natural laboratory for a child's education. To rob the school of this is to enforce upon it, in this day of activity education, a barren and ineffective program.

Ideally these two educational programs should be merged and the responsibility be placed in the hands of the county superintendent's office. To be worthy of this responsibility, rural educators need a new vision of education. The school has tended to formalize and make rigid everything it touches. It is constrained by stereotypes that seem to devitalize every experience and activity, every mental adventure that becomes a part of its program. Herein lies the curse of the past and the challenge of progressive education to the rural leader.

To safeguard the distinct contribution of club work, there should be provided an assistant county superintendent, responsible for promoting this type of work and aiding the teachers to utilize these out-of-school experiences and problems as a basis for a real integrated experience-activity curriculum. Pending this ultimate solution these two forces (county and state school officers and state and county club agents) should coöperate in such a way as to provide an integrated program with maximal learning for the child.[1]

Information for the organization of a local 4-H Club may be secured from several sources: (a) the local Farm Demonstration Agent whose office is usually located in the county seat; (b) the local Home Demonstration Agent; (c) the Director of Extension of the local State Land Grant College; and (d) the Chief of the Extension Service, United States Department of Agriculture, Washington, D.C.

NATIONAL YOUTH ADMINISTRATION

The Federal government has undertaken yet another program for youth known as the National Youth Administration.

[1] National Society for the Study of Education. *The Status of Rural Education*, *1930*, pp. 266–267, Public School Publishing Co. Quoted by permission of the Society.

While the program has been adopted as an emergency measure during the economic crisis, leaders in the field of education suggest that it may become a permanent feature of the educational service of the Federal Government. If so, the program will have many possibilities for the schools. At the present, the program is dominated by the necessity of providing financial aid to alleviate an economic situation involving the welfare of approximately 6,000,000 young people between the ages of 16 and 25. The educational program, therefore, has become secondary to the immediate one of providing jobs for needy youth. The nature of the tasks performed by these young people, while incidentally educational, is, at the same time, educationally significant because many of them are performed in the interests of children now in school.

Aubrey Williams, Executive Director of the N.Y.A. stated in a recent article that the service projects of the educational program were divided into several categories.[1] The greater part of them were recreational and provided young people with part-time employment in urban and rural centers in the capacity of leaders on playgrounds and in recreational centers, schools, and clubs. Other activities provided experience in handicrafts, machine crafts, and design. Others fell in the fields of research projects in social and scientific fields, many having a direct bearing on human betterment. Still other projects gave experience in such fields as crime prevention, parole, sanitation, and the care of crippled children. Another group of projects dealt with rural development in the field of experimental farming, reforestation, health practices, and home economics. The program thus outlined is basically educational, and an attempt is made to bring it to fruition through school facilities already in existence. It has set up no schools, no centers for training, no clubs, but has rather sought to use those already in existence and functioning.[2] If the program continues in

[1] "Youth and the Government," *Progressive Education*, Vol. 12 (Dec. 1935) p. 505.
[2] *Ibid.* p. 506.

the future along lines laid down in the present, the National Youth Administration will pursue a policy of integration with existing educational and social agencies. While such an integrated program lies in the realm of prophecy, the teacher is wise who seeks to understand its philosophic implications and its practical applications. In the event of its continuance the school should coöperate to make its program truly educational.

THE TEACHER'S RESPONSIBILITY IN THE COMMUNITY PROGRAMS AFFECTING YOUTH

While Pierce's study, referred to above, suggests a complexity of organizations for the small community, another side of the picture reveals: (a) the existence of wide differences in the educational opportunities offered through community agencies in the several supervisory districts studied, and (b) the actual poverty of educational agencies in some of the districts. Upon this point Miss Pierce states in part:

. . . In one unit $15,750 is spent in agricultural extension work, with eight paid workers, while one third of the supervisors report no agricultural extension work being carried on in their units. A similar situation appears under 4-H Club service where the range of money spent is from $9,800 to none; 97 per cent of the school enrollment is being served in one unit, while in several units there is no service. One unit is supporting five paid workers, while others have none.

. . . A like situation exists in Boy Scout work. Five out of twenty-four report no such activities, while thirteen paid workers are distributed among nine units, and a total of $30,400 is spent on such activities in ten out of the twenty-four units.

Some type of library service is found in all except three units. However, in units where money is spent for this service, the sum ranges from $32,000 to $500.[1]

In other words, the modern rural teacher may have one of two problems to face in dealing with the rural community. There

[1] *Agencies Contributing to Rural Education, Bulletin Rural Education.* Department of the National Education Association, pp. 38–39, Feb. 1932.

may be (a) the problem of the actual initiation and development of community forces for educational and social advance or (b) the problem of the use, the coördination, and the harmonization of community forces.

THE PROBLEM OF INITIATION OF COMMUNITY AGENCIES

Mr. Robert Clark, Assistant Superintendent of Schools, Monongalia County, Morgantown, West Virginia, presented the first problem in an address before the National Education Association in 1935. Said he:

In many rural communities today we find a decadent society. It is a natural consequence of the industrial era through which we have passed for the last half century, debilitating rural society by its constant drain of wealth and leadership into industrial and metropolitan centers. There is no greater need in the nation today than the rebuilding and revitalizing of many of these rural communities . . . The rural community is to be rebuilt, not as it was in a primitive and pioneering society, but as one in line with progress, enjoying the advantages of modern transportation, labor saving devices, and a public school program that offers advantages and opportunities that heretofore have been exclusively the possession of those living in urban communities. The leading factor in revitalizing rural communities is the community school.[1]

The rural teacher facing such a debilitated community life should decide his course of action in accordance with his philosophy of education. If he accepts the theory that children grow through manifold experiences, then he must accept the responsibility, since local leadership is lacking, for the development of opportunities for experiencing both in and outside the school. He will probably find it necessary, for instance, until local leadership can be developed, to organize a 4-H Club, to initiate a parent-teacher association, to develop a health center, or to encourage a program for community recreation. On the other hand, if the teacher interprets his task only in

[1] *National Education Association Proceedings, 1935*, p. 411.

terms of the school day and thus feels no responsibility for community participation and leadership, his teaching performance will become at the same time more simple and more difficult. It will be simpler because fact-getting is not difficult for the normal child; nor is fact-finding difficult for the average teacher. Learning and teaching under these conditions is a routine performance; it is likely to be dull, but in the hands of a skillful teacher of dynamic personality it may even be lively, agreeable, and gratifying to both teacher and learner. It will be more difficult because education is more than an accumulation of facts; interpretation of facts is important and the use of them a necessity. Such knowledge as we now have about the educating process indicates that we interpret and use facts in the light of experience. Consequently, learners may be actually beggared because of a narrow range of experiences. Teachers of the social sciences know the wide differences in the possibilities of teaching geography, for instance, when dealing with two groups of children—those who have traveled and those who have not. It is entirely possible that the teacher who "loses" time participating in community activities affecting children may "gain" it back in the economical learning time of his pupils.

THE COÖRDINATION AND INTEGRATION OF COMMUNITY FORCES AFFECTING EDUCATION

The improvement of human beings is the primary responsibility of a community. The school is only one agency charged with this task; its specialty is minor children, and to meet their needs the school is given about one-eighth of children's time. The other seven-eighths is spent in work, sleep, recreation, and worship where the child comes under organized and unorganized interests, some of which are good for him and some are not. It is easy to make time spent in school educational, but it is the leisure time of children which gives teachers increasing concern. Even where children belong to organized groups such as are outlined in this chapter, worthwhile results in desirable child development are not always forthcoming. Often the programs are unrelated, there is no unity and no integration, so that the child is tossed about from school to 4-H Club, to church, to the Boy Scouts without direction and guidance. All programs lose in effectiveness by such procedures. In 1902 Professor John Dewey pointed out the following in such a situation:

No educational system can be regarded as complete until it adopts into itself the various ways in which social and intellectual intercourse may be promoted; and employs them systematically, not only to counteract dangers which these same agencies are bringing with them, but so as to make them positive causes in raising the whole level of life.[1]

The employment of the various social, recreational, educational, and religious ways by which a community is organized suggests a systematic procedure. Many urban centers have met this difficulty with a community council, and rural communities with a community committee. Often the latter is composed of only three members: the teacher, the minister, and the 4-H Club leader; but its program of integration can be important. Leadership in integration need not necessarily come from the teacher. Various community factors, such as attitudes and personnel, will determine who should assume leadership. It seems desirable, however, that the program of coördination and integration be built upon well-defined principles. These are suggested as follows:

1. The integrated program should be initiated and developed in the interest of children rather than in the interest of organizations. This principle suggests that efforts should be made to study in each community the interests and needs of the children and that programs should be built to meet them. These needs, for instance, may be in the fields of health, recreation, economics, housing, crime, etc.

[1] "The School as a Social Center," *Proceedings of the National Education Association, 1902*, pp. 376–377.

2. It would appear desirable to integrate all programs around a yearly central objective or theme. If health, for instance, were selected as the outstanding need by the community committee, the programs of all community agencies affecting children might be properly directed toward the solution of the problem. The school would profit by such emphasis. So would the 4-H Club and so would the church. Programs could be developed so that they supplemented rather than duplicated each other.

3. Not only should the committee attempt to encourage programs of value, but it should discourage community activities which are considered undesirable influences for children. The best means of discouraging such influences is the substitution of worthwhile programs for them.

4. Each organization represented in the community committee should make a sincere effort to understand and to appreciate the worth of each program. Because life is complex, no one agency is able to supply all the needs of the modern boy and girl. Each community organization is important because, better than any other, in its own special field, it contributes to the total need of the community's youth. Essential to coöperation are mutual understanding and the respect of each organization for all, and of all for each.

SUMMARY

Modern education is conceived as a process which includes all the experiences of children, whether acquired in or out of school. The experiences out-of-school which affect youth, therefore, are of real importance to the modern teacher. In the small rural school, his responsibility may be three-fold: (1) He may find it necessary to initiate and stimulate community interest to the point of providing desirable experiences for the out-of-school life of children. In this matter, the responsibility of the rural teacher differs from the responsibility of the urban teacher, who looks to an administrator, usually his principal, for the initiation of community programs. (2) He may find it necessary to inform himself of the out-of-school programs affecting his children, and participate in them.

(3) He may find it desirable to give his major attention to the integration of programs, so that children may have the advantage of unified work organized for their complete development.

Available studies indicate that the church, the Boy and Girl Scouts, and the 4-H Clubs are the three organizations which most often influence the lives of rural children. While the aims of these organizations differ, each has points in common with the others. Each is interested in character education, and in the fullest development of the individual member. Each, with the exception of the youth organizations of the church, draws heavily upon the rural environment for much of its program materials. The concern for community welfare is the concern of all. The church specializes in the field of ethics and is concerned with the adjustment of the individual to his community, in accordance with the ideals set forth in the Christian faith. The Boy and Girl Scouts accept as their special function the development of recreational activity to the end that the leisure hours of children may be rich and meaningful. The 4-H Club is vocational, though modern trends are toward the cultural as well. These three organizations represent important and large areas in child development, spiritual, physical, and vocational. They cannot be ignored by the modern teacher. Organized education in the school completes the cycle of forces which work toward the well-adjusted child. To the end that the child may reach this goal in human achievement easily and efficiently, it seems best that the community programs affecting his development be integrated, with the school and the teacher as the unifying core.

SUGGESTED READINGS

Cooper, William John. "The Principal as a Community Leader," Department Elementary School Principals, National Education Association, *Eleventh Yearbook*, Vol. XI, pp. 151–153, Washington, D. C.

Dewey, John. "The School as Social Center," *Proceedings of the National Education Association, 1902*, pp. 373–383, Washington, D. C.

Jordan, R. H. *Extra-Classroom Activities in Elementary and Secondary Schools*, Chaps. II–III, Crowell Co., New York, 1928.

Kendrick, W. H. *The Four-H Trail*, Chaps. IV, VII, Part I, The Gorham Press, Boston, 1926.

Kolb, J. H. and Brunner, Edmund deS. *A Study of Rural Society*, Chap. V, Houghton Mifflin Company, Boston, 1935.

Lowth, Frank J. *Everyday Problems of the Country Teacher*, Rev. ed., Chap. XII, Macmillan, New York, 1936.

Stowell, Jay S. "Religious Training for Rural Youth," *Missionary Review of the World*, Vol. 54 (May, 1931), p. 349.

Warren, Gertrude L. "4-H Club Work with Rural Girls," *Journal of Home Economics*, Vol. 24 (Aug., 1932), pp. 686–688.

White House Conference on Child Health and Protection. Sec. III G, *Youth Outside the Home and School*, pp. 344–406, Century Co., New York, 1932.

Wyland, R. O. *Scouting in the Schools*, Chap. I, Bureau of Publications, Teachers College, Columbia University, New York, 1934.

MATERIALS FOR DISCUSSION

Consider the following statements. What changes would make them more acceptable to you? What significant issues arise from their study?

1. The school is only one activity in the educative process. Education is a continuous process which respects neither time nor place. Often the out-of-school activities are more educational than those offered by the school.

2. The aims of the 4-H Club program and the aims of the modern rural school are at many points the same. In view of this fact the two programs should be integrated and made a part of the school program.

3. The teacher who "wastes" time participating in community activities affecting children may "gain" it back in the economical learning time of his pupils.

4. All community programs should be developed for the welfare of children rather than for the promotion of organizations.

5. To the end that children grow toward well adjusted personalities it seems best that community programs which affect child development be integrated, with the school and the teacher as the unifying core.

CHAPTER XVIII

THE PARENT-TEACHER ASSOCIATION IN THE RURAL COMMUNITY

THE PARENT-TEACHER MOVEMENT—AN HISTORICAL BACKGROUND

To THE uninitiated the term Parent-Teacher Association connotes what it says: namely, that it is an association of parents and teachers organized for the purpose of promoting the welfare of children and the interests of schools. As worthy as such a program of promotion and coöperation may be, the Parent-Teacher Association, ideally at least, is more than this. Its program is more important, its functions more significant. The Parent-Teacher Association, as we know it today, is apparently a part of and an outgrowth from the larger Home School Movement which began to achieve significance in this country at the turn of the century and which had its source in the humanitarian movement of the nineteenth century. The latter concerned itself with reforms in education, health, prison conditions, and, indeed, in all spheres of activity involving minors. The movement was world-wide. In 1929 Mrs. A. H. Reeve, President of the International Federation of Home and School, stated at a conference on the Parent-Teacher Association held at Columbia University that organizations similar to the Parent-Teacher Association of America could be found in thirty-five other countries. There were many phases of the movement in the United States: the Rural School Improvement Association of the South; the Kindergarten Mothers' Club, whose interests were the interests of young children; study clubs attached to schools; and associations and other organizations similar to the Coöperative Education Association of Virginia.

The organization had, in a sense, a national beginning, since it had its inception in Washington, the capital city. The story of the founding of the Parent-Teacher Association is too familiar for details here. Briefly, the story was this: In 1896, Alice McLillan Birney, of Washington, D. C., conceived the idea of a Congress of Mothers, the program of which should be chiefly concerned with the care and training of children. The idea was perfected into an organization on February 17, 1897. While outlined in the interest of children it also gave recognition for the first time to a fact now commonly accepted, namely, that parenthood is a profession to which should be brought special training and study. The young organization soon discovered that in order to serve itself and the children it represented, some effort should be made toward coöperation with the educative forces affecting children. Hence, eleven years after the initiation of the Congress, teachers were brought into the organization through a parent-teacher department. At about the same time fathers were admitted also to the Mothers' Congress, and the name of the organization was changed to designate the new membership. In 1924 the present name of the national organization, "The National Congress of Parents and Teachers" was adopted. The growth of the organization has been almost phenomenal. In 1910 the total membership for the whole United States was less than thirty-two thousand; in 1931 the enrollment reached a million and a half.

CHARACTERISTICS OF THE RURAL PARENT-TEACHER ASSOCIATION

The Rural Association Is a Community Organization. Any parent may become a member of the Parent-Teacher Association of the school attended by his child. In some associations this privilege is extended to all in the community who are interested in schools and children, a policy almost essential in rural associations where the community problems are different from those in urban associations. Hence the average rural association is likely to be more than an organization of parents and teachers; rather it approaches a community organization whose chief interest is the school. At a meeting of a rural association there will probably be present grandparents, parents, children in school, and children in arms. There will be present also the young unmarried people of the community and married couples without children. The diverse ages and interests of the rural group have a significant bearing on the making of a program, but, while the difficulties of such a community meeting are obvious, so also are the opportunities. Educational programs develop in an interested community. To unite two powerful forces, the home and the school, in the interest of a third, the community, whose representatives are present is a service of the highest importance. Many reforms in rural education can be traced to interested members, not always parents, of the local Parent-Teacher Association. Two authorities bear out the above generalizations. Butterworth in his 1928 study of the Parent-Teacher Association reported that the per cent of non-parent membership decreased as the size of the community increased. Thus in schools of one and two teachers the per cent of non-parent membership was 16.3 per cent; in the schools with three to five teachers it was 10.5 per cent; in the schools with six to ten teachers, 12 per cent, and those of eleven or more teachers, 9.5 per cent.[1] William McKinley Robinson, National Chairman of the Rural Service Committee of the National Congress of Parents and Teachers, reported the same tendency in 1933 as follows:

The attendance at city association meetings is made up almost exclusively of parents and teachers. The rural association is a community organization attended by all age groups from babies to grandparents,

[1] Butterworth, Julian E. *The Parent-Teacher Association and Its Work*, pp. 101–102, Macmillan, 1928.

including a few bachelor uncles and visitors from neighboring communities.[1]

Membership in the Rural Parent-Teacher Association Represents a Large Percentage of the Parents of the Community. Representation from the homes in which children of school age live is recognized as an important factor in the local Parent-Teacher Associations. It is considered desirable if the percentage is high, and, compared with urban associations, the rural local groups have this desirable characteristic. The Butterworth study data for the one-teacher and two-teacher schools showed a median of 83.8 per cent of parents represented in the Parent-Teacher Association. In schools with three to five teachers the percentage was 53.7; six to ten teachers, 42.8 per cent; eleven or more teachers, 32.2. Parent membership consistently decreased as the size of the school increased.[2]

Teachers Join the Local Rural Associations in Large Numbers. Nearly all local Parent-Teacher Association groups make an effort to secure a one hundred per cent membership of its teachers. According to Butterworth this goal is most likely to be accomplished in the smaller schools. His study revealed that the schools of one and two teachers had a 100 per cent membership in 95.4 per cent of the associations; schools with three to five teachers in 88.5 per cent of the associations; with six to ten teachers, 73.9 per cent; with eleven or more teachers, 59.3 per cent.[3] Membership in an organization does not always mean helpful participation and constructive leadership, though it does indicate an interest which may conceivably lead to both. The fact that so large a number of teachers in small schools enroll in local Parent-Teacher Association groups also suggests that they have little choice in the matter of

[1] National Congress of Parents and Teachers. *Proceedings of the Thirty-Seventh Annual Meeting, 1933*, National Congress of Parents and Teachers, p. 188, 1933.

[2] Butterworth, Julian, E. *The Parent-Teacher Association and Its Work*, p. 102, Macmillan, 1928.

[3] *Ibid.* p. 103.

accepting considerable responsibility for the development of the association's program.

The Monthly Meetings Are Attended by a Large Number of Children. The custom of child attendance at the meetings of the rural Parent-Teacher Association was suggested in an earlier paragraph, but it is so pronounced that it forms one of the differentiating characteristics of the local rural group. This is brought about by a number of factors, chief of which is that farm families tend to move as a group. The isolation of the average farm home discourages the leaving of children, unchaperoned, in them, so that children either accompany parents to meetings, or all remain at home. The place occupied by the rural child in the average farm home, discussed at some length in Chapter III, and the fact that rural parents and children incline to identify their interests also apparently increase this tendency.

The Membership Is Likely to Be Composed of One Occupational Group. Contrasted with the membership of the urban association, with its cross-section of a community life including lawyers, doctors, ministers, business men, mechanics, and bankers, the rural association, with the sole exception of the teacher, usually represents one occupation. Robinson presents the situation as follows:

The city association has several occupational as well as various social, civic and cultural interests represented within its membership. The rural association, aside from the teacher, is made up usually of but one occupational group and represents but one mode of life. The attendants at the city association meetings are in many cases members of other social and civic groups. The members of rural associations have fewer affiliations, and therefore participation in the parent-teacher association is less likely to be a perfunctory duty.[1]

[1] National Congress of Parents and Teachers. *Proceedings of the Thirty-Seventh Annual Meeting, 1933*, p. 188, National Congress of Parents and Teachers, 1933.

ORGANIZATION PROCEDURE OF THE LOCAL UNIT

In line with other national organizations the Parent-Teacher Association has its local branches which are attached to local schools; its states' congress, composed of the locals; and the national congress of parents and teachers, composed of the state organizations. National headquarters for the congress is at 1201 Sixteenth St., N. W., Washington, D. C. Inquiries about the organization should be addressed there, though the community desiring to organize an association may nearly always find help nearer home.

Local associations are interested in assisting nearby schools to form new associations, and district and state officers are ready to give help to any community asking for it. Requests should, perhaps, be sent to the district officers, since they are near at hand. It seems to be the consensus of opinion that the organization of local units should proceed from a felt community need and that the school's part in such an organization should be indirect and suggestive only. This, however, while proper enough for urban situations, is not practical for the rural community. Experience indicates that nearly always the rural teacher in the small school must take the initiative for the organization of a parents' community group, and most leaders in the rural education field advise it. The reasons for this are evident to any student of rural sociology. In the average community of a small rural school, leadership is either lacking altogether or is undeveloped; and, with leadership lacking or dormant, the community is not likely to be aware of its own needs. In this event it is not only the privilege, but the duty, of the rural teacher to form and foster an organization through which the community may become aware of its needs and may have its potential leaders trained. There are many avenues open to the rural teacher for the development of community leadership, but perhaps the one most available is the local unit of the Parent-Teacher Association.

A practical question at this point, of course, is how a teacher, particularly one who is inexperienced, should proceed to organize the community into a Parent-Teacher Association. There is no pattern, unfortunately, to offer for the solution of the problem. All communities are different, and no one plan will fit all needs. However, the problem has similarities at so many points that a general plan may prove suggestive. By and large the procedure is as follows:

First Step. Try to induce an influential person in the community to organize a local Parent-Teacher Association. Any person or group of persons may act, and it seems wise for the teacher to seek first to work through a local group. This gives the movement importance, particularly if the person or group is prominent, and will tend to enlist other influential community members. In the event of securing the interest of local people the teacher will serve only in an advisory capacity. Failing here, however, he will himself assume responsibility for the initial organization.

Second Step. Solicit information and help from the nearest local district or state officer, and consult the district or county superintendent of schools who will be able to assist.

Third Step. Make careful plans for the first meeting. Success depends upon this. Seek a possible local candidate for president, interview him, and point out the reasons for a community organization and what may be accomplished by it. If a prominent local person will agree to accept the presidency of the organization, offered to him at the first meeting, half the battle is won. There is nothing more fatal to the auspicious beginning of an organization than to have person after person presented for president from the floor, only to have the nomination withdrawn for reasons good or bad. The wise teacher forestalls any such calamity. If he fails to secure a local desirable candidate, he will hold himself in readiness to assume the responsibility of serving as the first president. In any event, his gathered information and his willingness to take the responsibility for the organization at the initial meeting, and at subsequent meetings, if necessary, have armed him for any emergency arising at the first meeting.

Fourth Step. Enlist the help and advice of the children of the school, thus making the community meeting a school activity in which all the children share. They will make their plans in one of their conference periods and will discuss with the teacher such necessary items as the invitation list, how the invitations shall be sent and what part the children will play in the first meeting. All of these items call for committees and for more planning. They give opportunity for the development of potential leadership in children, the community leaders of the future, and furnish occasion for the joy and interest that are excited by a common task.

Fifth Step. Let the children coöperate actively in putting plans into action. Children of the upper grades may write the invitations to the community as a part of their English exercises. If the invitations are artistic, the art work for the whole school can be correlated here. The children may even send out a hectographed or mimeographed bulletin explaining the object of the meeting and urging the parents to attend. Committees on refreshments may make final plans and the committee on the program spur their efforts. The children may assume sole responsibility for the first program; theoretically, this practice is supposed to be bad, but child participation will guarantee a good audience, and the teacher who wishes to present a plan for a community organization will need to have the community present to hear it. Child participation, within reasonable limits, in a community organization is not bad, and in a rural community is desirable. Some of the strongest rural associations make a practice of having a short program by children precede the program by the adults; and this seems only fair to the children since they, as well as adults, attend the rural Parent-Teacher Association. The difficulty, of course, lies in the fact that adult organizations often find it pleasant to exploit children and in so doing abridge their own individual development. With the invitations out and the plans for the program perfected, the teacher is ready for the initial meeting and the organization.

Sixth Step. Be at the schoolhouse, with a committee of children to assist, in time to greet the people of the community as they come. Lack of social contacts make many rural people appear shy and timid; but, like all types of people, they respond to genuine friendliness and a real interest in their problems. The chances are strong, if the publicity has been good, that the community will be well represented. At this first meeting the teacher will preside until a permanent president has been elected. He will present the program, introduce the visiting Parent-Teacher Association officer, if one is present, explain to the group the purposes of the association, and outline the main objective for the year.

Seventh Step. Provide good refreshments for the social hour of the first meeting. These may be served by the children.

The teacher or local leader should remember that the organization in the offing is rural not urban, and as such presents peculiar problems. The rural Parent-Teacher Association does not need and indeed cannot efficiently handle the elaborate organization of the urban association. The latter generally has all the officers required by the National Congress and, in addition, sets up an elaborate committee system consisting of at least ten committees—four of them local and six of them standing committees coöperating with and reporting to the corresponding committees in the state organization. To attempt such an organization in a rural Parent-Teacher Association serving a small community would be folly. The average rural Parent-Teacher Association needs only three committees— the committee on hospitality, the committee on publicity, and the committee on the program.

The selection of a chairman for each of these three committees should be made with the greatest care. If the teacher has been able to secure a good permanent president, and is thus left free for further service, he can perhaps find no better place for it than on the program committee, upon the efficiency of which the future of the association often depends. Since the membership will probably be small, it is desirable to place each member on one of the three recommended committees. Once organized, the Parent-Teacher Association, generally speaking, should function in solving problems that are specific and urgent.

The seven steps thus outlined form a pattern of procedure, which consists, in the main, of group planning, group consultation, and group activity. While this procedure cannot always be followed, taken as a whole it is sound, and the young teacher would be wise to use it. He should keep in mind, however, a fact that is fundamental for all work in the rural school: every community, like every child, is unique and different; each has its individual problems, each its individual assets. The modern teacher attempts to discover both assets and problems and makes plans in the light of them.

PLANNING THE PROGRAM

The teacher in the small school who is actually engaged in parent-teacher work should keep in mind a few basic facts. The first of these is that the organization of the Parent-Teacher Association is the beginning and not the ending of his responsibility. The organization will not of itself run itself. It requires constant study, planning, and group activity. The second is that the regular meeting is only a part of the program, only one of the activities of the association. The association program which interprets itself in terms of a monthly meeting only is poor indeed. Ideally, the program grows out of a study of the problems of the community and is developed as a means of accomplishing what Butterworth calls "socially desirable ends" which may concern community health, public morals, community recreation, and countless other problems which plague the rural community. But the rural association needs to exercise vigilance lest it repeat in its individual program the mistakes which have hampered the National Congress from the beginning of its history.

HISTORICAL DEVELOPMENT IN PROGRAM PLANNING

Originally, the program of the Mothers' Congress concerned itself with child study. Upon the alliance of the Congress with organized education, however, trends in programs and activities changed. For many years the local associations spent most of their time and nearly all of their energy in providing equipment for the school. This was usually done by giving entertainments of all sorts for the purpose of raising funds, which were then expended for pianos, drinking fountains, library accessories, and various other items conspicuously lacking in the average rural school equipment. Mrs. E. C. Mason thinks the trend was inevitable in view of the dismal school which parents viewed for the first time in their monthly meetings of the Parent-Teacher Association. She thus sums up the situation:

The three R's were supplemented by the three D's, dull, dirty, dreary. Square rooms with bare walls. Monotony, stern right angles, lack of color and beauty everywhere inside. Bareness and bleakness outside. No wonder there were early campaigns to raise money, and enrich the equipment, even though it would have been wiser to arouse the school authorities to make the improvements from public funds.[1]

There is a further theory that principals and superintendents directed the energies of the new force in education into such innocuous channels in an effort to provide "busy work" for parents who felt called to do something about the schools, but lacked enough knowledge to formulate a program. Be that as it may, the fact remains that the association spent many of its early years in the endeavor to raise money, and newly established units in rural areas still tend toward the same procedure. This practice is not wholly bad. Within reasonable limits it stimulates interest in the school. It grows bad only when the program consists solely of money-raising for school necessities, and it is bad for two reasons.

In the first place the association assumes a responsibility which does not properly belong to it. Supplies and equipment

[1] "How the Movement Started and How It Has Developed," *A New Force in Education*, p. 26. Proceedings of a Conference held at Teachers College, Columbia University, Dec. 5 and 6, 1929, National Congress of Parents and Teachers.

for the school should be purchased by the local trustees and with public funds. Nearly all authorities in school administration are agreed that such a procedure is educationally sound. Education has suffered a great deal of harm because boards have in many instances depended upon parent-teacher associations to supply the necessities which they fail to provide. In the second place, the association thus turns aside from its real and primary functions—to provide an opportunity for the home and school to study their common problems and to develop in the study the potential leadership which lies in the average rural community.

In this equipment stage of the development of the Association the programs were usually stereotyped, consisting of a talk or lecture by an outside speaker; and each monthly program was separate and distinct from the others, so that there was no continuity in thinking or planning. Of this stage Mrs. E. C. Mason, then First Vice-president of the National Congress of Parents and Teachers, had this to say:

It has taken many, many years to foster the idea that the meeting is only a part of a program and that program planning is the planning of all the activities which contribute to the doing of something socially valuable and needed in the school community where the association is located. The meeting is one of the factors which is valuable in the carrying out of these activities.[1]

Today many rural associations have never progressed beyond the equipment type of activity and the lecture type of program. It indicates a lack of vision, lack of objectives, and lack of planning.

MODERN CONCEPTION OF PROGRAM PLANNING

Professor Julian E. Butterworth of Cornell University, writing on this problem in the *Child Welfare Magazine*, stated that all programs for the parent-teacher association should

[1] *Ibid.* p. 27.

begin with some educational problem of the community and end with the completion of those activities believed expedient in meeting the problems. The process involves four steps: (a) a determination of needs to which the association may properly devote itself; (b) the determination of existing specific problems; (c) acquainting the association with the existence of the needs of the community; and, (d) the development of activities which will solve the problems. Such a process Professor Butterworth points out in the same article will result in the following: it will reduce the diffusiveness in the discussions and activities of the association, it will place entertainment in its proper place, it will indicate to school officers that the association is interested in education and can do something educationally worthwhile.[1]

According to our present knowledge of education, Professor Butterworth's recommendation for program making is sound. It is, indeed, suited to the procedure in modern curriculum making for the organized school. The community provides another curriculum for the child and it seems only logical that parents and teachers recognize it as such and apply accepted educational procedures to it. If the program of the association is unrelated to the educational problems of the community, it will prove to be as uninteresting to the members as curriculum material unrelated to the interests of children proves boring to them. The association would likewise profit from an adoption of some of the modern techniques of teaching. If the procedure for program making, as recommended by Professor Butterworth, is followed, the association will find itself involved in many activities. This is also educationally sound. Adults as well as children learn through experiences. Both knowledge and leadership develop from participation, and the association which best serves the community is the one which has every member at work on a task individually satisfying and educationally worthwhile. As a rule, the yearly program of the

[1] "First Principles in Program Making for Parent-Teacher Associations," *Child Welfare*, Sept. 1929, pp. 23–24.

local association should be planned a year in advance. It should be set up in terms of objectives and the monthly programs integrated with them. The planning of the program is the responsibility of the program committee, but often in small rural associations the whole membership plans, discusses, and decides upon the yearly program. This procedure obviously has many advantages.

PRINCIPLES OF PROGRAM PLANNING

1. The yearly program should be planned so that local leadership can be easily developed. In the last analysis each local community is largely self-dependent, meager as its resources may be.

2. The program should be planned so that all groups are served. Parents, non-parents, and children should participate in programs and their needs should be met through them. This requires careful analysis and wise discussions in selecting program materials.

3. Efforts should be made, through programs, to stimulate in the group what Robinson calls an "awareness of local community needs." This is particularly important in rural associations because the average member of the community has a direct control over the social, cultural, political and educational environment. In a way rarely possible in urban situations, a single individual in a rural community can directly bring about environmental changes.

4. The program should encourage informal study groups for parents. Experience indicates that these are best fostered in private homes, when children are not present, and when discussions of their problems can be frank and free. These study clubs then become in effect small circles within the larger organization.

5. As in planning curriculum programs for children, the program for adults should include many worthwhile activities. Professor William McKinley Robinson in his 1933 Rural Service Report to the National Congress points out the desirability of this procedure for the following reasons: (1) "Unless accustomed to coöperative endeavor, most rural people work together more readily than they think or play together; (2) tangible activities

are the chief means of learning and expression to some people; (3) desired ideas and attitudes may grow out of participation in projects; as for example, the purchase of playground equipment should carry with it the belief that play is more than mere physical exercise." [1]

6. The program should be planned in terms of the persistent problems of rural areas. It will include many phases of health, such as clinics, hot noon lunches, tubercular testing, etc. It will also include the beautification of school buildings and grounds, library service, recreational needs, safety education, adult education, music and drama, and many other local rather than general desiderata.

7. Finally in the words of Professor Robinson "Only that rural parent-teacher association has a continuing and developing vitality which bases its program upon the needs 'of' the people as met 'by' the people. Neither the state nor National Congresses, neither the district, nor county councils, neither outside speakers, nor organizers and promoters can build a working program 'for' the people. These latter groups and individuals may guide the community in the recognition of its needs and ways and means of meeting those needs; but until the people themselves have an awareness of community well-being toward which they themselves are striving, the association program remains superficial and futile." [2]

WHY A PARENT-TEACHER ORGANIZATION IN THE SMALL SCHOOL?

To many teachers in small schools the responsibility for Parent-Teacher Associations appears only as another burden for their already overburdened shoulders. They usually ask, and quite reasonably two questions: (a) why is the Parent-Teacher Association important for small schools? and (b) what

[1] National Congress of Parents and Teachers. *Proceedings of the Thirty-Seventh Annual Meeting, 1933*, p. 189, National Congress of Parents and Teachers, 1933.

[2] National Congress of Parents and Teachers. *Proceedings of the Fortieth Annual Meeting, 1936*, p. 115, National Congress of Parents and Teachers, 1936.

returns may the small rural school expect from it? Each question is important and, in view of the multiplicity of duties of the average teacher in a small school, deserves an answer.

To the first question concerning the why of the Parent-Teacher Association the answer is four-fold. In the first place, the association offers those opportunities for social contacts so helpful to the adult farm group. Being a community organization, it is composed of neighbors and friends. Whole families belong, and the monthly meeting is more than an educational program. It becomes the place for an exchange of opinions, a time for the discussion of crops and politics. The social hour listed incidentally in many urban programs is vital for the rural group, a real need in the life of farm people.

In the second place, the rural teacher needs the social contacts and companionship of his community group. The life of the teacher in a small school is lonely at best. Unless he owns a car or is near a trolley or bus line, his contacts with adults are often limited to the family with whom he boards. The association provides him with the opportunity of making new friends—important ones, too, the people of the school and neighborhood.

In the third place, farm parents need to understand—as do all parents—the needs of child nature and the perplexing problems of modern youth. Modern parents have long been aware of these needs, but they need information about the latest discoveries in the field of health as related to growing children. They need the results of psychological investigations of the mental and emotional development of children and adolescents. They need an understanding of the modern problems in education—the changing curriculum and the changing technique in teaching. They need to know a great deal about the new movement in education called "progressive." Education cannot be progressive if parents are conservative, particularly if the conservatives are articulate in school elections, as is often the case in the small rural schools. The association should provide opportunities for this understanding of child and school problems through study, reading, and discussion. For example, it is folly for the schools to set up standards in emotional stability when the child at home lives with selfish, possessive parents who afford him no opportunity to reach those standards. The same holds true of standards in health, good taste in literature, and other phases of child and school life. Much of the effort in the development of good taste in music, literature, and art is lost when the standards of the home and the school are in conflict. The association should be a meeting-ground where parents and teachers may agree upon standards.

In the fourth place, the rural schools need improvement in a way not needed by the urban schools. A recent study covering seventy years of history in the rural educational field in the United States indicates that a large number of these problems are of many years standing. The reason lies in the slowness with which rural schools adjust themselves to changing conditions. The study concluded in part:

The industrial development with which the growth of cities is inevitably linked affected all of the national life. Within the years encompassed by the study the country changed from a simple agrarian order to a complex industrial one. Education was but one of the social institutions that felt the impact of the change. The fact that the rural schools changed slowly to meet the new order and were for a half century isolated and neglected is one of the tragedies in the historical development of American education.[1]

At the present time, as in the past, the average rural school needs improvement in nearly every respect—in the buildings and grounds, in equipment, in playground apparatus, in the curriculum, in the special needs of high school children, and in the care of atypical children. These are a few of the many problems which encompass the rural schools from all sides and call for answers. And, because the rural schools need improvement, they need the interest of a group of coöperating parents. The association offers the rural school such a group.

[1] Wofford, Kate V. *An History of the Status and Training of Elementary Rural Teachers of the United States, 1860–1930,* p. 23, Siviter Press, 1935.

Answers to the second question, what returns the school can expect from a parent-teacher association, are, of course in the realm of conjecture. No one can foretell the results of a community organization. Theoretically, what is expected of the rural Parent-Teacher Association in California has recently been well expressed in a bulletin issued by the State Department of Education. It reads as follows:

1. The most valuable contribution the parent-teacher association can make to a rural school is the creation of a sympathetic understanding on the part of the members of the community of the place of the school as an integrating force in the community. No tangible additions to the school equipment which a group of interested parents might give to the school could possibly serve the advancement of child welfare so powerfully as the faith and confidence of the people based upon a genuine understanding and appreciation of objectives, methods and outcomes of modern education.

2. It (the P.T.A.) can represent a larger vision of higher educational ideals. It can awaken interest in communities that have become apathetic or complacent toward the schools.

3. The rural parent-teacher association can afford an avenue through which the socially intelligent leadership of the community may express itself.

4. It can provide the agency through which may come not only an acceptance of, but an aggressive desire to secure for rural children what is generally conceded to be educationally desirable for all children.[1]

While California has set up these desirable objectives in terms of the future, Dr. Elmer S. Holbeck has reported in a recent study what a rural Parent-Teacher Association has actually accomplished in the past. His investigation was in the form of a case study of an association in a small rural community and showed the following significant results:

[1] *Handbook for Rural Parent-Teacher Association Activities and Relationships.* Bulletin 12, 1933, p. v, State Department of Education, Sacramento, California.

1. There had been a definite attempt to study needs and understand what responsibilities and opportunities were those of the Parent-Teacher Association in the education of the child.
2. The purchasing of equipment for the school.
3. The association had brought about
   (a) the reduction of turnover of teachers
   (b) higher salaries for teachers
   (c) correction of health defects in pre-school children
   (d) improvement in the curriculum
   (e) better community support of schools
   (f) better housing conditions.[1]

Any one of the several results seems worthwhile for the rural school, and the sum of them makes a heartening story. Each is worthy of the best efforts and coöperation of both teachers and parents. The work of the organization instead of proving a burden may be in the hands of a discerning teacher an educational lever with which to remove mountains.

SUMMARY

The National Congress of Parents and Teachers is a powerful force in the formation of public school relationships. Beginning in 1897 as a small group of mothers interested in the welfare of children, it had expanded by 1931 to a membership of a million and a half composed of fathers, mothers, teachers, and in some instances of all in the community interested in schools. Nearly all of the local rural associations belong in the latter group; for in the country the Parent-Teacher Association achieves community importance and the membership may include a cross section of community life. Ages, interests, and experiences of such a group are diverse and demand a varied program with contributions from both children and adults, and with entertainment features which have a general appeal. The rural Parent-Teacher Association has certain

[1] *An Analysis of the Activities and Potentialities for Achievement of the Parent-Teacher Association with Recommendations*, pp. 61–62, Bureau of Publications, Teachers College, Columbia University, 1934.

differentiating characteristics which set its needs apart from those of an urban association. These are: (a) the association is likely to be composed of all community groups, rather than of parents only; (b) nearly all parents will be members of the association; (c) teachers will compose a large part of its membership; (d) the monthly meetings will be attended by many children; (e) the association will be composed of one occupational group, whose interests tend to be similar.

Authorities advise that new associations be formed by local groups and that the teacher act in a coöperative and advisory capacity. This advice, however, can rarely be followed in a rural community because leadership in it is often dormant or lacking. In either event it becomes the duty of the rural teacher to assume leadership until it can be developed in the community. The seven steps for the formation of a new organization by a young and inexperienced teacher are given in this chapter; and may be briefly summed up as (a) group planning, (b) group consultation or discussion, (c) group activity.

Planning the program is the most important single piece of work for the association. This responsibility belongs to the Program Committee, one of the three committees recommended for the simple organization best suited to rural needs. On the whole, the program should develop out of a felt community need; it should be closely linked to community interests; it should be directed toward what Butterworth calls "socially desirable ends." Planning the program of the local Parent-Teacher Association bears striking similarities to the planning of the school curriculum. It begins with some educational problem of the community and ends with the completion of the activities believed expedient in meeting the problems. According to Professor Butterworth the process involves four steps: (a) a determination of needs to which the association may properly devote itself; (b) the collection of all data which seems feasible and necessary; (c) a regular meeting of the association at which the problem is presented; (d) the carrying out of activities to bring the problem to a solution.

Many teachers in small schools question the advisability of adding community responsibilities, such as the work of the Parent-Teacher Association, to an already overburdened schedule. However, results of such efforts seem to pay large dividends in (a) a new understanding on the part of the community of the needs of the child and the needs of the school; (b) an enlarged vision of educational ideals; (c) provisions for the development of potential leadership; (d) an avenue through which the socially intelligent leadership of the community may express itself; (e) a closer integration of two powerful forces, the home and the school, in the interest of a third, the community. These beneficent results, when translated into child welfare, indicate that all the efforts necessary to bring them to pass are eminently worthwhile.

SUGGESTED READINGS

Bain, Winifred E. *Parents Look at Modern Education*, Chap. XII, D. Appleton-Century, New York, 1935.

Baldwin, Sara E. and Osborne, Ernest G. *Home-School Relationships*, Chap. III, Progressive Education Association, New York, 1935.

Butterworth, Julian E. *The Parent-Teacher Association and Its Work*, Macmillan, New York, 1928.

California State Department of Education. *Handbook for Rural Parent-Teachers Association Activities and Relationships*, Bulletin 12, 1933.

Frasier, George W. and Armentrout, W. D. *An Introduction to Education*, Chap. III, Scott, Foresman, 1933.

Holbeck, Elmer S. *An Analysis of the Activities and Potentialities for Achievement of the Parent-Teacher Association*, Chaps. II, III, VII, Bureau of Publications, Teachers College, Columbia University, 1934.

Lowth, Frank J. *Everyday Problems of the Country Teacher*, Rev. ed., Chap. XII, Macmillan, New York, 1936.

Mason, Martha Sprague. *Parents and Teachers*, Chap. XIII, Ginn and Co., New York, 1928.

Robinson, William McKinley. "Report of Rural Service," *National Congress Parents and Teachers Proceedings, 1933*, p. 187, Washington, D. C.

Robinson, William McKinley. "Report of Rural Service," *National Congress Parents and Teachers Proceedings, 1935*, p. 45, Washington, D. C.

MATERIALS FOR DISCUSSION

Consider the following statements. What changes would make them more acceptable to you? What significant issues arise from their study?

1. The primary aim of the Parent-Teacher Association is the welfare of children. Any procedure at variance with this aim should be speedily abandoned.

2. Every community, like every child is unique and different; each has its individual problems, each its individual assets. It is futile, therefore, to attempt to fit the urban pattern for the Parent-Teacher Association upon rural areas.

3. The rural Parent-Teacher Association should develop community, rather than school programs. Since the association serves all age and interest levels within the community, the program should conform to the needs of all.

4. Since rural people work together better than they play or think together, it seems advisable that rural Parent-Teacher groups develop many activities in which adults participate.

5. The teacher in the small rural school should never serve as leader in the local Parent-Teacher Association.

CHAPTER XIX

THE LIBRARY—A CONTROLLING FACTOR IN MODERN EDUCATION

AN HISTORICAL STATEMENT

A STUDY of the modern library movement shows an interesting parallel with that of the development of the modern school system. Like the schools, libraries were originally established for the rich, the powerful, and the scholarly. Unless a man belonged to one or more of these social groups, neither books nor education was easy to obtain. Libraries were institutions where books were kept, and there was no vision of a program of library service. Likewise, education, especially in the institutions of higher learning, prided itself upon a cloistered existence and felt that a withdrawal from the world was not only desirable, but essential.

Approximately a half century ago there was begun in America a library movement to take books to the masses, just as there had been a movement some thirty years previous to take education to them. As in the educational movement, reforms in the libraries first took place in the cities. One has only to read the literature of that period to recognize the concern and zeal with which the libraries attacked the problem of providing books for people who lived in urban areas. Under the stimulus of their newly conceived responsibility and with the financial assistance of benefactors like Andrew Carnegie, public libraries began to take form in all cities and in many small towns and villages. The rural district, however, was untouched by this reform and, except for sporadic and ineffectual efforts, was destined to remain for many years without the benefit of organized library service.

BEGINNINGS IN RURAL LIBRARIES

As early as 1816 the constitution of the State of Indiana authorized the counties to sell some of the public lands and invest the proceeds in county libraries. The funds from such sales, however, were inadequate and the county libraries disappeared. Wyoming, in 1886, took similar steps with like results. Van Wert County, Ohio, 1898 organized a county library which had many of the characteristics of the modern county system of library service. To Melvil Dewey of New York State is generally credited the beginnings of the traveling library system which was destined to be of inestimable benefit to rural peoples. In response to the library needs of the rural areas, as he saw them, Mr. Dewey sought and secured from the legislature in the latter years of the nineteenth century enough funds to provide traveling libraries in New York State. Consequently, carefully selected libraries of one hundred volumes each were sent out for six months at a time to all parts of the state. Commenting on this movement, Miss Ethel M. Fair said:

Study clubs, small libraries, university extension centers, all availed themselves of this opportunity. Other states saw the light and took up the plan.[1]

It was not until after the Report of the Roosevelt Country Life Commission in 1909, however, that such scattered efforts reached the dignity and significance of a movement in American education and American life. Following the Report and for approximately two decades, a determined effort has been made to equalize opportunities as between urban and rural areas. One of the most significant developments in the process of equalization is the bringing of library facilities, long available to residents of cities and towns, to remote rural districts.[2]

[1] *Countrywide Library Service*, p. 13, American Library Association, 1934.
[2] Voght, Sabra W. *Biennial Survey of Education, 1928–1930*, p. 644, United States Office of Education (Dept. of the Interior), Government Printing Office, 1930.

FACTORS WHICH INFLUENCED THE LIBRARY MOVEMENT

The Country Life Movement. The reasons for the library movement to rural areas, were three: In the first place, as was suggested in a previous paragraph, the country life movement included in its plans the bringing of libraries to rural areas in the attempt to stem the drift from farm to city which characterized the early years of the twentieth century. A determined effort was made to ascertain the cause of this drift and, if possible, to curb it. This concern explains, in part, as developed in previous chapters, the appointment of the Roosevelt Country Life Commission and the enthusiasm and interest which greeted its report. Among other things the Commission stated that the dissatisfaction of the farmer came from a dearth of cultural advantages and from economic difficulties. He was restive in such an environment, and, in the effort to give his children a better chance in life, was moving to cities where they would have the benefit of good schools, good libraries, and other cultural opportunities. This convincing report was the beginning of many reforms in the rural field, and, of this general program of action, library service was a part.

Adult Education. Another factor influencing the growth of libraries has been a movement for adult education which is achieving importance in rural life; in fact, it has given to the library movement in the rural community much of its vitality. Adult education in rural areas is similar in purpose to adult education in urban areas, but the methods of procedure are different. In urban areas it takes form in a planned program. The administration of its curriculum, its courses and schedules are similar to those of the public school, whereas in rural areas it is not planned at all except insofar as rural agencies coöperate in the promotion of programs for self-development and growth. To the uninformed it would appear at first that rural areas in the United States have no program for the education of adults. As a matter of fact, they have a very effective adult program in the system of extension service to adults, sponsored by the United States Department of Agriculture. The ever-mounting enrollment of adults in evening classes is an indication of the strength of the extension service. In 1930, for example, there were in the United States 2,116 organized evening classes with an enrollment of 62,952; in 1931, there were 2,545 such class organizations with 85,688 farmers enrolled; and in 1932, the classes had increased to 2,975 with an enrollment of 87,138.

The program of service includes nearly all of the areas of adult education; and, while the emphasis from the beginning of the program has been vocational, it becomes annually more cultural. Farm people are going in large groups into the fields of music, drama, and art. This self-imposed study by adult rural groups is one of the significant facts in modern American life and has in it more potency than is sensed by the casual observer. The teaching of agricultural agents is informal and is by way of demonstration rather than exposition, but the program requires scientific facts and since these are to be found mainly in books, a demand is created for books which inform as well as entertain. Books for this purpose, however, have been secured against great odds. Mr. John D. Willard, authority on adult education, says:

Rural adult education has been retarded by isolation, which has prevented rural people from having much contact with the great accumulations of literature, history, and science; by the inadequacy both in number and quality of schools and libraries; by the lack of trained and well-equipped teachers and by extreme conservatism. On the other hand, rural America is a fertile field for adult education because rural people have in almost all places a self-elaborated and indigenous culture that is vigorous and individualistic, crude though it may be.[1]

Recent studies have indicated how seriously the farm group reads when it is given a chance. An opinion on this question reported in the *Saturday Review of Literature*, January, 1933, disclosed that in the selection of reading material by rural people, the choices stood in the following order: (a) history,

[1] "Libraries and Rural Adult Education," *Adult Education and the Library*, Vol. 4 (Jan. 1929), p. 5.

(b) general reference materials, (c) civics, (d) music, (e) encyclopedias.

Parent-Teacher Associations, the Grange, community clubs, and church groups are also eager for library materials. Each is an agency for adult education and each program is an evidence of a new and indigenous culture now in the process of development. Since all new cultures are constantly needing new standards and means of attaining them, library facilities take on here a new significance. Books give new visions, create new desires, set up new standards, and assist in growth toward the attainment of them. The library movement, at the present, is therefore seeking to meet these needs in rural areas. Wisely, it relates itself to all volunteer community organizations and forms, ideally at least, the integrating factor for much of the adult education in rural areas.

The Importance of Books in Modern Education. The third reason for the movement toward an equalization of library facilities in rural communities lies in the increasing value of books in a modern program of education—a point discussed at length in Chapter XIII. As rural teachers substitute the activity program for formal recitations, children need not fewer, but more books; indeed, success in learning depends in part upon the availability of library materials, and crippled indeed are the community and school which accept a modern philosophy of education and have not the means of putting their theory into practice.

As stated in Chapter XIII, the average rural school is in a state of "book poverty," and many of these small schools have but faint hopes of ever offering an adequate library, since it would be too great a drain upon their budgets. One dollar a year per pupil is about what the average rural school can be expected to spend for library books and supplementary reading materials. Since one book averages considerably more than this amount, one new acquisition a year for each child is prohibitive. Under the compulsion of these facts it was soon evident to those interested in the library movement that if children were to be adequately served with books, some plan to supplement the existing school libraries was necessary. The extension of libraries into rural areas was developed and so far has proved most successful.

EXTENT TO WHICH THE MOVEMENT HAS SPREAD

For the three reasons given above—(a) the library movement is a part of a reform program of the more powerful country life movement, (b) the library is essential for a program of adult education, and (c) modern education in the public school is dependent upon a large and adequate supply of books—it is important that teachers and community workers know the extent to which the movement has spread. A recent study sheds light upon this question. In 1926 the American Library Association, through its committee on Library Extension, made a comprehensive study of the library facilities in the rural areas of the United States and Canada. The report made some startling disclosures. Among other things the survey revealed that 83 per cent of the entire rural population was without public library service and that of the 3,065 counties in the United States 1,135 had no library services at all, except such as were offered by small local schools and churches. These counties, without a public library within their boundaries, represented every state in the Union save the New England states, Delaware, Iowa, New Jersey, and New York. This condition means that in the large number of communities for which there is no organized library service all educational programs for both adults and children are severely curtailed. Supplementing the study of the American Library Association, the Biennial Report of the United States Office of Education, 1928–1930, states:

Rural Schools have shared in the general awakening in school libraries during the decade. . . . educational and library surveys show that, in general, library facilities for rural schools score much lower than those for city schools.[1]

[1] *Biennial Survey of Education, 1928–1930*, p. 686, United States Office of Education (Dept. of the Interior) Government Printing Office.

Of later date was the Yearbook of 1936 of the Rural Education Department of the National Education Association entitled *Rural School Libraries*. It reported in part that less than 300 of the counties of the United States had county-wide service. On the brighter side, however, was the fact that of 39 states and territories which replied to a questionnaire, 23 reported definite legal provisions for the financial support of libraries, so that while the extension of library service to rural communities has been slow, hope can be found in the fact that it has been steady and persistent.[1]

LIBRARY AGENCIES WHICH SERVE RURAL AREAS

According to the study referred to above, reports from 27 states indicated that library service for rural communities and schools is being performed by one or more of the following agencies: (a) state library commissions, state departments of education, or boards of education; (b) county departments of education or county superintendents; (c) free public libraries, serving counties or local communities; (d) libraries maintained by single schools or groups of schools; (e) college libraries; (f) private organizations (Parent-Teacher Association, American Association of University Women, Women's Federations, etc.).

LIBRARY SERVICE AVAILABLE FROM THE STATE

Forty-five states, by statute, provide some form of library service, which is administered by state departments of education, state commissions, state boards, or state libraries.[2] The chief purpose of the state agency is to promote, either directly or indirectly, local community libraries in units sufficiently large to bring adequate library service within the reach of all of its people. In ten of the states offering this assistance the

[1] Lathrop, Edith A. and others. *Rural School Libraries*, pp. 6, 46, Department of Rural Education, National Education Association, Feb. 1936.

[2] *Ibid.* p. 19.

service to schools achieves such importance that full time librarians are employed to administer it. These states are as follows: Alabama, Indiana, Louisiana, Michigan, Minnesota, New York, North Carolina, Tennessee, Virginia, and Wisconsin. Three other states—Arkansas, New Jersey and Oregon—provide part-time supervision.[1]

The service of the state library agency usually functions in two ways. First, there is a direct mail service available to individuals, to schools, to groups, and to libraries. The majority give this service to isolated individuals and groups whose library units are too small to care for their reading needs. Often pictures, books, magazine articles, pamphlets, and maps form a part of the traveling library service. The traveling school library should not be confused with the traveling county library. Distinguishing features lie in its administration. The former is under the jurisdiction of the school system and is chiefly concerned with the interests of schools and children; the latter is administered by a local board, is concerned with the whole community, and attempts to serve all groups. The importance of this type of service to rural schools can scarcely be estimated. The attempt to bring library facilities to the state as a whole involves a broad program of activities. Second, in addition to aid offered to isolated individuals, it offers assistance to local and county libraries, particularly in the selection and maintenance of standards. Thus we find state agencies furnishing to local libraries book lists and devices for improving library technique. They also develop and enlarge, through gifts and loans, the work of existing libraries; they direct book service to schools, and act as advisers to school librarians and teachers. Many state departments of education, following Dr. Dewey's plan, send out traveling libraries to schools. In many of the states the majority of the libraries go to rural schools in lots of from fifty to several hundred volumes. In 1926 over

[1] National Elementary Principals. *Elementary School Libraries*, p. 388, Bulletin of the Department of Elementary School Principals, Vol. XII, No. 5, National Education Association, 1933.

a million books were circulated from state agencies to rural areas. Under this plan of library extension to rural areas, the school libraries become branches of the larger system, receiving and distributing books for both classroom and community.

The library services performed by principal state educational officers have been summarized as follows: [1]

(1) Promoting the establishment of libraries
(2) Organizing and supervising libraries
(3) Administering state financial aid
(4) Publishing book lists and aids for book selection
(5) Training and certificating school librarians
(6) Gathering and reporting information on school libraries
(7) Administering traveling libraries
(8) Making, adopting and approving rules and regulations for library administration and management.

LIBRARY SERVICES AVAILABLE FROM THE COUNTIES

The program which seems best to meet the difficulties of the rural area is the one known as the county library plan. Experience and the opinion of experts appear to bear this statement out:

Such a plan provides for centralized selection and purchasing of books, technical processing, organization and circulation, thereby bringing to the isolated rural schools an efficient and extensive library service which could not be provided by the district for itself.[2]

Edith A. Lathrop, Associate Specialist in School Libraries, United States Office of Education, who has given much study to the problem of library facilities for rural areas, reports on the county library as follows in the twelfth yearbook of the De-

[1] Lathrop, Edith A. and Others. *Rural School Libraries*, p. 20, Department of Rual Education, National Education Association, Feb. 1936.
[2] Heffernan, Helen. "The Administrative Control of School Libraries," *Rural School Libraries*, p. 23, Department of Rural Education, National Education Association, Feb. 1936.

partment of Elementary School Principals of the National Education Association:

Educationists and librarians are agreed that for most sections of the United States, county or regional libraries well supported and administered, provide the best means yet devised for insuring library facilities for small rural and village schools. County libraries in California, Indiana, Ohio and New Jersey and some other states have demonstrated that such library service insures a way whereby a minimum amount of money provides a maximum of school library service.[1]

Only 7.48 per cent of the counties in the United States have organized library service and 50 per cent of them are located in six states: California, Indiana, New Jersey, North Carolina, Texas and Wyoming. New Jersey and California are leaders in the movement to place library facilities within the reach of the remotest rural district. Forty-six out of the fifty-eight counties in California have a county library or receive county library service through contracts with nearby libraries. Since 1920 New Jersey has installed the county library system in eleven out of twenty-one counties. Three-fourths of the states in the union have had successful demonstrations of the plan, so that, with modifications to suit local conditions, it is, apparently, destined to meet the library needs of rural peoples in general. Of these adjustments to local conditions Miss Helen Heffernan, Chief, Division of Elementary Education and Rural Schools, State Department of Education, Sacramento, California, has said:

It is true that in some regions of the country, geographical conditions and distribution of population may make the county too small to be a satisfactory unit of library administration; however, effective library service for rural schools seems definitely to demand an administrative unit larger than the local school district. The selection of an appropriate region for library service will of necessity have to give attention to such considerations as the existing political units, the

[1] National Education Association, Department of Elementary School Principals, "Status of Libraries in Elementary Schools," Bulletin, *Twelfth Yearbook*, Vol. 12, p. 155, June 1933.

wealth of the region, and distance not merely in terms of area, but in terms of available types of transportation.[1]

CHARACTERISTICS OF THE COUNTY LIBRARY SYSTEM

An examination of the county library system reveals different characteristics in different localities. A central library is located in the county seat or a large town situated near the center of the county. It may be housed in a separate building, in rooms of its own, or in a school building. The central library, as in a city, maintains branches in towns, villages, rural centers or rural schools, and books are sent to the local units at regular intervals.

The service program of the county library varies greatly. Miss Lathrop reports that maximum service is represented by libraries employing several librarians who give freely of their time to the schools of the county, while the minimum service is represented by libraries supplying some of the schools in the counties with a small collection of books once a year. Transportation of books is usually made by a "bookmobile," driven in many cases by a librarian who acts as supervisor and adviser to the local libraries and units. The "bookmobiles" carry approximately five hundred books on a trip, the books assembled in accordance with the requests of teachers and students. Reference books are usually left in the local school libraries.

In addition to supplying a fresh supply of books at regular intervals, the county librarian also attempts other services to rural communities. Library supervision is provided which covers the promotion of reading circles and story-telling, the establishment of reading standards, and instruction in the proper use of books. In addition, the county library often provides current magazines, newspaper clippings, victrola records, globes, and other visual materials. Forty-one per cent of the

[1] National Education Association, Department of Rural Education, "Administrative Control of School Libraries," *Rural School Libraries*, p. 24, Feb. 1936.

county libraries in Miss Lathrop's study reported that special efforts were made to direct children's readings during summer vacations and to instruct children, teachers, and adults in the use of the library.

The library is usually administered by a county board. It is financed by an annual appropriation from the general county fund or by a special tax levy. The amount of support varies, but authorities recommend a minimum of one dollar per capita for good library service. At least one state, Pennsylvania, has voted state grants to the county library to supplement county funds.

The plan of the county library seems, on the whole, to match strength against weaknesses in the other plans in use throughout the United States. The system is largely centralized and responsibility is localized. A trained librarian is nearly always in charge of the unit. Financial support through county and state appropriations is adequate. Every school in the county is served. The program is sustained from year to year and thereby achieves the stability essential to both school and community service. For its possibilities of service to rural areas the plan has the endorsement of leading national organizations including the American Library Association, the National Grange, and the National Congress of Parents and Teachers.

THE COUNTY LIBRARY SERVICE OF CALIFORNIA

In view of the fact that California has been a pioneer in the establishment of county libraries, and since approximately 20 per cent of the county libraries are located within the boundaries of that state, an examination of the system in detail seems justified. Prior to 1911 the elementary schools of California had school district libraries. Each district purchased its own books, with such funds as were available and gradually accumulated its own library. No efforts were apparently made to serve the community. May Dexter Henshall, County Library Organizer, California State Library, Sacramento, describes the result of the localized effort as follows:

Each one of these libraries was practically duplicated by all the others because enterprising book agents systematically traveled from district to district throughout the state taking orders from the trustees for books and school apparatus. There was no legal provision for the circulation of books among the school districts of a county. Each school district kept building up a collection which soon became inactive because of the limited number of people who could use it. These libraries were uneconomical and ineffective. A library system was needed which provided for central libraries, professionally trained librarians and the circulation of books.[1]

In answer to this need of rural peoples the State of California passed legislation in 1911 which provided for them (a) a county library tax, (b) a certified county librarian, (c) headquarters at the county seat, and (d) branch libraries throughout the county. In order to extend this community service to children, legal provisions were made for affiliations between county and school libraries, professionally trained librarians were secured, and their services made available to adults and children alike.

According to Miss Henshall the following library services among others have been developed in California under the county library law: (a) a central school library department in each of the 46 county libraries; (b) a county librarian to supervise the school libraries; (c) a librarian as head of school library department with one or more assistants, if the county is a large one; (d) circulation of the books to the schools by the county library in place of the stagnation caused by inactive school district libraries; (e) a specialized library service to meet classroom needs; (f) equipment of schools with reference books approved by the county board of education; (g) home reading supplied to the children; (h) picture collections made available to schools; (i) music records and stereographs circulated to the schools.[2]

In order to ascertain the extent to which these services are

[1] National Education Association, Department of Elementary School Principals. "County Library Service of California," *Twelfth Yearbook*, Vol. 12, p. 377.

[2] *Ibid.* p. 379.

used in California, Miss Heffernan made a study of them in 1934. The study revealed that in the school year 1932–1933 a total of more than 2,300,000 books was furnished to 192,413 pupils in the forty-two counties studied This was an average of over twelve books per child. These books were selections which children needed in their school work and did not include those for their general reading, which they usually procured from branch community libraries. It is the policy in California to encourage the attendance of children upon the community library, since, as Miss Heffernan points out, this is the source of adult reading materials and it is desirable that children establish the habit of patronizing a public library and develop some skill in the proper use of its resources.[1] The survey concluded that the county libraries were rendering a commendable amount of service to rural schools, and upon this point Miss Heffernan commented as follows:

It is generally accepted that the library is indispensable in any program based upon socialized procedures and recognizing individual differences in children. The county library system makes it possible to meet these needs in rural schools. Upon this basis the county library system merits consideration from those states which do not as yet have legal provision for its establishment and wholehearted support from the schools experiencing its benefits.[2]

CONTRACTUAL ARRANGEMENTS WITH CITIES AND TOWNS

There is often an arrangement made by rural areas with public libraries in cities or towns, so that nearby communities may be served. This is one of the most common types of library service and is secured through local initiative and leadership. Usually found in cities of less than fifteen thousand population, the local organized library service accommodates neighboring schools, establishes branches, contracts with townships, or

[1] National Education Association, Department of Rural Education. "The Administrative Control of School Libraries," *Rural School Libraries*, Feb. 1936, p. 28, 1936.

[2] *Ibid.* p. 31.

serves rural subscribers by mail. Many towns in New York State and New England have locally worked out such a program. Here, also, various means of transportation are used. Parcel post, trucks, and occasional visits of interested local people are the means by which books go into areas where there are no organized libraries.

LIBRARIES WHOSE SERVICES ARE MAINTAINED THROUGH CIVIC GROUPS

Many urban libraries are the result of the philanthropy of individuals or groups; the same source is responsible for service to rural areas. An excellent example of this type of traveling library is found in Washtenaw County, Michigan. The movement to provide library books to rural areas was begun by a local Chapter of the Daughters of the American Revolution of Ypsilanti, Michigan. It contributed the idea and made a donation of fifty dollars. The idea was furthered by the Business and Professional Women's Club of that city whose members agreed to give books. Under the sponsorship of these organizations three thousand books were collected as a nucleus and were catalogued and put into readiness for circulation by a trained librarian who contributed her services. The schools that were served agreed to pay one dollar a year each to help defray expenses, and the teachers agreed to coöperate in the transportation of books. The schools in the county have developed into branches of the central library and the plan gives promise of fine returns.[1]

While such efforts of civic groups and the urban library appear laudable, the various plans have many weaknesses. The efforts are too scattered to be effective. They lack the stabilization which comes from the designation of responsibility and authority. Most serious weakness of all, they lack money to afford a sustained program. It has long been the experience

[1] Lamb, Cyril E. "A Library Nucleus that Serves One Hundred and Fifty Rural Schools," *The Nation's Schools*, Vol. 13, Jan. 1934, p. 32.

of small village and town libraries that no service program is possible without financial assistance from a larger civil unit. If a sustained program for the rural community is ever assured, appropriations for its support must come from a stronger group than a volunteer one, and a larger tax unit than the district, town, or village. Rural schools have long ago learned that lesson, and organizations which seek to serve rural areas must follow suit.

THE TEACHER AND SUPPLEMENTARY LIBRARY AGENCIES

The teacher in the small rural school bears many responsibilities in the efficient use of such library services as are available. If he is teaching in one of the counties where there is organized service, his responsibilities are clearly defined. He will coöperate in the program and participate intelligently in the administration of the service—responsibilities presupposing some knowledge of library materials, the ability to handle books, and the enthusiasm necessary to instill in children the love of good reading. Teacher-training institutions, aware of this need, are adding the requisite courses to the professional education courses of prospective teachers. If the teacher lacks the training, she should remedy the deficiency in summer session or in extension classes. Coöperation with existing agencies also includes some recognition on the part of the teacher of the interdependence of schools and libraries in a modern program of education. Libraries should keep closely in touch with current trends in education and chart their program of service accordingly. Conversely, according to Miss Heffernan:

. . . The school should realize that the increasing demands upon the library mean increased costs and should budget a fair proportion of available funds accordingly.[1]

A teacher in a small school in one of the 1,135 counties in the United States which have no organized library service

[1] National Education Association, Department of Rural Education. "The Administrative Control of School Libraries," *Rural School Libraries*, Feb. 1936, p. 32.

has different responsibilities. There are several procedures he can follow. He can do nothing about local conditions. Many teachers follow this course, and inevitably teaching degenerates into the hearing of lessons from assigned pages in the textbooks. The adults in the community suffer from lack of reading material and the programs of community organizations remain limited.

The teacher may importune the local board of trustees to make an appropriation for books for both children in school and adults in the community. If he is teaching in a state which supplements local library funds, he should investigate the state laws and take advantage of them. Many teachers adopt this procedure and, by following it consistently over a period of years, a good library can be accumulated. In a few states—Minnesota, New York, Oregon, and Wisconsin—collections of well-chosen books are generally found in rural schools, chiefly because these states have consistently followed the program of making yearly additions to the local school library. These local collections have often been supplemented by public funds in the form of state aid over a long period of years. In such a situation state supervision of libraries is provided. This supervision, while largely promotional, also offers aid in the selection of library materials and in giving direction to the program of reading. In addition, many teachers are required to have some training in library technique.

This plan, while superior to the first one, has its apparent disadvantages. The average small school is not financially able to supply the books necessary for a modern program of teaching. Aside from the financial limitation of the small school libraries, there is a tendency for individual libraries to stagnate. The children in small schools return year after year to the same school, and the library remains the same, save for the annual addition of a few books, which children quickly read.

The best solution to the reading problem of the small elementary school lies apparently in a combination of the individual and the county library. In this case the individual library would be composed of reference materials and the favorite books which children wish kept in the individual class rooms. From the county library would come a fresh inflow at regular intervals of recreational and informational materials, the latter assembled to meet the teaching needs of teachers and the learning needs of children. It is this combination which, according to the information now in hand, promises most for the future of library facilities in rural areas, and it is for this program that the teachers should plan and work.

SUMMARY

The development of the modern library system in America shows an interesting parallel with the development of the modern school system. In the beginning education and the library served the same social groups—the rich, the powerful, the scholarly. Similar to the movement to take education to the masses was the movement to take libraries to the people. Reforms in both the school and the library began in cities. Following the Report of the Roosevelt Country Life Commission, an activity of the Country Life Movement which began in the latter years of the nineteenth century, general reform took place in the institutions which served rural peoples. The school and the library shared in the reform.

Two other developments gave impetus and vitality to the library movement toward rural areas: (a) the development of a program of adult education; (b) the changing conception of the place of books in modern education.

In order to meet the needs of both adult and public education one of four plans of library extension service is usually followed:

Library services available from the (a) state and (b) counties, library services available from the (c) contractual services with cities and (d) libraries supported by civic groups.

The services secured through the county library apparently give promise of best meeting rural needs. The county library serves both adult and school groups and is organized as follows: The central library is located in the county seat and is available to all parts of the county; the branches are served by a book truck; a trained librarian and staff are in charge of the central unit and their services are available to local schools and branches; the system is administered by a local library board and is financed by county and state appropriations. Probably the best solution of the reading problem of the rural school lies in a combination of the individual room library as a part of the laboratory equipment of the school and the services of a county library which, at regular intervals, supplements the local library with fresh reading materials according to rural needs.

SUGGESTED READINGS

American Library Association. *Rural Public Library Service; A Handbook for Rural Leaders*, 2d ed., American Library Association, Chicago, 1928.

Fargo, Lucile F. *The Superintendent Makes a Discovery*, Bulletin, American Library Association, Chicago, 1931.

Felton, Ralph A. and Beal, Marjorie. *The Library of the Open Road*, Cornell Extension Bulletin 188, Ithaca, New York, New York State College of Agriculture, Cornell University, 1929.

Lathrop, Edith A. *School and County Library Coöperation*, Pamphlet, No. 11, 1930, United States Office of Education (Dept. of the Interior), Government Printing Office, Washington, D. C.

Lathrop, Edith A. *County Library Service to Rural Schools*, Bulletin, 1930, No. 20, United States Office of Education (Dept. of the Interior), Washington, D. C.

Lathrop, Edith A. *A Study of Rural School Library Practices and Services*, United States Office of Education (Dept. of the Interior), Government Printing Office, Washington, D. C., 1934

Lathrop, Edith A. and Others. *Rural School Libraries*, Department of Rural Education Bulletin, National Education Association, Washington, D. C., Feb., 1936.

National Education Association, Department of Elementary School Principals, *Elementary School Libraries*, Twelfth Yearbook, Chap. VIII, June, 1933. Washington, D. C.

Otto, Henry J. *Elementary School Organization and Administration*, Chap. X, Appleton-Century Company, New York, 1934.

Reavis, William C. and Others. *The Elementary School, Its Organization and Administration*, Chap. XII, University of Chicago Press, Chicago, 1931.

MATERIALS FOR DISCUSSION

Consider the following statements. What changes would make them more acceptable to you? What significant issues arise from their study?

1. Adults in rural areas face situations which make libraries less essential to them than to adults in urban centers. They have less leisure time for reading, they think in concrete rather than in abstract terms and they deal in things rather than in words.

2. The county system of libraries is the best one yet devised for the provision of adequate library facilities to rural people.

3. It is generally agreed that rural people in America are in the process of evolving an indigenous culture. Since all new cultures need new standards and means of attaining them, it is essential that libraries be taken to the country.

4. The community library should be attached to the rural school and should become a part of its educational program.

5. The education of every rural teacher should include adequate training in the efficient handling of library materials.

CHAPTER XX

COMMUNITY HEALTH FACTORS WHICH AFFECT CHILD DEVELOPMENT IN RURAL AREAS

As STATED elsewhere in this book, the child in a modern program of education is viewed as a whole. He is taught, therefore, not solely in terms of mental reactions, but in terms of wholeness of mind, body, and spirit. Thus the mental and physical health of children achieves a new significance in the teaching process. Techniques of healthful behavior, like those in the process of learning, are acquired at all times and in all places. It is not possible, therefore, to say that a child develops healthful techniques only in the school, or in the home, or in the community when he is in fact a product of all that he has met in the health habits, practices, and standards of all three environments.

Of these three environments, the home, and not the school, dominates the child. Ruth E. Grout in her recent book on health education in rural areas emphasizes this point of view as follows:

. . . The part played by parents in giving the child opportunity and encouragement to develop healthfully begins before the child is born and extends through adolescence. Moreover, since most of the fundamental habits, such as those relating to diet and sleep, are well formed before the child goes to school, the need for intelligent guidance by parents during this pre-school period is readily seen. Matters for which parents are largely responsible, both during the pre-school and school period, are:

I. Health practices of the child relating to amount and quality of sleep.

Provision for and encouragement of cleanliness.

Suitability and care of clothing.

Amount and adequacy of diet.

Opportunity for and proper use of leisure time.

Rest periods for the younger children do not require elaborate equipment.

Photograph by Jay W. Baxtresser

II. Medical care

Prevention of the spread of disease through isolation, proper care and willingness to immunize. Sanction must be given and arrangements made for medical attention.[1]

The health of the child, as affected by the school, is dwelt upon in several chapters of this book—in the discussion of the rural child himself, in Chapter III; in health practices, especially that of the hot lunch, presented in Chapter VII; and in the discussion of environmental controls in child development, specifically those of school buildings, grounds, and equipment. This chapter considers those factors in the out-of-school environment which affect the physical and mental well-being of rural children. In addition to the environmental factors there is general agreement that three others vitally affect health. These are: (a) control of communicable diseases; (b) correction of remedial defects; (c) health promotion and improvement. In an attempt to analyze the out-of-school environment in terms of the needs of rural children these factors will be discussed under (a) the environment and (b) the program of health promotion and improvement.

THE ENVIRONMENT

Its Assets for Mental and Physical Health. The rural environment naturally has in it the conditions considered essential to healthful living: fresh air, sunshine, and food of the right quality and abundance, if adults are willing to manipulate the environment to obtain it. Nature is generous in her gifts to make literally true what is now current belief that "The country is the healthiest place in the world in which to rear children." That the country is not always the best place for the desirable development of children is discussed in Chapter III of this book, entitled *The Status of the Rural Child.* However, educators, sociologists and physicians are in agreement that

[1] *Handbook of Health Education,* pp. 9–10, Doubleday, Doran and Co., 1936.

the rural scene has certain aspects which should be recognized and manipulated for the welfare of the children who are a part of it. In agreement with this assumption a recent, comprehensive study of farm children in Iowa was made, and in an examination of the rural child's environment the conclusion was reached that

influences, both favorable and unfavorable, make farm children neither better nor worse than city children, but different and doubtless equally valuable to the world.[1]

According to the study, the environmental factors which make farm children different from urban children are as follows:

(a) *Association with nature.* This influence has, for some time, been recognized as desirable and important from the standpoint of child development. The natural association of the farm child with birds, flowers, trees, and the stars, and his close personal contact with the weather tend to offer the rural child opportunity for developing a feeling of familiarity and security in the natural world.

Modern curriculum materials draw heavily upon the natural environment for units of work because it is rich in materials for teaching nature study, geology, astronomy, and agriculture. The difficulty in using this environment lies in the fact that few rural teachers are wise and sensitive enough to recognize its possibilities. Professor Fannie W. Dunn stressed this point in an article in the *Teachers College Record* when she said:

For the hardest lesson we have to learn—we who are stumblingly working out our techniques in the new mode of educating which we believe in, but which we have not yet learned perfectly to employ—is to see the educative experiences that lie in the child's environment, and to realize from each potentiality the best that is in it. A group of rural teachers were reading with their supervisor one of the charming reports of the Country and City Day School. They read of the interest of the children of that school in boats, and the range of activities grow-

[1] Baldwin, Bird T. and Others. *Farm Children*, p. 150, D. Appleton Co., 1930.

ing out of that interest, which led those children into far countries, and into reading, writing, music, and a host of other worthwhile experiences. And they wailed: "If only *we* had such an environment as she, we too could have our children do interesting things. *We* have nothing but trees!"

As a matter of fact, the school they envied was set in a crowded city street, near wharves which an unperceiving teacher might have seen as sordid and ugly, while she envied the trees and birds and lovely old colonial homes, full of suggestive relics of the past, which the rural teachers had all about them, and which they came in time to see and to use, in excursions and art, dramatization and verse.[1]

The children studied by Baldwin, like the teachers cited by Dunn, evinced but little consciousness of the power and beauty of nature and their very indifference to these powerful influences suggests both opportunity and responsibility for the rural teacher.

(b) *Companionship of pets.* No other group of children in American life, except the very rich who can afford both urban and country homes, has such opportunity for the wholesome and wide acquaintanceship with animals as have rural children. Companionship with dogs, kittens, chickens, lambs, and horses is a natural part of the everyday life of the rural child. Very early in his life he has the joy which comes from association with animals, and, as he grows older, he usually shares the responsibility for their care. Thus he develops feelings of sympathy, loyalty, and responsibility for creatures more helpless and dependent than himself. All of these emotional characteristics are desirable, and the rural child lives in an environment which makes their development easy and natural.

The care of pets has yet another advantage. Children learn through the experience the influence of proper food, sanitation, and temperature upon animal life. With proper direction, generalizations from this experience with animals may be developed in respect to human life, as well.

[1] Dunn, Fannie W. "Modern Education in Small Rural Schools," *Teachers College Record*, Vol. 32 (Feb. 1931), p. 414.

This asset of rural life has implications for curriculum making as well as for health. Little children are naturally interested in animals and efforts are made in many progressive urban schools to furnish them to children as a basis for their first reading experiences. Experience with animals may be secured through excursions, or the animals themselves can be brought directly into the classrooms. When rural children enter school for the first time they have already a rich background for the beginning of reading, and the wise teacher draws heavily upon these resources during the first year of the child's school life.

(c) *Responsibility for regular tasks.* One of the characteristics desired in the development of mental health is dependability, and we develop the trait through reacting satisfactorily to situations which require it. Fortunately for the farm youth there is no dearth of opportunity for developing this trait through the assumption of responsibility for regular tasks. In the average farm family there is usually a division of labor which includes all members of the group, even to the youngest children. Not only does the average rural child at an early age have his duties in the home, but he must perform them regularly and on time, or his group will suffer. Thus his daily routine tends to develop self-reliance, dependability, and a sensitiveness to his personal responsibility for the comfort and welfare of his social group. On this point Professor Fannie W. Dunn in a preface to a recent text in *Health Education* commented as follows:

Lacking the benefits of highly organized public services, highly mechanized system of heating, water supply and sewerage, and a complex organization of social agencies, the rural home and family still carry the major responsibility for the healthful living of their members. Of this responsibility the rural child bears a genuine and significant part. His efforts make a real difference in the health and sanitation not only of his immediate family but also of his neighborhood community, and to some extent even of the wider community.

To the son or daughter, in the rural home, fall the chores of filling of the woodbox, or caring for the stove or furnace; a share in the milking and handling of milk utensils; the bringing of water, disposal of garbage, and other tasks in maintaining sanitary surroundings; assistance in food preparation and serving; much responsibility for younger children; help in care of the sick and aged. Children and youth in rural communities may have an active part in prevention of soil and water pollution, in eradication of insect carriers of disease, in beautification of home and school grounds and roadsides, and in creating or developing recreational facilities, to an extent difficult to equal in the more complex organization of densely populated urban areas. Such experiences, moreover, come to the rural child not uncommonly or infrequently, but as constantly recurring events in his daily life.[1]

(d) *Rhythm of country life.* The need for security, paramount for the satisfactory emotional development of human beings, is satisfied in some particulars by what Baldwin calls the "rhythm of country life." This rhythm, an outgrowth of the relationship of man with nature, is exemplified in Gladys Hasty Carroll's romantic story of farm life, *As the Earth Turns.* The order of the seasons and the order of farm life which follows them have, according to the Iowa Study, beneficent effects upon the individuals who work under their influence. Economic and personal security develop from the land. The late depression brought this fact into focus when the United States witnessed a flight from the city amounting to an average of a million people a year, most of them the sons and daughters of farmers who found in the farm "a city of refuge" in a troubled world. Here were to be found food and shelter and the comforting rhythm of homely tasks—in short, personal security.

A further asset in the rural environment which has possibilities, not always realized, is the economic importance of the child. Not only are rural children important from the standpoint of numbers, but practically all rural sociologists are agreed that the vital family relationships of the average farm family have great influence in the development of child nature. Children on the farm have always been considered economic assets. From an early age they earn their own way; consequently, they

[1] Grout, Ruth E. *Handbook of Health Education,* p. v, Doubleday, Doran and Co., 1936.

are nearly always welcome which explains, in part, the fact that the farm family is larger than the urban family. To be wanted and to be valued are two necessities for complete emotional development. Taylor points out a difficulty developing here however of which the modern rural teacher should be aware and should attempt to avert:

But this mental and social security may sometimes be a handicap to rural youth, for, although everyone strives for it, a security which restricts an individual to submissiveness and complacency tends to thwart the broad development of his personality. It is probable that the security of farm life, particularly the shelter of the farm home and the assurance of some kind of employment, leads to some degree of stultification of the personality; and further, that many contributions to society as a whole, as well as to farm life, remain unmade merely because farm life is secure to the point of inhibiting stimulation by wholesome discontent.[1]

The child's place in the rural community also tends to develop in him certain attitudes of self-reliance and adequacy. As is pointed out in Chapter XVIII, the school child nearly always accompanies his parents to community meetings. He listens to the discussions of his elders, often takes part in them, and nearly always has his own opinion of the debates and the activities of his community. In the hands of a skillful teacher the participation of the child in community life may be made a sort of laboratory for instruction in government, for developing responsibility in the sharing of community tasks, and for education in good citizenship.

(e) *Liabilities and hazards in the environment which affect mental and physical health.* For many years leaders in rural education have recognized those characteristics of the rural environment which adversely affect the satisfactory development of children. In 1922 one of these leaders, Orville G. Brim, listed those liabilities apparent to him in an article entitled *The Handicaps of the Rural Child.* The Iowa Study of Baldwin revealed practically the same handicaps in 1930. These

[1] Taylor, Carl C. *Rural Sociology*, p. 309, Harpers, 1933.

in part were: (a) the limited number of social contacts in the school and community; (b) the low standards of control in the fields of community sanitation and health; (c) the absence of a proper amount of recreation, and the poverty of the community in providing for it; (d) the critical and conservative attitude toward change on the part of the rural community and its tendency to resist it when it comes; and (e) an unfortunate feeling of class consciousness, which tends to set country people apart from urban people. It is essential that these disadvantages be kept in mind in the planning of programs for rural children and this book has made practical suggestions for overcoming them. Chapter VIII, for example, attempts to suggest means whereby the lack of social contacts can be counteracted; Chapter XIII and Chapter XIX consider the problems of reading in the rural school and community; and Chapter XVII presents certain organizations which may supply programs of recreation and culture for rural boys and girls. A consideration of the handicaps exemplified in low standards of hygiene and sanitation is properly the concern of this chapter.

LACK OF SANITARY CONTROLS

There is disagreement among rural sociologists concerning the status of the health of rural children. Apparently all are agreed, however, that the sanitary and hygienic controls of the rural child are materially lower than those of the urban child. Sorokin and Zimmerman point out that nearly all of the physical defects among rural children are due to the poor sanitary conditions of the country schools and homes, and that a decrease in the physical defects of rural children during the past four years can be traced to a series of sanitary improvements recently installed in these two institutions.

This disparity of the sanitary conditions, coupled with almost equality in defects, testifies rather in favor of a better health for the rural children.[1]

[1] Sorokin, Pitirim and Zimmerman, C. C. *Principles of Rural-Urban Sociology*, p. 147, Henry Holt and Co., 1929.

Kirkpatrick in his 1926 study, *The Farmer's Standard of Living,* reported low standards in the sanitary and health conditions in the farm home. He found that, if one took as criteria for measuring the modern farm home (a) central heating and central lighting, (b) running hot and cold water, (c) sewerage disposal, only 1.7 per cent of the Southern farm homes, 8.3 per cent of the North Central, and 8.8 per cent of the New England were wholly modern.[1] Since these are the sanitary and safety fixtures which the humblest city apartment is expected to have, it seems a disturbing commentary upon the health and safety features of the rural environment in which over half of the Nation's children are reared.

The sanitary and safety conditions of the average rural school are likewise sobering. Recent surveys, as was pointed out in Chapter XV reveal the low status of the average small rural school building. The study of the school buildings of Utah made by Professor Julian E. Butterworth in 1926 was significant. The buildings were scored by using the Butterworth and Strayer-Englehardt score cards, each score card being built on a 1000-point scale and constructed to include the measurement of sanitary and health provisions for each school. Indeed it might be said that the score cards emphasized the mechanical features of school buildings as they relate to health and sanitation. The median score for the one-teacher schools of Utah was 677; for New York, 604; for Texas, 594; and for Oconee County, South Carolina, 333. For the two-teacher schools of Utah the median score was 731; for New York, 755; for Texas, 697; and for Oconee County, South Carolina, 418.

CHILD LABOR

As stated above, children in rural areas are considered economic assets, since from an early age they earn their board and keep. Unquestionably, much of the work thus performed is

[1] Kirkpatrick, E. L. *The Farmer's Standard of Living,* p. 21, United States Department of Agriculture, Dept. Bulletin No. 1466, Government Printing Office, Washington, Nov. 1926.

harmless and under proper conditions, discussed elsewhere in this chapter, may be actually beneficial to them. On the other hand, the gainful employment of children on farms is recognized in many quarters as constituting a social problem whose ill effects are felt in all fields concerned with child welfare.

According to the census of 1920 the number of children gainfully employed in agriculture was considerable, amounting to 647,309 between the ages of 10 and 16 years. Of this group 328,958 were under 14. Commenting on this group, the White House Conference stated that many people thought of farm work as consisting of light tasks carried on out-of-doors and in the sunshine. However, as the report indicates, there are other factors to be considered in determining the healthfulness or harmfulness of such work. As listed by the Conference they were as follows:

1. Whether or not the work is too heavy for the years and physical development of children, and whether or not it is too long continued.
2. Whether or not the work is hurried and, therefore, conducive to overstrain and excessive fatigue.
3. Whether or not the work requires unnatural postures for long periods or causes over-development of one set of muscles at the expense of others.
4. Whether or not the work involves accident hazards.
5. Whether or not children away from home are housed in sanitary and healthful accommodations.

By way of further comment the Report said:

There is little definite information about the physical effects of work in agriculture. Undoubtedly, many of the tasks done by children are quite harmless, provided they are not carried on by too young children or for too continuous a period. But in many cases, as child labor studies have revealed, this is exactly what happens. Little children are employed, the work is not suited to their strength, and daily and weekly hours are long, usually exceeding eight and often ten and twelve hours a day. In certain types of farm work, moreover, there are definite factors that are unhealthful such as the cramped position of workers pulling and topping beets or suckering and worming tobacco, the exposure to dampness and cold at the end of the beet and cranberry seasons, the danger involved in the use of knives and the operation of farm machinery.[1]

In recent years there have been two studies of children engaged in agricultural work. These were of the children employed in the onion fields of Ohio and the sugar beet farms of Colorado. Findings of these investigations were to the effect that the seven and eight year old onion workers in Ohio toiled from nine to ten hours a day with infrequent rest periods and only one hour of rest at noon. The study concluded that although no obvious defects were noted such working conditions were a hindrance to proper growth and that the continuous stooping posture tended to constrict the chests of children and interfere with the normal development of their organs and bone structure. Similar were the findings of the study of the Children's Bureau of the beet workers in Colorado. Here was discovered a high percentage of orthopedic defects in these workers; two out of three children were taxing the muscles of undeveloped shoulders, a practice which resulted in 676 cases of winged scapulae, and 21.6 per cent of the group had developed cases of flat feet at an early age.[2]

The statement of Dr. Charles Hendee Smith, Clinical Professor of Diseases of Children, Columbia University, and Director of Children's Medical Division, Bellevue Hospital, New York, is an example of the opinion of the medical profession on the exploitation of children in agricultural communities. Said he:

Long hours of tiring work like this (that is, beet cultivation and cotton picking) must result in chronic fatigue. This works serious harm to children in two ways. In the first place, the child's main business in life is to grow and gain weight. Excessive muscular work expends the energy which should be used in the natural process of growth.

[1] White House Conference on Child Health and Protection. *Child Labor*, Section III D, pp. 253–254, Century Co., 1932.

[2] *Ibid.* pp. 255–256.

The result is the child becomes undernourished and undersized. In the second place, chronic fatigue results in lowered resistance to disease. The various infections which are everywhere lying in wait for the growing child, find an easy victim in those who are overfatigued and undernourished.[1]

Thus scientific study and expert opinion agree on, and at the same time give warning of the ugly results resulting when agricultural work beyond reasonable lengths is required of children. The environment of the country sets a stage in which children naturally participate in the activities around them. Carried to reasonable lengths this participation seems desirable, but those interested in rural youth should so direct and control these activities that the point of exploitation is never reached.

HEALTH PROMOTION AND IMPROVEMENT

Modern public health practices in the United States may be said to have had their beginnings in the tensions resulting from the urbanization movement of the nineteenth century. Rapidly developing urban centers, unrestricted immigration, and the spread of industrialism tended to produce conditions which made the spread of communicable diseases easy and rapid. Under the soporific social conscience of that period, and hampered by inexperience in the field of public health, people died by the thousands from diseases we now know to be controllable.

This environment in its broad sense, as well as in specific ways, was fatal to thousands and disabled hundreds of thousands more, thus operating blindly as a selective agency which respected neither the weak nor the strong.[2]

The health necessities of this new urban environment tended to bring the problem of disease control into sharp focus, and the very urgencies of the situation hastened relief. Counteractive forces were set in motion as follows:

[1] *Ibid.* p. 257.
[2] Sydenstricker, Edgar. *Health and Environment*, p. 188, McGraw-Hill Book Co., 1933.

1. The establishment of public health departments in cities whose functions were (a) community sanitation and (b) preventative medicine and care.

2. The education of the public in matters of health.

3. Growth of an intelligent humanitarianism which developed into (a) social service work; (b) hospitals, clinics and social welfare; (c) the revolt of industrial workers against intolerable working and living conditions.

4. A program of health education in the public schools.[1]

The results of these counteractive efforts speak for themselves. Through them health has come to the cities. New York City offers an excellent example. In 1893 the death rate of that great city was nearly 25, the rest of the state approximately 17, per 1000. By 1923 the death rate for the city had dropped to 12, while the rest of the state was 14, per 1000.[2] The rural areas show no such progress. Dr. Frederick L. Hoffman, of the Prudential Life Insurance Company, reported in a recent study that the death rate in rural and urban areas per 100,000 in four controllable diseases were as follows: typhoid fever for rural areas was 24.4; for cities, 22.6; malarial fever, rural, 3.7; for cities, 2.6; influenza, rural, 27.8; for cities, 14.8; dysentery, rural, 10.2; cities 6.8. The mortality statistics for the same area showed that smallpox, measles, whooping cough and pellegra caused more deaths among the rural than the urban population.[3]

The problem of providing organized health services for rural areas is one of the most pressing of our social problems. It is the concern of the laity and the medical profession alike, a concern shared by teachers who see in this liability a threat to the welfare of childhood. Upon this point Dr. Winslow has made the following statement:

Only about one-fifth of the rural population have the benefits of any organized health machinery, and even in the 500 counties which boast

[1] *Ibid.* p. 188.

[2] Winslow, Charles E. A. *Health on the Farm and in the Village*, p. 20, Macmillan, 1931.

[3] Taylor, Carl C. *Rural Sociology*, p. 421, Harpers, 1933, Revised Edition.

of full-time county health services, budget and personnel are generally far below any reasonable standards of efficiency. Nor is this situation characteristic mainly of the United States. Recent meetings of the Health Committee of the League of Nations have shown increasing emphasis upon the urgent problem of rural health. In every country of the world the major administrative health need is the extension of modern health services to the country districts.

The chief difficulties in the path of rural health service are of two types, administrative and economic. In the first place, the isolated rural community cannot possibly develop a self-sufficient health unit. The ultimate minimum of effective sanitary organization includes a full-time health officer, at least three public health nurses, and a sanitary inspector, which will cost $15,000.00. Therefore, no population group of less than 6000 persons can possibly develop an adequate health service at reasonable cost. It is essential then, either to replace local health units by a county organization or to unite such local units into larger ones in some other way.[1]

While adequate health service in rural areas is pitifully lacking, there are a few centers throughout the United States where demonstrations are in progress which promise much for the future. These may be found in such services as are offered by Los Angeles and San Joaquin, California; Chatham and Clarke, Georgia; Monmouth, New Jersey; Marion, Oregon; Rutherford, Tennessee; and Cattaraugus County, New York. The rural health demonstration now in progress in the latter county under the auspices of the Milbank Foundation has set up a program which seeks answers to the following questions: (1) What is a rural health program of minimum adequacy, and how should it be set up? (2) What should be its relation to other public and private agencies and to the local medical profession? (3) What will it cost, and how much of this cost can the area itself be expected to bear? (4) What will be the concrete results of such a program? These are the knotty problems involved in providing health services to rural areas.

[1] Winslow, Charles E. A., *Health on the Farm and in the Village*, p. 20, Macmillan, 1931.

If the Cattaraugus demonstration succeeds in answering them it will render the whole rural field an inestimable service.[1]

PLANS IN EFFECT FOR MEETING THE HEALTH NEEDS OF RURAL CHILDREN

Obviously the health program suggested by Dr. Winslow is not possible of consumation at the present time. Administrative machinery, especially if dependent upon legislation, is ponderous and slow at best. Years must probably elapse before the rural areas are either willing or able to centralize local units for health administration and appropriate money for its support. In the meantime, the practical problem of how the health machinery now present in the rural areas may be efficiently manipulated for children obtrudes itself upon young teachers in preparation and teachers in the field. In general, there are two sources of help to which the teacher may turn: (a) agencies set up by governmental units through legislation and (b) supplementary agencies whose services are donated to schools.

HEALTH AGENCIES SET UP BY GOVERNMENTAL UNITS

Help Provided by Legislation. The White House Conference on Child Health and Protection made a study of the legislation affecting health in rural areas, and the results of the study have been made available. Briefly they are as follows: Thirty-eight states have some kind of statute or regulation either permitting or requiring the examination of children for physical and, sometimes, for mental defects. In 24 states there are mandatory laws for all school districts, rural or urban. In 8 states the laws are mandatory for certain districts, and in these districts all

---

[1] For an excellent report of progress of the Cattaraugus demonstration, see Winslow, C. E. A. *Health on the Farm and in the Village*, Macmillan, 1931; and for a stimulating discussion on Health Education, outgrowth of work in the country schools, see Grout, Ruth E. *Handbook of Health Education*, Doubleday, Doran & Co., 1936.

the states, except New York, exclude all or part of the rural children from the requirement.[1]

The study thus reveals that there is a tendency for the states to make legislation uniform in the application to rural and urban children alike, and in the face of the laws themselves, there is apparently equality of health opportunity for the two groups. It is in the administration of the law, however, that rural children suffer neglect. Experts in the field of public health state that equality in health education and protection will never come to rural children until legislation for health includes two features. Legislation should, first, provide for annual health examinations, health instruction and healthful environments. These practices should be mandatory and apply to urban and rural children alike. In the second place, legislation should provide for both groups of children continuous follow-up work. It is in the follow-up work that the rural health program most often suffers. Too often physical examinations are given to children, the results are placed on cards, and the cards filed away. The letter of the law is thus kept, but in the keeping children do not profit. The White House Conference reports on this point:

In studying the effects of such laws upon rural as contrasted with urban children we meet a decided handicap in the lack of available data since most states do not separate rural and urban statistics. Available data could be separated for the state of New York. . . Examination of this data of New York shows that the chief weakness of legislation intended to control the health of the rural child is in its lack of provision for adequate follow-up work, rather than in the statutory requirement itself.[2]

In the rural areas of this state, with a larger number of physical defects discovered, 24,255 fewer of them were treated than the number treated among city children during the same period. The cause of neglect in this follow-up work seemed to be wholly

[1] White House Conference on Child Health and Protection. *School Health Program*, Part III, pp. 298–299, Century Co., 1932.
[2] *Ibid.* p. 300.

in terms of rural problems. These were: (a) inaccessibility of agencies; (b) the lack of organizations which provided work gratis—an item badly needed among children of foreign parentage now living on farms and the children of tenant farmers; (c) distances which made travel difficult; (d) weather hazzards. Members of the commission who studied the problem of health legislation for children reported similar conditions in all the other states in the union.[1]

HEALTH SERVICE IN THE SCHOOL

In carrying out the provisions of health legislation the teacher in the small school plays no minor part. In many instances he is the deciding factor as to whether or not the children in his school receive any health service or experiences in healthful living. According to experts aggregate health service in school falls into the following categories:

The Daily Health Inspection. Many teachers allow this important activity to develop into a routine which means nothing to him or to the children. It is frequently characterized by such brusque observations as: "Mary, where is your handkerchief?", "John, you did not clean your nails," while the children sit primly in their desks and the teacher passes quickly from one to another on "an inspection tour." Fortunately, children are as immune to the comments, which from one adult to another would be an impertinence, as to the inspection, so that no great harm is done. The difficulty about this type of inspection, however, is that no good comes of it, either. To make this the vital activity it should be teachers should keep the following principles in mind: (a) the daily inspection is primarily a preventative measure; (b) it should be made as unobtrusively as possible, probably while children are entering the room and sitting down for work; (c) the activity has in it valuable ideals for health instruction.

Since the average rural school is far removed from physicians

[1] *Ibid.* p. 300.

and nurses, the teacher must comprehend quickly and easily from children the presence and significance of deviations from the normal. Many state departments of health or education have set up warning signs. One of the best is the list of easily detected symptoms of communicable diseases:

flushed face without normal cause
rash
pallor
red and watery eyes
swollen glands
running nose
listlessness
vomiting
frequent coughing
sneezing
sore throat
fever
chills
faintness or dizziness
headache

The characteristics of a healthy child are:

good posture
good skin color
bright eyes
abundance of vitality and good spirits
good teeth
firm, well-developed muscles
normal amount of subcutaneous fat
freedom from physical defects
freedom from chronic or acute illness. [1]

Health Examinations. Like the daily morning inspection, the periodical health check up should be made an educational experience. Miss Ruth E. Grout, Director of the Health

[1] New York State Education Department. *Health Education; A Manual for Rural Teachers*, 1931.

Education Study of Cattaraugus Experiment, so well presents this point of view that she is quoted somewhat fully:

The health examination, aside from its purpose of ascertaining physical conditions, may be made a valuable educational experience for a child, particularly if the teacher aids effectively in preparing for it, and in assisting during the examination and the follow-up. Physicians, dentists, and nurses who make the examination an educational procedure find their efforts well repaid. For best results, however, they need the special help of the teacher as outlined below:

1. *Preparation for the examination*

Help children to understand why the examiner is coming and what he or she will do. Consider the reasons for various aspects of the examination, using reference books, if necessary.

Seek to develop a sympathetic attitude toward the examiner and dispel any feeling of fear.

Invite parents to be present at the examination.

2. *Assistance during the examination*

Help examiner record findings, and utilize this opportunity to become intimately acquainted with the individual problems.

Assist the examiner with weighing, measuring height, and with other help which the examiner may need.[1]

3. *Follow-up after the examination*

Discuss findings of examination with nurse and doctor in order to understand the problems fully.

Study problems with children and, so far as feasible, work out possible means of solving them. Numerous suggestions as to how this may be done are contained in this book. See especially units of work on "Care of Teeth" and "Correcting Physical Defects" in Chapters IV and VII.

Talk over problems with parents and assist them in obtaining corrections.[2]

---

[1] Cattaraugus County teachers, after having proper instructions, are encouraged to do weighing and measuring and testing of vision and hearing previous to the examiner's visit.

[2] In New York the Public Welfare Department of the State is required to provide for correcting defects of school children whose parents are unable to provide funds. Article I, Statute 83, of the Public Welfare Law, 1933, reads:

Make necessary adjustments for the handicapped child at school, as, for instance, seating a near-sighted child at a front desk.[1]

Control of Communicable Diseases. Both the morning inspection and the physical examination will reveal symptoms of communicable diseases, should they be present. The control of these is a shared responsibility of the home, the school, and the community. It is the teacher who must act promptly, if he would protect both the ill and the well child at school. He should familiarize himself with the local health regulations and act in accordance with them. Observations should be made and records kept of all children exposed to the disease and steps in prevention taken, if possible. These steps also furnish material for health instruction and should be made an essential part of the curriculum materials as they arise.

Aid Should Be Available in Time of Emergencies. Fortunate is the rural teacher who never faces an emergency in a broken arm, a cut finger, or a bruised head. In the event of such accidents he cannot telephone a doctor, nor send the child to the school nurse, as is possible in urban schools. He must act quickly and intelligently upon his own best judgment. It is desirable, therefore, that all prospective rural teachers include somewhere in their own health education a short course in first aid. Such information should also be given to the older children so that they too can act intelligently in an emergency caused by accidents. To complement action there should be available in every rural school an adequate first-aid kit. Miss Grout has assembled such a kit and a list of the essentials may be found in the appendix.

The Follow-up Work in All the Above Named Activities. As stated previously in this chapter, children frequently suffer in

"The public welfare district shall be responsible for providing necessary medical care for all persons under its care, and for such persons, otherwise able to maintain themselves, who are unable to secure necessary medical care."

[1] Grout, Ruth E. *Handbook of Health Education,* pp. 7–8, Doubleday, Doran and Co., 1936.

rural schools from a lack of follow-up work after a physical examination. Indeed, many teachers consider their duty done when the examinations have been made and the results properly indexed and filed. As a matter of fact, the physical examination is merely the beginning of a teacher's responsibility for the physical well-being and health of the children in his room. The findings should be discussed with the attending physician or nurse and their suggestions for remedial programs should be carefully kept, along with the report of the physical examination, in the individual folder of each child and referred to frequently until his defect has been remedied. The problems of each child should be discussed frankly and freely with parents and with the child himself, so that the coöperation of all concerned may carry the remedial program agreed upon to a successful conclusion.

It appears essential that somewhere in his education the rural teacher receive training which will fit him for participation in these vital activities. The state of Virginia through the West Law of 1920 made such preparation on the part of teachers mandatory.

Under the provisions of this law every teacher in the state teaching in a public school must be prepared to make medical inspections and to assist doctors and nurses in giving medical examinations. Under this Act the employment of school nurses and physicians is permissive but in counties where such help is not provided teachers, especially trained for it give the inspections.[1]

COÖPERATING HEALTH AGENCIES IN RURAL AREAS

Fortunately, there are many coöperating agencies whose interest is wholly or partly that of the promotion of health. To them the rural teacher finds it helpful to turn in time of need. Every rural teacher should, therefore, survey his community, locate the coöperating agencies, make a study of them, and use

[1] White House Conference in Child Health and Protection. *School Health Program*, Sec. III, p. 301, Century Co., 1932.

their programs as need for them arises. According to the White House Conference the agencies most often found promoting health in rural areas are seven: (1) The Farm Bureau makes its contribution through the promotion of better food supplies, specifically through provisions for hot lunches in school. Individual members also coöperate on nutrition programs. (2) The local Parent-Teacher Association often proves of inestimable value because of its ability to secure the coöperation of parents in the establishment of proper health habits, and in follow-up and correctional work for individual children. The "summer round up" of children is an example of this coöperation. (3) The Anti-Tuberculosis Association through its advisory service, especially in the field of nutrition and functional health activities, has proved helpful to rural children. The supervision of health programs is frequently available. (4) The Red Cross finds its greatest value to rural schools in its distribution of health information and through the practice of promoting school nursing service to rural areas. Promotion of the Junior Red Cross is also valuable. (5) Child health and welfare associations are often available, their chief contributions nearly always being in the areas of the school survey and the dissemination of information. These surveys are excellent guides for charting programs. (6) Often there may be found helpful health committees in nearby women's clubs and fraternal organizations who will assist in providing school lunch equipment and help in a program for crippled children. Men's luncheon clubs are also frequently coöperative. (7) The education departments of life insurance companies are also available to the rural teacher, and probably, render their best service in the dissemination of health information. Often this information is available in attractive booklets, which children can use to supplement regular assignments. A vivid picture of coöperating agencies, exclusive of official educational ones, is furnished by the following listing from Cattaraugus County.[1]

[1] Grout, Ruth E. *Health Education*, pp. 266–267, Doubleday, Doran and Co., 1936.

LOCAL AGENCIES AND HEALTH SERVICES THEY PROVIDE IN THE RURAL
SCHOOLS OF CATTARAUGUS COUNTY
(Exclusive of Official Educational Agencies)

Agency	Services to Rural Schools	Mechanics for Bringing Services in Contact with Schools
I. Medical inspection of school children	1. Part-time locally employed physician inspects each child annually per State Law	Local trustee selects medical inspector and makes financial arrangements with him
II. County Dept. of Health		
1. County Commissioner of Health	1. Immunization against disease	At request of community through nurse
	2. Control of communicable disease	Visits schools or homes as needs arise, often at request of teacher, trustee, or superintendents
	3. Advisory services on individual health problems such as disease control, etc.	At request of teachers or others
2. Public Health Nurse	1. Assists with medical inspection in her district	Makes direct arrangements with medical inspector and teacher for schedule of inspection visits
	2. Control of communicable diseases as agent of the County Commissioner of Health	Visits school or home on request of County Commissioner of Health, teacher, trustee, or superintendent
	3. Assists in securing the correction of physical defects	Works in coöperation with family physician, parent groups, and welfare workers
	4. Interprets school problems to the home and vice versa	Through home and school visits
	5. Advisory services on individual health problems	Through home and school visits
3. Sanitary Engineer	1. Inspects water supplies	May be at request of superintendents, teacher, trustee or others
	2. Advises on sanitary improvements.	By request

LOCAL AGENCIES AND HEALTH SERVICES THEY PROVIDE IN THE RURAL
SCHOOLS OF CATTARAUGUS COUNTY (*Continued*)

(Exclusive of Official Educational Agencies)

Agency	Services to Rural Schools	Mechanics for Bringing Services in Contact with Schools
4. Director of Bureau of Tuberculosis	1. Clinical and X-ray examination of suspected cases of tuberculosis.	At request of physician, nurse, or others
	2. X-ray examination juniors and seniors in high school.	On permission of local school board
5. County Laboratory	1. Bacteriological examination of water samples	Routinely and on special request
6. Director of Maternity, Infancy, and Child Hygiene	1. Provides program for preschool child—a preliminary step toward a healthier school child. Also parent education through health program for preschool child, etc.	Conferences with individual parents. Talks before parent-teacher groups
III. Supervisory School Hygiene District		
1. Director of County School Health Service	1. Provides link between health and education department. Assumes responsibilities and directs policies for all health work in schools	Works through existing agencies in direct contrast with schools such as medical inspector, nurse, superintendent, director of health education, etc.
	2. Keeps all school health records in central office Sends annual reports to State Education Department	Summaries of reports used to promote further activities in schools
2. Director of School Health Education Project	1. Acts as consultant on school health education program	Through personal and group contacts with teachers, district superintendents, nurses, parents, and others
	2. Assists in curriculum building with special emphasis on health	Same
	3. Assists in unifying all health work in schools	Same

LOCAL AGENCIES AND HEALTH SERVICES THEY PROVIDE IN THE RURAL
SCHOOLS OF CATTARAUGUS COUNTY (*Continued*)

(Exclusive of Official Educational Agencies)

Agency	Services to Rural Schools	Mechanics for Bringing Services in Contact with Schools
IV. County Welfare Department	1. Relief program for needy individuals. In a few instances helps to provide lunches for needy school children	Largely through assistance to family
	2. Child welfare work including arrangements for child guidance clinics	At request of teacher, nurse, and others
V. Catholic Charities	1. Relief program for needy individuals	Largely through assistance to family
VI. Boy Scouts of America	1. Sponsors formation of scout troops	Contact of leader with individuals in community
VII. Camp Fire Girls and Blue Birds	1. Sponsors formation of groups of girls	Contact of leader with individuals in community
VIII. County Tuberculosis and Public Health Ass'n.	1. Provision of educational material related to control of tuberculosis	Individual contacts of secretary with health education director, teachers, and community
	2. Special services in community education such as preparing lists of health books in County libraries	In conjunction with school education program in general
IX. Home and Farm Bureau	1. Advisory and promotional services in relation to food and nutrition	Through general educational program. Special help at request of teachers
X. 4–H Club Work	1. Club meetings and projects to promote homemaking and agriculture	Limited to sections where high school teachers organize clubs in vicinity of their schools
XI. Parent-Teachers Associations Mothers' Clubs, Granges, *Etc.*	1. Support school programs in general and provide for such specific needs as hot lunches and defect corrections	Contribution of funds, community education, and other services

Help is nearly always available in coöperating health agencies if the rural teacher will but inform himself and make use of their services.

SUMMARY

This chapter presents the thesis that the child is heir to all that he has met and not of least importance in his birthright are those health factors which influence his life at home, in school, and in the community. An analysis was made of both the assets and liabilities in the out-of-school environment which most often affect child development. The assets presented were as follows: (a) association with nature, (b) companionship of pets, (c) responsibility for regular tasks, (d) rhythm of country life, (e) the place occupied by children in the rural family and community. The factors in the rural environment which adversely affect child development were listed as follows: (a) the lack of sanitary and hygienic controls, (b) child labor.

Modern health practices began as a necessity in cities in the nineteenth century. These are: (a) The establishment of health departments which provide community sanitation; (b) preventative medicine and care in illness; (c) education of the public in health practices; (d) programs of health education in the public schools. These programs, now well established in cities and bearing fruit, are difficult to establish in country districts largely because of economic and administrative difficulties. However, demonstrations, notably in Cattaraugus County, New York, now in progress indicate that with proper leadership and effort all four of the services now available in cities are possible and profitable in rural areas.

Such programs for all rural areas, however, apparently belong in a far distant future. The practical problem for the rural teacher at present is in the profitable use of the environmental resources in order that children now in school may profit from them. Help is available at present in two ways. First, in the legislation found in 38 states which looks toward an adequate health service for rural children. This health service usually falls into the following activities, for which teachers are held increasingly responsible: (a) daily health inspections; (b) health examinations; (c) control of communicable diseases; (d) first aid in emergencies; (e) and the follow-up work of such services. Second, help is available through the use of services of coöperating agencies. These sources vary with localities, but the White House Conference listed seven which are available most often: (a) The Farm Bureau, (b) the local Parent-Teacher Association, (c) the Anti-Tuberculosis Association, (d) the Red Cross, (e) Child health and welfare associations, (f) women's clubs and fraternal organizations, (g) educational departments of life insurance companies.

The end and aim of modern education is consistent and satisfactory growth in the three areas which make up the wholeness of childhood—body, mind, and spirit. The health factors of a community play a highly significant part in determining whether or not the "child in its midst" shall have a proper foundation for abundant and healthful living.

SUGGESTED READINGS

Baldwin, Bird T. and Others. *Farm Children*, Chap. X, D. Appleton and Co., New York, 1930.

Bennett, Thomas Gordon. *A Health Program for the Children of a County*, Chap. III, Bureau of Publications, Teachers College, Columbia University, New York, 1933.

Freeman, Allen W. *A Study of Rural Public Health Services*, Chap. I, Oxford Univ. Press, 1933.

Grout, Ruth E. *Handbook of Health Education*, Chap. I, Doubleday, Doran and Co., Garden City, New York, 1936.

Moore, Harry Hascall. *Public Health in the United States*, Chaps. XI, XII, Harpers, New York, 1923.

Sorokin, Pitirim and Zimmerman, Carle C. *Principles of Rural-Urban Sociology*, Chap. V, Henry Holt and Co., New York, 1929.

Sydenstricker, Edgar. *Health and Environment*, Chap. IV, McGraw-Hill Book Co., New York, 1933.

White House Conference on Child Health and Protection. *The School*

Health Program, Section III, pp. 3–34, 290–305, Century Co., New York, 1932.

White House Conference on Child Health and Protection. *Vocational Guidance and Child Labor*, Section III, pp. 213–312, Century Co., New York, 1932.

Winslow, Charles E. A. *Health on the Farm and in the Village*, Chap. II, Macmillan, New York, 1931.

MATERIALS FOR DISCUSSION

Consider the following statements. What changes would make them more acceptable to you? What significant issues arise from their study?

1. The environmental assets in rural areas outweigh the liabilities in the development of satisfactory mental and physical health in children. Consequently, the country is considered an ideal place in which to rear children.

2. The health hazards of agricultural labor are considerable and children should be protected from them. An adequate Federal child labor law would probably make the best solution.

3. The necessity for and the problem of providing adequate health service for rural areas is the most pressing social problem in the United States.

4. While it appears desirable to organize rural health services on a regional rather than a local community basis, it appears administratively impossible to fashion one pattern to fit all sections of the United States.

5. In the establishment of a school health program the family and the home rather than the school are the determining factors in the success of it.

APPENDIX

APPENDIX A

MODIFICATIONS OF DAILY PROGRAM TO ACCOMMODATE NEEDS OF FIVE AND SIX-YEAR-OLD CHILDREN [1]

In this school the five-year-olds are in group D.

Arrival—9 Perhaps not yet in the schoolroom. May be getting off coats and rubbers in hall under supervision of older pupil, coming quietly into the room when ready. May be playing outside until a second bell which calls all groups in to prepare for opening exercises. If in room, at seats or in own work center, getting out books or work materials, watering the plants, arranging flowers, feeding pets, or sitting quietly resting from walk to school, watching activity going on around them, or just waiting for morning inspection.

9–9:20 Opening exercises (suitable for primary children or for whole school). This period is planned and carried out by different groups of pupils, under the teacher's guidance. The five-year-old children take their part with other primary age children in grades 1 and 2 (group D) on days assigned to them. Time is provided here for reminding pupils of their plans for the day's work.

9:20–9:40 Language activities with teacher
Conversation developed from opening exercises; or
A continued conversation or a new conversation as a basis for planning and for board reading or textbook reading; or
Story telling in preparation for reading; or dramatization; or
Oral reading from class textbooks; or

[1] University of the State of New York, State Education Department. *Handbook for Rural Elementary Schools*, Bulletin Number 3, p. 79, University of the State of New York Press, 1936.

467

Reading from different books by different children, the rest of the group being an audience; or

Silent reading, responding by activity of various kinds; or

Any other type of reading exercise, using books, cards, or blackboard

9:40–10 Quiet work growing out of lesson just completed (unsupervised). May be representation, drawing pictures, cutting, pasting, reproduction, identification, advanced reading work, following board directions, etc. Where practicable, not all this need be at seats. A group might go to the hall or cloakroom to plan a dramatization together, or to the sand table to work out a representation or to the easel or blackboard to draw. Occasionally the five-year-olds during this period might be the audience for the second grade reading, listening to a story prepared to read to them, or seeing a dramatization prepared for them to see.

10–10:20 Toilet, lunch, such as crackers and milk, orange juice, etc., rest. Supervised and assisted quietly by an older pupil without disturbing other groups at work.

10:20–10:30 Outdoor period with whole school

10:30–11 Outdoor period continued, if possible; games, making playhouses, playing in sand, snow play and the like. Indoors when weather conditions require. Quiet play on the floor in the play corner, which may be covered with rugs, linoleum; standing or sitting around the table, or at the work table or sand table. Materials for use: dolls, blocks, large beads, weaving materials, pictures, picture books, scissors, paints, soft balls— anything suitable for five-year-olds at quiet play, unsupervised.

11–11:10 Putting away materials, or taking off wraps, cleaning up and getting ready for next period, assisted by an older pupil.

11:10–11:20 Stories with teacher

11:20–11:35 Language seat work (rest of school is having arithmetic). As the teacher moves from group to group, she stops at intervals to observe and check the seat work or other activities of these youngest children.

11:35–11:50 Informal activities or rest, if tired (unsupervised) except as indicated in previous period

11:50–12 Number games with teacher

12–1 Toilet and preparation for dinner, assisted by older pupil
Eating
Rest
Last part of period:
    (a) Children play—free period
        (Committee cleans up after lunch)
    (b) Teacher plans afternoon work

1–1:10 Reading with teacher—any type of lesson including word study and phonics as related to the material being read

1:10–1:20 Reading activities, continued (unsupervised), looking at picture books, etc.

1:20–1:35 Social studies with teacher two days a week, free period other days

1:35–2 Special work with entire school
Activity period continued from 1:20, begin to clean up and rest toward close

2–2:15 Music, rhythms

2:15–2:30 Toilet, play

2:30–4 Dismissed, if possible, for children to go home. If they can not go home, they should enjoy informal play and other activities at school. Young children should not be left to sit idly in their seats for the last hour and a half of school or to loiter aimlessly outside, because their "lessons" are finished. This period may be made educationally worth while, if a little thought and planning is given to it even though the teacher is at work with other groups and can not supervise these children to any extent. If a cot or bench for resting can be provided, a nap will be beneficial to many such children.

SUGGESTED PROGRAM FOR GROUPING PUPILS IN ONE-TEACHER SCHOOL [1]

MORNING

Time	Minutes	Time to Be Distributed According to Group Needs	Group D		Group C	Group B		Grade 8
			Grade 1	Grade 2	Grades 3 and 4	Grades 5 and 6	Grade 7	
9	20		*Opening exercises:* This period should be carefully planned by different pupil groups, under teacher guidance. Teacher should keep record of subjects covered. These should be alternated by days, weeks or by units of work.			1 *Music; Current events* 2 *Morning health check-up; Health discussions* 3 *Hygiene talks, stories etc.* 4 *Instruction in correct use of flag* 5 *Nature talks, kindness to animals*		
			English literature group of studies: Two periods each day, one 60-minute period before morning recess, one 30-minute period after morning recess (Suggestive arrangement offered below)					
9.20	60	10	*Reading* [1]* (Teaching lesson) *Reading S. W.* [2] *Reading S. W.*	Review preparation for reading	Activities based on social studies	Library period	Project work for 40 minutes, based on opening exercises, social studies or other work of the day For seventh and eighth grades	
		10		*Reading*	*Reading*			
		10	Reading S. W.	Reading S. W.	Reading S. W.	*Reading*		
		10	Reading S. W.	Reading S. W.	Reading S. W.	Reading S. W.		
		20	Library period for both grades or other informal activities, easel work, clay modeling, etc.				*Reading and literature, spelling and language study (alternated by days [3]);* grades 7 and 8 combined	

[1] *Ibid.* p. 82.

* For footnotes to all references within the table, see p. 474.

470

Time	Min					
10.20	10	Recess (drinks of water, toilet and play) Physical education, rhythms etc.: Smaller children, three days a week; larger children, two days				
10.30	10	Group D still excused, play directed by trustworthy Group B or seventh or eighth grade child[4]	Work on spelling and language—notebooks etc.	*Language and spelling*	Study reading and spelling etc.	Study reading and literature or spelling and grammar
	30	*Language work with teacher:* grades 1 and 2 combined	*Language and spelling*	*Language and spelling*	Study language	
	10		Study language and spelling	Study language and spelling	Study extra work	
	10		Study language and spelling	Study language and spelling		
		Arithmetic group: Work to be partly individual instruction, partly group teaching. All pupils, except group D, should work entire 40 minutes (suggestive arrangement offered below).				
11	15	Language seat work[5]	Work arithmetic		See note[10] below.	Work arithmetic
	15	Informal activities	After starting grades 7 and 8 as above, teaching whichever group needs teaching, turn to group B and C and do the same. Thus work down across the room until all difficulties are cleared up, and all pupils are busy with new assignments. Then take group D for last ten minutes.			
	40	NOTE. Grades 1 and 2 will need to have seat work changed during this period. For fuller explanation, see below.[5]				
	10	Group D: *Number games, short drills,* practice in counting actual objects, in reading or writing numbers as needed (twice a week, grade 2 alone for formal work), other days add time to activity period.				
11.40	20	Activity period—3 days a week Science work—2 days a week				

471

SUGGESTED PROGRAM FOR GROUPING PUPILS IN ONE-TEACHER SCHOOL—(Continued)

Time	Minutes	Time to Be Distributed According to Group Needs	Group D		Group C	Group B		Grade 8
			Grade 1	Grade 2	Grades 3 and 4	Grades 5 and 6	Grade 7	
12	60	*Recess* (dinner)	1 Hot lunch during winter months. At all times, if possible. Lunch, properly eaten at tables or desks. Clean hands. Social conversation. Music, on phonograph. Other social activities. Teach table manners. Short rest after eating. 2 Last part of period: (a) children play—free period (committee cleans up after lunch); (b) teacher prepares for afternoon work.					

AFTERNOON

Time	Minutes	Time to Be Distributed According to Group Needs	Grade 1	Grade 2	Grades 3 and 4	Grades 5 and 6	Grade 7	Grade 8
		Social studies group (History, geography etc.) *Science and arts group* (continued). Extra reading classes for younger pupils are also scheduled in the afternoon.						
1	75	10	Reading[1]	Number S. W.	Complete arithmetic work	Complete arithmetic work		
		10	Reading S. W.	Reading			Library period	Library period
		15	Social studies—2 days		Social studies—3 days			Library period

Special work (entire school): Drawing, penmanship, club meetings, etc.

1 Two days, art work—crafts, drawing etc.; teacher supervises entire group. (This work may grow largely out of activities.)

2 Two days, penmanship—school divided into two groups. All pupils practise each day; only one group taught by teacher. All written seat work, spelling etc. should be judged for good penmanship. One day for club meetings or discussions.

Music whole school:[6] Four days a week review of songs already taught. Period under pupil leadership. Teacher to relax, rest in rear of classroom, if her guidance of pupil control will permit. One day a week, music lesson for younger pupils.[6]

Recess (drinks of water, toilet, play): Physical education, rhythms etc.; larger children three days; smaller children two days

Time						
25	Special work (entire school) — see above					
15	Music whole school — see above					
2.15 / 15	Recess — see above					
2.30 / 70	Dismissed, if possible for children to go home. See below, note.[7]	Dismissed, if possible for children to go home. See below, note.[7]	Activities based upon social studies	*Social studies*	Activities for Social studies	Activities based on Social studies
20			Library period	Social studies	Social studies	Social studies
20				S.W.	*Social studies*	Social studies
15				Social studies	Social studies	S. W.
				S. W.	S. W.	

2 days—Health education
2 days—Elementary science[8]
1 day—Music, teaching new material[6]

Time	
3.40 / 20	Supervised study and planning[9] for groups C, B and grades 7 and 8. (Teacher helps pupils to catch up on all back work, explains assignments further, plans work with them for long periods next morning. Teaches how to study.)

Notes. [1] All items printed in italics are periods in which the teacher is working with the children.

[2] S. W. throughout the program means study work, seat work, or other between class activity.

[3] Silent reading class for older pupils who have not yet learned how to study should be conducted twice each week with group B.

[4] In open weather, let the pupils play outside. On other days, an informal play corner may be developed in the classroom, where quiet games with soft balls, dominoes and other materials may be enjoyed.

[5] As the teacher moves from group to group during the arithmetic period, she should stop at intervals to observe and check the seat work or other activities of group D pupils.

[6] The music work may follow any of the teaching plans which have been developed specifically for use in one and two-teacher schools, several of which are now available.

[7] The younger pupils should be permitted to return to their homes or to enjoy informal play and other activities at school when they can not go home. Such activities should be carefully planned by the teacher. Young children should not be left to sit idly in their seats for the last hour of school or to loiter aimlessly outside, because their "lessons" are finished. Play is an important factor in the young child's development and this last hour may be made a rich educational experience, if a little thought and planning

are given to it. If a cot or bench for resting can be provided, a nap will be beneficial to many such children.

[8] All pupils from grades 3 to 8 should be treated as one class, the younger pupils learning the easier facts such as identification of common wild flowers, birds, insects and weeds and observation of simple scientific phenomena. If group D pupils are present, they may join the class. On days when a field trip is planned, the period may be extended through the following study period.

[9] This period of planning for the next day's activities is essential, if the older girls and boys are to carry on a worthwhile program the following morning without supervision from the teacher. The plan for these activities should be discussed and may be written on the blackboard and left for the pupils' guidance when they return to school the next day.

[10] First 15 minutes begin with grades 7 and 8: alternate, one day eighth grade pupils may work at board, seventh grade pupils at seats. Each pupil's work is individualized; that is, each works under general topic, assigned his class, but completes as rapidly as possible, then takes up supplementary problems, practises speed drill, etc. When regular assignment is completed, and he is "up to standard performance" on topic, pupil may use rest of the 40-minute period as he wishes, reading, practising on his weakest subject, working on unit activities, etc.

FLEXIBLE DAILY PROGRAM ADAPTED FOR USE IN INTERMEDIATE OR UPPER GRADES OF A TWO-TEACHER OR THREE-TEACHER SCHOOL [1]

Hour		Time Distribution in Minutes		
		If two grades in the room (Grades 5–6; Grades 6–7; Grades 7–8)	If three grades in the room (Grades 4, 5, 6; Grades 5, 6, 7; Grades 6, 7, 8)	If four grades in the room (Grades 4, 5, 6, 7 or Grades 5, 6, 7, 8)
Hour	Subject Matter or Activity upon which pupils are working. Both recitation and study occur within the same block. The lowest grade or group has "class" first, then the next lowest, etc. In the case of a laboratory period the teacher works individually with all. She goes to the most dependent children first, then to the others.			
8:30– 8:45	Free period	15		
8:45– 9:00	Planning the day's work or Inspection and Opening Exercises	15		
9:00–10:15	Social Studies or the major unit being studied. This time may be divided between grades or groups as local or state curriculum and grading practices dictate. Or the whole group may participate in planning one large unit, divide and apportion the work among smaller groups, and engage in research, reporting, evaluating, drilling, etc. Club meeting—Fridays. The formal type of school should break this period by two minutes of setting-up drills at about mid-period.	40 35	25 25 25	20 20 20 15
10:15–10:45	Art, either fine arts or industrial arts	30		
10:45–11:05	Toilets, supervised play, preparation of hot lunch, washing hands, etc. (Mid-morning lunch for children who breakfast very early)	20		

[1] Bardwell, Muriel. Demonstration Teacher, Rural Education, Summer Session, State Teachers College, Buffalo, N. Y.

FLEXIBLE DAILY PROGRAM ADAPTED FOR USE IN INTERMEDIATE OR UPPER GRADES OF A TWO-TEACHER OR THREE-TEACHER SCHOOL—(Continued)

Hour	Subject Matter or Activity upon which pupils are working.	Time Distribution in Minutes		
		If two grades in the room (Grades 5–6; Grades 6–7; Grades 7–8)	If three grades in the room (Grades 4, 5, 6; Grades 5, 6, 7; Grades 6, 7, 8)	If four grades in the room (Grades 4, 5, 6, 7 or Grades 5, 6, 7, 8)
	Both recitation and study occur within the same block. The lowest grade or group has "class" first, then the next lowest, etc. In the case of a laboratory period the teacher works individually with all. She goes to the most dependent children first, then to the others.			
11:05–12:00	Arithmetic. Grade, group, or individualized teaching methods may be used, the teacher developing new work with not more than one group each day, and moving about to each group in turn. All may have certain types of drill together. Include two minutes of setting-up exercises at mid-period in the formal type school.	30 25	20 20 15	15 15 15 10
12:00– 1:00	Washing, serving lunch, eating together, clean-up, and quiet rest or play.	60		
1:00– 1:20	Music	20		
1:20– 2:20	English and Literature. Follow the grade or grouping plan and the curriculum required. All children may unite to plan and work on entertainment projects, a school news or literary sheet, book club, creative writing, etc. English should also be correlated with the major unit. Supplement with workbooks to meet the drill needs of each group. Include two minutes setting-up exercises at mid-period in the formal type school.	30 30	20 20 20	15 15 15 15

476

2:20– 2:40	Toilets, supervised play, housekeeping duties, etc.	20
2:40– 3:00	Science, agriculture, nature study, health courses, safety, library, or guidance courses.	20
3:00– 4:00	Reading, Writing, and Spelling skills. Divide the Grade IV should have a reading period daily. Divide the pupils of grades V, VI, VII, and VIII into two groups, placing all dependent readers in the so-called "B" group and independent readers in the "A" group. Alternate these groups so that one or the other has class daily. The "B" group may recite three days a week and the "A" group twice, or the "A" group may need but one real class a week and the "B" group four. By copying spelling words for different grades in parallel columns on a sheet of ruled paper the teacher may test all grades at the same time, pronouncing a word to each group in turn. Words requiring teaching may then be taught to all pupils needing them. Writing may be taught to the entire room exactly as to a single large grade, the pupils being grouped and seated according to the type of practice needed. Include two minutes setting-up exercises at mid-period in the formal type school.	15 min. intensive teaching of reading to all very dependent readers daily. 15 min. reading teaching to so-called "B" readers three days a week and to "A" readers one day a week. 30 min. writing and spelling divided any way the teacher prefers.

477

DAILY PROGRAM SUGGESTED FOR THE PRIMARY ROOM OF A TWO-TEACHER OR THREE-TEACHER SCHOOL [1]

NOTE: Time may be adjusted as daily needs require within the main subject matter blocks outlined at the left. The program shows adjustments suggested where there are four grades in the room. If there are three grades in the room, grades I and II may have an arithmetic period after the morning recess which would come at 10:00 to 10:20. Reading IV would be omitted as there would be no fourth grade in this room. (r) indicates that children are reciting.

Subject Matter and Hour	Duration in Minutes	Grade I	Grade II	Grade III	Grade IV
8:30– 8:45 A.M.	15	Free period			
8:45– 9:00	15	Bell, washing hands, health inspection, opening exercises, news, planning the day, etc.			
9:00–10:20 Reading	20	Reading (r)	Study reading	Study reading	Study reading
	20	Reading type seatwork	Reading (r)	Reading seatwork	Reading seatwork
	(02)	The formal type of school is required to provide two minutes of activity or setting-up exercises four times daily			
	20	Seatwork providing activity	Reading seatwork	Reading (r)	Reading seatwork
	20	Another type of reading seatwork	Reading seatwork	Reading seatwork	Reading (r)

[1] Bardwell, Muriel. Demonstration Teacher, Rural Education, Summer Session, State Teachers College, Buffalo, N. Y.

Time	Min.			
10:20–10:35	15	Mid-morning lunch, toilet, washing hands, supervised play outdoors. Recess.		
10:35–11:30 English and Literature	15	Reading (r)	Study English and Spelling	Study English and Spelling
	20	Spelling, writing and English study or seatwork	English	
	(02)	Second period for setting-up drills required in the formal type of school		
	20	English (r)		Study English
11:30–12:00	30	Dismissed	Spelling and writing. (All grades can be managed at one time)	
12:00– 1:00 P.M.	60	Lunch hour. Washing hands, eating lunch together, clean-up, toilets, quiet play.		
1:00– 1:15	15	Music		
1:15– 1:50 Reading	05	Self-drill	Reading seatwork	Divide in Reading Groups using easier afternoon readers, or audience type reading. Also free library period certain days. Spend the first five minutes of the period with the teacher
	15	Reading (r)	Reading seatwork	
	15	Reading seatwork	Reading and Arithmetic (r)	
	(02)	Third period for setting-up drills required in the formal type of school		

479

DAILY PROGRAM SUGGESTED FOR THE PRIMARY ROOM OF A TWO-TEACHER OR THREE-TEACHER SCHOOL—(Continued)

Subject Matter and Hour	Duration in Minutes	Grade I	Grade II	Grade III	Grade IV
1:50– 2:45 Social Studies or Science and Industrial Arts or Fine Arts	15	Social studies or arithmetic type of seatwork or study		Social Studies or Science (r)	
	15	Social Studies or Science (r)		Study social studies	
	25	Creative Art until dismissal at 2:30 P.M.		Industrial or Fine Art	
2:45– 3:40	15	Dismissed		Recess	
	20			Arithmetic	
	(02)			Fourth period for setting-up drills required in the formal type of school	
	20			Individualized drill or Arithmetic	

480

APPENDIX B

SUGGESTED CONSTITUTION FOR A RURAL SCHOOL CLUB [1]

CONSTITUTION OF THE SCHOOL CLUB OF SOUTH WALES, NEW YORK

Article I

Name

This club shall be known as the Gargoyles Club.

Article II

Purpose

The purpose of this club is:

1. To teach us how to put on plays.
2. To teach us stage terms and activities.
3. To practice good manners.
4. To show us a good way to spend leisure time.
5. To train us to be good club men and women.
6. To help us live together.

Article III

Membership

Persons desiring membership in this club should be in sympathy with the purpose of our club.

A person must be ten or over before he can join this club.

[1] Adopted by the School Club at South Wales, N. Y.   Dorethea T. Weeks, Teacher; W. R. Buell, District Superintendent of Schools.

Article IV

Officers

The officers of this club shall be President, Vice-President, Secretary, Treasurer and Sergeant-at-arms.

Article V

Meetings and Quorum

Section 1. Regular meetings of this club shall be held every Monday and Wednesday after school.

Section 2. Elections shall be held at the first regular meeting in the fall and the first regular meeting held after the mid-term examinations.

Section 3. Special meetings may be called by the president, or on special application of several members, the president shall call such meetings.

Section 4. Seven members of the association in good standing shall constitute a quorum for the transaction of business.

Article VI

This Constitution may be amended at any meeting of the organization by a two-thirds vote, a quorum being present.

By-Laws

Article I

Section I. It shall be the duty of the President to preside at all meetings of the club and perform all the duties of president, usually pertaining to that office.

Section II. In the absence or disability of the President, the Vice-President shall perform all the duties of President.

Section III. The Secretary shall keep the minutes of all proceedings and record the same. He shall keep notice of all meetings, notify officers, and perform such other duties as his office may require.

Section IV. The Sergeant-at-arms shall be responsible for the conduct of members at all meetings and shall submit the names of any people whose behavior is not as it should be to the Constitution Committee for judgment. He shall also give and receive the password and membership cards. He shall ascertain whether the member knows the Gargoyle Clap.

Section V. The Treasurer must be trusted and will be responsible for the collection and safe keeping of any money voted to be collected and the regular dues of one cent a week.

Article II

Election of Officers

Section I. Officers shall not be elected by ballot, but by the raising of hands after the candidate has withdrawn so that he can not see the vote.

Section II. Elections shall be held in the fall and after the mid-semester examinations.

Section III. Should an officer resign during the club year, the President shall appoint some member of the club to assume the office temporarily, and order the Secretary to send notice of a special election at the next regular meeting, when the vacancy can be filled.   An officer cannot resign without giving a good reason for his or her resigning. (A person resigning an office must hand a written resignation to the President.)

Article III

Membership

Section I.   To be a member of the Gargoyle Club one must be a pupil in the fifth, sixth, seventh and eighth grades of the South Wales School, Aurora No. 8.

Section II.   Members may be suspended or asked to drop the club for disorderly conduct or gross misdemeanor. Such action is taken by the Constitution Committee with the Sergeant-at-arms acting as chairman.

Section III. Any member absenting himself from three consecutive club meetings without reasonable excuse, will be dropped from the club and will forfeit the rights and privileges given to members.

Section IV. Persons desiring to join the club must apply for membership to the President, and receive some kind of appropriate initiation before coming into the regular meeting.

Section V. Only members in good standing in the club shall be eligible for office, committees, and parts in plays.

Article IV

Dues

Section I. Each member shall pay one cent a week to help buy materials for the club.

Article V

Committees

Section I. There shall be eight regular committees: constitution, school improvement, refreshment, ensignia, fun, program, initiation and clean-up.

Section II. The President shall be empowered to appoint such special committees as he thinks necessary at any time, for any occasion.

Article VI

Parliamentary Authority

Robert's *Rules of Order* shall be used to decide all questions of Parliamentary Procedure.

APPENDIX C

FORM FOR AUTOBIOGRAPHY [1]

MY AUTOBIOGRAPHY

I. *First Facts about Myself:*

My name is: last name...............middle name.......
first name..... My address is................ I was born in
the year.......on the......day of.............at..........
I live in open country, village, town (*underscore*). This has been
my home for.............years. Besides my birthplace, I have
lived in these places: .... My family
lived in................for............before I was born.
I have visited these places...........................

II. *My Family:*

My father's name is.............. He is.......years old. My
father's name was................. He was.........years old.
He died.......years ago. He was born in........... He has
lived here.........years. He completed............grades in
the elementary school; ....years in high school; ....
.....years in college; ....years in..... His present
occupation is..................... He has also been a......
He attends the............church of which he is (is not) a
member.

My mother's maiden name was................. She is
........years old. She died.........years ago. She was
.......years old. She was born in..............., and she
also lived in or near.............before I was born. She completed..............grades in the elementary school;........
years in high school; ....years in college; .....years in

[1] Gooch, Wilbur I. and Keller, Franklin J. "Breathitt County in the Southern
Appalachians," *Occupations, The Vocational Guidance Magazine,* Vol. XIV, No.
9 (June 1936), Sec. Two, pp. 1024–25.

.... Her occupation before her marriage was..............
Since marriage, besides the usual homemaking, she has also done
.... She attends the.............church of
which she is (is not) a member.

I have.........brothers and........sisters. I am giving
these facts about those who have left school: Name............
......, age......., grade reached............., occupation
............, living in city, town, or country...............
Married?.......... These are now in school or college: name
of school..................., name..................., age
........, grade........... These have not yet entered: name
..................., age........ Others living in our home
are...

III. *Our Home:*

We own (do not own) the home in which we live   We own (rent)
...........acres of land. The chief crops on our farm are
.... We have........car(s), ...
......truck(s), ...head of stock. I am allowed to
drive the......... I live a distance of.............from
school and reach it by.................... Our home is of
brick; frame, painted; frame, unpainted; logs. It is heated by
................and lighted by................ We have
running water. We get water from a.................. We
have........rooms. These include a (no) living-room, a (no)
bathroom, and...........bedrooms. I sleep alone, or with
.... We have the following conveniences in our home:
washing, ironing, sewing machines; outside help in cleaning,
cooking, washing, ironing, nursing (*underscore*). We have about
............books in our home. We take these magazines and
papers: .... We have these musical
instruments in our home: ....
Home duties: My regular duties each day or week, at home are
.... My occasional
duties are...

IV. *My Education Thus Far and Plans for More:*

I was............years old when I started to school. I attended
(did not attend) kindergarten. I began in the........grade

and I have repeated the................grades and skipped the
.................grades. I have attended the following schools:
(*Give name and location of schools. If doubtful give what you
think with question mark in front*)............................
We had........teachers. I attended......months. I
finished............... The grades were............ As a
rule I spend.......hours at home studying my lessons. I should
like to stay in school through the.....grade, and then take
........years in................ I am planning to stay in
school through the............grade, and then take.........
years in.............. My parents would like me to stay in
school through the............grade, and then take..........
years in..................... I have earned money in these
ways: kind of work..............; I earned about...........;
the date of this was.......................................

V. *What I Like—My Interests:*

When I have time of my own these are the things I like to do:
....
I like best these kinds of readings: ....
The studies I like best are these: ....

VI. *My Future Occupation—Occupational Preferences:*

The occupations in which I am somewhat interested for myself,
are: first choice...................., second choice..........,
third choice.................... The education needed for
each choice (report for each choice) takes............high
school years, ...college years, ...business or
professional training years. My father would like me to be a
.... My mother would like me to be a
....

VII. *Group Contacts:*

I have belonged or do belong to these clubs, teams, or societies:
name of club.............., years.........., number in group
......., office held............ I attend..................
church of the....................denomination regularly (irregularly) every.......and Sunday School regularly (irregularly)
every.............. I am (am not) a member. Our church is
..........miles from home. I do (do not) belong to the young

people's society of the church. I attend it regularly (irregularly). I take part in it by............... When I finish school, I should like to live in the country (a town) (a city) because

....

MY AUTOBIOGRAPHY[1]

Name...................... *Date*......................

1. Facts about myself
   My name is..............................
   My postoffice address is..........................
   I am...........years old.
   I was born at.................................
                          (give the place)
   I have lived in the following places:
   ....
   ....
   ....
   ....

   My family lived in........for.........years before I was born.
                       (place)
   I have visited the following places of interest:
   ....
   ....
   ....
   ....
   ....

   I have.........brothers and.........sisters.
   (Give names and information about your brothers and sisters)

NAME	AGE	GRADE REACHED	OCCUPA- TION	WHERE LIVING
....	....	....	....	....
....	....	....	....	....
....	....	....	....	....

[1] Compiled by the Coöperating Rural Critics of the State Teachers College at Buffalo, W. R. Buell, District Superintendent of Schools, Chairman.

Others living in our home are: (Give names, relationship and occupation) . . . .

. . . .

. . . .

. . . .

Names of children . . . .

(To be obtained BY THE TEACHER in conference with pupil)

2. Family data   Date. . . . .

Father's name. . . . .

Father's age. . . . .

*(Father's name was. . . . .

*(Father was. . . . . years old)

*(Father died. . . . . . . years ago)

Father was born in. . . . .

(Place)

Father lived here. . . . . years.

Father has completed. . . . . . . grades in the elementary school

. . . . years in High School

. . . . years in College

. . . . years in . . . .

Vocational School, Army, Navy, etc.

Father's present occupation is. . . . .

Father has also been a . . . .

Mother's name is. . . . .

Mother is. . . . . years old

*(Mother died. . . . . . . years ago)

*(Mother was. . . . . . . years old)

Mother was born in. . . . .

(place)

Mother has completed. . . . . . . grades in the elementary school

. . . . years in the High School

. . . . years in College

. . . . years in. . . . .

(Nurse, etc.)

Mother's occupation before marriage was. . . . .

Since marriage, besides usual homemaking, she has also done.

* To be filled out if parent dead, divorced. If "boarding child" record data on reverse side.

....

To what extent do parents coöperate.....................

3. Our home

We own (do not own) the home in which we live.

We own (rent)........acres of land.

The chief crops on our farm are:

....
....

We have....cars,....trucks,......head of stock.

I am allowed to drive the................................

I live......miles from school and reach it by..............

My house is heated by........and lighted by ....

We have (do not have) running water. We get our water from a....................

We have....rooms. These include: a (no) living room
                                  a (no) bathroom
                                  ......bedrooms

I sleep alone, or with......................

We have about......books.

We take these magazines and papers....................
....

We have (do not have) a radio and the following musical instruments:

....

Home duties:

My regular home duties each day or week are:

....
....
....
....

My occasional duties are:

....
....
....

4. My Education

I was......years old when I started school.

I attended (did not) kindergarten.

I began in the......grade.

I have repeated the........grades.
I have skipped the ....grades.
I have attended the following schools:

....

....

....

I would like to attend....years in High School in......course.
....years in College in.........course.
My parents would like me to................................
(leave   school,   complete   H.S.,
attend college)

5. What I like—My Interests:
When I have time of my own these are the things I like to do:

....

....

....

I like best the stories about:

....

....

....

The studies I like best are these:

....

....

....

My favorite radio program is............................
My favorite section of the newspaper is............ ....
I go to the movies....times a year, month (check one)
The pictures I have liked are:....... ....

....

Things I can do: play musical instrument dance sew   cook
write stories   handwork   sing   draw paint   garden
write poetry   skate   print   read carve   weave
build   play games   block print   act in plays

6. My future occupation—occupational preference
The occupations in which I am somewhat interested for
myself are:
First Choice...................................
Second Choice..................................

Third Choice...

When I finish school I should like to live in the country, town or city (cross out two) because:

....

....

....

7. Group Contacts

I have belonged or do belong to these teams, clubs or societies:

NAME OF CLUB	Years I have Belonged	Number in Group	Office Held
....	....	....	....
....	....	....	....
....	....	....	....
....	....	....	....

ILLUSTRATION OF CUMULATIVE SCHOLASTIC RECORD[1]

Name of Pupil....................... Date of Birth............

Year During Which Pupil Is in School

No. of pupils in class
Subject
Reading
Writing
Arithmetic
Geography
History
Spelling   (Use vertical rules
English   to indicate years)
French
German
Latin
Algebra
Geometry
Civics
History

[1] Strang, Ruth. *Every Teacher's Records.* p. 16. Bureau of Publications, Teachers College, Columbia University, 1936.

Home Economics
Shop
Typewriting
Stenography, etc.
Deportment
Effort
Citizenship
General Average
Standarized Intelligence
    and Achievement Tests

CARD REPORTING PUPIL PROGRESS[1]

MARION COUNTY, MO.
RURAL SCHOOLS
PUPIL'S RATING CARD

For the.......Quarter
1936–1937

Pupil..
    Grade.................... Age...............
Days present......... Days absent......... Times tardy......
This report is not designed for the purpose of comparing the pupil
with others of his class, but to inform parents as to whether or not he
is making satisfactory progress in his all round development.

SYSTEM OF MARKING

Habits needing improvements are marked......................(–)
Habits being satisfactorily developed are marked...............(+)
Items not marked do not figure in this report

Education is Teaching People to Live
Together

[1] Report Cards of Pupil Progress Recently Constructed for Elementary
Grades.   Circular Number 169.   Office of Education, United States Dept. of
Interior, 1936.

CHARACTER TRAITS

1. Is friendly, kind and courteous.........................
2. Is agreeable and coöperative.........................
3. Is truthful and dependable...........................
4. Is industrious.......................................
5. Has a keen sense of right and wrong ....
6. Has pride and is modest..............................
7. Is neat and orderly..................................
8. Is punctual in all duties............................
9. Depends on self.............. ....
10. Is a good school citizen.............................

READING

1. Likes to read.......................................
2. Masters the reading vocabulary.......................
3. Interested in correct pronunciation of words..........
4. Studies properly and holds book correctly.............
5. Reads orally so listeners enjoy it....................
6. Can read silently for meaning........................
7. Uses the dictionary..................................
8. Is up to the grade standard..........................
9. Shows improvement in reading ability..................
10. Requires special help...............................

Remarks:_____

_____

WRITING

1. Interested and strives to improve.....................
2. Forming habits of correct position....................
3. Holds pen or pencil properly.........................
4. Improving in neatness, legibility and speed ....
5. Up to grade level....................................

Remarks:_____

_____

ARITHMETIC

1. Interested in the subject.................................
2. Mastering the number combinations......................
3. Accurate in figuring....................................
4. Does neat work...
5. Can figure with reasonable speed.......................
6. Can read and understand problems......................
7. Reasons well in solving problems.......................
8. Can explain problems clearly...........................
9. Shows ability expected of his group.....................
10. Requires special help...................................

Remarks:_____

_____

LANGUAGE

1. Speaks clearly in a pleasant voice.......................
2. Interested in building a vocabulary......................
3. Studies the dictionary..................................
4. Can retell stories well..................................
5. Shows interest in writing...............................
6. Strives to correct common speech errors.................
7. Making satisfactory progress............................
8. Requires special help...................................

Remarks:_____

_____

SPELLING

1. Masters the assigned lessons............................
2. Spells well in all written work.........................
3. Uses dictionary to check spelling.......................
4. Making satisfactory progress............................
5. Requires special help...................................

Remarks:_____

_____

SOCIAL STUDIES
(History, Geography, Civics)

1. Shows ability expected of this grade in history . . . .
2. Shows ability expected of this grade in geography . . . .
3. Shows ability expected of this grade in civics . . . .

Remarks:_____

_____

HEALTH

1. Observes health rules . . . .
2. Acquiring habits of good posture and carriage . . . .

Remarks:_____

_____

MUSIC

1. Learning to appreciate good music . . . .
2. Has musical ability . . . .

Remarks:_____

_____

ART

1. Recognizes beauty in the world about him . . . .
2. Shows ability in art expression . . . .

Remarks:_____

_____

. . . . .Teacher

Parents, you are cordially invited to confer
with the teacher on any matters
pertaining to your child's progress
and welfare.

PROMOTION

This certifies that.....................................
has this day been promoted from grade.......to grade ....
.......................Teacher

E. C. Boxon, Superintendent

INDIVIDUAL RECORD FOR THE STUDY OF PUPILS' PROBLEMS [1]

THIRD SUPERVISORY DISTRICT, LEWIS COUNTY

(These records are used by the teachers and the superintendent.)

Name of pupil............... Age..... Grade...... School...... Teacher......
Note to the teacher: Check the items that apply and write in information where necessary. Use *pencil* not pen.

I. THE CHILD

1. *Physical status and characteristics*

General

Size: large for age.... average.... small....
Health: generally good.... generally poor.... varies....
Energy: active and vigorous.... inactive or lethargic .... varies....

Specific

Hearing: normal.... defective....
Vision: good.... poor.... needs glasses....
Tonsils: normal.... diseased.... removed....
Adenoids: normal.... diseased.... removed....
Teeth: good condition.... need attention....

Nutrition: normal.... underweight.... overweight ....
Speech: normal.... defective....
Skin: clear.... blotched or pimpled....
Posture: erect.... stooped....
Bodily movements: average.... quick.... graceful.... slow.... awkward....
Deformities: crippled.... How?....
Other deformities:............................

2. *Mental and emotional traits and characteristics*

I. Q. (if mental test has been given)....
Mentally alert.... sluggish....
Quick to respond.... slow....

[1] University of the State of New York, State Education Department. *Handbook for Rural Elementary Schools*, Bulletin Number 3, p. 90, University of the State of New York Press, 1936.

Consistent... erratic....
Superior ability... average... inferior....
Expresses himself well... poorly....
Memory good... faulty....
Vocabulary strong... weak....
Emotionally stable... unstable.... hysterical at times....
"Conquering hero" type.... "suffering hero" type....

3. General traits and characteristics

This child may be classified as:
attractive... unattractive... average....
bold... shy... average....
confident... timid... average....
courageous... cowardly... average....
careful... careless or destructive... average....
energetic or industrious... lazy... average....
governable... willful... average....
honest... dishonest... average....
obedient... disobedient... average....
poised... excitable or impulsive... average....

consistent... erratic... average....
appreciative... unappreciative... average....
serious... frivolous... average....
meek... domineering... average....
coöperative... noncoöperative... average....
social-minded... seclusive... average....
friendly... quarrelsome... average....
resourceful... helpless... average....
interested... indifferent... average....
truthful... untruthful... average....
respectful... disrespectful... average....
tractable... sulky... average....
mind of own... easily influenced... average....
normal sex attitude... abnormal... average....
high tempered... pouty... silly....

4. Special abilities

Musical... artistic... eloquent... mechanical ...dramatic... social... leadership....
Mention other special abilities: ....
....
....

II. The Child and the Home

Parents: Father (if living): age.......... nationality............ birthplace (country or state)............
occupation................. amount of schooling (grade completed or graduate of what)............

INDIVIDUAL RECORD FOR THE STUDY OF PUPILS' PROBLEMS—*(Continued)*

Mother (if living): age.......... nationality.......... birthplace (country or state)..........
occupation.......... amount of schooling (grade completed or graduate of what)..........
Brothers (living) number older.... number younger.... Sisters (living) number older.... number younger....
Family classified as: well-educated.... well-read, but lack formal schooling.... uneducated or illiterate.... cultured
.... semicultured.... uncultured.... very thrifty.... thrifty.... shiftless.... religious.... indifferent....
irreligious.... coöperative.... noncoöperative.... wealthy.... well-to-do.... self-supporting.... poverty-
stricken.... socially prominent.... average social status.... low social level.... permanent residents in community.... temporary residents.... move about a great deal....

Home Conditions

Father separated from family.... home occasionally.... not living.... Mother separated from family.... not living
....

Child has foster father.... foster mother....
Both parents work away from home....

Neighborhood: good.... medium.... bad....

Discipline of child: reasonable.... lax.... harsh....

Home responsibilities or duties of child: none.... few and light.... numerous and burdensome.... interfere with
school work....
Conditions for home study: good.... average.... poor.... impossible....

Health of father: good.... poor....
Health of mother: good.... poor....
Moral standards of home: high.... average.... low....
Parental supervision: excellent.... indifferent.... in-
adequate....
Parents agree on methods of supervision and discipline
.... disagree....

The home has suitable for child reading: daily or weekly papers.... magazines.... books....
Child retires during the school week at.... o'clock and arises at.... o'clock
The family is unusually interested in: music.... reading.... athletics.... the theater.... travel.... social activities
(parties, clubs, etc.).... movies.... church.... fraternal orders.... dancing.... high grade entertainment....
low grade entertainment....

III. The Child and the School

Present grade.... Number of years child has been in school including the present year.... What grades has the child
repeated?.... Skipped?.... Number of different teachers the child has had (in elementary grades only)....
Number of different schools the child has attended.... Days absent last year: on account of illness.... for other
reasons.... Achievement: good.... average.... poor.... Subject child does best in.... poorest....
Study habits: desirable.... undesirable.... Attitude toward school: interested.... disinterested.... attentive in
class.... inattentive.... coöperative.... noncoöperative....
Wants to continue schooling.... wants to drop out as soon as possible....
Interests and hobbies: music.... reading.... athletics.... collecting.... mechanics.... ownership and care of
animals.... Mention any specific interest or hobby ....
Apparent weakness or difficulties: None.... 1 Lacks ability to do regular school work.... 2 Lacks ability to make
progress in certain subjects.... What subjects? .... 3 Handicapped by poor health....
4 Home conditions unfavorable.... 5 Overage for grade and discouraged.... 6 Has language handicap.... 7 Feels
socially inferior to other children.... 8 Overconfident of abilities.... 9 Outside interests interfere with school
work.... 10 Wants to go to work.... 11 Receives no encouragement at home.... 12 Standards of work are too
low.... 13 Wastes time either in idleness or frivolous activities.... 14 Unable to concentrate on the work at hand.
.... 15 Does not apply himself (herself).... 16 Has perverted sex habits.... 17 Uses obscene language....
Comments: ....
....

501

FORM USED BY TEACHERS IN RECORDING INVESTIGATIONS [1]

Child's name...................................

SOCIAL PROBLEMS

Date of report......... Person reporting......................

Nature of report:

History of investigation:

Conclusions:

Recommendations:

Later reports: (Nature of case should determine frequency and number of checkings)

NARRATIVE REPORT OF INDIVIDUAL CHILDREN USED IN THE FOURTH SUPERVISORY DISTRICT, DELAWARE COUNTY [2]

Name of pupil..
Name of teacher..

September and October

————has had perfect attendance for September and October. She has been a good girl. She has read 78 pages in Peter and Peggy Primer and done 50 pages in her workbook. She can make the figures to 50. She can count to 100 by 1's, 5's and 10's. She can count by 2's to 20. She can spell 10 words which she has learned by herself with no help from me. [Here the words were listed for the parent.] She prints very well. She will not recite the poems we learn in school.

[*Signed by parent*]......................................

[1] *Ibid.* p. 93.
[2] *Ibid.* p. 86.

November and December

_____has had perfect attendance since school began. She has not been tardy. She is improving in her speed. In reading she has finished Peter and Peggy Primer. Read Fact and Story Primer, the F-U-N Book by LaRue, and Kitten Kat by Dearborn. Finished workbook. In number work, she is learning addition combinations. She needs more help on:

$$
\begin{array}{ccccc}
6 & 8 & 3 & 7 & 7 \\
7 & 5 & 5 & 8 & 6 \\
\hline
\end{array}
$$

She has done 114 pages in her workbook. She can spell 15 words now. [Here the words were listed.] In English she has written a letter to Santa Claus, sentences about pictures, copied short stories from the board, learned poems. In health she has improved in keeping her hands and face clean while eating and after. She keeps her desk and floor neater. She does not put her pencil in her mouth as much. She usually has a handkerchief. She has not been out of school with a cold. She plays out of doors nearly every day. She has recited one poem for the group. She enjoyed doing this.

PROGRESS CHART USED IN MENANDS SCHOOL, THIRD SUPERVISORY DISTRICT, ALBANY COUNTY [1]

Growth in Attitudes and Habits

Listens when others talk. . . . .

Answers when spoken to. . . . .

Works quietly. . . . .

Takes turns

    a On the playground. . . . .

    b With work materials. . . . .

Is a good winner. . . . .

Is a good loser. . . . .

Accepts corrections without sulking . . . .

Controls temper. . . . .

Meets and leaves others politely. . .

Asks favors politely. . . . .

* Makes things for sake of making them. . . . .

Makes things for use. . . . .

Wishes to improve quality of work. . . . .

* Asks questions to get attention . . . .

Asks questions to get information . . . .

Makes thoughtful suggestions

    a For individual work and play . . . .

    b For group work and play. . .

[1] *Ibid.* p. 87.

Is polite in passing and disturbing others....................

* Does his share in helping around room when reminded..........

Does his share in helping around room without being reminded...

Does his share in helping around room to best of his ability......

Keeps own locker in order........

Keeps wraps in order............

Comes to school on time.........

Puts on and takes off wraps without loss of time..............

Finds work materials readily.....

Is a leader....................

Is a follower...................

Takes initiative in expressing self through work materials........

Takes initiative in making personal contacts...............

Plans work...................

Asks for needed help...........

Asks for help only when needed ....

Follows simple individual directions.....................

Follows simple group directions..

Keeps hands and materials away from mouth................

Sits and stands in good position ....

Is clean in person..............

Is free from fear...............

Relaxes during rest period......

Is independent of teacher......

Is independent of other children ....

Is eager to work...............

Works steadily................

Is willing to play vigorously....

Makes good use of time........

A check after any item except the ones starred (*) indicates that we believe that that particular item of behavior is as satisfactorily and consistently shown as can be expected of a child of this age. Each item starred (*) is only an intermediate stage and should be disregarded when the item next below it in the same column is checked.

Below this report there is space for comments from the teacher and comments from the parent.

APPENDIX D

SUGGESTED PROCEDURE FOR ORGANIZATION AND ADMINISTRATION OF THE LIBRARY IN CLASSROOMS AND IN SMALL RURAL SCHOOLS[1]

1 Sort books as to value.
   a Useful
   b Not useful
      To determine use consider (1) the interests and reading ability of the children in the school, (2) curricular needs, (3) the subject matter, authority, treatment, copyright date and physical make-up of each book.
2 Sort useful books as to condition.
   a Good condition
   b Suitable for mending (to be set aside for mending when time permits)
   c Suitable for rebinding (to be set aside for sending away to a bindery)
   d Worn or soiled
3 Discard books.
   a Set aside for discarding.
      (1) The books which are not useful
      (2) The books worn and soiled beyond repair
   b Make entry in accession record (and other records) to indicate that these books are being discarded.
   c Decide what to do with discards. For example, some may be useful in a public or reference library; others may be taken apart for separate pictures, poems or stories.
4 Prepare books for shelves.
   a Open new books.
   b Stamp, write or insert the marks of school ownership inside the front cover.

[1] *Ibid*. p. 50.

505

    c Accession new books and find out whether the accession record is complete and accurate.

      (1) Enter author's name (surname first), title, publisher, date and price of each book in the accession record.

      (2) Write the accession number in the book at the foot of the first right-hand page following the title page.

    d Classify each book by subject.

      (1) Write the subject heading in the book at the top of the first right-hand page following the title page and inside the back cover at the upper right corner.

      (2) Teach pupils to match the subject heading written inside the back cover of a book with the subject heading on the shelf label.

    e Provide a charging system by

      (1) Pasting "date due" slips on end sheets opposite back covers

      (2) Writing book cards, either deposit station cards or individual book cards

        Author's name (surname first), title, accession number and subject heading should be included.

        If individual book cards are used, paste book pockets inside of back covers of books.

    f Wash soiled books, remove labels etc.

    g Shellac book covers.

5 Arrange books on shelves.

    a Arrange books

      (1) By subject

      (2) Under subject arrange alphabetically by authors' names (surname first), (books of biography form an exception in that they are arranged according to the person written about rather than by author)

    b Shelve books as arranged.

      (1) Use shelf labels. Shelf labels are narrow strips of lightweight cardboard on which the subject heading is written or printed. They are attached to the shelves with thumb tacks or by means of shelf label holders and are used as guides in finding books as well as aids in shelving books.

      (2) Use book ends to keep books standing straight, with backs plumb with the edges of the shelves.

6 Consider book needs.

  a Keep on cards a list of needs for particular books or for material which the collection does not supply.

    (1) Use information gained from sorting, discarding and classifying books to make up this "want list."

    (2) Use information gained from noting needs shown when working with children and books.

    (3) Consult notes regarding important, practical and attractive books seen at meetings, library exhibits, etc.

  b Plan so that in the book collection there will be titles for ages, sexes and different degrees of reading ability found in the school and so that there will be that variety of subject matter, point of view and treatment which the pupils' present and potential interests demand.

  c Consult recognized book selection aids.

  d Weigh relative values and uses of

    (1) Individual titles

    (2) Reference works

    (3) Periodicals

7 Administration

  a Ordering books

    (1) Consult "want cards" before making up order. (See preceding section.)

    (2) List books selected for purchase on book approval forms furnished by Education Department through superintendent's office, and send list for approval to district superintendent, who will forward it to Albany.

    (3) When the list is returned with approval for purchase, make a duplicate list and order the approved books.

    (4) When books are received, check them with the duplicate list and with the bill.

  b Preparing books for shelves (see 4 above)

  c Borrowing books. Plan to obtain books from

    (1) Local public library

    (2) Near-by schools and school libraries

    (3) New York State library

    (4) Traveling Libraries Section, Library Extension Division, State Education Department, Albany (A one-teacher school may borrow at least 25 books each year from this division).

  d Lending books

    (1) Advertise and display books so that children will wish to read

(2) When charging a book to a child, write (1) borrower's name and date due on deposit station card or on book card, and (2) date due on date due slip.

(3) Keep a circulation record and note which books are most popular with children, also which children are reading.

(4) When book is returned, discharge it, by checking deposit station card or returning book card to book pocket.

(5) Return it to proper place on shelf.

Housekeeping to keep library or library corner clean, orderly and attractively arranged.

8 Provide opportunity for

  a Reference lessons when needed

  b Reading guidance and stimulation

  c Reading for information

  d Reading for recreation

APPENDIX E

SUGGESTIONS FOR THE SUBSTITUTION OF INEXPENSIVE FOR EXPENSIVE MATERIALS [1]

ART

FINE ARTS

Art easel for painting: Large piece of cardboard folded makes an easel.

Card board box, remove two sides or two opposite ends, clamp top of remaining sides together and set on desk or table or box for easel.

Four boards, two pair hinges, two pieces beaver board, twelve screws, one piece of cardboard are sufficient for a homemade easel.

Colors: Talens Company easel paints.

Alabastine (washable paint in powder form), calcimine, and hot water soaked with one part glue to sixteen parts water.

Tea, coffee, onion skin, beet juice, walnut juice, berry juice, dye, bluing, crepe paper soaked in water substitute for show card colors.

Short crayon pieces substitute for long crayon in flat work.

Stiff feathers, stick to which cloth or cotton batting is tied, or the bare hand, with thick paint, may be used for paint brushes.

Can covers or a jelly glass substitutes for watercolor dish or dish for mixing paints.

Tin cigarette box substitutes for a crayon box.

Fine paper for silhouettes, designs, window transparencies, or cards: Tissue paper, crepe paper, tinfoil, cellophane, birch bark, wrappers from Kodak films, lining from greeting card envelopes.

Paper for painting: Large size paper from unprinted newspaper which may be obtained from newspaper offices or print shops.

---

[1] The compilation is the result of the work of many people. Gathered item by item from many sources each succeeding class in the author's course in *Rural Education* has added its bit to the growing list. In the summer of 1937 Misses LaMar Johnson and Marie Hofman organized the items, gave them unity and presented the result of their work to the author to be used as she wished. She is pleased to add it to the appendix of this book.

Large rolls of commercial paper, such as stores use for wrapping paper.

Back of unused wall paper.

Card board, such as, suit boxes, hat boxes, cracker boxes, tablet backs, carton fillers.

Paste: Two cups flour, two cups water, one tablespoon powdered alum, ten to twenty drops oil of cloves. Mix until smooth, add a cup of boiling water. Cook in double boiler until thick. Add oil of cloves. Strain into small jar.

Ointment jars and cold cream jars substitute for paint jars.

Pictures: Posters made with green or brown oatmeal paper for background. Paste child or animal pictures on background.

Make several frames 42″ × 19″ or of any uniform size. Change pictures within each frame monthly.

Paintings from magazine covers. Save from year to year.

Pictures painted by members of class. Use unprinted newspaper to secure large, free work expressive of child.

Prints mounted on construction paper.

Print of art work with glass front and card board back secured by paper.

Silhouettes with crumpled tinfoil for background.

Wall silhouettes of black or colored enamel.

INDUSTRIAL ARTS

An African hut outdoors. Use cornstalks and make it life size.

Balsam ends may be plucked for pillows or cushions.

Boats may be made from wooden plates, butter trays, and milkweed pods.

Book and booklet covers may be made from pieces of cloth, wrapping paper, wallpaper or sample books, rolls of wallpaper, card board from boxes. Paste on design.

Christmas Tree Ornaments

Save tinfoil tea wrappers, cut in circles of uniform size and string by spacing double (so both ends of it show the tinfoil at intervals).

Cut animals from red paper and string at 6″ intervals or alternate animals and tinfoil.

Cover bottletops with silver paint or paper, inserting a cord for hanging.

Make red paper chains.

Paint cattails or milkweeds with aluminum paint.

Cover the shells of tiny walnuts (halves) with tinfoil and paste or tie together inserting a cord for hanging or paint with aluminum paint.

Place pine cones in oven until they spread apart, then spray or paint with aluminum paint (mixed in powder form)

String popcorn.

Materials for designs may be worked out with berries, dyed corn, dogwood berries, rose hips, buckeyes, walnut hulls, seeds and leaves previously colored. These may be used for chain materials also.

Beads may be made from short pieces of wax crayon melted, small pieces of paraffine and spools of various sizes, macaroni.

Clay: Use ordinary soil clay, modeling clay, pulverized chalk tinted and mixed with a little vaseline.

Handicraft Straw: Birch bark, honeysuckle vines, grapevines, grasses, trimmings from fruit trees, willows, corn husks, hickory splits, ravelled yarn, swamp grasses, rags torn in strips, straw (wheat preferred) scraps of twine, string binder twine, strips of old dresses, hose sheets or knitted underwear may be used in baskets, mats and woven rugs.

Hooked rugs: may be made from burlap and ravellings. Strips of old dresses and burlap foundation may also be used.

Indian: Feathers from poultry may be used for decorations, head dress designs.

Make a life size wigwam or tepee outdoors using poles and burlap.

Old inner tubes may be used for many things. A tin can covered with a piece of inner tube makes a fine tom-tom.

Kites: may be made from flour sacks.

Linoleum may be carved with a safety razor blade.

Masks may be made from brown paper bags.

May baskets may be made from cereal boxes.

Nails: Flatten and file pointed ends to various shapes. Can be used for clay modeling, soap carving and leather tooling.

Pieces of flannel or felt become pen wipers.

Take a *plaster of Paris* imprint of animal or bird tracks, use as a mold, and make designs for bookends, etc. (See Cornell leaflet for details)

Portfolios may be made from wax-paper folders.

Sand table scenes: Fruit, vegetables, match sticks, cloves, etc. may be used as animal figures for the sand table.

Carved soap (Ivory) figures, wooden or celluloid toy imitations and figures made from clay may be used for animals.

Milk bottle tops or spools become the wheels to a wagon, train, cart, etc.

Cotton sprinkled with snow; such as, isinglass used under Christmas trees, or card board covered with wet salt and sprinkled with artificial snow may represent snow.

Tissue paper may be crumpled and dipped into paraffin to make icebergs.

Butter pipe may become a canal.

Half a grapefruit makes the foundation for an igloo.

Corks may be used to make floats and water toys.

A mirror in the bottom of a sand table looks like water.

Colored excelsior or straw represents grass.

Sawdust: May be used for stuffing cloth animals, bean bags, etc.

May be used in place of sand in the sand table.

Store: Construct from canned goods boxes.

Use emptied packages, fruit and articles made by the children ("for sale").

Cut price tags from card board and paste on figures from calendar.

Make paper money or use milk bottle tops.

Tin cans: May be flattened out and used for metal work.

Bird houses may be made from them.

Weaving: For the loom use an old picture frame with nails at uniform intervals to hold the warp or woof.

Card board with pins or cuts.

An old slate frame.

A homemade frame.

Use rags cut in strips of uniform size, stockings, yarn unravelled from old sweaters, mittens or socks, and colored twine and string.

Cotton and flax from the field, wool from the sheep's back may be used for cording, spinning, and weaving.

Drive nails in a short board to make a carder.

BUILDING MATERIALS

Roofing, tile, shingles, fireplaces, hollow tiles, plaster board, beaverboard, and scraps have many uses in illustrative work and play.

Crates, boxes, sawmill scraps provide material for building.

Orange crates and tin cans are always valuable.

FURNITURE AND FIXTURES

Adjustable seat: Box to be placed under the feet, board placed under desk.

Bookcases, book racks, dish cupboards, shelves, lunch counters, individual lockers: Orange and apple crates piled up neatly and decorated. Wooden boxes from grocer, wooden packing boxes, piano boxes, etc.

Bulletin board and display wires: Wire stretched under blackboard, above blackboard or along wall. Plaster board or beaver board, painted a dull color, preferred.

Newspaper tacked to a board and covered with burlap. Frame with strips of flat molding.

Cement bird baths, flower boxes, aquariums, bookends, sun-dial, etc. may be made by constructing a wooden frame and pouring in the cement.

Doormat: Braided rug of corn husks, woven or braided strips from burlap.

Folding screen: Home made screen of three or four panels, 65″ × 25″, made of beaverboard or burlap on frames and fastened with double action hinges.

Increased space: Make distinctive use of closets, coat rooms, halls for library, kitchen work room, play corner, or committee room.

Add planks for seats or work bench, tables, shelves, oil stoves, box for dishes, window curtains, etc.

Unscrew stationary desks. Fasten to runners so that they may be moved to one side to make space for indoor play at recess, moved together for tables for noon, moved into circle formation for class reports, etc.

Space may be made in the corner for church bench; library table made of orange crates and small orange crate chairs for the smaller children.

If the church bench is placed with the back to the room, it serves to isolate the play corner.

Screens may be made from sheets of wall board hinged together. Support these on a plank on which are nailed two strips of wood into which the fitted strips of wall board go.

Erect bookcases about ten feet from the end wall, but low enough so that the teacher may see over them. These may be double with book shelves or cupboard space on both sides, and really make possible a workroom under the teacher's supervision while she remains in the classroom, without any alteration to the building.

For cupboard space, use wooden boxes, hopechests which can serve as both window seats or benches and as boxes for supplies, boxes stowed away under tables or sand boxes when not in use, and orange boxes in tiers.

Window sills may be used for library book displays and exhibits.

Movable desks: Old stationary desks, unscrewed from floor and screwed to one-half inch board runners in pairs. Cover disfigured desks with individual blotters.

Mudscraper: Block of wood nailed to side of steps.

Waste basket or storage basket: Peach basket, bushel basket, tin can.

Window shades: Heavy wrapping paper fastened to roller of shade. Dye heavy packing twine a gay color, fold bottom of shade about a piece of lathe, and punch a hole for curtain pull. Put ring in end for finger.

Work tables, work benches, chairs, drop leaf tables, recitation chairs: Wide board supported by double-hinged, elbow-jointed brace to permit dropping shelf table when not in use.

Small keg, barrel, potato crate with wall seat and back, or stout orange crate without top as chairs.

Vases, flower pots, bowls: Mayonnaise jars, tin cans may be enameled or lacquered or decorated by pasting small three cornered pieces from bright envelopes in irregular designs and coated with shellac. Cut colored paper to fit jelly glasses or flower pots and paste or draw designs in contrasting color for temporary use.

HEALTH AND CLEANLINESS (*Lunch and Nutrition*)

Cleaning and dusting: Lygnaphol is better than floor oil because it does not rot or deaden the wood. If not available or if floor is poor, equal parts of kerosene and motor oil may be substituted.

A floor mop might be made from oiled cloth. Use underwear for dust cloth.

Folded cardboard becomes a dustpan.

Either cold dry snow or sawdust mixed with a little oil that has been drained from an automobile to which a few drops of antiseptic have been added may be used as a sweeping compound.

Crude oil and vinegar may be used to polish desks.

Coatroom equipment: Homemade coathangers.

Broomstick across corner of room as rod for coathangers to hang on.

Simple trellis or screen to separate place where coats hang from class-room proper.

Orange crate or box for each child (stacked to save space) for rubbers, mittens, and dinnerboxes. These should be at a height most convenient for the respective children. Place name labels on each.

Bags for rubbers may also be used, suspended from coathangers. Use any stout cloth, or hold rubbers together with a spring-type of clothespin.

Cupboard: A drygoods box with a cretonne curtain. Use for dishes. Use tin boxes and cans to store food. Enamel and initial individually.

Cups: Enamel cups are best.

Jelly glasses may be used for individual drinking cups.

Waxed paper may be folded into individual cups.

Dinner boxes: Make from coffee cans. Enamel and initial individually.

Dishwashing: Use sugar bags or flour sacks for dish towels.

Use old underwear for washing and wiping kettles.

Boot or shoe scraper: Worn down floor brush may be used. Nail to edge of step. (Extension Service or U. S. Department of Agriculture for details.)

Flytraps: Homemade wire flytraps. (Send to Cornell University, Department of Agriculture.)

Homemade fireless cooker: Bring food to a boil on the top of a stove, then put in the fireless cooker to complete cooking. You will require (1) a good-sized airtight box or bucket with a tight cover for the outside container, (2) hay, sawdust, or crumpled newspaper packed closely to form a nest for the cooking vessel, (3) a metal or enamel bucket and a sheet of asbestos to cover the bucket. The bucket must have three straight sides and a lid. At top, bottom, and sides there should be three inches of packing material between the inner bucket and the outside cover. (4) a cooking vessel with a tight lid. It should fit article number three closely, yet slip in and out easily. (5) cardboard to make a collar, (6) a cushion of muslin stuffed with packing material and pressed down across the top under the outside lid. (7) two separate soap stone dishes, if possible, as you can cook more quickly and in greater variety with them.

Hot lunch: Each child should bring a small glass jar containing soup or cocoa. Set these on a wire rack in the bottom of a large dishpan, loosen the top of each jar, fill the pan with water so it comes up about an inch around jars, and heat.

Liquid soap: Shavings of soap melted up with water. Or add olive oil to soap.

Milk: Skimmed milk may be used.

Napkins and tablecloths: Use newspaper or oiled cloth or paper napkins. Make mats or enamel small wooden pieces to keep hot dishes off the desks.

Tinted flour sacks, etc. for table covers.

Refrigerator: Homemade window box.

Running water: Five gallon oilcan with spigot in bottom. Granite tea kettle to contain water for drinking purposes.

Rugs: For primary grades to sit on in play corner or during rest period. May be woven or braided from rags.

Soap container: Coffee can with hole punched in top.

Stove: A three burner ("Perfection") oilstove is most satisfactory if gas or electricity is not available. Properly managed it will not smoke or burn food. Potatoes may be baked in a small tin over the top of a coal stove or inside the coal stove on the doorsill. Soup or water may be warmed somewhat on almost any type of stove.

Washbench: Old washstand or bench, orange crate may be used.

Towels kept on homemade wooden towel rack.

Box for small children to stand on.

Mirror at convenient height for children.

A long bench with several wash basins and drawers for individual soap boxes underneath may also be used.

Washing: Save scraps of soap and sew up in a muslin bag for washing.

HEAT AND VENTILATION

Fuel room: Stout box to hold stove wood. Coal bin.

Humidity: Homemade water container inside stove jacket. Tea kettle, basin, or kettle of water on top of stove.

Jacketed stove: Sheet of metal (may be a car door hammered out) bent to make homemade jacket.

Window screen or ventilator: Homemade frame covered with cheese cloth or netting, fine mesh cloth stretched over old screen frame.

Six inch board inserted to deflect fresh air and prevent draught.

LIBRARY CORNER

Library books: Travelling library from the state should be ordered in April for September use. Country, city, and village may have books to lend to teachers and to schools also.

Old books may have stories, words, and pictures which can be mounted or put into attractive cardboard (corrugated) carton or covers and used for supplementary reading by lower grades. Silent reading exercises may be prepared to accompany them.

There is a wealth of reading material, to fit into the work of any grade on almost any subject, to be found in the five and ten cent stores for five or ten cents. No teacher can afford to pass this up.

Library equipment: A filing cabinet for pictures and pamphlets may be made from a large packing box or corrugated cardboard sections cut to fit and the labels are adhesive tape, doubled over and lettered.

A shoe box makes a small file for cards.

Pictures may be obtained from magazines, travel folders and advertisements, Sunday picture sections, postcards, etc.

Bookends may be made of wood, metal or stones. Two alike, well-shaped stones may be painted. Bricks, covered or uncovered, may be used.

Book plates may be made by the children out of plain paper.

A piece of paper 4″ × 4″ pasted at three corners makes a card envelope; while wrapping pages, pictures cut from magazines, and paintings may be made by the teacher.

To repair torn pages, use a small amount of the following paste and cellophane (to which ordinary paste will not adhere) in place of transparent adhesive tape: one gram Knox gelatine, two grams cane sugar, one gram sodia benzoate, twenty-five centimeters water. Stir to prevent burning. Preserve in a cold cream jar and use as required.

Book shelves may be made by placing boards (painted) on bricks. You can vary the size and shape according to need. It is also very convenient as it may be moved around. A second type is made by nailing boards to the wall. This type is not movable. The third type is made from orange crates.

A set of chairs may also be made from orange crates. They may be painted and the seats covered with a strong material.

A few field flowers in an artistically shaped, painted jar add color to the corner.

MUSIC

Piano: Old piano donated by someone in the neighborhood.

Old piano purchased from Good Will Industries (sometimes as low as $5.00)

Rhythm band instruments: Tin cans or covers to hit together for drums.

Hollow box with heavy paper stretched over the top for a drum.

Oatmeal box decorated with Indian designs for tom-tom. Also coffee can covered with rubber tube.

Pan, dishpan, or old boiler for bass drum.

Stick with padded knob for drum stick.

Two small kettle covers for cymbal.

Two embroidery hoops with cloth stretched between them, and with or without bells sewed to the outer hoop, for tambourine.

Bones, seeds or pebbles in a box for a rattle.

Cigar box or other small, hollow, wooden box secured to a stick with bridge and stretcher to hold wire or string taut, for primitive stringed instrument. Cut a small hole in the top.

Harness bells, school bells for chimes.

Bottles of uniform size filled to various heights with water and suspended from a long bar supported by uprights. Strike with a wooden hammer protected with a felt cover.

Homemade xylophone: Strip of wood laid in v shape with cross pieces of metal strips cut to various lengths to give tones of the scale.

Marimba: Homemade.

Triangle: Homemade.

Comb with thin paper folded over it, through which child hums.

Willow whistles of various sizes whittled by the boys. This can be done early in the spring when the bark is loose so that it can be removed and afterward replaced intact.

Songbooks: Paper covered books of community songs. Children copy the words into a notebook, the teacher, only, having a copy of the music.

Melody on blackboard or chart made from wrapping paper and used as in chart prepared for primary reading classes.

Rote songs taught by teacher. If teacher is not musical, she may use a victrola and records for rote singing. If she can play the violin or piano but cannot play well, she may still be able to give simple pattern well enough for children to get it.

Hectographed or mimeographed sheets fastened together.

Victrola: May be given by someone or purchased from the Good Will Industries. Many rhythms may be taught with it.

PLAY MATERIALS (*Playground Equipment*)

Indoor: A *checkerboard* may be made by coloring blocks of paper. Buttons may be used for checkers.

Dolls and doll furniture: Scraps of agar boxes, wood, cardboard, and wallpaper may be used for doll furniture. Crepe paper or wall paper may be used for paper doll dresses. Rags, cornhusks, shoe buttons, cornsilk straw, clothespins, yarn, corks, toothpicks, burnt matches, hairpins, spools, pipe cleaners, sucker sticks, wooden beads, copper wire wrapped in yarn, cloth with stuffing for stocking dolls, rag dolls, etc.

Bean bag: Straws or beans.

Outdoor: In good weather many activities may be carried out by groups out of doors, but within sight of the teacher. The side of the woodshed becomes an easel. The stone wall or stump serves as a seat, table, etc. Indian wigwams, African huts, snow maps of the Antarctic, sand maps, and maps of primitive life are possible.

Balls: Roll strips of rags and cover with stout canvas or leather, making a soft ball for use of lower grades.

Save string and make a ball, covering in same way.

A solid rubber ball may be used as the foundation, if desired.

For bean bags, fill stout cloth with beans.

Baskets: Baskets for basket ball may be made from butterfly nets with the bottom cut out, or from chicken wire fastened around a hoop. Rings of reeds or hoops may also be used. Support with wire as required.

Giant Stride: Erect an upright pole with a wagon wheel at the top from which ropes are suspended. A shorter pole may be used with wagon wheel to make a merry-go-round.

Playground: Use a vacant field. Lay off court with sticks or white lime.

Ring games: Use rings of reed or hoops. Make a hole in a flat heavy board and insert a stick for the upright to catch the rings.

Sandpile for lower grades: Confine the sand in an old box or make a wooden frame without a bottom. This prevents wasting the sand. Bring sand from the lake shore or from a sand pit nearby.

Swing: Secure a stout pole between branches of a tree or between two trees. Use a rope for the seat, or erect poles or planks from which to suspend the swing, according to the same principle used in commercial swings.

Automobile tires make a swing.

Teeter-totter or see-saw: Place a small long log across a short flat log. Place a plank across the log. Nail wooden cleats a foot apart on the under side of a long plank so that the plank will balance.

Tether ball set: A pole, ropes, and bats.

Vaulting and jumping, etc.: Use poles from the woods, a homemade bar, a rope held lightly at desired height by two children, a broom handle, or a clothes line.

Volley ball net: Use canvas or burlap.

Willow whistle: Use willow.

Quoit: Use horsehoes and wooden stakes.

PLAY PRODUCTION

A wooden box may be draped with cloth for a throne.

Costumes may be made from old potato sacks, old bran sacks (Indian costumes with Indian designs painted on with glue plus easel paint), worn sheets, curtains, turkish towels, and old dresses. These may be dyed to make gorgeous costumes or background curtain. Tights may be made from old union suits dyed a dark color.

Folding screens may be used for a background.

Movies, peep shows, shadow plays, puppet shows, etc.: Use corrugated box or wooden box for stage settings. For a movie, use a corrugated box, two pieces of broomstick for rollers, and wrapping paper or unprinted newspaper pasted together for the combined curtains. Films reeled on the rollers. This may be made as elaborate as desired.

Shields: May be made of cardboard or large tin cans.

Wands may be substituted by pointers or yardsticks.

SEATWORK

Arithmetic: Large calendar figures may be pasted on cardboard, used in number card drills, arranged, matched, and combined in various ways.

Berries from dogwood, rose hips, buckeyes, stones, macaroni, and toothpicks may be used for counting and seatwork.

Flash cards may be made from backs of tablets or from backs of advertising cardboards from the local store.

Homemade games and puzzles, anagram cards, and homemade drill cards may be used in many ways.

Spools on a heavy cord may be used to count and add. Also colored
peach stones.

Scraps of lumber may be substituted for blocks for kindergarten and
first grade.

Utilize number games and dominos owned by the children.

Reading and language: Old textbooks may be cut into sections, with
questions about each and put in paper or cardboard folders.

A collection of animal and paper doll forms cut accurately from cardboard. Seatwork directions involving dressing, selection, and tracing
of these may be evolved by the teacher.

Yes and no questions may be matched with "yes" and "no."

Words may be matched to pictures.

Stories may be written about pictures.

SCIENCE AND NATURE STUDY

Aquarium: An aquarium may be made from a galvanized laundry
tub painted with aluminum paint. Better still, use a five or ten
gallon glass water bottle. Make a deep file mark around the top,
place upper part of bottle in the fire, and the top will crack off.
Protect the edge with adhesive tape, and you have a good jar.

Baskets (hanging) and plants: Make hanging baskets for a fern from a
sweet potato or carrot. Scoop out the center of the carrots, or a
turnip, fill the depression with water, and fasten with a string from
the ceiling. This will grow.

Soak a sponge, and sprinkle with grass seed, clover seed, flaxseed, or
oats.

Plant grapefruit, lemon, or orange seed in a small flower pot, after
soaking them in water for a week.

Use a gourd for a vase or bowl.

Birdhouses: The birdhouses should not be bright in color, should not
leak, and should not be draughty or hot. Old weatherbeaten
boards, slabs from the sawmill, stout wooden boxes that will not
warp, or tin cans suitably insulated from the hot sun may be used.

Bouquets: Dip dried weed tops, cattails, or milkweed pods in melted
glue and water, then dust with colored aluminum powder for winter
bouquets.

Feeding tray: Use a large round cheesebox. Look in the Cornell
leaflets for other details about feeding stations.

Insect jars: For insect jars cover a show box or chalk box with wire netting or stretch cheesecloth over the top of a glass jar, keeping it in place with a jar rubber. A glass bottle or can makes a good herbarium.

Labels: Labels may be made from brown paper, pasted on a stick, and then protected by a coat of shellac.

Garden markers may also be made thus.

Sectroscope: Make a sectroscope from a tin can, a light bulb, and a mirror.

Seed tester: Homemade seed-testing trays may be made by marking off spaces on an old oilcloth or on blotting paper and numbering the spaces to correspond with the ears of corn or whatever seeds are to be tested. Cornell leaflets contain directions in full.

Siphon: Use rubber tubing to siphon water from the fish bowl.

Window boxes: To decorate the room, use small cheese boxes for window boxes.

SUBJECT MATTER (*Illustrative Material*)

Aluminum

The Aluminum Cooking Utensil Co. New Kensington, Pa.
1. Samples of crude and refined aluminum.
2. Test materials for conductivity of heat.
3. Booklet—"The Aluminum Age"—describing process and telling about Hall's work.

Aluminum Goods Manufacturing Company. Manitowac, Wisconsin
1. Exhibit—Manufacturing of Aluminum and making one article
2. Booklet—"Aluminum"

Asbestos

Johns-Manville Co. 22 East 40th St., N. Y. City
1. Exhibit—Manufacture of asbestos
2. Booklet—to illustrate processes.

Asphalt

Barber Asphalt Co. Philadelphia, Penna.
1. Booklet—"The Wonderland of Trinidad"

Automobiles

H. Ford Motor Co. Dearborn, Michigan
1. Booklet—Making of a car with pictures to illustrate each step.

Baking Powder

Standard Brands, Inc. New York City
1. Booklet—Behind the Scene with Royal Baking Powder.

Batteries

Electric Storage Battery Co. Allegheny Avenue at 19th Street, Philadelphia, Penna.
1. Excellent chart on a "Storage Battery"
2. Numerous pamphlets

National Carbon Co. 580 Henderson St., Jersey City, New Jersey
1. Exhibit—Sectional cut of a dry cell battery

Birds

Divinell-Wright Co. 311 Summer St., Boston, Mass.
1. Bird booklets—3¢ each

"The Farm Journal," Washington Square, Philadelphia, Pa.
1. Sponsors "Liberty Bell Bird Club" especially for young people.
2. Publishes booklets on building bird houses, economic importance of birds and bird pictures.

Brass

Copper and Brass Research Ass'n. 205 Broadway, New York City
1. Booklet on Copper and Brass

Brick

American Face Brick Ass'n. 205 W. Wacker Drive, Chicago, Illinois.

Carbon—see batteries

Carborundum

Carborundum Company, Niagara Falls, New York
1. Exhibit of raw materials used in manufacture of abrasives.
2. Booklet to describe process.

Cereals

Kellogg Corn Products Co. Battle Creek, Mich.
1. Exhibit—Steps in making corn flakes
2. " — " " " bran "
3. " — " " " Kaffee Hag
4. Booklets to describe processes
5. Nutrition pamphlets on iron, vitamin, etc.

Quaker Oats Co. 141 W. Jackson Blvd., Chicago, Ill.
1. Source list of material which can be obtained from them.

Ralston Purina Co. St. Louis, Mo.
    1. Large wall chart on wheat
Hecker-Jones-Jew. 11 Milling Co., 40 Corlears St., New York City
    1. Exhibit—showing steps in the manufacture of flour.
    2. Booklet—Adventures of a Kernel of Wheat.
National Biscuit Company 449 W. 14th Street, New York City
    1. Chart—Manufacturing Shredded Wheat
    2. Booklet—The Wheat Grain Tells You Its Story
The Wheatena Co. Wheatenaville, Rahway, N. J.
    1. Chart—Whole Wheat for Health
    2. Book—Feeding child from crib to college
Southern Rice Industry New Orleans, La.
    1. Two charts on Rice and Its Growing
    2. Booklets—rice in the diet, the story of rice.
Pillsbury's Cooking Service 1000 Hodgson Bldg. Minneapolis, Minn.
    1. Booklet—The Story of Bread
    2. Wall chart—showing above process
Standard Brands Inc. New York City
    1. Booklet—Bread and its Importance
Louisiana State Dept. of Agriculture and Immigration, Baton Rouge, La.
    1. Exhibit—Rice, sugar cane, cotton
    2. Booklet to describe processes and growing
International Harvester Co. 606 S. Michigan Avenue, Chicago, Ill.
    1. Booklets on bread and wheat
Corn Industries Research Foundation. 150 Broadway, New York City
    1. Chart on Corn Refining
    2. Booklet—"Industrial Corn."
Corn Products Refining Co. 17 Battery Place, New York City
    1. Exhibit—Corn Products
    2. Booklet—Corn Yesterday, Today, and Tomorrow
    3. Chart—Corn

Chemicals—see laboratory supplies

Chocolate and Cocoa

Hersey Chocolate Corp. Hersey, Pa.
    1. Booklet—Story of Chocolate and Cocoa
    2. Exhibit—Small charge

3. Chart—"Chocolate and Cocoa"

Coffee

Associated Coffee Industries of America   11 Water Street, New York City

    1. Booklets—On Growing of Coffee

    2. Set of excellent photographs on coffee growing, roasting, and importing (12 in set)

Reid-Murdock & Co.   Chicago, Ill.

    1. Booklets—"Coffee Blossoms"

Bureau of Coffee Information, 230 Park Avenue, New York City

    1. Exhibit—Steps in Roasting of Coffee

    2. Chart—Showing steps in process

    3. Booklet—To describe processes and illustrate it for notebook work

Communication

American Telephone & Telegraph Co., 195 Broadway, New York City

    1. Booklets—The Telephone in America, Behind your Telephone, The Magic of Communication, Making of a Telephone

Copper see brass

Cork

Chicago Cork Works Co., 2600 N. Crawford Drive, Chicago, Illinois

    1. Cork exhibit—$1.00

Cotton

American Thread Co.   New York City

    1. Booklet—Story of Cotton Thread

Esmond Blanket Mills, 21 E. 26th St., New York City

    1. Exhibit—Steps in making blankets—50¢

    2. Booklet—to describe processes

Pepperell Mfg. Co.   160 State St., Boston, Mass.

    1. Booklets—How Cotton is Made, Textile List of Common Cottons, Samples of Cotton, Uses of Cotton.

Pequot Mills, Salem, Mass.

    1. Booklet—Teachers Textbook of Sheets and Pillow cases, Story of Pequot

    2. Chart—Bed making

Louisiana State Dept. of Agriculture   Baton Rouge, Louisiana
    1. Cotton boll and booklet

Dr. Denton Sleeping Garment Mills, Centerville, Mich.
    1. Exhibit—process of making garments
    2. Booklet to describe process

Knit Underwear Industry   395 Broadway, New York City
    1. Exhibit—Making underwear

Electricity (see also batteries)

Western Electrical Instrument Corp., Newark, N. J.
    1. Wall charts of electrical equipment
    2. Booklet—describing instruments and magnets in electricity

Niagara Hudson, Buffalo, New York
    Mr. Walter Thompson will give personal interviews to anyone desiring information in regard to electricity, its generation, or transmission.

Films—see motion pictures

Flax

South Dakota State College, Brookings, S. D.
    1. Booklet—on flax in America

Flour—see cereals

Food—see also special headings as cereals, meat, etc.

Reid-Murdock & Co.   Chicago, Ill.
    1. Booklets describing how each "Monarch" brand product is prepared and packed.

American Can Co.   230 Park Avenue, N. Y. City
    1. Booklet—Story of Salmon

Postum Cereal Co.   Battle Creek, Michigan
    1. Charts on composition of foods.

Forestry—see housing

Fruits

California Fruit Growers Exchange, Box 530 Station C, Los Angeles, California
    1. Booklets about all kinds of citrous fruits
    2. Posters—Oranges and Lemons and How They Grow, Oranges and their Importance to Health

The Hills Brothers Co.   110 Washington St., New York City
    1. Booklets—Dates growing, etc.

United Fruit Co., 1 Federal St., Boston, Mass.
    1. Assortment of booklets on bananas
    2. Charts on bananas

Glass

Kimble Glass Co. Vineland, New Jersey
    1. Exhibit—showing steps in making a test milk bottle
    2. Booklets—New development in American glass industry.

Owens-Illinois Pacific Coast Co., San Francisco, California
    1. Chart showing process of glass making from raw materials to finished product

Pittsburgh Plate Glass Co. Brant Bldg., Pittsburgh, Pa.
    1. Booklet—on "Carrara"—Modern structural glass
    2. Excellent pictures of processes

Glue

Russia Cement Co. Gloucester, Mass.
    1. Exhibit of manufacture of fish glue

Grain—see cereals

Granite

Granite Mfg's. Ass'n. Barre, Vermont
    1. Booklet—"A letter to Junior about Barre Granite"

Great Scientists

Ford Motor Co. Dearborn, Michigan
    1. Booklet—Greenfield Village (Edison, etc.)

Aluminum Cooking Utensil Co. New Kensington, Pa.
    1. Booklet—"The Aluminum Age"

Metropolitan Life Insurance Co., New York City
    1. Booklets on "Lives of Famous Scientists"

Health

American Medical Ass'n. 535 N. Dearborn St., Chicago, Illinois
    1. List of publications and sample copies of "Hygeia"

Metropolitan Life Insurance Co., New York City
    1. Booklets on diseases, health, and great scientists

Housing

American Walnut Mfgs. Ass'n. 616 S. Michigan Blvd., Chicago, Illinois
    1. Booklet—Raising and milling walnuts

The Barrett Co. 40 Rector St., New York City
    1. Booklet on roofing

Johns-Manville Co.   22 E. 40th St., New York City
    1. Exhibit—samples of all their products
    2. Booklets—several to illustrate processes
National Lumber Mfgs. Ass'n.   1337 Connecticut Avenue,
   Washington, D. C.
    1. Exhibit—$1.95 wood samples (48 in set)
    2. Booklets—on lumber and its uses (10¢ each)
Pittsburgh Plate Glass Co., Brant Bldg., Pittsburgh, Pa.
    1. Booklets and pictures on "Carrara"
Southern Pine Ass'n., Madison, Wisconsin
    1. Booklets—Following pine through the laboratory, what
       it is, and how used
Ford Motor Company, Dearborn, Michigan
    1. Booklets on "Brazilian Hardwoods"
Inspirational
   International Harvester Co.   606 S. Michigan Ave., Chicago,
   Illinois
    1. Booklet—Inspiration to Young People
Iron—see also steel
   Phila. & Reading Coal and Iron Co., Philadelphia, Pa.
    1. Booklets on iron products
Kodak
   Eastman Kodak Co., Rochester, New York
    1. Booklets—several on amateur photography
Laboratory Supplies
   J. T. Baker Chemical Co., Phillipsburg, New Jersey
    1. Catalog of their products
   Camabasco Co., Waverly, Mass.
    1. Chemistry stencils for lab. work
   Chicago Apparatus Co., Chicago, Ill.
    1. Catalog of supplies
   Globe Book Co., New York City
    1. Chemistry drill sheet (5¢ each)
   J. H. Winn Mfg. Co. 2255 Broadway, New York City
    1. Magic Chemistry Booklet
   E. H. Sheldon & Co.
    1. Catalog of supplies
   Kewauneo Mfg. Co. Kewauneo, Wisconsin
    1. Catalog of supplies

Merck & Co.   Rahway, New Jersey
    1. Chemical almanac

Lead—see zinc

Leather
    American Leather Producers, 41 Park Ave., N. Y. City
        1. Booklet—"The Romance of Leather"

Linen—see also flax
    Klearflax Linen Looms, Inc. Duluth, Minn.
        1. Exhibit—small charge

Lumber—see housing

Measurements
    Ford Motor Co., Dearborn, Michigan
        1. Booklet—"History of Length"

Meat
    Swift & Co., Chicago, Ill.
        1. Charts on meat. Booklets—describing processes

Metal
    American Rolling Mill Co., Middletown, Ohio
        1. Booklets on steel alloys, iron, etc.
    Berger Brothers Co. 229 Arch Street, Philadelphia, Pa.
        1. Catalog of tinners' and roofers' supplies
    Fansteel Products Co., Inc. North Chicago, Ill.
        1. Booklets on newer metals and samples of molybdenum
    John A. Roebling's Sons Co., Trenton, N. Jersey
        1. Booklets on wire making, bridges, etc.

Milk
    Borden's   350 Madison Avenue, New York City
        1. Wall chart on values of milk and correlated subject
           matter for each grade.
    Evaporated Milk Ass'n.   203 Wabash Avenue, Chicago, Ill.
        1. List of available free material on all subjects
    Dairy Men's League
        1. List of available material on milk

Mohair
    L. C. Chase Co., Inc., 295 Fifth Avenue, N. Y. City
        1. Booklets on mohair, its mfg., and uses

Motion Pictures
    Castle Films, R. C. A. Bldg., New York City
        1. Catalog of free films on all subjects.

Nature Crafts

Boy Scouts of America Service Library, 2 Park Ave., New York City

1. Booklet—Nature Collections—40¢

Cocoa Cola Co., Atlanta, Ga.

1. Visual Instruction in Nature Study—free

Slingerland-Comstock Co., Ithaca, New York

1. Field books on all nature crafts

Women's Press, 600 Lexington Ave., N. Y. City

1. Nature crafts by Emily Veazie—25¢
2. Nature Study—Louise Brown—15¢

Nature Study

Whitman Publishing Co. Racine, Wisconsin

1. 10¢ guides on birds, flowers, etc.

Iowa Pupils Reading Circle 415 Shops Bldg., Des Moines, Iowa.

1. Bird Study Field Book—25¢

Harter Pub. Co., Cleveland, Ohio

1. 10¢ guides—Seeing Stars, "Talking Leaves," etc.

John C. Winston Co., Philadelphia, Pa.

1. 60¢ books on "Coal," "Houses," etc.

Nickel

International Nickel Co. 67 Wall St., N. Y. City

1. List of available material, which is authoritative but above level of children

Oil—see petroleum

Paper

Hammermill Paper Co., Erie, Pa.

1. Exhibits—Teachers' packet—10¢, Classroom exhibit —25¢, Chemistry & Science exhibit—$1.00, College and museum—$3.00

Pencil

Eberhard Faber Pencil Co. 37 Greenpoint Avenue, Brooklyn, New York

1. Exhibit—showing steps in making a lead pencil and soft gum erasers—50¢

Pens

Esterbrook Pen Mfg. Co. 99 John St., N. Y. City

1. Exhibit—Mfg. of pens from sheet steel
2. Booklets to illustrate each step

Petroleum

Quaker State Oil Co., Oil City, Pa.
1. Exhibit—different grades oil
2. Wall chart—showing difference in oil
3. Booklet—describing process

Sinclair Refining Co. 45 Nassau, N. Y. City
1. Exhibit of oil
2. Booklets describing manufacture

Rayon

The Viscose Co., 200 Madison Avenue, N. Y. City
1. Rayon exhibit
2. Booklet to describe process
3. Bound book on "Story of Rayon"

Dupont Rayon Co. 350 Fifth Avenue, N. Y. City
1. Skein of rayon
2. Booklet to describe its manufacture

Rice—see cereals

Roofing—see housing

Rope—Twine

Columbian Rope Co., Auburn, New York
1. Sample of hemp
2. Booklet on manufacture of rope
3. Knot chart for scouts

International Harvester Co., 606 S. Michigan Ave., Chicago, Illinois
1. Booklet on rope and twine

Rubber

B. F. Goodrich Co., Akron, Ohio
1. Exhibit—"From Plantation to Highways"

Kleinert's Rubber Co. c/o Homemakers Educational Service, Freeport, New York
1. Exhibit of rubber

Salt

Morton Salt Company, 208 Washington Street, Chicago, Illinois
1. Booklet—History of Salt

Worcester Salt Co., 40 Worth St., N. Y. City
1. Exhibit of Salt

Science Publications

American Education Press 40 South 3rd St., Columbus, Ohio
1. Current Science Leaflet

See list at end under *Miscellaneous Material*

Shellac

>   William Zinsser & Co.   516 W. 58 St., N. Y. City
>   1. Booklets—"The Story of Shellac"

Silk

>   Belding-Homingway-Corticelli Co., 119 W. 40th St., New York
>   City
>   1. Chart and exhibit of silk and its mfg.
>   2. Silk cocoons
>   3. Booklet—Romantic story of silk

Spices

>   McCormick & Co., Baltimore, Maryland
>   1. Booklet and map—"From Singapore to Baltimore"

Sponges

>   Schroeder & Tremaine Inc., 500 N. Commercial St., St. Louis, Missouri
>   1. Booklet—"Men Who Fight Sharks"

Steel

>   Alleghany Steel Co.   Brackenridge, Pa.
>   1. Booklets—Alleghany Steel

Sugar

>   Louisiana State Dept. of Agriculture, Baton Rouge, La.
>   1. Sample of sugar cane
>   2. Booklet to describe process
>   Californian & Hawaiian Sugar Refining Corp., 215 Market St.,
>   San Francisco, California
>   1. Booklet—Something about Sugar

Synthetic Fibres—see also rayon

>   American Bemberg Corp.   261 Fifth Avenue, N. Y. City
>   Booklets—Mechanical silkworm, suggestions for a class
>   project on synthetic fibres, identification of synthetic
>   fibres, knitted fabric facts.

Tea

>   Chase & Sanborn Co., Boston, Mass.
>   1. Booklet—Tea, Where and How it Grows
>   India Tea Co., c/o Homemakers Service, Freeport, N. Y.
>   1. Chart and booklets on tea.

Telegraph & Telephone—see communication

Textiles—see each one; as, wool, silk, etc.

Tin—see also metals

>   American Sheet & Tin Plate Co., Pittsburgh, Pa.

1. Booklet—Evolution of a Tin Can

Tooth Care

Pro-phy-lac-tic Brush Co., Florence, Mass.

1. Booklet—A handbook for teachers

Trees—see housing

Varnish

National Paint & Varnish—Lacquer Ass'n., 2201 New York Avenue, N. W., Washington, D. C.

1. Booklet on mfg. of paint, varnish, and lacquer

Wood—see housing

Wool

Kenwood Mills, Albany, New York.

1. Exhibit—Making an all wool blanket.

Wire—see metals

Yeast

Northwestern Yeast Co., 1750 North Ashland Avenue, Chicago, Illinois

1. Charts on action of yeast in bread making

Zinc

Eagle Picher Sales Co., 1030 Broadway, Cincinnati, Ohio

1 Samples of zinc and lead
2. Charts showing mfg. and uses of each

MISCELLANEOUS MATERIAL

American Museum of Natural History, 77th Street at Central Park, West, New York City

1. List of free motion pictures
2. List of publications

Comstock Publishing Co., Ithaca, New York

1. Books on all nature subjects with from 10-25% discount to teachers

National Ass'n. Audubon Societies, 1775 Broadway, New York City

1. Samples of all kinds of materials for nature study

National Advisory Council on Radio in Education, New York City

1. Programs dealing with science

National Recreation Ass'n., 315 Fourth Avenue, New York City

1. All types of pamphlets on play and equipment, some games good in science

South Dakota State College, Brookings, S. D.
   1. List of available material
Cornell University, Ithaca, New York
      1. Rural School leaflets on all nature subjects
      2. State publications on related work

TEACHING EQUIPMENT

Blackboard: Use sheets of shale, hyloplate, composition board, manilla
   paper with two or three coats of liquid slating, oilcloth slated on the
   back, composition board coated with slating, or a high black board
   fence may be used for the primary children.

Blackboard Erasers: may be made from a block of wood covered with
   felt, with cloth, or with fleece lining from a glove or coat.

Compasses may be made from chalk and a piece of string, or a pencil
   and a piece of string.

Clock face dial may be cut from card board.

Counting aids are peach stones enameled different colors. Spools
   may also be used.

Display rack may be made from a wooden towel rack with six arms.
   Posters, pictures, or charts may be thumbtacked to both sides.

Flash cards, phrase cards and number cards may be made by the teacher
   from oak tag or card board cut $3'' \times 6''$ in size and with large letter-
   ing or printing.

Flash card holder may be made from strips of oak tag held together
   with gummed paper and bound at the sides. Half inch big full
   strips of inner tubes stretched and tacked to the wall will hold
   flash cards so they do not topple over.

Hectograph: 2 oz. sheet gelatine and 1 pint glycerine. Boil two hours
   in a double boiler, pour into shallow pans and let set over night.
   Push bubbles to edge with edge of a sheet of paper while hot. In-
   delible pencil may be used instead of hectograph ink.

Maps: Outline maps may be made to scale and mounted or hectographed.

Tough wrapping paper serves as the base for product maps.

Wall maps and blackboard outline maps may be drawn on the back of
   a piece of oilcloth previously slated, the outline painted in white
   paint, then tacked on a window shade roller and hung where needed.

Measurement: Wet and dry measure may be baskets, jars and tins
   very carefully measured and marked according to size, or real
   measures donated from home.

A small swinging scale is composed of a balance bar, two baskets suspended by a string exactly in the middle and string supports.

For weights (1 oz. 20 oz. ½ oz. etc.) fill small bags with sand.

Pencil Sharpener: Use razor blade or knife.

Printing: Old felt hats provide pads of felt for ink printing.

Slides and Projections: White sheets may be used as a screen for lantern slide projectors.

Slides may be made from plain window glass cut to regulation size and drawing ink, or frosted glass with drawings in crayon or pencil. Put plain glass over.

A crude projector may be made from a magnifying glass, a box and an electric light bulb, cord, etc.

TEXTBOOKS

Atlas: A homemade atlas made in a scrap-book form from using maps from steamship companies and statistics from texts or the World Almanac copied neatly will prove useful and may be kept up to date.

Music: Mimeographed or hectographed sheets make good music books.

Notebooks: Textbooks made in outline form in notebooks from the teacher's dictation and class discussion may be a last resort.

Readers: First grade children may make their own primer stories based on their experiences. These should be printed for them and clipped together in booklet form.

Charts may be printed on oak tag or wrapping paper.

Typed sheets of original stories.

Spelling: Spelling books are unnecessary if teacher mimeographs or hectographs the words for each week.

Workbooks: Teacher-made workbooks may be substituted for commercial workbooks. Also all children in a class may use the same workbook, or individual workbooks for all members of the class may be provided but not written in, and saved for use from year to year.

APPENDIX F

A LIST OF EQUIPMENT SUGGESTED FOR THE
SMALL RURAL SCHOOL [1]

Supplies and Equipment Kept Mainly in the Janitor's Room, Tool, and Supply Closet

- 1 eighteen inch long handled floor brush
- 1 fourteen inch long handled floor brush
- 1 counter brush
- 1 heavy broom (3 lb. or heavier)
- 1 light broom (2 lb.)
- 1 heavy dustpan
- 1 window squeegee with both short and long handles
- 1 large wash basin
- 1 mop
- 1 mop pail with wringer
- 10 yds. cheesecloth for dusters
- 1 ten foot step ladder
- 1 long handled coal and snow shovel
- 1 axe
- 1 hatchet
- 1 coal hod
- 1 ash sifter
- 1 incinerator
- 1 lawnmower
- 1 garden rake
- 1 hoe
- 1 garden trowel
- 1 pr. pruning shears
- 1 long handled pointed shovel
- 1 stove shovel

[1] This list was assembled by Miss Muriel Bardwell, Demonstration Teacher in Rural Education, Summer Session, State Teachers College at Buffalo, N. Y.

1 barrel soft wood sawdust *or* sweeping compound
5 gals. corn oil and raw linseed oil mixed in equal parts *or* floor oil
1 qt. mineral oil *or* furniture polish
2 qts. clear ammonia
5 lbs. sal soda *or* tri-sodium phosphate *or* water softener and paint cleaner
2 qts. compound solution of cresol *or* disinfectant
100 lbs. lime *or* permanganate of potash *or* chemical recommended for type of chemical toilet in use. Unnecessary with flush toilets.
1 qt. ink bottle with filler top
ink or ink powder
1 fireproof metal container for oiled dust cloths
fly exterminator, if needed
mosquito exterminator, if needed
rat exterminator, if needed
1 pr. rubber gloves
extra window glass and putty
extra fuses and electric light bulbs

Equipment and Supplies Kept Mainly in Furnace Room or Fuel Room

1 furnace *or* jacketed stove with approved properly installed fresh air inlet, foul air outlet, stovepipe, and chimney, and humidifier
1 stove poker
1 concrete floor or zinc sheet underneath stove or furnace
fuel room (near stove or furnace) of sufficient size to hold the year's supply of fuel
½ cord dry kindling wood
2 cords dry wood (more wood and less coal in warm climates)
4–12 tons anthracite coal (depending upon climate, size of building, and efficiency of stove or furnace and janitor or teacher. More will be required in very severe climates.)
1 shovel.

Equipment and Supplies Kept Mainly in Entry, Coatrooms, and Toilets

teacher's coatroom equipped with rod, coat hangers, hooks, and hat shelf
children's coatrooms. (Noiseless warmed and ventilated wardrobes may serve as the partition between kitchen and classroom. The noiseless doors may be equipped with slate or cork to provide needed

blackboard or bulletin space. The back of the wardrobe may serve also as the back of the kitchen cupboard base, drawer base, and wall cupboards.)

rods

coat hangers—for each child	1 door mat
hat shelf or rack—space for each child	1 outside flag
rack for rubbers—space for each child	1 school bell
umbrella rack or drip pan	1 lock and key for outside door

Equipment Where Running Water Is Installed

2 flush toilets—boys' and girls' separate
low toilets or curved foot stools for convenience of small children
2 lavatories (low enough to be reached by all unless footstools are used by smallest children)
1 drinking fountain
1 sink

or

Equipment Where Running Water Is Not Installed

1 water pump
eave troughs and fittings
1 cistern or storage tank for rain water
1 sink provided with straight drain pipe leading to rock filter and drain bed or cess pool
1 stone jar for drinking water
2 water pails
1 wash bench
3 wash basins—medium size
2 chemical toilets properly installed *or* ventilated open-pit toilets suitably concealed
1 cess pool, septic tank, or approved drain
2 mirrors placed at height convenient for children's use
2 toilet paper holders
soft toilet tissue paper
1 paper towel holder
paper towels
1 liquid soap container

First Aid Equipment (May be kept in classroom or kitchen)

2 ounce bottle tincture of iodine, half or quarter strength
¼ pound boric acid crystals
¼ pound sodium bicarbonate
    ipecac if likely to be needed
2 ounce bottle spirits of ammonia
1 pint ethyl (grain) alcohol 60–70%
    petroleum jelly
    tannic acid (Make absolutely fresh solution when needed. 25
       grams tannic and 4 grams sodium carbonate, 500 cc water,
       spray on with atomizer)
    sterile gauze pads   ⎫ 1 inch, 1½ in.
    sterile gauze bandages⎭ and 2 in. sizes
    sterile absorbent cotton
    sanitary napkins
    adhesive tape—1 inch size
    scissors
    forceps
1 package needles, assorted sizes
    white thread
    black thread
1 package razor blades
1 box matches
1 clinical thermometer
1 cabinet to hold the above first aid supplies

Pamphlets:

Poisonous Snakes of the U. S. from Dept. of Agriculture, Washington,
    D. C.
Poison Ivy, Circular 154, N. Y. State Agricultural Experiment
    Station at Geneva, N. Y.

Equipment and Supplies Mainly Related to Windows or Lighting

Adequate window space so planned as to provide sufficient light on even
    the most remote desks, without glare or cross lights anywhere at
    any time. Also window locks on all windows
Translucent center roll window shades to exclude direct sun
Dark shades to darken room for stereopticon slides or motion pictures
    (Some prefer that these roll from the bottom)

Shade pulleys and cords

Draftless window ventilators if needed to supplement ventilation

Window screens where needed

Storm sash where needed

Curtain rods wide enough so that curtains may be adjusted at the sides without excluding light

Furniture, Equipment and Supplies Kept Mainly in the Classroom Proper

Movable desks, table style, in five sizes (22″, 23″, 24″, 25″, 26″). All tops should be 18″ × 24″ and entirely flat, with edges and corners slightly rounded.

Chairs designed to promote comfort and correct posture. One chair for each child's desk and extra chairs for library table and class circle should be provided. Five or more sizes (12″, 13″, 14″, 15″, 16″).

3 teacher's chairs for teacher and visitors

1 teacher's desk—kneehole office type having two or more drawers fitted with locks

2 boards 18″ × 6′ hinged to sidewall so that they may be raised and supported by locking-elbow type hinged braces to provide extra table space or dropped out of the way like a drop-leaf table leaf

1 sand table, 24 inch height for primary children

blackboards with chalk ledge

blackboard erasers

chalk, dustless for children's use and soft for teacher's use

2 bulletin boards

globe

wall maps—world, continents, state, county, United States

[noiseless ventilated wardrobe (see note under children's coatrooms)]

[library—(see page 547)]

[indoor play equipment—(see page 542)]

[lunch equipment—(see page 549)]

[first aid—(see coatrooms)]

1 steel filing cabinet, standard office size, with file cards, folders, and envelopes

cupboard space for all books, supplies, and children's projects. (Drawer base, cupboard base, work space on the top, with wall cupboards above are economical. The well-equipped school will need at least 120 feet of library and book shelving and 60 ft. of deep shelving for paper and supplies.)

flag and staff

hectograph (or ditto) pans

hectograph refill

pencil sharpener

pointer

thermometer

clock

typewriter

3 waste baskets

teacher's rubber type chart printing outfit and stamp pad

health cards

permanent record cards

teacher's plan book or desk file

fire extinguisher

Playground Equipment for Outdoor Use

1 sandbox 8′ × 8′ × 10″ deep for primary children

2 cubic yards of clean sand

70 unsharpened fence posts 6″ × 6″ × 8′ long. (These should probably be soaked in creosote to prevent weathering as they will be used for outdoor building—huts, ships, forts, stockades, doll houses, play houses, etc. for years)

2 soccer balls

1 ball bladder (extra) or rubber cement and old inner tubing for patches

1 bicycle pump

2 indoor baseballs

1 bat

1 catcher's glove

2–3 swings

2 see-saws

rope

3 rubber balls (3″, 6″, 16″) for primary children

1 flagpole (not for play)

1 bicycle rack (may be in fuel room for greater safety), stable, or garage if needed by pupils and teacher

The following may be justified in some schools: tricycle, wheelbarrow, kiddie car, large wagon, small wagon, ladder, junior horizontal ladder, walking board, jumping board, fixed hobby horse, slides, giant stride, Indian clubs, hoops, basketball or volley ball with baskets or net and posts.

shade trees

drained playing area—as level as possible

parking area

garden

fence if traffic hazard is present

outdoor table and benches

fireplace or council circle, amphitheater, etc. where convenient

Indoor Play Equipment

Primary children's corner featuring a set-up for (1) rest, (2) educative self-checking seatwork, and (3) quiet self-amusement as follows:

couch, double bunk bed, or comfortable cot or bench

washable rug

blanket

hassock, ottoman, or upholstered footstool

sturdy doll house or store or garage or hangar (or materials for building)

primary work table with linoleum top

cupboard space for books, materials, games, tools, etc. nearby

self-checking seatwork, either commercial or homemade, in variety and quantity

self-teaching seatwork, workbooks, etc.

materials such as clay, plastecine, cotton roving or rags, soap and clay pipes, enlarged beads, colored sticks, counting blocks, crayons, paste, and paper

playthings such as washable toy animals, dolls, rag dolls, paper dolls, doll clothes, doll furniture, doll dishes, Noah's ark, peg board, Tinker-Toys, Lincoln logs, crazy-ikes, the Blox that Lox, wooden toy train, ten pins, spools, floor blocks, erector sets, toy money, etc.

games such as dominoes, ring toss, jigsaw puzzles, etc.

Equipment Used Mainly in Science

    seeds and bulbs
    wire insect cage 2′ × 2′ ×2′
    animal cage suitable for pets
    water and food pans for pets
    fernery with removable metal pan
    flower pots
    watering pot
    collection of vases, bowls, and flower stem holders
    aquarium
    wooden flat for germinating seeds
    microscope, also one tripod lens
    telescope or bird glasses
    flat pieces of glass 4″ × 4″ and 6″ × 6″
    plaster of Paris for making casts and molds
    weather vane
    outdoor thermometer
    barometer or
    hygrometer
    yardstick
    scales
  6 wax candles 6″ long
    magnets—different sizes and shapes
    saucers for holding specimens
 12 glass test tubes with cork or rubber stoppers to fit
    medicine dropper
    hydrometer jar 15″ × 1½′
  2 one-liter battery jars
  1 two-liter battery jar
    fruit jars with covers
    rubber tubing—large
 ½ lb. soft glass tubing
 10 ft. thin wall tubing to fit glass tubing
100 ft. insulated bell wire, electric fuses
    electric wire
  4 dry cell batteries
    electric door bell
    push button
    rods of glass, amber, vulcanite, sealing wax for static electricity

1 gross assorted corks
triangle file
alcohol lamp and denatured alcohol
litmus paper
1 pt. lime water

Supplies and Equipment Used Mainly in Industrial Arts

workbench planned to hold all tools required in the small school
vice
hammer
screwdriver
bitstock
bits
pliers
wire cutters
steel square
chisels—$\frac{1}{2}$ inch and $\frac{1}{4}$ inch
gouge—$\frac{1}{2}$ inch
dividers—8 inch
tape
level
saw
coping saw
coping saw blades
compass saw
assorted round head screws, sizes 1–12
nails, sizes $\frac{1}{2}''$, $\frac{3}{4}''$, $1''$, $1\frac{1}{2}''$
finishing nails—$\frac{1}{2}''$, $\frac{3}{4}''$, $1''$, $1\frac{1}{2}''$
brads—$\frac{1}{2}''$
glue
soft wood, as pine or basswood
pieces $\frac{1}{2}'' \times \frac{1}{2}'' \times 10$ ft.
                     $\frac{1}{2}'' \times \frac{3}{4}'' \times 10$ ft.
                     $\frac{1}{4}'' \times 1'' \times 10$ ft.
                     $\frac{1}{2}'' \times 1\frac{1}{4}'' \times 10$ ft.
                     $\frac{3}{8}'' \times 9'' \times 10\frac{1}{2}''$
                     $\frac{1}{2}'' \times 9'' \times 18''$
                     $1'' \times 2\frac{1}{2}'' \times 12$ ft.
                     $\frac{1}{2}''$ diameter dowel wood
                     $1''$ diameter dowel wood

linoleum scraps
soap (fresh large size Ivory) for carving
passe partout binding
clay
5 gal. crock to hold clay
warp—colored and white
rug wool—variety of colors
curved steel weaving needles
fiber weaving shuttles
cold water dyes, variety of colors
needles
pins
safety pins
thread
thimbles
hand loom
model airplane outfit (patterns, wood glue, directions, etc.)
raffia, pine needles, etc.
turpentine
lacquers or enamels—variety of colors
varnish
brushes for painting with lacquer and enamels—round and flat
set of tools for block cutting
(binders board—See Art)

Art Supplies and Equipment, Paper and Writing Supplies, etc.

2 good pictures which make esthetic appeal to children, such as
    "Galahad the Deliverer" by Abbey
    "The Calmady Children" by Lawrence
1 piece of sculpture
2 lovely pieces of pottery
1 tapestry of real beauty
1 scarf for piano, desk, or table
wax crayons with crayon boxes
water colors with cups *or* alabastine paints with water jars
tempera paints *or* tempera for mixing with water colors, *or* poster
    paints
Shaw finger paints
pastel crayons

charcoal
India ink and white ink
drawing pencils—hard and soft
primary pencils—large for small children
writing pencils—No. 2
pen points for writing
pen holders
round nib drawing pens No. 3 and No. 5 (square or shading nibs
    may be preferred by some teachers)
hectograph ink or ditto ink
paint brushes (water color brushes) Sizes No. 1, 4, 8, and 10 (or all
    sizes if possible)
paste brushes
individual paste jars (small ointment jars will serve if kept covered)
5 qts. paste
rulers and yardsticks
scissors and shears
eyelets and eyelet punch
picture wire and hooks
hectograph pans and filler
burlap
erasers—ink, pencil, and art gum
2 easels
roll of gummed paper
Scotch tape
brass fasteners (¾″ and 1½″)
suspension rings
gummed labels
rubber bands
atomizer and fixative
wire staples and stapling machine
Ideal paper clips—medium size
Gem paper clips No. 1 size
thumb tacks
binder's board
20 sheets oak tag (24″ × 36″)
news print paper, 1000 sheets in package, 18″ × 24″
1 roll heavy wrapping paper
heavy white drawing paper 18″ × 24″ and 24″ × 36″
manila drawing paper, 9″ × 12″ and 12″ × 18″

bogus paper 12" × 18"
charcoal paper 19" × 25"
construction paper—all colors—12" × 18"
poster paper—all colors—18" × 24"
1 pkg. coated colored paper—all colors
1 pkg. carbon paper
1 pkg. tracing paper or onion skin tissue
10 reams mimeograph paper (good quality that will not leave fuzzy
    coating on the hectograph)
cellophane wrapping paper
lithograph paper 18" × 24" rough on one side and coated on one
    side for finger painting
writing or composition paper, lined for primary children, unlined
    for older children
notebooks or looseleaf paper—unlined, lined
arithmetic paper 6" × 9"
desk blotters
notebook covers

Library Supplies and Equipment (Books Not Included)

1 (steel filing cabinet—also listed under classroom equipment)
    book cases or shelves within easy access of children. (If these
    are not built in, a satisfactory substitute may be built by teacher
    and children from 50 face bricks of standard 8" size and 5
    boards each 1" × 8" × 48". The boards may be painted
    white to contrast with red bricks.)
1 library table and chairs for small children (round type)
1 library table for larger pupils
12 book ends
1 desk card file or steel card cabinet
1 accession book
    shelf labels (or Scotch tape and paper scraps or thumbtacks and
    paper scraps)
    book pockets (or heavy paper)
    loan cards
    filing cards
    white ink (may be added to art supplies)
    India ink (See Art)
    librarian's lettering pens

finish remover (alcohol, ammonia, or turpentine may be substituted)
sponge
brush
colorless shellac
transparent adhesive tape
gummed sewed tape—for loose pages
gummed mending tape
gummed binding tape

Equipment Used Mainly in Music, Dramatics, or Community Festivals

1 stage curtain, curtain rings, wire *or* folding screens *or* a building so
planned that kitchen, coatrooms, and fuel rooms may be used
as dressing rooms with easy entrance and exit to stage
portable stage
string of stage lights
spot light
1 Santa Claus suit
1 Christmas tree support
3 strings electric light bulbs for Christmas tree
2 boxes Christmas tree ornaments
(1 five gallon coffee pot, coffee bag, and dishes. See under Lunch
Equipment.)
3 benches for small children (while their chairs are occupied by the
audience) 13″ × 8″ wide × 8 ft.
8 (or as many more as needed) planks 2″ × 8″ × 8 ft. (May be
covered with carpet for adult seating and supported on stools,
chairs, or potato crates at each end.)
   *stereopticon or balopticon or lantern to show slides
   *motion picture projection machine
1 radio (with loud speaker remounted behind a suitable baffle board
or wall panel), ground wire, aerial, leadin strip, etc.
1 phonograph—set of records for music appreciation; set of records
for physical education
1 piano
rhythm band instruments, as xylophone, drum, cymbals, tri-
angles, chime bells, sleigh bells, sand block, variety of pieces of

*These need not be school property but should be available from central
office or larger school.

ringing steel, standard to hold hanging bottles, wooden hammer, etc.

variety of colored cheese cloth, percale, cotton broadcloth, sateen, etc., remnants for costumes

variety of wood for framework of puppet stage

large pieces of light wall board useful for display of exhibits, as screens, and for temporary construction as scenery

Lunch Equipment

kitchen cabinet or equivalent consisting of 1 drawer base, 1 cupboard base, and 1 or more wall cupboards. (Top of bases will be needed as work space and when serving food on dishes.) Should contain shelves, racks, cutlery box, box for knives, forks, and spoons, etc.

convertible kitchen table—work table with linoleum top

3 burner oilstove (Perfection No. 2) *or* electric plate, *or* gas stove properly connected to pipe line or tank where bottled gas is to be used

detachable oven

linoleum sufficient to cover floor of "kitchen"

2 garbage cans (3 or 4 gallon size for school use, also largest possible size for community functions)

5 gallon kerosene can, or gas or electric installation approved by fire insurance company

vegetable bin (metal-perforated)

2 18 qt. dishpans

2 dish drainers with drip pans underneath

8 dish towels

1 dish mop

whiting

steel wool

2 dish cloths

1 clothes dryer (rack)

1 clothes line

1 toaster

1 corn popper

1 teakettle

1 12 qt. kettle with cover

1 8 qt. kettle with cover

1 5 gal. coffee pot, cloth coffee bags
2 saucepans—any size
2 2 qt. metal pitchers for pouring
2 half-pint ladles
1 mixing bowl
2 strainers (small and large)
1 can opener (or more)
2 long handled mixing spoons
2 4 qt. milk pails with tightly fitted covers for delivering milk from
    farm to school
1 jar rack for lifting pan full of hot half-pint jars and to prevent
    breaking
1 pair hot jar tongs
1 opener for screw top jars
  plates (enamel if not chipped)
  cups (enamel if not chipped)
  spoons, forks, knives
  wooden cup slides to place under hot dishes
1 bottle opener
1 flour sifter
1 egg beater
1 potato masher
1 spatula
2 vegetable brushes
1 bread knife
2 stainless steel vegetable knives
2 case knives
2 steel forks
1 long handled fork
  set measuring spoons
1 quart measure
1 cup measure
  tin food receptacles
  pepper shakers
  flour sieve
  cream pitchers
  sugar bowls
  paper napkins
  oil cloth or Dupont table covers
  sugar, flour, beans, salt, pepper, soda, etc.

APPENDIX G

AN EMERGENCY KIT FOR THE SMALL SCHOOL[1]

Container: A small tin or pasteboard box with cover. A candy box will do.

Contents:

1.	A half ounce bottle of two per cent mercurochrome, with a rubber stopper and a glass rod...............	$ .10
2.	One tube of unguentine or vaseline...............	.10
3.	Two and one-half yards of one-inch adhesive......	.10
4.	One one-inch bandage...............	.05
5.	One two-inch bandage...............	.10
6.	One dozen safety pins...............	.05
7.	One pair of blunt scissors...............	.10
8.	Absorbent cotton...............	.10
	Total	$ .70

Additional gauze bandages, triangular bandages, and aromatic spirits of ammonia may be added, depending upon the funds available and the number of pupils. Metal cases, ranging in price from $.50 to $1.00, may be purchased. Occasional checking is necessary to assure a constant supply. Older pupils should know how to use contents of kit.

[1] Grout, Ruth E. *Handbook of Health Education.* p. 272. Doubleday Doran & Co. 1936.

APPENDIX H

THE TEACHER AND THE COMMUNITY SURVEY

Teaching in terms of the environment of children cannot be accomplished until the teacher knows it thoroughly and in some detail. Nor is knowledge of the community achieved through cursory visits and incidental questions. The environment must be studied, and the results of the study placed in workable form, if children are to be served. The social studies, perhaps more than any other school subject, profit from environmental studies. It is easier for children to understand lumbering in general, for example, if they know the processes of the lumber mill in their own neighborhood. Knowing the processes of the neighborhood mill, however, can never be achieved by a school excursion to it, nor by a visit of the mill president to the school. These activities are desirable, but they are not enough for a program of environmental teaching. Many progressive teachers have attacked this problem in recent years, and the teaching profession is profiting from their techniques in the discovery and in the accumulation of information. One of the outstanding developments in the study and use of the environment has taken place in the Bethlehem Central School at Delmar, New York. How this study came about is given below in a Case Study.

CASE STUDY [1]

In June 1936, the teachers of the Bethlehem Central School decided to make a long view plan for group study. In order to facilitate action on this decision a steering committee was appointed, and instructed to develop plans for the monthly teachers meetings to be held the following year. At the June meeting the teachers had decided to study the community environment of the centralized school in order to (a) understand the environment in which the school was located, and (b) develop the findings in the construction of a curriculum. Both

[1] Reported by Bethlehem Central School, Delmar, New York.

of these aims seemed desirable and practical. The committee felt that educational theorists had long presented the theory that teaching was most effective when accomplished in terms of the local milieu. The group of teachers subscribed to this theory, and felt that they would profit from the experience of putting it to a practical test. A search for previous practical applications of the theory revealed a discouraging paucity of them. Without past experiences for guides the committee was forced with the necessity for original and detailed planning for the September meeting. Not only did it feel the necessity for constructing a long view plan, but also the advisability for suggesting practical techniques for developing it.

The group accepted the plan of the steering committee and decided to study Rural Sociology as a background for an intelligent understanding of what might be found in the environmental study. Following this study, the group also attacked the problem of survey making, and specifically the techniques by which information could be accumulated in a community survey. For this latter study, the group met every two weeks, on Monday. At this time comparisons of readings were made, conclusions reached, and discussions engaged in. In the meantime, a listing of the community enterprises had been made and the group had divided itself, on an interest basis, into small committees. There was, for example, a committee on lumber, a committee on printing, another on grocery stores, another on bakeries, etc. Indeed, each individual industry had its own special committee of teachers. These smaller committees met on the intervening Monday between the group meetings, and developed definite plans for surveying their own particular industries. On each of these sub-committees there served a member of the Steering Committee. In this way the Steering Committee knew at all times the development of each sub-committee, and thus achieved a grasp and an over-view of the whole undertaking. The Steering Committee met as a group each Tuesday in order to plan for the needs revealed after (a) the bi-monthly general teachers meetings, and (b) the sub-committees on coal, lumber, printing, etc. held on alternating Mondays. The Steering Committee, by these techniques, planned and guided the whole program.

The field work of the undertaking, however, was performed by the sub-committees, but not until each committee felt prepared for the responsibility. This preparation consisted of (a) reading and discussions of general survey methods in the large group meetings, (b) specific readings on the special industry in which individual groups were interested, (c) a list of questions for securing information from the owner of the plant, (d) and a visiting date agreed upon by the industry owner and the survey group. The trips to the plants were taken on general faculty meeting days, the results were recorded at subsequent group meetings and then reported at the general meeting of all the teachers. The large group thus had the benefit of the activities of each small group, and in turn each group received help from all of the others. All activities were checked with the sociological principles learned earlier in the study and an effort was made to interpret local findings in the light of these principles.

A general plan was accepted for reporting data. This tended to give a uniform, clear and workable form to the findings. The outline generally used for these reports was as follows:

Part I

I. Historical background of local enterprise.
II. Reasons for choice by the founder.
III. Community needs filled by the establishment of the enterprise.
IV. Social, economic, industrial and religious trends.
V. Original equipment.
VI. Growth.

A further step was taken in Part II of the completed report. This gave a Pre-plan for a possible unit which might develop from the study. This Pre-plan followed the outline given below:

A. Possible approaches to the study.
B. Resources available.
C. Acquired information.
D. General principles.
E. Specific principles.
F. Children's questions.
G. Possible activities.
H. Possible outcomes.
I. Possible attitudes.

The actual translation of the outline into classroom procedure was postponed until 1937–1938. At this time, the teachers planned to experiment with this phase of the curriculum in their regular meetings. As an example of how an outline developed the report of the Committee on The Sawmill is given below.

SAWMILL

Part I

I. Historical background of the local commercial enterprise.

   A. Reason for choice by founder.

      1. Centrally located for obtaining raw materials. Woods thereabout furnished the raw materials needed.

      2. Centrally located for distribution of sawn lumber. The farming community was the principal market for the lumber.

      3. Stream nearby furnished power for running the machinery.

      4. The topography facilitated the transportation of materials. The mill, located at the foot of a hill, made it comparatively easy to get the logs to the mill.

   B. Community needs which were filled by this enterprise.

      1. It filled a definite need for the people of the section. The lumber was used in the construction of their farm buildings.

      2. It provided a means of making a living for the owner.

   C. Trends.

      1. It was a definite trend toward industrialized labor as apart from home labor. Where, heretofore, the home was considerably independent of industry outside the home, now it was becoming dependent on outside agencies for certain types of work being done.

      2. Tended to be the forming of a social, agricultural community due to the advantages of climate, soil, nearness to river and city.

   D. Original equipment.

      1. Machinery using water power—water wheel.

      2. Later, steam power—then, electric power.

   E. Growth of local commercial enterprise.

      1. Founded by a man named Dietz about 50 years ago.

2. Transferred to other owners, the last of whom is Mr. Frazier of Cohoes.

3. Change in type of power and machinery used.
   From water power to steam and then to electric.

4. Needs.
   a. Shelters.
   b. Barns.
   c. Ice houses.
   d. Buildings generally used for agricultural purposes.

5. Due to more modern methods of sawing, this small sawyer was unable to meet the fast growing requirements of the industry. Consequently the undertaking of other activities involving the use of the same power, location and building was necessary in order for his sawmill to survive, namely, cider press and the grinding of grain.

6. Better roads and better facilities for hauling greater distances have served to prolong the life of the sawmill.

7. Competition.
   a. Traveling sawyer.
   b. Small saw mill on Feura Bush road.

II. Present condition of the local commercial enterprise.

A. Present location.

Kenwood Avenue between Delmar and Slingerlands.

B. Description of housing facilities.

1. Rough wooden shed consisting of one story and loft, with lean-to for lumber. Loft is used to hold the motors. Building is open on north and east sides. Corrugated iron sheathing is used on the west side as a wind break.

2. No provision for artificial lighting as the work is done by daylight.

3. No heating facilities in the mill. There is a small heated building nearby on the grounds.

4. There is sufficient space for own work. Little storage space is needed as the lumber is called for soon after it is sawed.

C. Description of equipment and process.

  1. The farmers of the vicinity haul their logs, formerly by
     team, now generally by truck, to the mill where they are
     rolled off later to be sawed. The butts of the logs are at
     that time stamped with the owner's initials to prevent
     error. If there is considerable work on hand, the logs are
     sawed in order of receipt except for rush orders. The logs,
     one at a time, are rolled onto the carriage by the aid of
     cant hooks. Having been properly placed, the log is
     clamped onto the bed of the carriage by steel spikes which
     are a part of the carriage. The log is then ready to be sent
     toward the 50″ circular saw run at 550 r.p.m. by electricity.
     The bark is first removed in four cuts, thus squaring off
     the log before the boards are removed. The boards of the
     desired thickness are then removed. Mr. Frazier estimated
     that about 100 bd. ft. could be obtained from a 15″ log,
     figuring on obtaining 10″ boards. All types of wood are
     sawed the same except oak. This is quarter sawed.

  2. Files are used to sharpen the saw. The teeth are removed
     and sharpened. It is often necessary to replace worn out
     teeth.

  3. The planer is used to smooth the sawed lumber. It is also
     used to make grooves in the wood as desired. Four different
     operations may be done by this machine.

  4. The sawdust is blown through pipes to the rear of the mill.

D. Materials and sources.

  1. Logs are brought in by farmers of the immediate vicinity
     and surrounding communities. Some have been brought
     from South Schenectady and Poestenkill near Troy.

E. Products and markets.

  1. Sawed and planed lumber.
     Farmers of immediate vicinity as before mentioned.

  2. By products and uses.
     a. Saw dust—bedding for animals.
        floor covering for chicken houses.

floor covering for butcher shops.

ice house.

insulation.

    b. Slabs—fuel.

    c. Shavings—kindling, floor covering for chicken houses.

  3. Local markets, principally.

     Farmers of Elsmore, Delmar, Slingerlands, Glenmont.

F. Trends.

  1. Changes in enterprise to meet present conditions. Insufficient saw mill work makes it necessary to widen the scope of activities using same machinery in order to make the enterprise financially profitable.

    a. Grinding grain and making cider are also done here.

    b. This indicates that stationary saw mills will eventually give way to portable saw mills.

    c. It also indicates that anyone in a small village enterprise must be a jack of all trades and able to see relationships so he may have varied activities involving same type of equipment.

    d. Scientific development brought about change in methods.

      (1) Invention of new machinery. Greater specialization due to more technical machinery.

      (2) Water power lessened due to lessening of stream.

      (3) Demand of locality decreased.

G. Workers.

  1. One employed at time of survey.

  2. Physical requirements.

     Strong, healthy, able to stand long hours of work practically out-of-doors the year round.

  3. Education needed.

    a. Ability to keep saw in good working condition.

H. Employment conditions.

  1. Occupational hazards.

    a. Possibility of being injured by:

      (1) Partially guarded machinery.

        (2) Saw breaking due to metal imbedded in log.

        (3) Flying sawdust and chips.

        (4) Poor or improper lighting.

        (5) Intense cold.

    b. Work is seasonal. Possibility of unemployment during part of year.

    c. Possibility of fire due to carelessness of smokers.

  2. Advantages.

    a. Out-of-door work.

    b. Physical exercise.

    c. No special crowding for time. Work may be done as desired in this special sawmill.

  3. Government regulations.

    A. Employer #2: anyone employing workmen in hazardous employment. Subject to this chapter.

        #3: Hazardous employment subject to this chapter: long list of those given, occupational diseases; descriptions.

        #13: Treatment and care of injured employee.

        #14: Weekly wages, basis of compensation.

    B. Labor Laws.

        a. Article #4: Employment of children and females. Children under 14 prohibited. Employment certificate.

        b. Article #146: Prohibited employment of children under 14 to 16.

        c. Article #160: Hours of labor.

        d. Article #250: Accident prevention.

        e. Fire door, fireproof window, fire partition, fire building, fire wall, exterior enclosed fireproof stairway.

        f. Inspection of building and limitation of number of occupants.

        g. Fire alarm signals and fire drills.

III. Probable outlook for the enterprise.

  A. Summary of trends and probable effects.

    1. Establishment of the saw mill was a definite trend toward

the forming of a community centered around such enterprises.

2. The necessity of doing other types of work using same type of equipment shows necessity of the small business man to be able to see relationships in order to keep enterprise financially sound.

3. A definite trend is seen away from stationary saw mills to the use of portable saw mills.

B. Activities of the mill.

1. Cider.
   Grain.

2. 2000 ft. of hard lumber alone in one day.

3. $8.00 for soft wood.
   $10.00 for hard wood.

SAWMILL

Part II

I. Preliminary plan.

A. Possible approaches to the study of the local commercial enterprise.

1. Samples of lumber.

2. Story about a sawmill.

3. Gift of a small tree.

4. Exploratory trip to a sawmill.

5. Slides.

6. Pictures on the bulletin board.

7. Display of books.

8. Forest fires.

9. Floods.

10. Dust storms.

11. Sawdust from children's work.

12. Movie such as "God's Country and the Woman."

13. Conservation movement.

14. Newspaper clippings.

15. Radio program.
16. Any government movement.

B. Resources available.

1. Easily accessible.

  a. Bethlehem Center.

    (1) *Compton's Encyclopedia*
    (2) *World Book*
    (3) *Geographical Readers*
    (4) *Pathways to Science*
    (5) *Nature Magazine*

  b. Elmsore.

    (1) *Compton's Encyclopedia*
    (2) *Geographical Readers*

  c. Delmar Library.

    (1) Picture files (Lumber—title).
    Logs being floated into sawmill.
    Getting timber out of swamp.
    Tractor picking up unsawed logs.
    Scenes in life of log.
    (2) Magazines.
    Back numbers and recent copies *Nature*.
    (3) Books.
    Craig, Gerald S. *Pathways in Science* (in all classrooms).
    Hardy, May *Stories of Industry*.
    Read, Helen S. *Story about Big Trees*.

  d. Slingerlands.

    Carpenter *Our Neighbors Near and Far*.
    Dorrance, J. Gordon *Story of the Forest*.
    Russell and Smith *Human Geography*.

2. Less accessible.

Albany Public Libraries.

  a. Wood and fuel:

    (1) "Cordwood helps to solve the fuel problem," *Illustrated World*. December 1919.
    (2) "Fuel value of wood," *Scientific American*, May 1920.

(3) "Machinery for cutting fire wood," *Farmer's Bulletin*, 1919.

(4) "Occupational diseases in wood industry," *Monthly Labor*, 1932.

(5) "Properties of common woods," *Independent Arts*, April 1929.

(6) "Wood as food," *Literary Digest*, December 28, 1929.

(7) "Alcohol from wood," *Literary Digest*, March 5, 1932.

(8) "Timbers and peculiar odors," *Independent Educational Monthly*, June 1925.

(9) "Tropical hardwoods with special reference to their uses in American Industries," *Bulletin Pan. American Union*, May 1927.

(10) "What is meant by hard woods and soft woods?" *Independent Education*, May 27, 1925.

(11) "Woods used in house construction," *Garden and Home*, May 1927.

b. Wood preservation.

(1) "Disease and pests—How to prevent wood rot," *Popular Mechanics*, 63:946, 1935.

(2) "Protection of log cabins, rustic work, and unseasoned wood from injurious insects," *Farmer's Bulletin*, 1582; 1–9, 1932.

c. Books.

(1) Craig, Gerald S. *Pathways in Science.*

(2) *Forest Taxation.* Bulletin No. 8, Conservation Department, New York State.

(3) Josephson, M. *Robber Barons.*

(4) King, J. *Talking Leaves.*

(5) Noyes, W. *Design and Construction in Wood.*

(6) *Reforesting.* Bulletin No. 2., Conservation Department, New York State.

(7) Waring, R. G. *Principles of Mill and Paint Shop Practice.*

3. People.

a. Mr. Frazier.

b. Mr. Mott Keyser.

       c. Mr. William Tompkins.

  4. Lists of places to visit.

       a. Saw mill at Slingerlands.

       b. "The Lone Oak" Saw and Cider Mill, Feura Bush.

       c. Saw mill at Coeymans Hollow.

       d. Libraries.

       e. State Museum.

       f. Breakabeen Mill (old type).

  5. Acquired information found and recorded.

       a. Early process industry and trade by Bishop and Keller.

       b. Beginnings of forest exploitation in U. S.

       c. Lumber industry today.

       d. How lumber is made—Pack and Gill.

       e. Log rules.

       f. Uses of lumber.

C. Specific principles.

  1. The establishment of the saw mill encouraged the growth of the community and social life.

  2. In the beginning of the saw mill industry the brawny, physically fit type of individual was necessary to overcome the hardships and take advantage of nature's resources.

  3. A stationary saw mill must be located where there is a demand, where there are raw materials, and where there is a source of power.

  4. The stationary saw mill, in order to survive must take unto itself diversified activities using approximately the same power.

  5. With industrialization there has been a lessened demand for the products such as are produced by this saw mill.

  6. Modern machinery of the saw mill has lessened the number of workers required.

  7. Capital in a small stationary saw mill is a minor consideration.

  8. The machine in the saw mill has tended to increase the facility with which the product is produced.

9. Modern inventions have caused a decrease in demand for rough, hewn local lumber.

10. With community settlement there tends to be development of industry outside the home.

11. Some industries tend to locate where there is the greatest market demand.

12. Where there is a trend toward industrialization along one line, there is a general tendency to industrialize along other lines such as: man stopped sawing own lumber and stopped building own home.

D. Children's questions.

E. Possible activities:

1. Mental.
   a. Reading for pleasure, information, answering questions, etc.
   b. Knowing sources and where to look.
   c. Knowledge of correct use of reference books.
   d. Knowledge of correct use of dictionary—drills.
   e. Giving reports, oral, written and dramatized.
   f. Letter writing, both friendly and business.
   g. Bibliography.
   h. Anthology.
   i. Labeling and filing of materials.
   j. Use of board feet.
   k. Computing age of tree.
   l. Collection of different kinds of wood, labeling and reports on each as to use, etc.
   m. Stories of trees, both nature myths and original myths.
   n. Correlating rings in trees with dates in history.
   o. Personal interviews with those who can give further information.
   p. Vocabulary list.
   q. Dramatizations.
   r. Original poems.
   s. Microscopic studies of different grains of wood.
   t. Experiments to show density of different kinds of wood.

2. Manipulative.
 a. Saw a board to get sawdust.
  (1) By hand.
  (2) By electricity.
 b. Scrap books.
  (1) Newspaper clippings.
  (2) Pictures of trees, etc.
 c. Collections of:
  (1) Fungi.
  (2) Mosses.
  (3) Fossil prints.
  (4) Seeds.
  (5) Leaves.
  (6) Different kinds of wood
 d. Making paper.
 e. Relief maps.
 f. Source maps.
 g. Industrial maps.
 h. Historical maps.
 i. Product map.
 j. "How to go" maps.
 k. Pictorial maps.
 l. Make some article of furniture needed in room.
 m. Work with both soft wood and hard wood to note difference.
 n. Charts.
  (1) Products of trees.
  (2) By products.
 o. Time line to show correlation of rings with dates in history.
 p. Models of saw mill, etc.
 q. Reproduction of old time saw mill.
 r. Displaying, showing use of the products.

3. Fine arts, music and art.
 a. Collecting and mounting pictures.
 b. Sandtable scene.
 c. Frieze showing work of sawmill.
 d. Rhythms.
  (1) Buzz of the saw.

(2) Rolling down of logs.
(3) Chopping of trees.
(4) Roll of the wheels, truck or train.
(5) Sound of the trucks, trains.
(6) Wind in trees.
   e. Songs of the lumber camp.
   f. Songs of woods.
   g. Radio programs.
   h. Original songs.
   i. Conservation posters.
   j. Various types of maps.
   k. Textiles.
   l. Fossil plants.
   m. Spatter prints of leaves, etc.
   n. Scrapbooks.
   o. Drawings to show different phases of the lumber industry.
   p. Play musical saw.
   q. Frieze showing processes "from woods to ice house," etc.

F. Possible outcomes.
   1. A general understanding of the truths to be developed in such a study.
   2. Knowledge of facts (concerning our enterprise and all related facts).
   3. Skills, techniques and knowledge.
      a. Social Science, health, civics, geography, history.
         1. History of saw mill.
         2. Development of the saw mill as an enterprise.
         3. Sources of raw materials.
         4. Distribution of finished products.
         5. Use of woods and by products.
         6. Importance of health to success in enterprise.
         7. Supplying a civic need.
         8. Healthy outdoor work.
         9. Contribution to community life.
        10. Inventions relative to the enterprise.
      b. Language arts.
         1. Letter writing.

         2. Word meaning.
         3. Reading.
         4. Oral and written composition
         5. Dramatization.
         6. Original and collected poetry.
         7. Bibliography.
         8. Filing properly.
         9. Use of source material.
      c. Natural science.
         1. Recognition of different kinds
         2. Microscopic studies of differe
         3. Knowledge of formation of fo
         4. Knowledge of harm done to
            animals, etc.
      d. Physical science.
         1. Causes, results, and preve
            floods, erosion.
         2. Influence of climate conditic

G. Possible attitudes.

   1. Realization of value of conservation
   2. Broader point of view of problems t
   3. Sympathy toward people of other w
   4. Realization of inter-dependence of p
   5. Natural curiosity for information, e
   6. Initiative in individual research.

INDEX

Ability Grouping Plan, of individualized instruction, 111.

Accession record, in school library, 279.

Accomplishments, record of, 189.

"Activity program," described, 128.

Adams, C. F., on reading, 274.

Administration, rural teachers and, 73–74.

Adoption, of textbooks, 231.

Adult education, and rural libraries, 418–20.

Agencies, educational, 370–73; library, for rural areas, 422; health, in rural areas, 456–61.

Agricultural Extension Service, agency for community service, 355–56; as educational agency, 371; and adult education, 418–19.

Agricultural work, effect on child, 444–47.

Alabama, aids to school building in, 324; rural libraries, 423.

Alexander, M. E., on picture collections, 293–95.

American Country Life Association, on play periods, 148–49.

American Library Association, on rural libraries, 421.

American School of the Air, described, 310.

Anecdote, as record, 189–90.

Anti-Tuberculosis Association, as educational agency, 371, 372; as health agency, 457.

Arithmetic, rotation of materials in, 257–58; under Hoffman Plan, 117–18. *See also* Tool Subjects.

Arizona, marital state of teachers in, 57; religious education in, 375.

Arkansas, sex of teachers in, 57; aids to school building in, 324, 325; educational agencies in, 371; rural libraries in, 423.

Armstrong, C. P., on tests for rural children, 43, 44.

Arts, practical, the teacher and, 68; equipment for, 545–47.

Ashbaugh, E. T., on scoring rural schools, 330.

Askew, S. B., study of reading comprehension, 272–73.

Autobiography, as record, 186; form for, 488–92.

Bailey, L. H., and drift of rural youth, 235.

Baldwin, B. T., and Others, on tests for rural child, 41; study of farm children, 50–51; study of play periods, 147–49; on rural environment, 438, 439, 441; on handicaps of rural child, 442–43.

Bardwell, M., list of suggested equipment, 536–50.

Batavia Plan, of individualized instruction, 111.

Bathurst, E. G., on organization in groups, 86; on adapted curriculum, 250.

Behavior, general, of rural children, 48–51; problem child, 204.

Bennett, A., on retarded children, 208–209.

Bible schools, as educational agency, 374.

Birney, A. McL., and Congress of Mothers, 395.